D1317187

WHOSE SCHOOL IS IT, ANYWAY?

Praeger Studies in Ethnographic Perspectives on American Education

General editor: Ray C. Rist

WHOSE SCHOOL IS IT, ANYWAY?

Parent-Teacher Conflict over an Innovative School

Barry A. Gold
Matthew B. Miles

PRAEGER

PRAEGER SPECIAL STUDIES • PRAEGER SCIENTIFIC

PRAG 1981

Library of Congress Cataloging in Publication Data
Gold, Barry A.
    Whose school is it, anyway?

    (Praeger studies in ethnographic perspective on
American education)
    Bibliography: p.
    Includes index.
    1. Open plan schools.   2. Parent-teacher relationships.
I. Miles, Matthew B.   II. Title.   III. Series.
III. Series.
LB1029.06G64   372.16′232   81-8562
ISBN 0-03-059674-2   AACR2

Library
I.U.P.
Indiana, Pa.

372.13   G563 w

c. 1

Published in 1981 by Praeger Publishers
CBS Educational and Professional Publishing
A Division of CBS, Inc.
521 Fifth Avenue, New York, New York 10175 U.S.A.

© 1981 by Barry A. Gold and Matthew B. Miles

All rights reserved

123456789   145   987654321

Printed in the United States of America

To Bonita

STUDIES FOREWORD

Our understandings of American education are undergoing profound and swift changes. Instrumental in this process is the turning away from a near-exclusive reliance on quantitative research as the only acceptable means by which to analyze and interpret the realities of education. In fact, one of the basic themes of this shift is that there are multiple ways of "knowing", and no one method can answer all our questions or offer all the necessary perspectives.

As those interested in education begin to explore alternative frameworks and approaches, one gaining increased attention and utilization is that of ethnographic research. This approach of intensive, in-depth investigation by means of direct naturalistic observation has a long and honored tradition in the social sciences, especially sociology and anthropology. Only in the past decade, however, has this method gained new adherents who are applying it to the study of education. The impact has been immediate. The call for ethnographic case studies now comes from the academic community, from practitioners, and from policy-makers. All are interested in explication of the day-to-day realities of education, the micro-level issues which influence the lives of teachers, administrators and students, and in understanding of the school as a social system.

This present book is one in a series, ETHNOGRAPHIC PERSPECTIVES ON AMERICAN EDUCATION. The series is aimed at bringing together an exemplary set of recent studies employing ethnographic methods. This collection has singular importance, because it constitutes perhaps the first "critical mass" of such studies of American education. Further, the various volumes span the formal organizational structure of the educational experience, from the early grades through higher education. The topics covered are among the most pressing now confronting our educational system: school desegregation, how to sustain innovations, social class stratification, the future of rural education, and multicultural education.

This series comes at a most opportune time. As the popularity of ethnographic research continues to increase, it is important for those concerned with education to have ready access to an outstanding collection of books employing this methodology, both to become more familiar with the approach and to study the insights it can provide. These studies seek not only to chronicle current conditions, but to articulate explanations of why the situations are as they are. Each moves beyond the descriptive to the analytic. Their contributions reconfirm the absolute necessity of our continuing to observe American education as it is and where it occurs.

I am particularly pleased to include this volume, WHOSE SCHOOL IS IT ANYWAY? as the fifth in the Series. It represents an important contribution to one of the most vexing problems of education -- the matter of school improvement. As Gold and Miles note, there are at least seven distinctive strategies available to those who would improve educational practice. These include curricular innovation, role-shaping strategies, comprehensive planning, supported implementation, organization development, redesign, and creating new schools. It is the last of these alternatives -- that of creating new schools -- that this present study addresses.

The pages to follow provide a careful and thoughtful study of the process by which a new, open space elementary school came into severe conflict with its suburban community, Lincoln Acres. In this study, we find a myriad of important insights on how new schools are thought to solve problems not addressed elsewhere in school systems. Further, we are presented with an accounting of the painful process that those who created the school went through in coming to the realization that they did not share the same assumptions and beliefs about open education as did those in positions of local power. The institutionalization of any innovation is difficult. We are able to share in the difficulty, but the authors also provide us with more -- insights on how one needs to respond to organizational variables to sustain change.

Lincoln Acres was a community with many cross-pressures, not all (or even the majority) of them on the surface. Systemic school reform is akin to walking through a minefield. You are never quite sure where the next explosion is going to come from. Gold and Miles do an exceptional job of leading us along, pointing out the causalities of political battles in that community. The point of their excursion is not to caution us to beware of our enemies, but to encourage us to look out for our friends. Good intentions and initial enthusiasm can rapidly wane if there are not constant efforts at communication, at taking seriously the concerns of the key constituencies, and at finding the means to demonstrate the goals and objectives of the school in clear ways.

The authors are to be congratulated for their sensitive attention to the human factor in efforts at school involvement. Their ability to weave through their analysis an understanding of the school as a microcosm of constant pressures, expectations, and adaptations is exceptional. They not only take us back in time to the origins of the planning for the new school, but forward through two years of observation of the plan being implemented. The strength of a longitudinal perspective on educational innovation is dramatically reinforced by this approach. Were they to have left the field as the innovation was drastically changed at the end of the first year, one could conclude that the effort had failed. But their persistence in the field was rewarded with the finding that the initial reaction was not the last word. Key elements of the initial innovation reappeared. Though the school was not as it began, it was also not as those who were its most severe critics had hoped it would become. The respect of these authors for the study of school innovation as an on-going dynamic has been amply justified.

Washington, D.C.
May, 1981

vii

PREFACE

This is not precisely the book we intended to write. But we wish to report that the surprises we encountered were, if not always pleasant, rather productive. Our surprises followed from two hopes. Our first hope was to document the successful planning and implementation of a new, innovative public school. We wanted to see what <u>worked</u> in the planning, design and implementation processes of educational organizations. Too often studies of failed educational change projects assume blithely that creation of the "obverse" conditions, applying principles opposite to those used by the hapless innovators, will somehow avoid recurrent failures. But all that is speculation, and we wanted to see, concretely, what success looked like -- what would be reliable guidelines for <u>doing it right</u>.

Our second hope was to understand the creation of new schools by focusing on what those people closest to the action did. We reasoned that we should pay most attention to the administrators and teachers who were actually envisioning and putting together the new school, and living and working in it together with their students.

But we were surprised on both points. First, though we located a group planning a school with all the attributes we thought would make for success -- a history of innovation in the school district, adequate planning time, sufficient material resources and motivated, well-trained personnel -- the school they created, in the opinion of all groups involved, was not immediately successful. Indeed, after two years, though it was a good school, it was still a good distance from achieving its original vision.

The second surprise was that we found we could not focus solely on what the professional educators were doing within the school. Instead, we, like they, had to confront the fact that the school's fortunes as a newly-developed system were intimately bound up with its immediate environment; the ebb and flow of conflict between citizens and educators had profound effects on the nature and functioning of the new school.

These surprises make, we think, for a much more powerful and useful study, one which avoids the twin traps of empty prescription about what "should" be done, and the shallow, "if only" reinterpretation of innovative failure. There is enough success in the case, and enough understanding of the effects of environmental political pressure to make for useful knowledge.

In brief, one of the main conclusions reached in the study is that the planning and implementation of innovative public schools is as much a political process as it is a matter of coordinating the technical components of education or of effective leadership. In the next few years, if resources allocated for education continue to diminish, and the political climate retains a conservative temper, it is likely that educational innovators will, more and more, be confronted by experiences similar to those described in this book. In these circumstances, regardless of their level of expertise, educators' political skills will ultimately determine their ability to re-shape schools.

This book, then, should be of interest as a detailed case study of organizational change to several audiences. In colleges and universities, teachers and students whose concerns are in the areas of educational administration, sociology of education, curriculum, management sciences and organizational behavior can use the case as material for learning and teaching about organizational change. In communities and school districts, school administrators, teachers, consultants and parents who are either planning and creating new schools or innovating new programs should find numerous examples of the pitfalls and successes that are likely to occur in any large-scale innovative effort. Finally, researchers (based in any of the disciplines above) with interests in educational organizations will, we hope, find this book stimulating, perhaps maddening, and useful.

Many people contributed to the preparation of this book. The students, parents, teachers and administrators of the Lincoln Acres School deserve our warm thanks. We owe particular debt to the teachers and administrators without whose trust, patience and introspection this study could not have existed. Through all the vicissitudes of change, their primary interest remained: the education of the children. The fact that parents too shared that motivation may account for the courtesy and cooperation we encountered from them. Happily, we should note that though life was sometimes stressful for Lincoln Acres students, they proved resilient and adaptive -- and performed at high achievement levels during the time of the innovative effort.

Members of the Social Architecture in Education Project who made valuable contributions to this study and provided regular, colleaguely support are Ellen W. Sullivan, Sam D. Sieber, David E. Wilder, Beverly Loy Taylor, and Wamboi Kironde. Professor Rein van der Vegt of the University of Nijmegen, as visiting research associate, was especially helpful as a semi-detached observer of the Social Architecture Project and this study.

Dale G. Lake collaborated closely in the creation of the Social Architecture Project, and was a strong co-investigator during the first year, with staff members Bunty Ketcham, Denise Burch, and Julie Quain.

Jolene Vrchota, Thomas Cook and Joan Charles provided coding and clerical assistance. Administrative and secretarial support were amply supplied by Ann Wechsler, Anita McCabe, and Gay Gaskins. We also appreciated very much the competent fiscal and administrative services of Stephanie Clohesy, Sophie Sa and Marcia Kroll of the Center for Policy Research. Parallel thanks to Paul Collins and Jay Sexter of Fordham University, who administered our Teacher Corps funds.

Joe Lopatin and Peter Abrams of Calculogic, Inc., managed our quantitative data processing with competence and speed.

This book was typeset with much patience and skill by Judy Woolcock. Our thanks for the graphics to Janice Poretz.

Mary Milne, Charles Thompson, Elisabeth Hansot and Fritz Mulhauser, our project officers from the National Institute of Education gave thoughtful commentary, steady stimulation and sustained support. William L. Smith of Teacher Corps encouraged our early exploratory effort, and helped expand our vision of what good learning materials would look like.

A version of this study served as the senior author's Ph.D. dissertation at Columbia University. For valuable comments during its preparation, and for serving on the examination committee, thanks are extended to Professors George Z.F. Bereday, Amitai Etzioni, Herbert J. Gans, Francis A.J. Ianni, David E. Wilder and especially Professor Eugene Litwak, who served graciously as dissertation advisor.

Finally, we would like to thank each other: for five years of sustained energy, for interesting arguments and long meetings, for revision after revision, and for a book that we both like.

New York City
June, 1981

B.A.G.
M.B.M.

CONTENTS

LIST OF CHARTS

LIST OF DIAGRAMS

LIST OF FIGURES

LIST OF TABLES

I'll ultimately run my own kind of school anyhow. Whatever is decided in the political arena doesn't matter. They will come out with a school that I can run; I can run an exemplary school in an outhouse if necessary. I shouldn't get too hung up about politics. I will do things the most efficient way that people want things done. Open education is an efficiency device. The dispute was about if I can deliver what is expected by the means I choose.

> Ellis Brown, Lincoln Acres School principal -- after three months of planning the new school.

As I was telling you this thing, it occurred to me that it would be an interesting play or novel. It's almost like a little tragedy with sub-plots weaving back and forth. So many little elements. At the end of the whole thing you say: How did this really happen? How did such a fine thing go bad? It's really kind of a fascinating story.

> Sy Golden, Lincoln Acres PTA president -- five months after the school opened.

1

INTRODUCTION

A. WHAT'S IN THIS BOOK

Designing a new school from the ground up has been a favorite strategy for educational reformers: Pestalozzi, Montessori and Dewey each had a new educational vision, and believed the best way to advance it was to exemplify it in a concrete setting. Today, after the flood of new schools in the innovative sixties has waned, and though enrollments and resources are dropping, there are thousands of American school districts designing and carrying out comprehensive school programs, from minischools to work experience programs, magnet schools and alternative learning centers.

The problem is that new schools, which are complete educational environments more substantial than the "part-innovation" represented by the introduction of new textbooks, materials or courses, are not at all easy to create, and may even be failure-prone. This book aims at deepening our understanding of what it takes to envision and implement a total school. It has three basic aspects.

1. A Natural History

The book is first of all a basic case study: it is a detailed account of hundreds of events that took place during the planning and first two years of operation of an innovative new elementary school, Lincoln Acres, in a suburban public school district. The events are presented in chronological flow, as they were observed, described and reconstructed by ourselves and by the school people and citizens who were most closely involved. At many points, we also present participants' reactions, commentary and analysis of what happened. The aim is to be as rich and as thorough as possible in providing a detailed account.

2. A Systematic Analysis

The book also offers a set of explanations for the events at Lincoln Acres school, couched in more general terms. Our objective was to make conceptual sense from the welter of empirical detail that fills the pages ahead. Our explanations are drawn both from general sociological theory, and from a more specific conceptual framework we developed to account for the processes of development of new educational systems. (The framework is outlined in Chapter 2.) Our explanations are concerned not only with the dynamics of planning and implementation as such, but with the sources and nature of conflict between school and community, and how it affected the school's transformation over time.

Our explanations are decisively marked off from the main account. That way the basic case can be examined in its own terms, and alternative explanations generated by readers. Our work was essentially exploratory, so we treat our explanations as stimulative and encouraging of further inquiry, rather than as final.

3. Implications for Research and Practice

Finally, the book also contains occasional advice. At various points we try to speak to people -- educational practitioners, consultants, and citizens who are struggling with problems of school improvement through the creation of new educational settings, suggesting what our data and our explanations may mean for their work. Similarly, we suggest for researchers of educational change what our findings, our theory and our methods may mean for their future work. However, we are modest -- and realistic -- enough to believe that the really useful derivation of implications will be carried out by each reader.

B. WHAT'S SIGNIFICANT IN THE BOOK

This book does several things that deserve the reader's attention. We point to them directly to save time and energy, and to offer some "handles" for reader use.

1. The Creation of New Systems

The book supplies a strong working feel for (and a clear framework for understanding) just what is involved when groups of people are trying to develop a new social system. Starting a new system is not like operating or repairing an existing system, and until recently there has been almost no literature devoted to this topic (see, for example, Sarason, 1971; Nystrom & Starbuck, 1981; Kimberly and Miles, 1980).

2. The Dynamics of Educational Innovation

The book also shows very clearly the problems that are involved along the way when a substantial educational innovation is envisioned, planned, and implemented. The literature on educational innovation is very large. But most of it refers to limited "part-innovations", rather than to large-scale, whole-school innovation. Furthermore, much of this literature overemphasizes "adoption" -- the decision to try something new -- and under-attends to the complex problems of implementing new ideas in the context of a social organization called a "school" (Berman, 1981; Miles, 1981). This book, like most case studies, is longitudinal. But it improves on past innovation research by extending backward into the history of the change effort, and further forward into two years' worth of implementation. A number of prior case studies of whole schools (for example, Smith and Keith, 1971; Gross, Giacquinta & Bernstein, 1971; Deal, 1978) ceased their descriptions relatively soon after the school was launched, concluding that failures had occurred, (and, implicitly, that the change effort had terminated as well). In our study, after what looked like initial failure, it appeared that stabilization, salvaging, and reimplementation occurred: the life of the new school continued, and deserved, it turned out, our continuing attention.

3. The School as an Organization

The book also focuses on the school, not just as a place where individual "teachers" offer something called "instruction" to others called "students", but as a network of structures and relationships that constitutes a certain kind of organization: one that may (as ours did) turn out to be collegially-oriented, coercive, conflictful and bureaucratic by turns.

4. School-Community Conflict

Every organization exists in an environment. When we began this study, however, the environment (read community) was in the background. We expected to study mainly those people -- educators, with some aid from citizens -- who were planning, and then implementing the new school. But the reality we examined rapidly became much more complex. The central social process that took place during the development of the Lincoln Acres school was a prolonged, sometimes bitter conflict between professional educators -- both teachers and administrators -- and the parents of children attending the school. At the core, the issue was whether educators or parents had the right to determine the sort of education the school would offer: hence the title of this book. More generally, the book explores the problem of how formal organizations (such as schools) with power based on expertise relate to primary groups (such as neighborhoods, voluntary associations and families) with power based on participative rights. There was a basic tension in Lincoln Acres between professional judgment and citizen participation in decision-making: the conflict was in many respects one between expertise and democracy as a basis for decision-making.

5. A Comprehensive View

Finally, the book takes an integrated approach: it examines all four of the preceding factors in educational change, as they affect each other: a new system, planned and implemented over time, that, as an organization, influenced and was influenced by conflict with the environment.

C. NEW SCHOOLS AS A CHANGE STRATEGY

There are many ways to improve the performance of educational systems. In America, these have included curriculum change through the introduction of new teaching materials and practices (Miles, 1964); role-shaping efforts (skills development through in-service training) (Rubin, 1971; Edelfelt & Johnson, 1975); comprehensive planning at the district level for change and improvement (Berman & McLaughlin, 1976); supported implementation (technical assistance with the process of adoption and implementation of proven practices) (Emrick et al., 1977); organization development (building a "self-renewal" capability in schools through self-study and problem-solving efforts) (Schmuck & Miles, 1971; Fullan, Miles & Taylor, 1980); redesign (structural changes in schools to support improved functioning) (Parker, 1977; Charters et al., 1973); and, our subject, the creation of new schools (the development of a complete new educational organization). All of these strategies have strengths and weaknesses (see Miles, 1974), which should not detain us here. We might note, however, that creating a new school, a comprehensive, organizationally-focused strategy, may well turn out to include activities drawn from any of the other school-improvement strategies just listed.

We should review briefly how widely the new-school strategy is used, as well as comment on its strengths and inherent difficulties.

1. Current Use

The prevailing stereotype is that because of declining enrollments and a "back to the basics" mood, few new schools are now being created -- in contrast to the vigorous flowering of "free schools" (Graubard, 1972) and alternatives of all types during the late 60's.

But there is a good deal of evidence that the new-school strategy for educational change is being used rather extensively. Recent studies (Bass, 1978; Broad, 1977) show that at least 25 percent of the 16,000 American public school districts have created "alternative" programs substantial enough to be considered complete new schools. A recent survey (Flaxman & Homstead, 1978) easily located 1,300 specific programs. Such programs, as Cohen and Farrar (1978) have pointed out, are not only politically popular, since they offer parents greater control over the sort of school their children are attending, but are satisfying to the teachers who volunteer for them, since they can shape the curriculum, work with students who have "chosen" to come, and operate according to their preferred teaching styles.

In addition, in the wake of declining enrollments, many districts are finding innovative educational uses for underutilized buildings, and not a few, believe it or not, are still putting up new buildings. The new-school programs being tried have a wide range: minischools, career academies, alternative learning centers, schools-within-schools, environmental studies centers, work-experience programs, the "city as school," magnet schools, and experimental schools focusing on foreign language, the arts, or science.

So the creation of new schools represents a considerably more substantial portion of current educational practice than is commonly assumed.

2. Advantages

Developing a complete new school has some decisive values as an approach to school improvement. First, in a new school, the constraints of the established system can be bypassed, and the vested interests of various parties set aside for the moment. Second, personnel favorable to the new school can be recruited, so that resistance is absent, and the energy of well-trained true believers brought to bear. Third, protection of the new school from the environment means that all energies can be fully focused on the task; experimentation and "fine tuning" are possible, so the vision can be actualized in something like its "pure" or optimal form, freed of expedient alterations. This actualization is often better because of strong participant motivation. There are "process benefits" for members of the new school -- the excitement of sharing in a new enterprise, the freedom to innovate, and the autonomy involved in creating something for which one is responsible. As Sarason (1972) remarks:

> Practically everyone...assumes that becoming a principal of a new school is much to be preferred to assuming leadership of an older school....the fantasy that one is starting "fresh" engenders a great deal of motivation, enthusiasm, and much hope that life in this school will be different.

Finally, most reformers believe, with some justification, that an actual demonstration of a new educational set-up can do far more to diffuse their ideas and vision than any amount of writing: the test of a new educational idea in this sense is whether potential adopters can actually see it working.

3. Difficulties

But creating new schools does not appear to be a simple or well-understood process, or a miracle cure for what ails education. Published accounts suggest many difficulties.

High energy requirements. Nearly all accounts of new schools -- especially those with an innovative mission -- describe overload and stress as typical, especially in the early stages (for examples, see Center for New Schools, 1975; Gross et al., 1971; Smith and Keith, 1971). As Stinchcombe (1965) has pointed out, there are many liabilities of newness, not least the fact that familiar roles and procedures which ordinarily make for economy of effort are lacking.

Failure-proneness. As one new-school planner said, "If someone wants to show that you've screwed up, they probably can -- because you probably have" (Carr et al., 1977). Careful scrutiny will always reveal that any human enterprise has fallen short of its hopes in some respect. Perhaps new schools are no more likely to fail than the other change strategies we have discussed, but it is notable that there are many more new school failure cases in the literature than successes.

There seem to be many ways to fail: regression to ordinariness (Sarason, 1972); slippage between the original vision and the final reality (Levin & Simon, 1973, 1974); incoherence and inadequate coping (Gross, et al., 1971). Most generally, new schools sometimes fail to survive at all (Deal, 1975). A substantial portion of the alternative and "free" schools created in the late 60's are missing today. In the public school sector, what may happen is that the principal and a large proportion of the staff leave for other jobs (Smith and Keith, 1971); the vision simply disappears with them and the new staff runs an "ordinary" school in the same physical plant.

Dissemination weakness. Even when a new school is successfully mounted, does well by children, and resembles the vision of its planners, it is not at all clear that it can serve well as a beacon of educational reform -- which is usually cited as one of the reasons for embarking on the enterprise in the first place. Kritek (1976) has shown that the need to build a cohesive staff with strong commitment works against the need to be open to the immediate professional environment in ways promoting dissemination. And beyond this, a school is a complex social system that takes much art and craft to produce. It cannot be "diffused" like a specific teaching innovation -- and, as experience suggests, even that process is slow and energy-consuming (cf. Walton, 1975). So although a few schools (such as Bremer's Parkway School in Philadelphia, Montessori schools, IGE schools) have successfully replicated themselves, the process does not happen easily or quickly; the latter two examples have taken years and a strong supporting "infrastructure" for widespread dissemination.

As we have noted, the literature on the creation of new schools is small: we have been able to retrieve fewer than thirty studies. It is not surprising that the reasons offered for the difficulties noted above are quite diverse: they range from environmental uncertainty (Biagioli, 1977) through over-ambitiousness (Bredo & Bredo, 1975), internal conflict (Sarason, 1972), managerial inadequacy (Gross, et al., 1971), lack of self-corrective capability (DeTurk, n.d.), and missing support systems (Green, 1975; Eastabrook, et al., 1974), to the simple failure to design the organization explicitly (Perlmutter, 1965). While all of these explanations may have validity, it seemed very clear to us as we launched this study that the new-school strategy was not at all well understood, in spite of its attractiveness and its prevalence as a method of school improvement.

D. THE RESEARCH PROJECT

The study reported in this book was a part of a larger enterprise, the Project on Social Architecture in Education. Beginning in 1974, it was funded by The National Institute of Education's Group on School Capacity for Problem-Solving, who were actively supporting many studies of what local schools and school districts could do to improve themselves, and by Teacher Corps, who were much interested in the development of materials to aid educational practitioners with change projects.

1. The Research Questions

Briefly, the project's goals were: (1) to describe empirical stages in the social-architectural process, defined as envisioning, designing and bringing into being the new social system of an innovative school; (2) to assess the success of innovative intent; (3) to study linkages between stages of the social-architectural process; and (4) to study methods of facilitating effective school design and start-up. As the study proceeded, it added another objective: (5) the production of learning materials to aid those planning and implementing new schools.

2. The Research Approach

The project, designed for three years, but extended to 4½, was staffed by a principal investigator (Miles), three field workers (among them Gold), two part-time research associates, a materials developer (in the 3rd and 4th years), and secretarial and clerical support.

Retrieval of prior research and experience. The available literature, eight recently-opened schools, and 11 experienced planners and consultants were studied to locate recurring issues.

Acquisition of research sites. Working from a pool of 58 possible sites where planning for a new school was under way, the project formed contractual agreements with six schools, which we list (pseudonymously) as follows:

Westgate Schools #2 and #3: two open-space elementary schools in a suburban district.

Lincoln Acres: suburban open-space elementary school.

College High School: a campus-based school uniting the resources of a college and the Lakeport urban school district. (This site never opened for students.)

Appelbaum High School: an experimental high school for business careers, also in Lakeport.

Arts Co-op: an experimental half-day arts program for students from one urban and six suburban school districts.

Site agreements promised full access, confidentiality and anonymity; the project provided matching funds for use of any of a pool of consultants to aid planning/implementation (P/I) work.

Conceptualization. Conceptual development occurred continuously over the life of the project, and included early concept papers, convention papers, the listing of variables needed for field work and survey instruments, and the development of propositions into a general framework (Chapter 2).

Instrument development. The project developed a number of interview guides and questionnaires on particular aspects of P/I work; a series of staff, parent and student surveys to assess the "state of the system" in implemented schools; and successively elaborated and refined methods of coding and storing the results of field work (see below).

Data collection. Each field worker had a primary site, and a secondary site shared with another worker. Sites were visited once or twice weekly, for periods of up to two years. Non-participant observation, informal and formal interviews were used; available documents were collected. Running notes were written up, then coded and stored. Systematic coding ran behind and was eventually discarded.

In each opened school there were from one to three waves of survey data collection from staff (and often parents and/or students as well). Wave 1 was after three or four months of implementation, with following waves at the end of Year 1 and, where feasible, Year 2.

Data analysis. The qualitative data, originally broken into incidents/excerpts, were coded as noted above. This method gave way to field workers doing summary ratings and analysis of each contact. Informal data analysis methods, such as written "site summaries," regular staff meetings to review status in each site and propose hypotheses proved more useful. The survey data were used to assess the degree to which the implemented schools were congruent with their planners' hopes. A systematic review of eight texts on field methods showed clearly that few formal guidelines for the analysis of qualitative data exist: the project developed some proposed ones, but found that case studies were largely produced in a very labor-intensive fashion, using an outline generated from the general conceptual framework described above. Confidence* in the

---

*We should also note that our conclusions were strengthened in an unexpected way; the process of developing supportive learning materials (Taylor, 1978) for people planning new schools forced us to clarify our conclusions and test their validity.

case analyses was improved by staff review and revision, and through feedback of draft versions to personnel in all the sites studied, who were invited to provide correction and commentary. Cross-site generalizations were drawn using the conceptual framework. (See Miles, 1979, for further description of analysis methods used.)

E. THE NATURE OF THIS BOOK

1. Overview

Lincoln Acres was one of the six sites in the Social Architecture study. This book tells the story of a new open-space elementary school: the community context in which it existed (Chapter 3); the early planning and the vision that emerged (Chapter 4); the formation of the faculty and the intensive "final planning" that took place during the spring and summer before the school was to open (Chapters 4 and 5), accompanied by the gradual development of an acute conflict between school and community; the opening of school in September (Chapter 7); the reorganization of the school as a response to the conflict between educators and parents (Chapter 8); the subsequent events of the first school year (Chapter 10); and the reconstructive processes that occurred during the second year of the school's life (Chapter 11). Our conclusions and explanations are spaced throughout the text, but are summarized in Chapters 9 and 12.

2. Research Methods

The reader needs a clear idea of how the data that fill these pages were collected, so he or she can know how much confidence to place in the account. Those methods, and the data analysis methods, are described in more detail in Appendix A, but here is a brief overview.

The research relationship. Research in the Lincoln Acres school and community began in December, 1974, and ended in June, 1977.

On January 3, 1975, three days after the principal arrived to begin work on planning the school, a contract was signed by him, the superintendent of schools and the research project staff. The important elements of the contract were that the researcher* be permitted to observe and collect data at all meetings relevant to the planning of the school, that questionnaire data could be collected, that the researcher would maintain the confidentiality of all informants, and that all individuals as well as the school system and community would remain anonymous.

---

*"Researcher" as used throughout this study refers to the senior author, who was the primary field worker in the site. The project director (Miles) was closely familiar with the site through occasional visits, and through regular project staff discussions.

The agreement also included an offer of periodic summary feedback reports, to be made upon the request of the school.* Finally, the agreement stated that no ongoing advice, help or reaction would be supplied by the researcher.#

The relationships that developed between the researcher and the faculty and community members were direct, trustful and as far as can be determined, open. In several instances, the researcher was asked by informants not to take notes, while especially revealing information was being presented. In other cases, information that would eventually affect the school deeply was given only to the researcher, even with the speaker's knowledge that it was being recorded. There was more than one instance in which the researcher was treated as a confidante by conflicting parties; he often had more information about a situation than any single person involved. Of course, there were also instances when people withheld data, as there always are in any social system being studied.

The researcher never discussed information obtained from one person with another. Additionally, he made a steady -- and, it seems, successful -- effort to avoid interfering with the operation of the school in any way.

Data collection techniques. A field researcher's interaction with the people he is studying can range from total involvement, being an actual participant, to total non-involvement, being a passive, unobtrusive observer (Gold, 1958). For the most part, this study was conducted toward the passive, or near-complete observer, end of the continuum. Classrooms, faculty meetings, PTA meetings and Board of Education meetings were attended without the researcher's contributing directly to the business transacted in them.

Field methods also involve interviewing people. In this study, two kinds of interviews were used: retrospective interviews, in which the respondent was asked to describe historical events, usually guided by a set of pre-designated questions; and informal, unstructured interviews, which

---

*One such report was prepared for the faculty near the end of their intensive summer planning workshop. Another report, on community attitudes toward the school, was made available to interested parents during the spring of the first year of operation.

#The researcher's role was thus defined as decidedly non-interventive. One objective of the larger project was to understand the role of consultants as facilitators of new-school planning and development. Toward this end, the project made modest funds (usually under $1,000) available to its sites on a matching basis for hiring mutually-agreed-on consultants. We wished to study their work -- and also thought their presence might increase the "success" of implementation, and thus usefulness of the project's findings to others.

We also expected that the consulting funds might serve as an extra inducement for schools to permit the research. At Lincoln Acres, this was not initially the case; the principal was skeptical about the use of consultants. He did use some funds for a residential workshop for faculty, but did not otherwise take advantage of the offer.

occurred after meetings, during teaching hours, in the principal's office and at social events.

Notes from field work were recorded -- whenever possible, verbatim -- on pads and later typed by the researcher, or occasionally dictated and transcribed. A few interviews were tape recorded.

The researcher tried to be present at all faculty meetings, all PTA meetings and all Board of Education meetings that had the new school as their topic. He also attended several Lincoln Acres Homeowners Association meetings where the school was discussed. The school was also frequently observed in operation. In addition teachers and citizens* often provided information on events the researcher could not attend either because of their confidential nature or his schedule. Over the course of field work the researcher contacted the site 190 times in person and another 25 times by telephone. Site visits ranged from a few hours duration to several full-day contacts in a particular week.

Documents collected and used fall into five categories: (1) internal organizational communication; (2) organizational communication with external groups (for instance, parents, the Board of Education, the local newspaper); (3) communications from parents and parent organizations to the school or related organizations; (4) local and state newspapers; and finally, (5) miscellaneous (for example, a former mayor's autobiography, articles by residents appearing in professional journals, and articles in national mass media).

In addition to these major sources of qualitative data, a substantial amount of quantitative data was collected. In February, shortly after the faculty was formed, a short open-ended questionnaire on their expectations for the new school was administered to the teachers. In June, during an intensive faculty workshop, a "goals" questionnaire was administered to the faculty.

In December and June of the first year of operation, and in May of the second year, lengthy questionnaires were administered to all faculty members. At approximately the same times a mail survey was sent to all parents of children enrolled in the school. Findings from the surveys are presented in the text.

Sources of validity. Wherever possible we have used "triangulation" among data sources to reconstruct the natural history of the school. For instance, newspaper accounts of events have been compared with participants' accounts as well as with the researcher's experiences of them. It should also be noted that this study is based primarily on observation of behavior, supplemented with people's reports and interpretations of their own and other's behavior and their attitudes; not, as is often the case in educational research, only on subjective responses constrained by standardized instruments.

---

*All faculty members served as informants. Some, of course, were more articulate, willing to talk about and speculate on events than others. In Chart 1.1 a "+" next to a community member's name indicates that fairly regular contact was maintained with this person as a primary informant throughout the study.

CHART 1.1

MAJOR ACTORS IN LINCOLN ACRES SCHOOL AND COMMUNITY
(All names are pseudonyms)

Staff of the school:

Ellis Brown - Principal
Sam Pennington - Resource Teacher
Monica Selwin - School Secretary
Lee Whitmore - Physical Education
Lindy Braun - Art

Alice Houghton
Sarah Fox — Kindergarten Team
Louise Hargrove

Katie Neustadt
Jane Baylor — Primary Team (NBC)
Sally Candler

Wanda Molloy
Priscilla Talbot — Primary Team (MTK)
Dori Kraus

Rebecca Barone
Glenda Jacobs — Intermediate Team (BJW)
Norbert White

District staff:

Dr. Robert Biddle - Superintendent of Schools
Anthony Smith - Assistant to the Superintendent
Astrid Little - Assistant to the Superintendent
Bob Haines - Head of Maintenance
Harriet Stein - Learning Consultant
Alberta Bard - Assistant Principal, Junior High School
David Hauptman - Principal, Fernwood School

Community members:

Barbara Berger+ - Co-chairperson, Lincoln Acres Homeowners Association
Marie Bonomi - Parent
Barbara Collins+ - Community Leader, (LAHA) Education Committee
Paul Elfenbein - President of LAHA
Irena Farrell - Board of Education Member
Charles Frisch+ - Education Expert, Board of Education Member
Alex Georgiades - Parent
Sy Golden+ - Board of Education Attorney, PTA President, second President of LAHA
Rob Goldman - Parent, Board of Education Member
Gerrie Holden - Board of Education Member
Estelle Hunter - Board of Education Member
Michael Karalis - Founder of LAHA
Robert Klahr - Board of Education Member
Charles Minetta - Community Leader
Sylvia Peabody - Board of Education Member
Sam Schwartz+ - Former Co-chairperson, LAHA Education Committee
Virginia Vitelli - Parent

+Primary informant, with regular contact maintained.

As noted earlier, we have additional confidence in our descriptions (and associated explanations) because we gave a semi-final version of this study to the principal and teachers in Lincoln Acres school, to the superintendent of schools, and to several citizens. They supplied corrections for factual errors. As might be expected, they also had interpretations or explanations for events that differed from ours at times. When that happened, we incorporated these alternate meanings in footnotes. For a further description of how the feedback process went, see Appendix B.

The book is full of quotations from the actors and excerpts from documents. We hope the reader can grasp the reality of the situation as the actors defined it and acted upon it, with minimal re-interpretation by the authors. Our selection of quotes and accompanying text of course constitutes a sort of interpretation, but we have tried to be as thorough as possible, and to mark off our analyses and interpretations explicitly.

One final point: many fairly routine events are reported here -- in a style that we hope is not mundane. They occurred in the creation of this school, as the do in the everyday life of human beings in any organization; to exclude them would be to bias our view of life in the school toward the exciting, unpredictable and novel (of which there is much, as the reader will see). We aimed to understand the "daily grind" of life in this school, along with the moments of stress, anger, crisis and joy. We hope we have succeeded.

3. How the Book Is Organized

The next chapter reviews the general conceptual framework which gradually evolved during the course of the four years of the larger study.

Then we proceed to a discussion of the Lincoln Acres context -- past and present -- as a backdrop for the chronological account that follows. (For chapter headings see Overview, above).

Throughout the text, analysis and commentary sections and chapters are clearly separated from description; the headings are marked off by parentheses, with titles such as (Comments), and (Analysis and Commentary).

A concluding chapter contains our final reflections on the case. To help the reader on the journey, we provide both a detailed table of contents and an index of concepts used. To make reference to particular sections easy during discussion with others, we use letters and numbers for subheads throughout.

4. How to Use the Book

A reader's approach to the book will naturally depend on what purposes are in play. For what might be the professional equivalent of a "good read", one can simply proceed sequentially through from start to finish.

The book can also be used to sharpen one's skills at diagnosing complex social situations and making workable predictions about what will happen next. To do this, proceed on a segmented basis. Read through the book from Chapter 3 onward until a set of parentheses ( ) is encountered around a section or subsection heading. Stop.* Write down an <u>analysis</u> of what has been happening in the situation, accompanied if wished by a <u>prediction</u> of what will happen next in the case. The analysis can then be compared with the analysis offered in the ( ) section, and the prediction can be compared with the next events that occur in the case. Appendix C discusses how to do this in a bit more detail. Continue with the next bit of description until the next analysis section is encountered, and so on. (We can testify that our own powers of prediction during the events themselves were often sorely tested, and think the reader will find this mode of using the book a challenging and profitable one.)

Some readers may prefer to have a general overview of the events involved in the Lincoln Acres forest before proceeding to the daily trees. To get this, review Chapter 3 on context, review the list of actors in Chart 1.1, skim the planning chapters (4,5 and 6), examine the chronology of events after school opened (Chart 9.1), skim Chapter 9 on the dynamics of reorganization, sections G, H and J in Chapter 10, and sections F, G and H of Chapter 11 on the second year's work. Then proceed to the concrete events. We should note that such an approach will bias the reader toward our conclusions, and may make it more difficult for alternative interpretations to be generated.

The next chapter provides an overview of the conceptual framework that came to guide our thinking as we learned more and more about the process of new-school creation.

---

*The reader with this interest should also stop before Chapters 9 and 12, which contain major analyses.

2

THE CREATION OF NEW SCHOOLS

A. OVERVIEW

This chapter provides a general introduction to our thinking about new schools and how they come into being. The key concepts outlined here will be used repeatedly during our analysis, so we want to acquaint the reader with our language.

We should note that this general framework emerged only gradually over the four years of our study, informed by our field work, our coding, and our analysis of data from each of our six sites. Thus it is reasonably generic and comprehensive. However, it certainly does not serve to "explain" all the events and dynamics that took place at Lincoln Acres, as the reader will clearly see in Chapter 12. Rather, it is a sort of accounting scheme that enables a clear look at what happened. Our discussion of the framework will necessarily be rather compressed; for a full account with many examples, see Miles (1978b).

Figure 2.1 outlines the general pieces of the framework, which will be detailed in following sections. It shows that the outcomes of planning and implementation efforts for new-schools are caused by a network of prior factors. These include, at the left of the figure, essential features of the enterprise (such as the fact that whole, new, innovative systems are being created), and the context of the enterprise (for example, the idea that American public schools are systems with diffuse goals and weak boundaries). These features and the context both generate a series of primary tasks (such as political stabilization, and development of a vision for the new school), and an associated series of key dilemmas (such as whether to make innovative or traditional choices, or whether to contact the environment actively or withdraw from it).*

These tasks and dilemmas are dealt with in what we came to call the planning/implementation group (P/I group) through decisions made by key actors (such as an agreement to ask parents to serve as volunteers, or to fire a teacher, or hold an in-service workshop). The quality of these decisions, as the figure suggests, is conditioned by P/I group capabilities (such as

---

*We are much indebted to Sam Sieber for this way of thinking.

FIGURE 2.1

FRAMEWORK FOR CONCEPTUALIZING PLANNING & IMPLEMENTATION

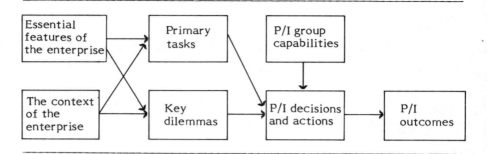

political skill, or decision-making ability).   If those capabilities are high, good <u>outcomes</u> (such as satisfaction of all concerned stakeholders, student achievement, and congruence with the original vision) are achieved.

For clarity, the discussion below begins with outcomes, so the reader can see what is being aimed for. Then it moves to the left of Figure 2.1 and proceeds through the several boxes. (The reader who wants an overview of the complete forest can jump forward and examine Figure 2.3 at the end of the chapter before proceeding.)

B. OUTCOMES

1. New Schools as the Context

Our focus in studying planning and implementation was on new schools. "New" has several meanings, to which we will return shortly. Here it should be emphasized that we mean a <u>total school program</u> (not a minor project, a course, or other innovation) which is <u>created</u> more or less <u>de novo</u> (is not simply an existing school being tinkered with) and which its creators experience as <u>different</u> from their own past practice. The new school may or may not be housed in a new building: the issue for us is the <u>social</u>, not the physical architecture (though the latter, of course, may influence the former).

2. Definitions

"Planning" and "implementation" are both activities intended to induce a desired future state of affairs, and cannot be easily separated. Most people would agree that "planning" is devoted to activities such as forecasting, envisioning the future, constructing verbal or graphic pictures of a desired aspect of that future, and specifying possible steps toward that aspect -- and that "implementation" requires the taking of <u>action</u> on the real and present world in order to shift it toward the desired aspect. But the two activities are usually closely intermixed in reality.

For our purposes, we considered that "planning" of a new school begins when someone decides that the new school should exist, and a legitimate body charged with designing the school starts work.

Naturally, "planning" does not stop when the school opens for students; it continues in parallel with "implementation," which, in our terms, begins as soon as a manager for the new school is appointed, with the right to spend money. Subsequent implementation actions include such things as selecting staff and students, actualizing the design for the school, opening for students (start-up), and early operation.

Both planning and implementation continue indefinitely, as far as we can see. Assuming that the new school survives, most participants will come to agree after a few semesters that the school has "settled down" and does not need further major adjustments. By that time, planning and implementation functions have receded to become a minor part of the life of the school, which has become institutionalized, and is operating as a more or less steady-state system.

We have used the term "planning/implementation group" (P/I group) to refer to whatever subsystem is most responsible for the enterprise at any given point in time: it may include an initial planning committee, principal and key assistants, principal and the total faculty, etc., depending on the situation and the stage of work. "P/I group" is thus an elastic term, with different meanings in different schools, and at different stages of the effort.

3. What Is Good Planning and Implementation?

We had to face the question of defining the major outcomes of planning and implementation efforts, so that we could specify better and worse results.

First, we identified four markers of good planning and implementation that could be noted during the process of P/I work; these are intermediate outcomes. They include:

1. Adequacy of obtained financial resources. A new school, to be successful, must have enough money to support planning and implementation efforts -- not to mention routine operations.

2. Environmental endorsement. Since P/I groups exist in a bureaucratic, social, and professional environment, salient pieces of that environment must approve of the decisions being made. Without endorsement, the risk is that P/I efforts can be blocked or thwarted. Though endorsement is not the same thing as financial support (note, later, for example, the difficulties faced in Lincoln Acres, where money was assured, but parents vigorously attacked the plans and actions of the faculty), it may well have back effects on the adequacy of financial resources.

3. Quality of planning/implementation decisions. Dozens, even hundreds of decisions are made as a new school is

designed and actualized. The "goodness" of such decisions is a slippery concept, and many criteria can be applied: Were all the available facts and information used? Would experts applaud the decision? Is it congruent with the planners' goals and hopes? Is the decision implementable? Will undesired outcomes of the decision be minimal? We settle for the idea that stakeholders (and observers) would concur that the decision is "good," technically "right."

4. Ownership of planning/implementation decisions. Since planning new schools is a complicated, even chancy process, often without much clarity or certainty, and since the implementation of planning decisions presents a thicket of unforeseen issues, it seems to be important that the decisions have commitment behind them. Key planners (and later, implementers) need to believe in their decisions; otherwise these decisions can too easily be set aside, walked away from, or unendingly re-made.*

These four intermediate outcomes might be seen as necessary prerequisites for P/I outcomes seen in a more ultimate, "bottom line" sense. Here we can identify four main sub-variables, adding up to planning/implementation success, once the school is operating.

1. Congruence with goals. First, the implemented school should have features which are reasonably congruent with the essential or core goals which planners had for the school. Much adaptation and shifting usually -- often desirably -- occurs along the way (Berman & McLaughlin, 1976) but good implementation should protect the original vision, not abandon it. The results of the P/I process should not conflict with what might be called the "meta-goals" (central or essential hopes) for the school. In short, "core" ideals should not be betrayed, assuming that it seems clear that they could have been actualized (that is, were not "unrealistic").

2. Problem-coping ability. Second, since any new school will have problems (situations which are "out of program" and require corrective or inventive action by implementers), good implementation should show us a school able to cope with problems -- so that they get solved with reasonable energy expenditures and do not recur. To put it another way, we can say that all efforts to plan

---

*This discussion follows the distinction made in much of the literature on small group decision-making (Collins and Guetzkow, 1964). Note that quality and ownership are jointly-needed: a high-quality decision not owned (accepted) will run into implementation problems; a highly owned decision will run into trouble when implemented if it is technically poor.

a new school have unanticipated consequences. How effectively these consequences are dealt with may be as important as whether "goal-congruent" implementation has occurred.*

3. Stakeholder satisfaction. Third, in good implementation efforts, we should note that key figures related to the new school feel reasonably good, believe that the enterprise has achieved (and is achieving) things important to them and their constituencies. Since stakeholders are diverse, we cannot demand uniformly high levels of satisfaction. But in the presence of significant dissatisfaction from parents, or students, or teachers, or Board members, we would conclude that planning and implementation had not been successful.

4. Goal achievement. Finally, for good planning and implementation, we should be able to note that the implemented vision does in fact accomplish what it is supposed to: enhance pupil self-esteem, serve as a beacon of change for other schools, provide certain community services, etc. This might be seen as a criterion of "objective success" -- one which is often given short shrift because educational outcomes are diffuse, difficult to measure, and so on, but one we cannot ignore.

Our working definition is that all four of these components must be present for implementation to be considered "good," "successful";# if the new school has lost the original vision (not just minor aspects of it), or is

---

*The reader familiar with the literature on eductional innovation will note that the "goal-congruence" criterion is quite similar to the "fidelity perspective" (Fullan and Pomfret, 1977), in which the success of an innovation is judged by whether it is implemented as its developers/planners intended. The "problem-coping" criterion is similar to Fullan and Pomfret's "process perspective," in which the nature of what happens during implementation is more crucial than "fidelity."

#There are some value-laden questions here, beyond the scope of this discussion. For example, what if the goals are trivial, not worth anyone's attention, but are well and congruently achieved? More pointedly, what of a school that was doing well on all four dimensions of P/I success, but was devoted to ethically dubious goals? Fagin's school for thieves is easy enough to cite, but depending on one's larger value framework, one might applaud or condemn, say, schools for CIA agents, for American Nazi sympathizers, "free children," or only blacks, or only whites. Or one might applaud or condemn schools using "dubious" methods, such as behavior modification, rote learning, or "letting kids do their thing."

In our study, we de-emphasized value and ideological issues of this sort by choosing to study schools built around (to us) significant and

floundering or overwhelmed with current problems, <u>or</u> has dissatisfied stakeholders, <u>or</u> is clearly not achieving its hoped-for goals, we are seeing an implementation failure of some degree.*

The remainder of this chapter turns to the question of what might be the determinants of P/I success or failure, taking the boxes of Figure 2.1 one by one.

C. ESSENTIAL FEATURES OF THE ENTERPRISE

The sort of social system we are studying in this book involves the actual creation of a whole new, innovative school, within a school district.

1. A Whole School

The fact that a whole school (rather than the introduction of a specific innovation such as a textbook) is involved, makes for a good deal of task complexity for planners and implementers, and requires substantial financial resources. The task at hand is a formidable one: thus, a good deal of expert knowledge must be mustered, and the P/I group must be powerful enough to obtain the money needed.

2. A Subsystem of the Local District

The schools we studied were not freestanding, but embedded in a local public school district. Thus they automatically had to compete for limited resources with other schools and programs, and had to deal with a wide variety of bureaucratic constraints -- rules, regulations, approved ways of doing things. These problems place a premium on political skill -- the ability to fight for and obtain resources within, around, and in spite of the rules of the game, against or with the other players.

The local district also includes a surrounding community populated by parents and other citizens, with characteristic sets of values and ideologies

---

(footnote cont'd) acceptable goals, and <u>then</u> to judge planning/implementation success by asking whether these goals were achieved, and how people acted and felt about their work. That stance is, of course, a decisive value position in itself.

*As David Cohen pointed out to us, the creation of new schools occurs for other reasons than "success" hopes: they serve <u>latent functions</u>, such as career advancement for their planners and implementers, or sheer boredom reduction; they serve as a sort of arena or theater for the <u>expression of cultural conflicts</u>; and they may be an expression of <u>innovation for its own sake.</u> We expect ourselves, and the reader, to stay alert to data consistent with these alternate views, even as we examine the "success" of planning and implementation in the terms we have described.

about education, which set the stage for conflicts over various aspects of the emerging new school. Here too, political skill is crucial to maximize endorsement for the enterprise.

3. Innovative: New and Different

The schools we studied were not only new (in the sense that they did not exist until they were brought into being), but they were to a greater or lesser degree different from past versions of schools in these districts (cf. Kimberly, 1980).* That meant that uncertainty would be considerably higher, and many skills needed would by definition be lacking, since something new and different was being attempted. In addition, the P/I group could expect opposition to their efforts from more traditionally-oriented parts of their environment.

These problems are likely to create certain needs -- not only for courage in facing the unknown, and for surmounting opposition, but for political skill, techniques for reducing uncertainty, and extra investment of energy (which, as Stinchcombe (1965) has suggested, is always required in innovative enterprises). The "economy of effort" of the familiar is missing. New roles and procedures have to be constructed, and people must learn them through training and socialization; habit is not enough. Once again: we were studying developing, rather than fully-developed organizations. We could expect to see a good deal of stress and difficulty.

4. Actual Implementation

The schools we studied were intended to be actualized, to appear, to be created; their creators were not engaging in an abstract planning exercise. In addition, the processes of implementation took place at different times, and were often carried out by different personnel than was the case for planning. Thus, certain problems would inevitably appear: the existence of gaps between planners and implementers, and the fact that surrounding conditions could change considerably over the life of the project. These problems created needs for careful linkage between planning and implementation, and for flexibility and adaptation as the P/I enterprise continued.

---

*It is fair to say that none of our sites was seen by its planners as basically "innovative" for the general field of schooling (in the sense, say, that Neill's Summerhill, or Bremer's Parkway School, or Montessori's first school, were at the time of their creation). Instead, our P/I groups were attempting a local, novel, adaptation of school forms and practices which were more or less available, professionally known in the larger educational environment. Even with this more modest definition of "innovative", however, planning and implementation proved difficult and stressful in many of our sites.

D. THE CONTEXT OF THE ENTERPRISE

The processes we studied were taking place in a larger, historically given context: American public schools. Certain features of this context serve, we believe, both to provide energy for and to constrain innovative efforts. These features can be briefly summarized:*

Goal diffuseness: educational goals tend to be vague and diffuse, hard to measure, and "loosely coupled" to educational procedures.

People-processing mission: schools are supposed to alter persons, rather than affect the shape of physical objects or accumulate money.

Structural constraints: schools in America are restricted by the presence of many formal macro-system structures (laws, courts, state regulations, unions) and less-formal structures (tests, accreditation procedures, standard texts)

Professionalism: Schools are staffed by people defining themselves as trained experts working from formal knowledge.

Weak knowledge base: The linkage between desired goals and appropriate "technology" is not well known, and/or not well diffused among educators.

Domestication: Schools are "owned" by the public, and have guaranteed survival.

Boundary permeability: Schools are "thin-skinned", can be entered easily by their clients and patrons, feel "vulnerable" from inside.

Table 2.1 summarizes what we consider to be the possible effects of these contextual features; we will not review it in detail.

E. PRIMARY TASKS FOR PLANNING/IMPLEMENTATION GROUPS

The nature of the new-school enterprise, and the contextual features surrounding it, help to define a series of primary tasks for the P/I group. They are, in brief:

1. Political stabilization: obtaining money, environmental endorsement, and a place in the local power structure.

---

*The relevant prior analyses drawn on were those of Miles (1967, 1977); Miles and Schmuck (1971); Bidwell (1965); and Sieber (1968). More recently, Miles (1981) has synthesized the available empirical data bearing on such features and their consequences for schools as organizations.

Library
I.U.P.
Indiana, Pa

372.13   c.1   G563w

TABLE 2.1

THE CONTEXT: AMERICAN PUBLIC EDUCATION

CONTEXTUAL FEATURE	EFFECTS
Goal diffuseness	Promotes diffuseness in goals for school Heightens uncertainty
People-processing mission	Induces tendency toward control of students Batch processing emphasized
Structural constraints	Constrain use of innovative procedures Force for choice of traditional practices
Professionalism	Commitment to goals; goal conflict Protection of vested interests of role Energy investment
Weak knowledge base of education	Unawareness of needed skills Minimization of expertise Inadequate mapping of planning/ implementation task Reliance on traditional forms, myths
"Domestication" (ownership by public)	Guaranteed survival Non-competition for students (guaranteed clientele) Legitimacy of community pressure pro or con innovation
Permeability to environment	Vulnerability when district or local bureaucracy is hostile

2. Knowledge utilization: acquiring and using technically-good information, expertise.

3. Vision development: developing coherence among basic philosophy, goals, and desired identity or image of the school.

4. Social-architectural design: creating an organizational plan, and selecting people to be part of it.

5. Actualization: linking the plan to start-up and early implementation, developing the real social system of the school.

6. <u>Institutionalization</u>: stabilizing the school, including its methods for continuing self-renewal.

These tasks are especially demanding and complex in the case we are studying: schools which are both new and different for their environments. The more innovative the effort, the more energy will be required to confront and deal with these primary tasks.

Each of the tasks is discussed here in more detail, and we show how they tend to sequence over time. They are arrayed in a roughly developmental order: reasonable success on each task is required for effective work on later-numbered tasks. Naturally, any particular P/I group may or may not see it this way, and we are not positing firm rationality as the guiding light. But it does seem (for example) that coherent design of the school's structures is less likely when the background vision, the collective hope for the school, is diffuse or still in contention. Or, if a P/I group working on staff training just before start-up suddenly finds that their political fences are not as well mended as they had thought, they will have to "return" to the political stabilization task, since political support is essential for effectiveness in the current situation.

Primary Task 1: Political Stabilization

The task here is essentially that of obtaining and assuring a continued flow of financial resources and environmental endorsement, to support not only the planning/implementation process itself, but continued operations of the implemented school. It is essentially one type of input assurance.* The task of assuring a <u>continued</u> flow of resources implies more than short-run political success: the P/I enterprise, and the new school itself, must be built in to the immediate power structure, find an ecological niche, so to speak.

---

*We should stress something important here. Our field work taught us that political issues were extremely salient, and that we could not stay inside the organization and ignore its environment, if we were to understand what was happening. That realization in turn has strong implications for one's model of organization.

Much past research on organizations has in effect utilized a closed-system model (for example, see Taylor, 1922 on "scientific management"; Gulick & Urwick, 1934 on public administration; or Weber, 1947, with his classical definition of bureaucracy). Such a model implies that environmental variation can be ignored, that all the variables that count are under the control of administrators, and that there are more or less standard structures and functions in all organizations.

An open-system model (see, for example, Buckley's (1967) systems theory formulation, or Katz & Kahn's (1978) social-psychological view), or Lawrence and Lorsch's (1967) analysis of organization-environment relations implies that the organization is steadily receiving inputs from and emitting outputs to its environment, and that environmental variation (as well as internal structures and functions) are a steady source of uncertainty,

Primary Task 2: Knowledge Utilization

A second basic type of input to the planning process is that of valid, technically competent knowledge. Since the schools we studied (and indeed all but a very few groundbreaking new schools) are not de novo creations, but rely on the importation and adaptation of educational practice from elsewhere, there is a steady need for P/I groups to locate, interpret and use the best available technical information from outside themselves.

If the two preceding primary tasks are essentially input-assuring, the remaining four can be seen as assuring various outputs of the P/I effort. Figure 2.2 shows them graphically; they will be discussed one by one.

Briefly, Primary Tasks 3, 4, and 5 can be seen as achieving effective linkage* among various outputs or products of the P/I group's work, such as a statement of goals, or the organizational design. The corresponding numbers of Figure 2.2 show where these linkages take place.

Primary Task 3: Vision Development

Vision development involves the development of coherence among several products of the P/I group's work: their underlying educational-philosophical position, the goals they hold for this school in particular, and their vision (a sort of rough sketch for or image of the school). The linkage question is: do these products match or fit well with each other? Do they form a coherent whole, or are there internal contradictions?

P/I groups naturally vary widely in how cleanly or systematically they go about vision development. But the task will not go away if it is not addressed: our thesis is that incoherence here will show up in confused organizational design and uncertain or expedient implementation. (We are not advocating a sequential, step-by-step planning model, only pointing out that vague or poorly-linked visions will influence organizational design and implementation -- and may have to be corrected (or at least acknowledged) later on).

(footnote cont'd) requiring adaptive coping. Our study is, not surprisingly, built around open system ideas. They have important implications: (1) the environment-organization relationship can be expected to be central, not peripheral; (2) uncertainties in new schools will always arise both from the environment and from the organization's technologies; (3) it is unlikely there is any single effective way to structure a new organization.

These implications may seem obvious, but it is fair to say that much prior research on new schools has underplayed them. See, for example, Gross et al., (1971); Smith and Keith (1971); Myers (1973); Cooper (1973); Simon et al., (1973); Center for New Schools (1975); Eastabrook et al., (1977).

*We are grateful to Rein van der Vegt for his active help in proposing and clarifying these ideas.

FIGURE 2.2
PLANNING/IMPLEMENTATION OUTPUTS

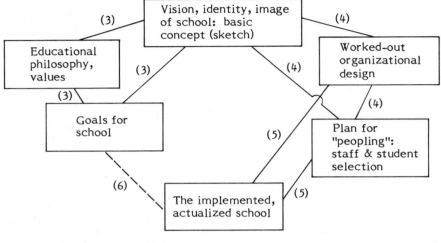

Primary Task 4: Social-Architectural Design*

This task involves the development of an organizational design which is linked to (follows from, is congruent with, is matched to) the goals/philosophy/vision; and a relevant plan for "peopling" the design with staff and students, which is well linked with the vision, and with the design.

---

*This label is drawn from Perlmutter (1965) who first proposed the idea that organizations being created could benefit from the sort of systematic planning attention that the "architecture" metaphor implies. The most recent and useful treatments of organizational design are found in Clark (1972); Kilmann (1977); Kilmann, Pondy & Slevin (1976); Burack & Negandhi (1977); Pfeffer (1978); Kimberly & Miles (1980); and Nystrom & Starbuck (1980).

In passing, we might note some things about this literature: first, we concur with Cherns (1976):

> The art of organization design is simultaneously esoteric and poorly developed. Most existing organizations were not born, but "just growed"....There is, of course, no lack of available models and no one seeking to set up an organization need invent the wheel. But organization design is generally an outcome, not an input.

In fact, the bulk of what is written about organization design is

Primary Task 5: Actualization

This task involves implementing or actualizing the school, bringing about a congruent realization of the organizational and peopling designs. Essentially, the linkage involved is between planning and implementation. Such linkage may be accomplished by various structural means (such as involving implementers in late planning, having the organizational plan on paper, using key planners as advisors, etc.), as well as by active diagnosis and trouble-shooting of the organization in its early stages, to insure that it is functioning congruently with the P/I group's hopes.

Actualization is a formidable, complex task, occupying a good deal of energy if P/I groups choose to take it seriously (i.e., care about achieving a real school that is congruent with the design and the original vision).

Primary Task 6: Institutionalization

The actualized school needs to be stabilized, routinized in a way that enables continued achievement of the original core goals (or, at the minimum, those goals that have survived the exigencies of the P/I process to date). Some aspects of this task will have been dealt with during social-architectural design work, naturally, but some will not be seriously faced until actualization is confronted. Envisioning an aspect of a new school is a different matter from actually starting it up, which in turn is different from ensuring its continued health and viability -- and its real connection to original goals.

Completing these six primary tasks is essential to implementation success. That is, if the linkages among the various products of the P/I group (tasks 4-6) have been adequate -- and if adequate inputs (tasks 1 and 2) from the environment have occurred -- we would presumably note success of the school (achievement of our four outcomes): goal congruence, satisfaction, goal achievement and problem-coping capacity. As with other chains, weak links make for vulnerability. So it is not surprising that dreams do not always become realities.

F. KEY DILEMMAS IN PLANNING AND IMPLEMENTATION

As P/I groups work on the primary tasks described above, they tend to encounter some chronic dilemmas. Though we do not have the space to give specific examples,* we should explain that these eight dilemmas are

---

(footnote cont'd) retrospective -- is about designs, not designing. Furthermore, the literature says little about the design of people-processing systems, is excessively rational, and generally avoids the political issues which as we shall see, are crucial in the design of new schools.

*For the full range of examples illustrating not only the dilemmas, but primary tasks and P/I group capabilities, see Miles (1978b; 1980). The first reference also shows through "force field analysis" how dilemmas arise from basic problems of the enterprise and its context.

empirically generated: they arose from our observations of P/I groups in Lincoln Acres and our five other research sites. They represent pervasive issues which must be faced repeatedly. The dilemmas of P/I groups are partly a result of their efforts to confront the barriers and constraints of the American public school setting, and partly a result of conflict and paradoxes generic to the process of creating a new school as such.

Dilemma 1: Innovative vs. Familiar Choices

This dilemma seemed so pervasive in our sites, so much at the center of what we observed, that it can be seen as a kind of "master dilemma," infusing the others that follow. As P/I groups proceed, they must repeatedly consider whether to choose the unfamiliar, new and different when making planning and implementation decisions, or to elect for the familiar and well-tested alternative.*

Dilemma 2: Goal Adherence vs. Revision

New schools usually have somewhere early in their history a more or less explicit vision, an outline of certain basic goals it is felt the school should accomplish. P/I groups often find themselves caught between the desire to retain certain goals as crucial, and the need to let go of them as stern exigencies arise during the course of planning and implementation, or as "better ideas" emerge.

Dilemma 3: Environmental Contact vs. Withdrawal

The new schools we studied existed in an environment, including the local school district organization and the community. It was by definition necessary for them to obtain financial resources and endorsement from their environments. Yet they were at the same time deeply preoccupied with the internal dynamics of designing and building an educational social system. We often noted rather different responses by P/I groups, as between proactive, outgoing, environment-confronting action on the one hand, and reactive-avoidant, inwardly-oriented responses on the other.

---

*There is a temptation to consider that one horn or another of any particular dilemma is better: in this case, that innovation is better than familiar practice. But the defining characteristic of a dilemma is usually that a chooser is struggling between two goods, rather than a good and a bad. Thus the choice is not between innovating and giving up -- but, given a generally innovative intent (the case we are studying), whether to choose an innovative (untested) solution or a familiar one (safer, and perhaps more likely to achieve the innovative goal).

Dilemma 4: Expertise-seeking vs. Self-reliance

A fourth dilemma we recurrently noted in our sites focuses on a different sort of environmental relationship. P/I groups steadily find themselves in need of expert knowledge, information from what might be called the professional environment. The choice regularly presenting itself is whether to actively seek for, and import such knowledge to the P/I effort, or to rely on the group's own internal resources. The issue is not precisely parallel to that of the preceding dilemma, where activeness/passiveness in relation to obtaining money and support from the environment is the crucial issue. Here the question is whether the P/I group will open its boundaries, reach out for assistance, allow the content of its decisions to be influenced by externally developed and validated knowledge and/or knowledge-bearers -- or conclude that sufficient expertise exists internally.

Dilemma 5: Feedback Utilization vs. Intuitive Action

We noted in our sites that P/I group members often face another dilemma: should they collect thorough, careful, systematic data on the results of their efforts, to guide subsequent planning and decision-making -- or should they make the practical assumption that things are okay and just proceed intuitively and directly? The feedback collected and used may deal with the functioning of the P/I group itself, with the functioning of the school, or with the environment's relation to the school. Getting feedback is supposedly the rational, effective way to proceed -- but collecting and using data can be an energy-consuming, threatening, fallible process.

Dilemma 6: Implementation Constraint vs. Autonomy

Should plans be specific, crisply formulated, with definite provision for linking planners to those who will carry out the plan? In short, should the hand of the past control actions in the present?

Or, on the other hand, given human fallibility, unanticipated outcomes of decisions, and unexpected events (in our sites, these included floods, heart attacks, and the scrupulousness of fire inspectors), perhaps it is more sensible to leave a good deal of flexibility, and autonomy for those who must carry out plans.

Even where planners and implementers are the same people, the question of firmness, specificity and explicitness of plans, and how much constraint should be exerted over day-to-day implementation (as contrasted with providing slack, or "loosely-coupled" execution of the plan) is at issue.*

----

*Weick's (1976) analysis of "loose coupling" carries the clear implication that "loose coupling" is not necessarily a defect in organizations, but a strategy with positive value, enabling better adaptation, more inventiveness, self-determination, and resistance to "trouble spread" -- all at less cost than for tightly-coupled systems.

Dilemma 7: Laissez-faire vs. Intervention

Once implementation begins in earnest, another characteristic dilemma appears: should implementers be active or easygoing in correcting difficulties and problems? One position is that the plan and its early implementation are mostly OK, and should not be seriously questioned or re-oriented. People will "work things out"; all that's really needed is a little oiling of the machinery here and there, plus routine maintenance.

But in most new, innovative enterprises, active intervention may often be needed. If the staff's skills are inadequate, they need active support, resocialization or training; if this does not work, the possibility of firing people must be considered. Or perhaps the basic plan is not really workable, and some form of reorganization is indicated. Perhaps additional personnel will be required. Implementation, says this horn of the dilemma, will not just "happen" naturally or easily, but may need active assistance -- or even surgery or reconstruction.

Dilemma 8: Routinization vs. Flexibility

A final dilemma centers on whether to stabilize, solidify, and universalize working procedures and the structures which support them, or retain maneuvering room for the unique, the unforeseen, and the particular. Without a reasonable degree of clarity and shape, much energy can be wasted, wheels are steadily re-invented and as steadily discarded, and things will not "settle down".

But institutionalization, it goes without much saying, can be the death of innovation. Uniform treatment for idiosyncratic situations dries up inventiveness; habitual responses to problematic events cause people not to notice what is really there. Poetry is submerged in the machinery.

In fact, we have come full circle from our first dilemma: whether to make the innovative or the familiar choice. A sort of meta-question is now raised: can our new innovative school be routinized, stabilized, institutionalized in a way that protects and furthers its originally innovative intent -- or will that intent be lost among the standard operating procedures?

The implementers of new schools are not immune, in their micro-societies, to the general dilemma of stability and change in human affairs. Though P/I groups begin with the hope (and assumption) that they can "make things new," they must ultimately face the question of how far to stabilize whatever newness they have achieved, and how far to keep pressing into new newness.

G. PLANNING/IMPLEMENTATION GROUP CAPABILITIES

Though all P/I groups face these dilemmas as they cope with their primary tasks, the solutions they come up with vary rather widely -- and not just because of the situations they face. We believe that the idea of "capability" -- greater or lesser amounts of operating skill -- must be invoked. Here we list briefly six capabilities that seemed important in the sites we studied.

The capabilities can be seen as "bundles" of more specific skills (for example, decision-making skill includes skills of summarizing, getting participation, forecasting decision effects, etc.). And they are exercised, not just by the P/I leader, but by other members, or the P/I group as a whole. Our list includes:

1. Legitimacy development. Can the P/I group gain a "license to plan", (and later, a license to implement)? It must be able to get the right to proceed, to spend money, to make decisions that will not be capriciously overturned.

2. Investment development. The P/I group must be able to evoke energy and time from its members, who are signing on for a difficult voyage; commitment must be developed, and cannot be assured by selecting only "true believers" (Kritek, 1976; Sarason, 1972), because the voyage is full of uncertainty.

3. Meta-planning. The P/I group must be skilled at developing a "plan for planning", or background strategy, which covers such matters as P/I membership, timetabling, P/I linkage methods, and use of data for steering. Meta-plans also include, implicitly, how the future will be approached, and how much adaptation is expected, and regulate the degree of design specificity (see Miles, 1976).

4. Political skill. The P/I group must develop strategies that succeed in getting needed financial resources and endorsement from the environment; they may include circumvention, cooptation, bargaining, coalition-building and buffering (Sullivan & Kironde, 1976).

5. Reflexiveness. Can the P/I group learn from what it is doing, by data collection, self-examination and self-correction?

6. Decision-making skill. The P/I group is faced with hundreds of decisions. Will they be technically good, and owned by the members? There are many sub-skills here; resource utilization, contingency analysis, variety protection, clarity of decision-making model itself, final decision clarification.

H. P/I GROUP DECISIONS

To recapitulate: the general context and the demands of the enterprise generate a series of primary planning and implementation tasks, with characteristic dilemmas involved. How these tasks are dealt with depends, we have suggested, on the presence of P/I group capabilities. As these capabilities are exercised, decisions and actions emerge in a steady stream.

A decision, to quote our instructions to field workers, is "a reasonably explicit agreement to do something, usually involving commitment of resources, in the immediate or near future."* And actions are the "do something" component.

Decisions and actions are the basic instrumental means through which P/I groups, using their capabilities, bring about more or less successful intermediate and ultimate outcomes.

I. FINAL COMMENTS

By this time, the reader may be overloaded, wandering among lists of dilemmas, primary tasks, capabilities, outcomes. Figure 2.3 suggests how all these may be related.

It suggests several things: first, that we believe that some primary tasks are more likely (see lines) to generate certain dilemmas. Second, the capabilities fall into two families: externally-oriented ones (legitimacy development and political skills) that assure resources and endorsement, and internally-oriented ones,which apply to all outcomes. Third, we do not know enough to suggest precise causal links (just how a particular capability is applied to a particular task and its most prominent associated dilemmas).

We hope this recapitulation of our conceptual framework has taught the reader enough about our ideas and our language so they will be familiar as the case proceeds. Concepts from the framework will be used regularly to analyze the concrete events as they unfold. So, on to the events of Lincoln Acres!

---

*The reader with worries about over-rationality should be reassured that field workers in our sites also attended to implicit or tacit, "as if" decisions, and to "non-decisions" -- failures to attend to issues which seemed to deserve work, on the face of it.

FIGURE 2.3
RELATIONSHIP OF MAJOR VARIABLES IN OVER-ALL FRAMEWORK

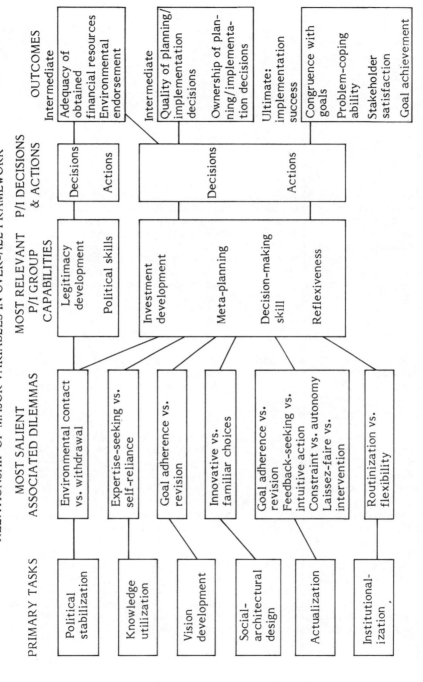

3

THE CONTEXT OF THE SCHOOL:
PAST AND PRESENT

We have already stressed that educational innovation cannot be adequately understood apart from the environment in which it takes place. We cannot ignore, either, the relevant events which have preceded it (Sarason, 1972). This chapter focuses on the township, local community and education system in which the new school is located. Throughout the study, forces from the context -- in particular the local community -- will surface repeatedly; they influenced the school's development actively, and thus help to explain much of the behavior we noted during its planning, implementation and continued operation.

A. A LOOK AT LINCOLN ACRES SCHOOL AND ITS COMMUNITY

Surrounded by a park on three sides and woods directly in back of it, Lincoln Acres School is located in the middle of the Lincoln Acres community. It is a one-story brick building of austere, functional design. Children's art work displayed in the windows, and the usually-filled bicycle racks on the side of the building identify it immediately as an elementary school.

Inside, on a typical day, there is a steady hum of activity. Almost all areas of the school are used continuously during the day for instructional purposes; intermittently, so are the hallways. In the classrooms, there is usually a variety of activities in progress: a teacher working with a small group of students on a reading lesson, another small group of students working independently on a science project, pairs of students playing quiet games, and others feeding animals or working alone. Each classroom area has an adequate to abundant supply of learning materials, old sofas (for relaxed studying), plants and animals. Student art work decorates the walls. In general, the atmosphere in the school is one of cooperation between teachers and students; there is minimal emphasis on discipline; it is rare to see a teacher scolding or closely directing students.

It is in this setting that three hundred and fifty Lincoln Acres children, sorted into grades Kindergarten through six, their 18 teachers, principal and parent volunteers spend the 180 days a year the state law requires for the process of education.

The Lincoln Acres community is a moderate-size suburban housing development. Construction began in 1971, and by 1976, when building was finished, there were nearly 600 single-family homes in the community.

Residents take great care to maintain the appearance of their houses and property. The houses, most of which cost between $50,000 and $70,000 in the mid-70's, are freshly painted with bright colors, and often have elaborate ornamentation (for example, wrought iron work, planters and large, fancy mailboxes at the curb). Lawns are kept trimmed, and carefully-arranged bushes and shrubs provide landscaping in an area nearly devoid of mature trees, which were leveled to provide easy, less-expensive construction.

Late-model automobiles -- usually two for each family -- dot the driveways, and periodically a recreational camper sits alongside the house or an above-ground swimming pool protrudes in a backyard. Beyond these few visible displays of material possessions that, presumably, either enhance or maintain family status within the community, little else besides the model of house separates one dwelling from the other. The lasting impression one gets from driving through the curving streets of the development is not so much the feeling of sameness that early "mass society" critics of suburbia complained about, but a suggestion of a kind of intentional equality; the individuality of each house, despite obvious attempts at differentiation, falls within what seems to be a limited, acceptable, range.

On a typical week-day afternoon, it is not unusual to see two or three Indian mothers dressed in saris walking down a street, with their pre-school children either following behind or being pushed in a carriage as their mothers talk. Other people, generally mothers, and almost always Caucasian, can be seen unloading groceries from cars, walking dogs, or, depending on the time of year, working in the garden. But for the most part, during the months that school is in session, between 9:00 a.m. and 3:00 p.m. few people are to be seen on the streets or in the yards of Lincoln Acres. All fathers, and an increasing number of mothers, are away from home working. Three quarters of the mothers identify their primary role as "housewife".

These impressions tell little about Lincoln Acres' surrounding physical and social context, and nothing about its history. The community of Lincoln Acres is part of a township, Washingtonville.

B. THE TOWNSHIP

Lying on a plain in the middle of an industrial eastern state, Washingtonville, which was organized as a township by Dutch settlers in 1685, stretches for more than forty square miles. An hour's drive by automobile brings its residents to a large metropolitan center, and it is only fifteen minutes to one of the large cities in the state. On its northern and eastern borders are sprawling suburban communities, and to the south is a university town. Small dairy farms still operate in the communities on the western boundary, and the clusters of older houses that dot the area retain a rural character.

Passing through Washingtonville is a major interstate highway that separates the older, rural part of the township from the recently-settled suburban communities. About one-third of the township's 15,000 residents live in the rural areas. Several small villages and isolated houses intermingle with swaths of family farms, many of which have fallen into disuse in the last 15 years. During the period of agricultural decline, large industrial complexes were built by local and multi-national corporations, mainly in two communities which have access to major highways, with others scattered throughout the area. In the last five years small tracts of new, expensive, houses have been built on the fringes of the villages. But despite the abandonment of farming, the increase in industrial and residential land use has been gradual. For the most part, this older section of the township has not changed much from the way it was in the 1880's.

Permanent mobile trailer parks have cropped up along the interstate highway. The population of these camps is mainly older, retired people; young, transient, semi-skilled factory workers; laborers; and a few college students. In some respects, these trailer parks, which are steadily expanding, have replaced the migrant labor force (and the temporary quarters they occupied) which disappeared along with the farms. Otherwise, with the exception of a few widely-separated diners, factories and gas stations, the highway serves mainly as a truck and commuter route between cities.

The largest community in the township, Allwood Green, was built in 1956 by a single construction company. When the mass-produced housing was finished, the community included fifteen hundred single-family houses of similar design, three schools (paid for by the builder), and a church and synagogue. On the main road that borders Allwood Green, a modest shopping center -- it has no major department store -- was built. The houses originally sold for $14,000 and today, twenty years later, sell for between $40,000 and $50,000.

The families in Allwood Green, many of whom were first attracted to it by the low house price and proximity to the metropolis, are fairly well established, with middle-aged parents whose children are mostly in junior high schools, high school or college. In terms of occupation, this community is diverse: truck drivers, technicians, salesmen, middle-management workers and college professors are the largest groups among the adult males. Quite a few wives in Allwood Green work full time outside the home. In general, family incomes in Allwood Green are lower than those in Lincoln Acres.

Although some additional houses and businesses have appeared in Allwood Green, it has not significantly changed since it was first built. Many of the current residents are the original owners of their houses.

At about the same time that Allwood Green was built, a small number of garden apartments, the only multiple-family dwellings in the township, were built nearby. Together, these two new residential areas increased the population of the township from an estimated 4,528 in 1955 to approximately 14,500 in 1966. This population growth did not, however, keep pace with the rapid expansion of many of the surrounding townships, and compared to them Washingtonville township is still mainly rural and underdeveloped.

C. THE LOCAL COMMUNITY

When Lincoln Acres, the community in which Lincoln Acres school is located, was proposed by a builder in 1962, the project met with strong resistance, and a lengthy court battle. The Washingtonville residents who initiated the lawsuit feared a situation similar to the one that followed the construction of Allwood Green: inadequate provision by the builder of municipal facilities, with the result of increased taxes throughout the township. In fact, opponents of further construction were powerful enough to succeed in barring all large-scale building in the township from the completion of Allwood Green in the early 1960's until 1969, when the Lincoln Acres tract was approved for residential use. Because of this resistance, part of the arrangement to get residential zoning approved included the developer's donation of land for an elementary school in the community, and $80,000 toward its construction.

The first residents moved into Lincoln Acres in the summer of 1970. By January, 1975, when this study began, there were approximately 500 single-family homes occupied, with another 60 scheduled to be built. Five basic models of homes were available, which in 1970 cost between $38,000-42,000; prices increased to $50,000-70,000 in 1975. Purchasers of homes in Lincoln Acres were mainly young, upwardly-mobile families. Few elderly or middle-aged people bought homes in the development.

Of those families answering our first survey,* 59% answered that the most important reason for moving to Lincoln Acres was "the house". This was followed in importance by the nearness of the community to place of work (17%), and the school system (17%). "To live near friends or relatives" and "low property taxes" received 3% and 0% respectively.

Where did these families live before coming to Lincoln Acres? 53% of the respondents had moved from large urban areas, 35% from suburban areas and 12% from rural areas. For the majority of families, this was the first home they had owned.

Occupationally, as in the age of its families, Lincoln Acres is, relatively speaking, homogeneous. A large percentage of male heads of household reported themselves as professionals working in private businesses; only 9% of them owned businesses or identified themselves as self-employed.

---

*Three mail surveys were sent to all parents of children in Lincoln Acres school. The first survey was administered in February, 1976 and had a response rate of 52%. The second administration, in June 1976, had a response rate of 35%. A third wave, in June 1977, was returned by 44%. The survey data, then, do not represent a random sample, but a proportion of the total population. We should also note that these data do not provide information about the entire community, but only on those families with children in the school. However, participant observation suggests that the majority of families without children in school are young and as yet childless or with infants. In major dimensions, these families appear similar to those with children attending school.

Despite recent trends toward increased employment of women, 85% responded that they were primarily involved in keeping house. Only 8% were working full time outside the home and 14% part time, with 2% temporarily out of work. Of the respondents, 6% of the females were attending school. An interesting and significant finding is that 29% of the respondents (male and female) currently were, or had been, teachers; familiarity with educational practices was extensive among parents.

Ethnically and religiously, the community is heterogeneous. In response to a survey question, 30% considered themselves as being members of minority or nationality groups and 46% did not. Within the minority groups, 12% identified themselves as Chinese, 4% as East Indian and 5% as Black. Family religious preference was 19% Protestant, 31% Catholic, 27% Jewish and 13% Buddhist. But the data on ethnicity and religious preference are incomplete, since the question was marked "optional", and 25% did not answer the ethnic question and 11% the religious question. From talks with community members, there seems to be an agreed-upon estimate that about 20% of the population is Oriental, 30% Jewish, 10% East Indian, 5% Black and the rest of varied racial, religious and ethnic backgrounds. Although the figures may be inaccurate, it is clear that in these important areas of life -- race and ethnicity -- Lincoln Acres does not fit the popular stereotype of the suburban community.

Besides these demographic differences, orientation toward, and expectations of, the community vary considerably. Many families, especially those in management, or highly technical occupations such as those in the electronics or chemical industry, view Lincoln Acres as a place to live for only as long as a company assignment is in the locality. Others have selected it as a place to settle in permanently; although they are new residents, they feel an attachment to the community and township, and actively participate in local associations and politics. Yet others view the home as an investment above all else, and are prepared to move if real estate values fluctuate or decline.

Related to property values is the fact that Lincoln Acres is on the same side of the interstate highway as Allwood Green. The two communities have the same postal address, but are separated by a strip of farmland about a half-mile wide. This separation, along with higher house prices in Lincoln Acres, its newness, and the builder-assigned name, gives the two communities separate identities, as well as a sense of being self-contained. Indeed, many Lincoln Acres residents exhibit a form of class bias toward Allwood Green, commenting that the houses there are smaller, less expensive and not as carefully maintained.

Countering the ability of Lincoln Acres residents to establish and maintain exclusivity is one of the peculiar features of the township: all of the communities in it are dependent for basic services on outside areas. In the case of Lincoln Acres, aside from the elementary school, no other institutions -- churches, the police, hospitals, libraries or stores -- are located within the development. They are sited in other parts of the township or nearby communities. Recreation is similarly limited. Surrounding the Lincoln Acres School is a park with a ball field and tennis courts, but there is no motion picture theater in the township, and the only sources of entertainment are a roller skating rink and a few restaurants. Most residents, if they do not make their own entertainment, seek it in nearby cities or at one of the elaborate enclosed shopping malls in the region.

Perhaps the matrix of institutional arrangements that ties Lincoln Acres most closely to the life of Washingtonville township is local government. Lincoln Acres is limited in actions it can take with respect to services supplied by the community, and to the policies that operate the local school. Essentially, Lincoln Acres is dependent on the township for two reasons: its ecology limits its autonomy, and it is part of a larger political unit.

From this brief account of the local community, it can be seen that Lincoln Acres is significantly different from the other sections of Washingtonville in two important respects: social class and life cycle (Gans, 1962). In terms of social class, Lincoln Acres is a more affluent community than any other settlement in the township. This is reflected in the house prices as well as the occupational structure of the community. From the perspective of life cycle -- an important and often-overlooked variable -- the residents of Lincoln Acres are, for the most part, young families in the early to middle period of child rearing. As in most American families in this stage (especially middle-class ones), education of the young is a primary concern.

D. THE EDUCATIONAL SYSTEM

In 1975 there were 2,025 elementary school pupils in the Washingtonville district, with 97 elementary teachers. Tradition in Washingtonville supports neighborhood elementary schools. As a result, there are seven elementary schools in the township, each with grades Kindergarten through six, with enrollment ranging from 220 to 612. Two of the rural schools were built in 1928 and another in 1950. Three other elementary schools, each of which has had a recent addition, were built in 1957, 1959, and 1961 to accommodate Allwood Green. The most recent one, Lincoln Acres school, was completed in 1975, almost five years after the first houses were occupied.

A junior high school was opened in 1966; it has 821 students currently attending school, with a faculty of 58. Before 1960, when the high school was built, students attended school in neighboring communities. The high school has since been enlarged, and currently has a student body of 1,266 and a professional staff of 96. In sum, the school system is not large, but has increased in size and complexity since the early 1960's.

Organizationally, the township school district is relatively free of bureaucratic positions, especially when compared to the administrative structures of large cities. The central administrative staff consists of the superintendent, three assistants to him, a business manager, and various heads of system-wide programs such as special educational services and maintenance. Each school has its own principal. Only the high school and junior high school have vice principals and department chairmen.

In the elementary schools, besides classroom teachers, there are learning disabilities consultants and teachers of specialized subjects such as music and art, who usually work in more than one school. Washingtonville elementary schools have a position not usually found in other school districts in the state, called a "resource teacher", whose basic job, beyond limited teaching, is to aid teachers in program planning and facilitate their work. Lunchroom and custodial personnel complete the staff. Volunteer parents are frequently used as either classroom or clerical aides.

Governing this educational structure is the Washingtonville Board of Education, a township-wide policy-making body. It is composed of nine members, three of whom are elected each year for a three-year term. After the board is re-constituted each year, a president is elected from among the members for a one-year term. Board members receive no payment for their efforts. The superintendent of schools attends the board meetings, but only in an advisory capacity, and does not vote. Operating under a "sunshine" law, designed to encourage citizen participation and discourage secrecy in local government, the Washingtonville Board of Education must conduct all business in public sessions, unless personnel matters or individual students are the topic of discussion.

The county board of education, the state department of education and federal agencies such as the Department of Education form an overlay on this local structure. Despite their regulations and ability to dispense funds, their control is usually indirect and weak; the local school district, partly because of tradition, retains autonomy -- especially in the critical area of the content of educational programs. However, in recent years, primarily through attempts to equalize education among localities through tax reform, the state has exerted more control over local school districts.

E. LOCAL SCHOOL POLITICS AND EDUCATIONAL PROGRAMS

The rural areas of Washingtonville township have been, and continue to be, more politically conservative than the newer suburban communities. In elections for the township council, the local Republican party, which favors, among other things, minimal municipal services and thus low taxes, wins seats with the aid of rural votes. The predominant Democrats, whose philosophy is also fiscally conservative but favors some governmental services, court and receive votes in the suburban areas. One knowledgeable, politically-active resident claims that the rural areas are no longer even considered important by the Democrats, who don't actively campaign there, since they can win enough power with the suburban vote. The political pattern is not significantly different from this when educational issues are at stake.

School board elections, reflecting the view that education is above politics, are non-partisan; an attempt is usually made to at least appear to follow this tradition. While candidates do not run on political party tickets, they do, however, often represent well-defined constituencies. Since school board policies and the way they are formed will have importance for understanding the origin and development of Lincoln Acres school, it is worthwhile at this point to recount the trend of recent Washingtonville school politics. Educational programs are also discussed in this section, because they have often generated the motivation needed for various individuals and groups to enter school politics.

Allwood Green, as mentioned earlier, had an extensive impact on the rural areas of the township, particularly in education. In 1961, Allwood Green residents occupied enough seats on the Board of Education to control it; responding to their constituents, they wanted to hire a superintendent of schools who could improve and guide the rapidly-expanding educational system. After a search they selected Dr. Robert Biddle, who was appointed superintendent of Washingtonville Schools in 1962. Biddle, a jovial, expansive, folksy man, was a graduate of a leading school of education. Prior to coming to Washingtonville he was chief administrator of a school district 30 miles away that experienced rapid suburbanization during his tenure. Eight years after this appointment, in an interview for a national magazine, Biddle recalled Washingtonville at the time he accepted the position as a

> ...highly centralized district with an extraordinarily good Board of Education. The principals had no authority, the teachers were scared of everybody, including themselves; all curriculum decisions were made in the central office. But it was obvious that the Board was interested in good education. The members wanted to change, to meet the needs of kids. They wanted to set policy and not be nine administrators any longer. I had had interviews all over the country -- big cities, small towns. I came here because of the Board.

1. Changes Introduced by Biddle

Early in his tenure, the school board supported Biddle's efforts to introduce educational innovations. He emphasized human relations training and an organization development program for administrators and teachers; in the early 60's he and all principals and central office administrators attended sessions at the National Training Laboratories in Bethel, Maine.

Two outgrowths of Biddle's stress on human relations training and organizational development have been a program of using internal personnel for the training of other staff members, and a careful effort in the design and implementation of the junior high school. In the latter project, outside consultants were used; the intervention and training were documented in a research report presented at the annual meetings of a national education association. This and prior training were supported with Title III federal funds.

Organization development, according to Biddle, has also increased trust between teachers and supervisors. "When I came here in 1962," Biddle said in the article quoted earlier, "no one trusted anybody. Now we're using some videotape machines so teachers can evaluate their own performances. They're looking for help; they're not afraid."

Along with personnel-enhancing programs, Biddle also introduced instructional innovations. One of his favorites is a developmental physical education program for children with learning disabilities which is unique in the state. Another is a community-based, work-study program for high school students, created in part to alleviate overcrowding in the high school (students work in the community, and are thus out of the school for part of the day). The district also housed and supported a state-funded summer program for the high school-aged children of migrant farm workers; it began in 1965 and is still operating. Other programs initiated or supported by Biddle were: outdoor education, a pre-school program, research and development time for up to 25% of the faculty during summers, and a large student intern program in collaboration with a nearby state teachers' college.

Changes in the structural arrangements of the schools were also introduced. Shortly after Biddle took office, Washingtonville instituted multi-graded elementary school classes. These combined students of several ages and achievement levels in an environment where each was encouraged to work at his own pace. There was also movement toward open-space education, in several instances including the use of team teaching. These innovations were not found in all schools, or for that matter, throughout an entire school, but only in classes where teachers were either predisposed to undertake them or wanted to change from the traditional pattern of teaching. By the early 1970's, the elementary schools had moved far enough in this direction that when two additions to existing schools and a new elementary school were needed because of population pressures, they were designed with open space architecture.

Biddle also created a new role in the district elementary schools: the resource teacher. This person, usually recruited from the older, more experienced teachers, provides assistance to teachers, administrators and students in the instructional program.

Finally, Biddle's administrative policy -- which reflects to some extent his educational philosophy -- is best stated in his own words.

> I believe in a strong degree of autonomy for a school building because it is an organic unit. There are certain things, however, that I will not permit; labeling kids and homogeneous grouping. We have tried to get away from blanket use of texts and workbooks -- to have a high degree of sophistication on the part of teachers and decision-making at an operational level. The major function of the central office is not to control but to expand. To provide for ongoing planned change. The principal and central office ought to be facilitators, planners, and give help in human relations skills.

This philosophy of administration has, according to many district educators, been followed, and not only through the human relations training experiences. For example, individualization of instruction has proceeded far enough that there is no uniform, standardized district-wide curriculum, even though there has been occasional vocal opposition to this development -- and to other innovations introduced by Biddle -- by various groups in Washingtonville township.

2. Political Changes

Beginning in 1965, a Taxpayers Association led by a resident of a rural community worked successfully to defeat the Washingtonville school budget in the hope of lowering taxes. In the process, there was criticism of the school system as being too permissive, too change-oriented and too involved with experimentation. After the defeat of the school budget, a group of Allwood Green residents formed an association called Citizens for Education. It was intended to serve as a means for disseminating information about the school system, and for identifying people it considered to be qualified candidates for the Board of Education.

Dissatisfaction with the school system remained despite the efforts of Citizens for Education, which disseminated information in an attempt to defuse conservatives. In 1967 the Taxpayers Association changed to Alert Ladies Take Action (ALTA), a group formed to defeat a bond issue for additions to the high school. ALTA was unsuccessful, but the bond issue only passed by a narrow margin. Two years later, the leader of both these groups organized a slate including herself, a teacher in an Allwood Green school and an architect to run for the Board of Education. Because of resignations five seats were open. The slate members ran on a platform criticizing the lack of a district-wide standardized curriculum for the system, and questioning the value of organizational development. Allwood Green residents, eager to maintain influence in educational matters, campaigned strenuously against the ALTA candidates, and retained their seats on the Board.

In 1970, the rural-based group again made a bid for seats on the Board and again had no success, in part because of weak organization. Later in the year, however, after an incident involving the arrest of two high school students for publishing an unauthorized newspaper that contained profanity and Biddle's defense of their rights, a group called Citizens League for Education and Normalcy (CLEAN), was formed by the ALTA leadership. This effort differed from the previous ones; it recruited from a broader spectrum of the population, and influential residents of Allwood Green took active roles. Moral indignation rallied the previously-inactive rural population and solidified it with conservative elements in the suburban communities.

A petition signed by 800 residents, Board of Education meetings, private meetings, and letters to the editor of the local newspaper served as a platform for the controversy and sustained it. Soon, what had begun as a response to a specific incident developed into an attack on the "permissiveness" of the educational system. Innovations in general were ridiculed, and criticism of Biddle was extensive. One resident, Charles Minetta, led a campaign to have Biddle removed as superintendent.

Citizens for Education responded by defending the schools' programs. But in the next Board of Education election in 1971, CLEAN supported three candidates and won two seats. From their new positions of power, they pressed for fiscal conservatism and questioned Board educational policies.

According to a regional newspaper, "the situation calmed down considerably in 1972 and the beginning of this year, but both men on the Board continued to press for more conservative board policies in education and finance." In June, 1973, both of the CLEAN-sponsored candidates resigned from the board because of business obligations.

Since Lincoln Acres became part of the township, it has displaced Allwood Green as the center of active liberal politics. Political power has been aggressively sought by residents of Lincoln Acres; by the time the community was only a few years old it had already either elected or appointed several key officials in town government. As we shall see in detail later, Lincoln Acres residents have taken an active role in local educational affairs, especially through the Board of Education.

Aside from the acceptance or rejection of educational innovations, another indication of political philosophy and broader cultural attitudes appears in the voting record of the various communities for annual school budgets. The rural areas consistently defeat the budgets, while the suburban residents vote for passage (although by increasingly smaller pluralities in the past few years). The suburbanites, it appears, are more willing than the rural population to support education, including some of the so-called "frills," like organization development.

3. School Finance

In this state, financial support for schools comes almost wholly from local property taxes, and substantially less from state aid; only a minor portion is from the federal government. In Washingtonville, local support has stayed at 85-88% of the budget for the past fifteen years. Compared with other school districts in the state, Washingtonville spent somewhat more money per pupil. In 1974-75 the school cost per pupil, which does not include transportation and tuition, averaged $1,201* for the state. For the county including Washingtonville, the average was $1,399, compared with $1,594 for Washingtonville. For comparison, East Lincoln, a suburban area, spent $1,313 per pupil; Jefferson Township, predominantly rural, spent $1,395; and Kingstown, one of the wealthiest communities in the nation, spent $2,020 per pupil.

Teachers' salaries, which form the bulk of the costs of education in Washingtonville, are about the same as those in surrounding communities, and range from an entry level of $10,000 to a maximum of $17,400.

In summary, we can say that, to a large extent, the type of education the Washingtonville schools currently offer reflects the educational philosophy of the superintendent of schools. Incremental, cumulative innovations -- human relations training and organization development, open space education, team teaching, individualization -- have marked his term in office. But, as we have seen, opposition to key aspects of Biddle's programs has occurred (with the effect of slowing their growth, not eliminating them). Out of this context came Lincoln Acres school.

---

*All figures are from the annual report of the state commissioner of education on financial statistics of school districts in the school year 1974-75.

4

THE EARLY PLANNING

A. THE INITIAL PLANNING GROUP

In 1970, shortly after plans for construction of the Lincoln Acres development were approved, planning for the new school began. The Board of Education hired an architect, prospective home owners were asked to fill out census surveys for an estimate of the potential school population, and Superintendent Biddle formed a committee to develop the physical design of the school.

Local educators, including those considering transferring to the new school, were asked by Biddle to volunteer if they were interested in contributing to the design of the school building. At early meetings, approximately twelve educators attended, but this rapidly narrowed to a regularly-attending group. Its members were Lois Ballantine, an elementary teacher in the district; Sam Pennington, who became the resource teacher in the new school; Sandra Georgine, who joined the faculty as a primary teacher in the second year; Lee Whitmore, who was one of the physical education instructors during the first year; and Brenda Spencer, who considered applying for a position in the school, but decided not to. Anthony Smith, an assistant to the superintendent, and Mal Portnoy, the principal of a rural elementary school, also participated regularly. Astrid Little, also an assistant to the superintendent, who later became a candidate for the new school's principalship, coordinated this committee and acted as a liaison between the committee, Biddle, and the architect.

No citizens were asked to participate on this committee; the only person not a local educator who had continuous input into the project was the architect.

Since this group had been formed by the superintendent of schools, it had considerable power, in the sense that its recommendations would influence design decisions. There was no question of its legitimacy; the task of the group was to design a school that would, in all probability, be constructed. Indeed, those with the most formal authority in the school system, the superintendent and his staff, not only granted authority to the group but participated in the decision-making themselves.

The plan was to formulate a physical design that reflected the committee's current educational thinking. There was pressure for quick action: in a short time the first residents would be occupying homes in Lincoln Acres, and a school was proposed and expected as part of the new community.

B. INITIAL DESIGN WORK

The basic question the initial planners posed for themselves was: "What should the school allow us to do with the new faculty?" The answer, quickly arrived at, was that the building should allow for "flexibility": its physical design should be one that, in Astrid Little's words, "will be useful fifty years from its construction." Generally, the educators' thinking reflected the open space concept of education that the district had gradually been moving toward since Biddle's arrival. In fact, by this time, open education had become so much a part of the thinking of district educators that two additions to existing elementary schools to be built at the same time as Lincoln Acres school were also open space facilities. "Eggcrates," the term used by Biddle and his assistant, Smith (and eventually by the principal of the new school) for self-contained classroom buildings, were not included in the plans for the future of education in Lincoln Acres.

As the planning group saw it, the basic design support for open education, which also coincided with the desire for flexibility, was a minimum use of stationary walls in instructional areas. As it turned out, only one person in the design group thought the school should be built with stationary internal walls. The general concept agreed on emphasized a building that would permit either self-contained classrooms or open space, depending on the preferences of the yet-to-be-hired faculty. This was a key decision in the physical design of the school.

The committee did not use school design consultants to aid with creation of the instructional area plans. However, State Department of Education specialists were used to provide the specifications in technical areas such as kitchen design. In other specialized areas, such as the first aid room, district school nurses were consulted. The head of school maintenance for the school district contributed ideas for the layout of the building and fixtures, such as desk and table design. The constraints in the planning were those of state space, construction and fire-law requirements, and the size of the local budget, which eliminated features such as sunken instructional areas. Basically, the committee designed the outline of a building, which in the case of the instructional area was four permanent exterior walls.

Biddle had acquired expertise in school construction planning early in his career, as an administrator in a district that had built a school each year. He made the dominant input into the design. As Sam Pennington recalled:

> Bob Biddle is a powerful figure. He is one of the brightest people I have ever met in education. Sometimes it's hard to tell how much a comment by Bob influences a decision. Bob

doesn't come down on you. He comes out with interesting and good ideas, defends them well and it's all based on what is good for kids -- within constraints.

Another influential figure in the design process was Mal Portnoy, the principal of the Sawyer elementary school. He spent a substantial amount of time reviewing the plans with Biddle, as did Anthony Smith. Portnoy, perhaps reluctant to experience the problems associated with a new school, did not apply for the position of principal of Lincoln Acres school.

From all accounts, the design process, which lasted approximately six months, was smooth; the committee's major participants, all volunteers, were essentially in agreement. The result was that the committee, including Biddle, Little and Pennington, were reasonably satisfied with the final design, even though budget constraints meant they got less than they had hoped for.

The architect's plans, worked out in interaction with the committee, were approved by the Board in late 1971.

C. BIDDLE'S VISION: A SUMMARY

Bob Biddle was so central in the initial planning that it is instructive to recount his vision of the educational program for the Lincoln Acres school, as he saw it nearly three years after the initial planning. When the new principal was about to appear on the scene, Biddle was asked what he thought the school would be like. He responded with a broad overview:

The major focus is on educational change and the change process. How do you create an institution that responds to the changing needs of society and the needs of individual kids, but at the same time planning and creating a situation where change is the main process and the focus of the institution? Innovations in this country have been taken as ends in themselves, rather than as answers to problems. In this school we want a re-definition of education, a re-definition of the institution of the school, a re-definition of the parents' involvement in the school, and a re-definition of education as opposed to instruction, which is all that education is today. Reading and writing are not education.* What is my view of education? Education is a set of learning experiences designed to help each youngster learn how to do, how to create a better society.

---

*After reading this, Biddle said he did not want to be understood as being unconcerned with cognitive learning. "Reading, writing and arithmetic must be deliberately taught and learned as efficiently and effectively as possible," he noted.

This is an idealistic image of what the school can become, cast in the moral, world-changing and redeeming rhetoric that educators often use to legitimate their efforts. Stripped of inflated claims, however, this statement strongly suggests that Biddle viewed the school as a step beyond the other schools and educational programs in the district; it would be, in his view, an active attempt to change education in a way that would make it more responsive to student, teacher, parent -- even societal -- needs.

According to Biddle, to achieve these goals the new school would:

> ...need an organizational structure, not a vertical one that presently exists in the schools, but a horizontal one -- kids with groups of adults. The function of the adults here would be to help the kids become involved. Groups would be autonomous. Decisions would be made on the basis of a systematic analysis of data. We'd use an assessment rather than an evaluation of classes because evaluation implies a value judgement. All that stuff that comes from industry -- management by objectives -- that's all bullshit. The most important thing is the relationships people work within.

The curriculum or learning activities of the new school, as he had envisioned them, would reflect his view of the importance of people as educators.

> My definition of curriculum is the interaction of people in the process of studying something. We need a high degree of trust, competency, planning skills, imagination and creativity. A complementary relationship develops between school, home and community. We will organize in teams, each responsible for a group of kids. It would be a multi-age group, the focus would be on the developmental aspects of the kids, their motor development, sensory development, etc.

As a result of his emphasis on human relations in the school, Biddle tended to see the curriculum in terms of the organizational structure of the school and the non-cognitive needs of children. Indeed, he seldom mentioned traditional curricular areas -- reading, writing, arithmetic -- and minimized their importance.* Again, underneath what appears to be fanciful speculation is a vision of education that is fundamentally different from much educational practice in America.

Concerning his relationship with the school and the role of the principal, Biddle's remarks were:

> The principal will have most of the decision-making power and I will serve as catalyst, monitor, helping person, freeing-agent, in a supporting role helping process clarification.

---

*After reading this, Biddle said the characterization was "inaccurate," but did not elaborate.

Biddle clearly had a holistic image of what he thought the school should become. In his view, however, the bulk of the detailed planning was to occur when the faculty had been selected and formed: in effect, they would fill in the sketch of the school that he had developed. He emphasized the incompleteness of his vision by saying:

> Concerning the new school building, Lincoln Acres is just a barn, a warehouse. It's got to be flexible, that's all. The biggest restrictions on the project are in the minds of people.

When viewed in the context of the educational programs and administrative policies that Biddle had developed since he became superintendent of Washingtonville schools, this outline of the new school is less a radical departure from his previous efforts than a logical extension of them. In effect, it combined elements of various programs that were scattered throughout the district; placed together in one school, these programs would form a cohesive unity, complement each other and, it was anticipated, reach their full potential. However, the particular educational practices and programs that would be put into the new school were left unspecified. Team teaching, multi-graded classes and the use of a resource teacher, among other things, were all likely candidates -- but were not definite parts of the plan. As we have seen, even open-space education was intended to be an option for the faculty. Instead of concrete practices, the key goals or "vision" of the school, as Biddle and the early planners saw them, were the concept of flexibility, and an opportunity for the faculty to fashion their own brand of education -- as long as it contained substantial portions of the innovations that had been introduced into the district and were becoming more widely used.

In sum, then, the need for the new school came primarily out of the local tradition of neighborhood elementary schools: a new population needed a new school. The educational ideas that informed its design, at least in the early stages, were a collection of practices, objectives, and philosophies that already existed in the school district. What made this school different, that is, "innovative," was that for the first time in Washingtonville all of the varied programs being developed in the district could be located in one school, and used throughout the entire school, not only by a few interested teachers.

So much for the initial planning work carried out by the school district's professionals. We need to turn back now, to an event in the community that came to have a strong influence on the making of the Lincoln Acres school -- the formation of a voluntary community association.

D. THE FORMATION OF LAHA

No community-based organizations existed when the first residents arrived in Lincoln Acres in 1970; aside from township-wide organizations such as the Jaycees, Boy Scouts and religious associations, there were few formal opportunities for neighbors to meet each other or discuss common problems. During the fall of 1971, when there were nearly two hundred families in the community, a group of fifteen residents began the formation of what was to become the Lincoln Acres Homeowners Association (LAHA). The basic purpose of the organization, as conceived by its organizers, was enabling homeowners to obtain better services from the builder. A central organizer, Michael Karalis, explained:

> There was no community interest or civic pride. The only binding interest was the developer and problems over him. Over the back fences we came to realize we had similar problems. People became familiar with each other.

In October, 1971, a hall was rented in a local parochial school and flyers announcing a meeting were distributed. One hundred and fifty people, representing approximately half of the homes in Lincoln Acres, attended. At this meeting, the organizers presented the association's primary purpose as an attempt to create a stronger relationship with the builder. During the course of the meeting, however, it became apparent that there were other concerns in the community: some residents complained that they didn't know their neighbors, several wanted "STOP" signs installed at dangerous intersections, and others were interested in arranging car pools for getting to work.

Three hundred people attended a second meeting in January 1972. The vote for a constitution was 140 in favor and 160 opposed. Many residents felt the constitution defined the activities and powers of the organization too narrowly. Problems also developed over the amount that should be collected for dues, the name of the organization and membership regulations.

A second constitution was drafted which changed the dues, specified membership privileges and gave strong authority to the president. The new constitution was ratified overwhelmingly by about three hundred Lincoln Acres residents in April, 1972. A month later, elections were held; Michael Karalis, one of the initial organizers, became LAHA's first president. The membership at this time was three hundred and fifty, representing almost two thirds of the households in the community.

The new organization's first action was to form committees for civic and community affairs, cultural and social activities, youth affairs, membership and education. Shortly after the organizational structure was completed, LAHA turned its attention to several local problems. A proposed extension to the East Coast Parkway was to border Lincoln Acres, and zoning variance was being sought for construction of a shopping center on the interstate highway near the development. These projects, which would increase traffic through the new community, were perceived as threats to local property values, and LAHA lobbied against them. Both projects were stopped. It is not clear that LAHA's influence actually caused the halt; it seems safe to conclude, however, that their efforts had some impact.

Karalis, as LAHA president, participated actively at township meetings, but according to him, "it meant nothing." As an alternative strategy to obtain local power for Lincoln Acres, LAHA began a voter registration drive: three hundred and ten residents were registered. Following this, LAHA was successful in getting the township to redistrict what was formerly the Jefferson Park polling section, so that Lincoln Acres would have its own voting district.

Adhering to its original intent, LAHA also sent a questionnaire to residents to find out if they had problems with the builder. From the data collected, homeowner concerns were presented to the builder; his cooperation with LAHA then, as now, was good.

E. THE BOND ISSUE

Once the architectural plans had been completed and approved by the Board of Education, the problem shifted to finding financial support for the school construction. The builder had donated land and $80,000, but a bond issue was needed for construction to begin. In the proposed referendum, $1,520,000 was estimated for construction of the Lincoln Acres school, $1,061,000 for an Oxford school addition, and $747,000 for an Eastland Junction addition. Enrollment was in fact expected to increase in the latter two schools, but the political reality was that unless other parts of the township were included in the bond issue, it was unlikely they would vote to support a project that would enhance only one area of the township -- especially the most affluent one.

To begin creating support for the bond issue, Biddle contacted the head of the LAHA education committee, Sam Schwartz, and arranged a meeting with committee members and other residents interested in the school. On July 18, 1972, at Schwartz's house, Biddle presented the plans for the school. The concept of open space education was discussed and presented as being "flexible."

Two weeks later, at the invitation of LAHA, Biddle presented the school plans to the entire membership. He told them that for the school to be built the bond issue would have to be approved by the township voters in October, 1972. At this meeting the LAHA education committee distributed a questionnaire to its membership titled: "What Turns You On or Off About the New School Proposal?"

LAHA education committee members collected the questionnaires a month later, and the results were presented at the next general membership meeting, September 14, 1972. Two hundred people were present.

The response rate to the questionnaire was low, but some of the information was helpful. For instance, many people said they would like a lunch program in the school. No lunch facility had been originally planned, but in response to this finding one was added. Two other concerns surfaced at the September 14 meeting. The first was raised by a group of about 25 residents, who didn't want a neighborhood school; they preferred having their children continue attending Fernwood school in Allwood Green. These parents thought the distance of the Fernwood school from Lincoln Acres would insure their children's eating in school, not returning home in the middle of the day and thus preventing mothers from holding jobs. A more general concern was fear that the new school's construction would cause a substantial rise in property taxes.

Biddle and Board of Education members who attended the meeting answered questions on these and other issues to the satisfaction of most people present. Afterward, a motion from the floor that LAHA support the bond issue was approved. At the same meeting, the members formulated -- and in the following weeks conducted -- a campaign of home visits, advertisements in the local paper and coffee-klatches to promote the bond issue passage. LAHA was assisted in this by members of the central administrative staff and several of the educators who had participated in the initial physical design of the school.

In the course of the LAHA-sponsored campaign for support, the primary detailed information concerning the bond issue most residents received appeared in the Board of Education's pamphlet, "Crowded: And More to Come!" This eight-page pamphlet described all three proposed buildings -- the two additions and the new school. In it the Lincoln Acres school is described as a 500-student elementary school with the following facilities:

> 18 Classrooms
> 2 Kindergartens
> 1 Library
> 1 Multipurpose room
> 1 Music room
> 1 Physical Development room
> A Kitchen
> Administrative office
> Small instructional area
> Music area and storage

Under a heading in the pamphlet called "design," the following paragraph appears:

> These buildings are designed as simply as possible in order that the community may profit from new construction methods and materials and reap whatever benefits may be obtained in lowered construction costs. Such construction will also permit us to provide a great deal of flexibility in future building use. For example, most of the inside walls will be demountable partitions. These partitions will reduce costs somewhat and will permit teachers to rearrange spaces in order to meet specific teaching and learning needs which develop during the next 25-50 years.

Included in the pamphlet is a schematic diagram of the Lincoln Acres school. It is reproduced as Diagram I.

Notes to Diagram I: The instructional area appears as the large rectangle at the left. The school as constructed varied in several respects from the diagram. First, the instructional area went through several rearrangements; these will be detailed in subsequent diagrams. Second, the block of rooms including the principal's office and faculty room was exchanged with the block for physical development and music.

DIAGRAM I

ARCHITECT'S OUTLINE FOR LINCOLN ACRES SCHOOL

TOTAL SQ FT = 58,990

FLOOR PLAN

SCHEMATIC DIAGRAM

PROPOSED
LINCOLN ACRES ELEMENTARY SCHOOL
FOR THE
BOARD OF EDUCATION WASHINGTONVILLE

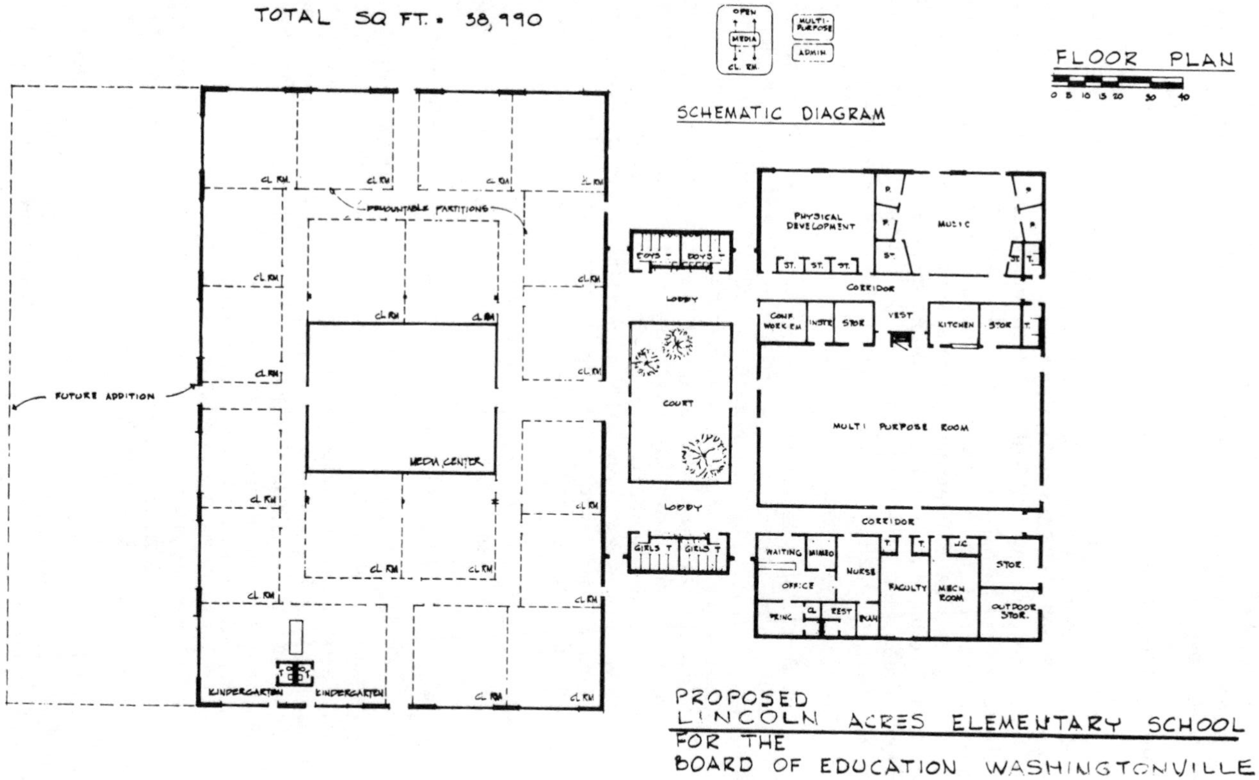

On October 17, 1972, Washingtonville voters approved the bond issue, by a large margin in Lincoln Acres, and with a narrow endorsement in the rest of the township.

F. PRINCIPAL SELECTION

With the bond issue approved, construction of the school began; the social system of the school now increasingly became the focus of attention. In May, 1973, Biddle began recruiting members of an advisory committee to the superintendent, which would screen candidates for the position of principal of the new school. The committee was to be composed of parents from the Lincoln Acres community and an equal number of local educators.

To select the community members, Biddle asked for help from LAHA. The LAHA education committee co-chairperson at the time, Barbara Berger, began recruiting, as did Sam Schwartz, the former chairman. Barbara Berger recalled the recruitment for the advisory committee as follows:

> Dr. Biddle approached me as the head of the LAHA education committee. We had a committee meeting and asked people to sign up and write questions they would ask of a candidate. Charles Frisch was the co-chairman of the education committee at the time, but didn't have time to participate in the selection. I felt that everyone on the list had the same point of view as me -- liberal. So, I asked people with other viewpoints. All those who signed up originally were my friends. So I asked Sam Schwartz and Michael Karalis, who were both conservatives, and they said they would do it.

In addition to Schwartz, Berger and Karalis (who was no longer president of LAHA), Shirley Potter and Carol Witterstein, both former teachers, were selected for the advisory committee. This group reflected an attempt to represent the ethnic, religious, educational, and political views of the community.

Biddle then requested teacher volunteers for the advisory committee. Selected for the committee were Sam Pennington, Lois Ballantine, Bobbie Hanson, Barbara Soames and Jane Marsten. Pennington, a teacher at Oxford school, had participated on the building design committee and was interested in transferring to the new school. All the others were teachers in Washingtonville elementary schools; Jane Marsten was also a resident of Lincoln Acres. Anthony Smith, an assistant to the superintendent, was given the task of coordinating the work of the committee.

With instructions from Biddle that their task was to screen candidates and make recommendations to him, the committee began meeting in mid-December, 1973. It met twice and sometimes three times a week until February, 1974.

The group began by developing a set of criteria for the position of principal. The procedure used was "brainstorming"; that is, anyone could suggest items, and these were listed without premature criticism. The finally-agreed-on list, presented in Chart 4.1, is fairly comprehensive.

CHART 4.1

CRITERIA FOR PRINCIPAL SELECTION

The Screening Committee is looking for the following characteristics in the candidates, and will rate them on a scale of 1-5, 1 representing few of the characteristics, 5, most of all.

I.   EDUCATIONAL PHILOSOPHY

A. Individualized approach:
1. She/he encourages <u>positive</u>, <u>relaxed</u> environment
2. She/he fosters <u>innovation</u>, <u>creativity</u>
3. She/he is concerned with the <u>total child</u>, not just curriculum
B. Commitment to growth:
1. She/he seeks <u>community involvement</u> and <u>participation</u>
2. She/he is committed to <u>teacher-training</u> and on-going growth
3. She/he is receptive to <u>change</u>

II. ADMINISTRATIVE ABILITY

A. The administrative process:
1. She/he <u>makes decisions</u>
2. She/he <u>delegates</u> some decision-making powers
3. She/he <u>completes tasks</u>, showing <u>consistency</u>
4. She/he is <u>flexible</u> and <u>accessible</u>
5. She/he <u>facilitates</u>
6. She/he is <u>supportive</u> of, to, for teachers
B. Technical skills:
1. She/he is trained in <u>planning</u> and <u>budgeting</u>
2. She/he is skilled in <u>organizational development</u>
3. She/he uses <u>evaluation</u> and <u>supervision</u> for <u>growth</u>
4. She/he has a <u>good track record</u> and uses <u>experience</u> wisely

III. HUMANIST

A. Personality:
1. She/he is <u>intelligent</u>, <u>sharp</u> and <u>inventive</u>
2. She/he has <u>warmth</u> and is energetic
3. She/he is a <u>listener</u>
4. She/he is <u>secure</u> and <u>self-confident</u>
B. Viewpoints:
1. She/he believes <u>people</u> come before products
2. She/he <u>relates well to children</u>
3. She/he reacts in a <u>calm</u>, <u>analytical</u> manner
4. She/he is <u>sensitive to teachers'</u> strengths and weaknesses

Following the development of criteria, each member of the committee went through the folders of the approximately sixty candidates who had responded to advertisements in the New York Times and professional education journals. Eight other applications were from people already employed in the district.* The central administration's policy was that all in-district candidates were to receive an interview. That is, they would not be screened and possibly rejected at the early stages of the selection process. After the initial screening, each member of the committee (with the exception of Anthony Smith, who only facilitated the task) made up a list of fifteen out-of-district candidates. Members then presented their choices to the rest of the group, with a discussion of each candidate's strengths and weaknesses. Since the ten initial lists had a high degree of overlap, there was little difficulty in arriving at a consensus for a single list of fifteen candidates to be interviewed by the committee. Anthony Smith scheduled interviews for the candidates, and the committee formulated a set of questions and procedures for conducting the interviews.

The interview guide, completed on January 16, 1974, was used for all candidates, with only minor changes. The seven questions that composed the interview (typically a half hour or more) appear in Chart 4.2.

The committee decided to rotate leadership, have each interview last at least a half hour, and allow each member of the committee to ask one of the pre-selected questions or a probing question. After the interview, each member was to rate the candidate on a scale of 1-5 for each response.

Once the candidates had been interviewed, the committee had to decide on a method for narrowing the list to the four or five the superintendent had requested. In addition, they needed a way to present the recommendations to Biddle. They decided to have each member rank-order the five he or she considered most qualified. Again there was a considerable overlap of candidates on these lists. Using aggregated ratings and rankings, a list of five candidates# was put in order of preference and given to Biddle on February 12, 1974. The memorandum from the screening committee to Biddle read:

> During the past several months we have reviewed approximately sixty applications for the position of Principal of the Lincoln Acres Elementary School. We have interviewed fourteen candidates for the position and discussed the qualifications of each rather thoroughly.
>
> It is the recommendation of this Committee that the following applicants be considered by you for this position. They are listed in the order of choice by the Committee.

---

*The eight in-district candidates were David Hauptmann, the principal of Fernwood school; Alberta Bard, an administrator at the junior high school; Astrid Little, an assistant to Biddle; Imogene Miller, the director of CIPED (a student work-experience program); and Robert Stewart, Michael Pierce and Anne Heinz, teachers.

#Of these candidates only Alberta Bard and Astrid Little were in-district people. The outsiders were all from other states.

CHART 4.2

INTERVIEW GUIDE FOR PRINCIPAL CANDIDATES

Introduction of the committee to the candidate. Candidate asked to tell about him/herself.

1. What is your concept of the administrator's role in getting the school going, and in continuing its development? What skills do you have to make that happen?

2. What is your idea of how children learn?

3. A parent calls you to say that their child has brought home a book which the parent feels any child should not be reading, and asks you to prevent teachers from using this material. What would your reaction be?

4. How do you see children with special needs -- gifted to learning disabled -- functioning?

5. You'll be hiring teachers for the new school. What will you be looking for?

6. How do you see the principal's role in evaluating teacher performance and fostering teacher growth? Specifically, what would you be looking for, and what procedures would you use?

7. How much and in what way would you utilize community and/or parental involvement?

Mr. Ellis Brown
Mrs. Alberta Bard
Mr. Martin Haber
Mr. Peter Hess
Mrs. Astrid Little

It should be noted that conflicts had existed in the screening committee. One was over the different views of the process the group should use to accomplish its task. The teachers, two of whom were trained in group dynamics methods, wanted adherence to a particular set of meeting rules and procedures. Parent members, uncomfortable with this, developed a ritualized response to reduce the threat they felt; when the teachers used terms such as "facilitator" and "hidden agenda," parents joked about it. Parents and teachers had different backgrounds and thus dissimilar approaches to the task: Karalis, a labor relations negotiator, was a skeptical, businessman type and some other parents were similar. In contrast, Pennington and the other teachers wanted an open, "trustful" atmosphere on the committee and toward candidates. The parents' suspicion of the ethic of "trust" was reinforced by some evidence that teacher committee members had briefed the in-district candidates before they were to be interviewed.

Generally, although cooperation and productivity varied over the course of the committee's life, all members interviewed recalled many meetings, especially the early ones, as being full of tension between parent and teacher members.

To gain a better image of the finalists and provide a basis for an informed decision, the committee members decided to visit their schools. One group, headed by Smith, went to upstate New York to visit a principal. Biddle, Berger, Pennington and Potter visited Ellis Brown's school in Colville, New Hampshire. The school was an open space building in a rural area and Brown was a teaching principal. After talking with teachers and students and observing the school, Biddle and the members of the committee assessed the situation positively and regarded Brown as a good candidate.

On the way to New Hampshire, when Pennington, the only teacher in the group, was out of the car, Biddle told Berger and Potter that he would like to see Imogene Miller, an in-district candidate, become the principal of Lincoln Acres school. When Barbara Berger returned to Lincoln Acres, she reported Biddle's preference for principal to the LAHA executive committee. At about the same time, Karalis had heard rumors that Biddle was going to recommend someone to the Board of Education who was not on the screening committee's list of finalists.

After he returned from New Hampshire, Biddle refused to accept the list of candidates that had been presented to him by the committee, claiming that he wanted criteria for the selection of finalists, and reasons for rejection of the other people interviewed. He then submitted three names to the Board of Education for possible appointment as principal. His first choice, Imogene Miller, did not appear on the committee's list of five top candidates, but the other two, Astrid Little and Alberta Bard, did.

The parent members of the committee were infuriated by Biddle's action. In violation of Biddle's ground rule that the selection process remain within the committee, Karalis asked to discuss the matter with the Board of Education president. A meeting with a group of parents at Karalis' home was arranged; after hearing their complaints, the Board president indicated that he was concerned with what had occurred. The LAHA education committee then sent a letter to the Board of Education; it did not endorse a candidate, but insisted that the superintendent make his first-choice recommendation from the list of candidates. Several weeks later, after the Board had interviewed the finalists, it was announced that Ellis Brown had been appointed principal of Lincoln Acres School.*

---

*Biddle said to the researcher late that year that Brown had been his second choice.

In 1975, when he reflected on the events around the hiring of the principal, Karalis said:

> We worked hard, and then not to take our recommendation hurt. But some superintendents aren't as earnest as Biddle -- they wouldn't even have a committee. I think that Biddle wanted to promote somebody from within. That can be a good policy.

Biddle, too, formed a lasting impression of the Lincoln Acres selection process.

> The hiring process that I used I will never use again. I believe ideally and theoretically in the involvement of parents, teachers and educators on the committee level, but, I'll never use it again because I do not find, unless people are trained as observers and in group process, that it works. Next time I will do it myself.

G. (ANALYSIS AND COMMENTARY)

1. Vision Development

The original vision of the school, as it was expressed in the architectural design, remained largely unaltered four years later when the principal was selected. "Flexibility" was still the cornerstone of the plan, the community was informed of the plans for open space education, and the principal who was hired had had experience in a similar school. At this point, the vision remained a deliberately rough sketch, rather than a complete design.

2. Actualization

The linkages between plans and implementation were not strong. Although other teachers participated with the expectation of joining the new faculty, the only teacher involved in all planning phases was Sam Pennington. Biddle had either been directly involved in, or closely monitored, all aspects of the planning and thus provided continuity in the plans. His general intent to serve as a "catalyst..... helping person, freeing agent" in relation to the new principal was a proposed form of planning-implementation linkage; whether it would materialize remained to be seen.

Finally, the criteria used in the search for a principal were intended to maximize selection of a person whose views would act as a linkage between planning and implementation.

The vagueness of the initial plans reduced the possibility that they would be altered, or that they would not be implemented; at this time nothing seemed specific enough to change, or to fail in achievement. The plans for flexibility were themselves flexible.*

3. Political Stabilization

The implicit strategy of this period was one of incremental educational change; the school was not presented as a radical departure, but as the combination of several educational innovations that were already standard practice in the school system. Whether it was intended or not, the political strategy also was a gradualist one. Educators were included in the process initially, warding off the possible charge that an innovation was being foisted upon them without warning or consultation. Similarly, the school administration included LAHA peripherally in the funding process, and then as co-equals with the educator members of the advisory screening committee for the principal.

Relations with the community were cordial during the bond issue campaign, but somewhat strained during the process of selecting a principal. If we compare the two processes, we note a striking difference. In the case of the bond issue, the important decisions -- to have a flexible school with a particular physical design -- were made by educators and presented to the community for ratification. In the instance of the principal selection, Biddle gave both educators and parents equal advisory powers, though not the power to make the actual selection. Apparently, however, both groups, but especially the parents, developed a sense of investment in their nominees, and subsequently a feeling that Biddle had not seriously considered their advice when he proposed a person not on their final list of candidates. They demanded, and finally received, more power than they had been initially granted when the opportunity to make an important decision arose.#

Biddle's strategy for coopting the community leadership was successful in the case of the bond issue. But the strategy set a precedent for continued participation; it may also have felt less like cooptation to the

---

*After reading this, Biddle commented that there was nothing at all vague about the plans. So to him they were explicit and clear.

#An interesting aspect of this is that Karalis and Berger seem to have been fully aware at the time that they were overstepping the role in principal selection which they had agreed to. Karalis claimed that objections to Miller, Biddle's first choice, were so great that "the community would have eaten her alive" had she become principal. He also felt that she would be a puppet for Biddle. These predictions may have been reasonable, but they were also rationalizations for his actions.

Interestingly enough, Biddle said after reading this that the committee did not receive more power. That seems to be formally correct, but the committee did in fact take more power, exerting more influence than they originally had a license for.

community than an opportunity to actually influence the plans for the school. Whether this interpretation is correct or not,* it is clear that the community leadership successfully exercised its power and thwarted Biddle's effort to place his candidate in the principal's office of the new school.

4. Knowledge Utilization

Utilization of outside knowledge was minimal in the design of the school building. State Department of Education specialists and the architect were the only outside experts. Of course, Biddle had developed expertise in school construction planning through previous experience, and the other educators who participated had developed similar stocks of knowledge. But no systematic attempt was made to survey the design of other open space schools, nor were any educational consultants used. The basic operating principle was to use internal resources as much as possible.

The pattern of reliance on internal resources is also apparent in the principal selection process, but in a slightly different form. The three names that Biddle recommended to the board were all in-district educators. Biddle's policy may have been to promote an inside person and thus provide opportunities and incentive within the district. Additionally, he could have preferred Miller because he was thoroughly familiar with her, or because he wanted to be able to retain control over the school through a hand-picked principal. At any rate, he displayed a local orientation, while the committee, for any number of possible reasons, went outside of the district. (Only two of their five recommendations were for insiders, and their first choice, Brown, was from another state.) Perhaps the parents on the committee thought an outside person would be likely to develop the school as they wanted it, and would be less dominated by Biddle than would an insider beholden to him for the position.

In sum, the vagueness of the early plans, together with the gradualist approach to realizing them, permitted considerable maneuverability for the central administration. Avoiding firm commitments also created the impression that every constituency would eventually be satisfied. With these conditions, there was much potential for later misunderstanding.

---

*Biddle thought this was a "bad observation," and said:
> I never coopted anyone in my life, nor
> deliberately set out to do so.

We are using the word "cooptation" simply to refer to the process of gaining the support of opposing forces. But the question of whether Biddle approached this deliberately or not (or even expected that having the committee would help to defuse opposition) remains open.

5

INTENSIVE PLANNING BEGINS:
FORMING A FACULTY

Orderliness, a dimension of reality frequently imposed in retrospect along with meaning, was not especially characteristic of the principal selection process. But it did find its way into several other early processes of planning for the Lincoln Acres school. After Brown had been selected, the next major events were his arrival and selection of a faculty for the school. Before we describe the teacher recruitment process, however, a brief account of the new principal's background, and his vision of the new school should prove instructive.

A. THE NEW PRINCIPAL'S BACKGROUND

Before he accepted the principalship of Lincoln Acres school, Ellis Brown was a young teaching principal in Colville, New Hampshire, a rural town near the Canadian border with a population of approximately 1,000. Colville is an old Yankee village with a faltering dairy-farm economy, some lumbering and a recently-built furniture factory which employs a large portion of the local labor force at wages below federal minimum. Farms have been sold piecemeal, as urbanites have purchased parcels for summer homes, while the farmers, reluctant to leave, turn to factory work and till their reduced acreage part time. Many French Canadians have recently filtered into the area in search of work. Generally, much of the population of Colville is underpaid, transient, and poorly educated; some are non-English-speaking.

A new elementary school was built in Colville to replace a ninety-year old building. Open space education and the architectural design of the new building had been presented to the community by the regional superintendent primarily as an economy measure; fewer internal walls and less heating meant reduced construction and operating expenses. Open space construction was also acceptable because it recalled a familiar image -- the one-room school. Beneath the publicly-stated reasons, the school district administration also had a hesitant interest in trying new forms of education.

In a recruitment process which included probes at nearby colleges and universities, Brown had been contacted by the Colville school district and asked if he were interested in the position of teaching principal. At the time, he was a doctoral student in educational administration at the University of Massachusetts. After interviews by the assistant superintendent and the Board of Education, Brown was offered the position, accepted it, and began work in September, 1972. According to Brown:

> My biggest qualification for getting a job in New Hampshire was that I was a graduate of a New Hampshire high school, not that I was a doctoral student at the University of Massachusetts. I took the Colville position because it was more interesting than other offers. It wasn't an egg-crate school .

During the summer before the school opened, Brown hired five teachers for the new school and retained two who had worked in the old building. He also hired four parents as teacher aides. In the hiring process, he looked for people who were young, with a considerable amount of time to spend in school, and with some specialty such as outdoor education, physical education or musical ability. The newly-recruited faculty was then arranged into two teaching teams: the lower team had four teachers and two aides, working with seventy children in grades Kindergarten through four, and special education. The upper team, working with eighty children in grades five through eight, also had four teachers (including Brown) and two aides. According to Brown, the teams decided how they were going to organize and deliver instruction; decision-making was primarily by consensus and often involved the students.

Relations between the school and community were fairly good. After a few weeks of school, several problems with individual parents arose: individualization of student work was not clear in a few cases; parents questioned the idea of a fifth grade student working with an eighth grade student in academic areas. When Brown arrived, the parents' association was almost non-existent, and he succeeded in encouraging more participation in it. This group became primarily involved in fund-raising activities, and was especially successful with sponsoring and organizing Bingo nights. About half of the faculty attended these and other fund-raising events, giving teachers and parents an opportunity to know one another on a face-to-face basis. However, only four or five families out of the eighty families with children in the school became extensively involved with school activities. "It was," Brown recollected, "a surprisingly quiet community."

In November, 1973, as he was starting his second year at Colville, Brown responded to an advertisement in the New York _Times_ for a principalship in Washingtonville. His motive for seeking another job was professional advancement; when he left Colville after a year and a half as principal, he felt the school was "in good shape." On January 1, 1975, Ellis Brown began work in the position of principal of Lincoln Acres Elementary School. He was 26 years old.

Brown looked somewhat older than his years. The impression he tended to create in others was one of assurance. His usual manner was crisp, sometimes a bit aloof, and always "professional."

Brown's experiences in Colville fitted remarkably well with the demands of his new assignment: he was the first principal of a new open-space school, he had hired the faculty of the school, he had worked with parents in the community, and had taught in, as well as administered the school. Only the community contexts differed: Colville was a rural, nearly-poverty-stricken community, and Lincoln Acres was a new, affluent suburban community. So, on the hiring criterion of "relevant experience", the screening committee had done an admirable job.

B. PRINCIPAL RECRUITMENT AS SEEN BY THE RECRUITEE

Brown's reflections on the recruitment process, shortly after he arrived for work, are illuminating. In general, he thought that the process took too long, with the result that the best candidates, because they were in demand, might have taken other positions while waiting for Washingtonville to decide. Including parents on the screening committee was in his view a good idea, but not having other principals participate was a weakness.

And from his perspective, by the time the principal was to be hired the open space concept for the new school was a "fait accompli", because of the way it was constructed. He felt that some members of the screening committee, however, represented a conservative view and wanted less diversified curriculum and teaching methods, while others favored the open space approach. It is worth quoting a portion of an interview with Brown ten days after he began work in Washingtonville:

Researcher: How did the two viewpoints balance?

Brown: They didn't strike any balance. I don't feel that either is legitimate. They don't know enough about education. They might change their point of view. The progressives are blindly attached to change with no foundation as to how it's done.

Researcher: What about the conservatives?

Brown: They patently don't know a damn thing about education. Yet they can possibly change. Both groups are opinionated and neither knows what they're talking about.

Researcher: What about the administration's goals or visions?

Brown: None. Bob Biddle is going to react to things that he likes or doesn't like. He gives the principals a huge amount of autonomy. Because of this he has some good and some strangely bad things in his schools. When they hired me they bought a product that fit their picture. This saved everyone involved from being explicit. They compromised. I have a free hand in what the school will become. I could keep everybody pleased, or I could please the community or Biddle.

Nobody has ever defined the position clearly enough. There is no accountability.

C. BROWN'S EARLY VISION FOR THE SCHOOL

These accounts of Brown's background as an educator and his impressions of the process by which he was recruited for his new position provide us with a perspective from which to consider his early plans for the school, those he had upon arrival in Washingtonville. Below we review what he hoped to accomplish in his new position, including his goals for the new school, and his educational and administrative philosophies. Then we outline his strategy for planning and implementation.

1. Goals for the School

The overarching goals for Lincoln Acres school as Brown viewed them were:

> To be very adaptive. I really see openness in schools as openness to needs and opportunities. If we get somebody on the staff with abilities we can use them well. For example, in the past there was no art teacher, but a third grade teacher did the whole school and others also used their abilities. Generally, not to follow any general prescription of what kids need. Idiosyncratic needs have to be identified.

Adaptiveness, openness and individualization, then, were the general goals. Brown intended to accomplish these goals with certain structural arrangements: use of the open space, team teaching, and multi-age grouping of students.

In relation to other schools in the district, Brown's aim was for Lincoln Acres to serve as a model: "I would like to become a 'lighthouse' school. People could borrow ideas."

2. Administrative Philosophy

Central to Brown's administrative philosophy was his belief in a charismatic leadership style:*

---

*The fact that Brown rarely stated his philosophy of administration illustrates a dilemma in field work. He was never directly asked what his philosophy was, since we expected that the result would have been an idealistic, not a realistic answer. The statements that he did make about it were volunteered, often in another context, and therefore more likely to reflect what he actually believed in and attempted to do. (See Appendix A for elaboration.) There is still ambiguity, though: the fact that he seldom elaborated a philosophy may have meant either that he did not have a highly developed one, or that it simply wasn't important to him to let others know what he thought.

> People need to believe in the spirit of what is
> going on. I believe in a charismatic leader.
> Mechanics can crank out the same old things. I
> want people to take a chance. A principal's job
> is to lead people.

It is not entirely clear what meaning Brown attached to the label "charismatic leader", but presumably he meant someone whose personal qualities subordinates found so attractive that they granted authority because of those qualities, not because of the formal power of office.

Brown also wanted to maintain autonomy from the central administration. His view of the superintendent's administrative policy was that Biddle did grant a substantial degree of autonomy to building principals. He felt this freedom from tight administrative control could be used to aid the development of the new school's educational programs as the principal and staff desired.

Somewhat at odds with his preferred administrative style, however, was Brown's desire to have the faculty participate in making important decisions. During the initial stages, the mechanism for faculty decision-making was not explicitly stated, but Brown clearly implied that a way would be found for the faculty to influence the goals and plans for the school. To a researcher, there was thus some tension between democratic norms on the one hand, and the demands of an inspiring, strong leader on the other.

Brown's intention to teach as well as administer, as he had in Colville, could be seen as a device to use this tension constructively. In Washingtonville, extra demands on his time, such as attending a weekly all-day principals' meeting, would be interfering with his being able to teach on a regular basis. He did succeed in doing so for a while, and we infer that he wanted to communicate his image of the principal's role as being that of an educational leader, rather than simply an "administrator".

3. Brown's Educational Philosophy

Individualization of instruction was the core of Brown's educational philosophy. The idiosyncratic needs of children, as noted above, were to be identified, and the instructional program developed around them. In Brown's view the most efficient means, but not the only one, to accomplish this was open education, carried out via team teaching. To a large extent, the architecture, Brown's background, and what the Screening Committee and Biddle were looking for, cast the school firmly in the mold of open space education with a staff arranged in teaching teams.

In these early stages, "curriculum" was unspecified. Individualization seemed only to imply that each child would have a curriculum shaped to his or her needs.

A few weeks after the faculty was selected, Brown was to distribute

a short article to them which examined the philosophy of open education.*
He drew a box around the following quote from John Dewey:

> There is always the danger in a new movement that in
> rejecting the aims and methods of that which it would
> supplant, it may develop its principles negatively rather than
> positively and constructively. Then it takes its clue in
> practice from that which it rejected instead of from the
> constructive development of its own philosophy (Experience
> and Education, p. 20).

Other passages in the text are also underlined. In all cases they caution
against unexamined assumptions in open education, and the uncritical
rejection of past practices. For example:

> Some kinds of structure and efficiency make the environment
> more comfortable and less frustrating for pupils as well as
> teachers. Structure or efficiency are not necessarily self-
> serving. (p. 282)

On the article, he also wrote a short message to the staff, part of which
was, "The authors show obvious vision as to where we ought to go and what
the common tasks are along the way."

4. Brown's Plan for Planning

In characterizing his strategy for innovation, or meta-plan, Brown
emphasized that he was flexible, and that he would do what the teachers
thought they were capable of, instead of forcing innovations upon them. At
one point he termed the strategy he would use "incremental," starting with
the teachers where they were, and working from that point toward more
open education. Including teachers in decision-making, as we have seen, was
part of the strategy.

The community, as already noted, had been involved in the early
stages of planning, primarily in the bond issue and principal selection.
Brown was aware of past community involvement and the eagerness of many
parents to participate in planning the educational program for the school.
His strategy toward parents was one that he struggled with in the early
stages. Still uncertain how to treat them, he said:

> I'll be responsive to them, but I don't know what they can tell
> me. Do we need their input for making decisions? The answer
> is clearly "No." Do we need input for input's sake? "Yes."

---

*Czajkowski and King, The hidden curriculum and open education.
Elementary School Journal: 75 (5): 279-83.

> I don't want to be bound by what they want us to do. I'm also concerned about having the community get a drop on the teachers -- goals should get worked out among teachers by themselves.

On the other hand, however, Brown viewed his largest problem as establishing the relationship of the school with the community and other schools in the district.

> I feel that we are being looked at a lot. I would not like to see the school go through a long period proving ourselves as in Colville. I hope that nobody gets worked up enough to start making noise in public.

Brown's plan for planning was a sketch, to be filled in as planning progressed. In brief, the superintendent would allow for autonomy, Brown would permit teachers to have input, and the community, though not a welcome member of the group, would be able to influence the planning. The timetable included faculty meetings to take place during the spring, and a month of paid planning time for all teachers during the summer, which were to be used to fill in, and possibly alter, the existing rough design of the Lincoln Acres school.

(Comments.) This section concludes with some notes on the meta-plan. First, the plan as formulated in the early stages of the enterprise reflected an incremental approach to the future. As we have seen, the plan was sketched only on a general scheme or framework level, rather than including more details and substance; they would be decided on as planning progressed. Second, teachers, and possibly parents, would participate in the detailed phases of planning. Significantly, little or no use of outside experts was contemplated; planning would be the province of local educators.* A third dimension of the meta-plan, then, was utilization of predominantly internal resources.

A fourth aspect of the plan for planning was that operational linkage (that is, continuity between planning and implementation) was to be accomplished by having the eventual operators of the school do the planning. There was also the possibility (unclearly stated at this time) that community members who had participated in the bond issue campaign and the principal selection process would participate, thus providing another source of continuity with the initial vision.

Fifth, (although Brown did muse briefly to the researcher about the possibility of a community survey), the meta-plan contained no systematic

------

*Our project's offer of "human systems" consulting help, which included a small amount of money on a matching basis, was rejected in favor of having the personnel who would eventually staff the school do the planning alone. Lack of money was not an issue.

way of collecting data from parents to steer the course of planning and early implementation. An associated point is, finally, that Brown's meta-plan was silent on the issue of how much change and adaptation could be expected in the plans and the developing school after it opened.

Overall, it seems fair to say that the two key administrators, the superintendent and the principal, were in fairly close agreement in their initial conception of what the educational programs of Lincoln Acres school should eventually become. They also agreed on the organizational design through which these should be reached. Of course, this agreement was not coincidental. Even though Biddle said he would not have selected Brown as his first choice for principal, he found Brown's approach to education acceptable and compatible with his own, and voiced only minor regret in having him as the principal. This regret did not reflect on Brown's abilities, but on what Biddle still regarded as the qualities of his preferred candidate that made her uniquely suitable, in particular, her demonstrated ability to work with people. The fact that Brown was considerably younger and less experienced than his superior probably increased Biddle's influence and thus the degree to which his vision was shared.

One curious phenomenon, however, is that when Brown was asked about the administration's -- that is, Biddle's -- goals and visions for Lincoln Acres school, Brown said that there were "none". As we have seen, this was not the case; Biddle did have a vision for the school. It is possible, of course, that Biddle never indicated what his goals and visions were to Brown, or if he did,* Brown chose not to regard them as goals or a vision, but only as an outline, not a set of objectives he was required to meet. But this does not seem to be entirely probable. A plausible explanation is that Brown was asserting his independence from, or lack of dependence on, Biddle for assistance in what the school would become. We shall have other occasions to see the same dynamic at work.

As the narrative progresses, we will return to the goals and visions for the school that various individuals and groups had formulated -- and to their revision and alteration as planning and implementation moved forward.

D. TEACHER RECRUITMENT

In the fall of 1974, Superintendent Biddle sent an announcement to all elementary teachers in the district, explaining that if they were interested in transferring to Lincoln Acres school they should attend a meeting Ellis Brown was going to have soon. At an October meeting of thirty teachers, Brown briefly explained what he thought the school might be like, and said that those interested in becoming part of the faculty should write a letter of interest to the superintendent. By the time Brown arrived in January to begin working full-time, twenty letters from teachers requesting transfer to Lincoln Acres had been received. Fourteen teachers, including a librarian and a resource teacher, were needed for the professional staff of the school.

---

*Biddle said after reading this that he did do so.

1. Constraints

Three constraints affected the teacher selection process. First, all teachers had to be within-district transfers; teachers from outside of the district would not be considered. Enrollment was declining in the township, and many students who would eventually attend Lincoln Acres school would be transferred from a nearby school, resulting in a loss of teaching positions there. Biddle's policy of transferring stemmed from the contract, which specified that going outside was not possible if any already-employed teacher wanted a vacant position. This policy was also highly sensitive to teacher needs; the job market for elementary teachers was not good at the time. It was Brown's opinion in early January, however, that the staff "would be better if I could go outside to recruit."

The second constraint was that all transfers had to be voluntary. Under this condition Brown could not "actively" recruit teachers, nor could other principals actively seek to retain their teachers. According to Brown, these norms were broken by both sides in several instances.* The third constraint Biddle set was that staff should be hired for the new school by February 1, 1975, a month after Brown assumed the principalship.

2. Criteria

The criteria Brown developed for selecting teachers as he reported them in an interview, were:

(1) Experience at a particular grade level, yet equipped for a multitude of levels, for example, grades 1, 2, 3.

(2) Previous experience with team teaching.

(3) Previous experience in using the classroom in an open way -- establishing functional areas in the classroom.

(4) A teaching style allowing the students to develop independence and responsibility -- choosing what they want to do. A highly directive teacher is not desirable.

(5) A style that involves a lot of social interaction in the classroom.

---

*Biddle's retrospective view of the process was quite different. He said after reading this that the issue was, in effect, that all parties had to be satisfied (the teacher who applied for transfer, the "sending" and the "receiving" principal). He saw no barriers to active recruiting efforts, nor to efforts to retain teachers.

(6) Experience in dealing with parents, especially parents who are critical of the school, and who have worked with parent volunteers.

(7) Indication that the individual is working with children in some socially constructive way as well as /having/ a simple, basic emotional response to kids. The kind of person who likes being around kids and has a mature view of what the business of the school is. Can't be juvenile -- must understand what the school ought to do.

(8) Good control tactics in the classroom. Not spending a lot of time on control. Either because of interest or personality, the class is under control in a positive way.

(9) A familiarity with curriculum materials.

These nine characteristics used in selecting teachers provide further insight into Brown's educational philosophy, and into how he intended to operationalize it. Multi-graded classes, team teaching, giving students independence and responsibility, socially constructive relationships between teacher and student, and experience in dealing with parents fit into a general model of the school, which if still vague, is clearly different from the traditional one of isolated self-contained classrooms with thirty children and one teacher.

3. Methods

To select fourteen teachers from the pool of twenty, Brown visited their classrooms, talked with them informally and interviewed them. By January 10, 1975, he felt that some teachers whom he would have liked at the new school had received subtle hints from their principals that they wanted them to stay. He also guessed that a half-dozen other teachers wanted to transfer to Lincoln Acres only because they feared being fired because of enrollment decreases. He estimated to the researcher:

> The staff will be very female, probably young, not many old. More married than unmarried. No blacks probably, since there are only two in the pool and they are both marginal.

By January 16, 1975, Brown had identified two groups of three teachers in Fernwood School who wanted to come to Lincoln Acres as two teams. They had worked together in Fernwood to some extent, though not in an open classroom, and wanted to try team teaching at the new school. Brown felt that although the potential team members were already familiar with each other and had worked together, he was not getting a "ready-made product"; they had a long way to develop before they could be called teaching teams.

In mid-January, the resource teacher* had also been identified. Imogene Miller and Sam Pennington had applied for the position. Miller, it will be recalled, had applied for the position of principal; she was Biddle's first choice, but was unacceptable to the parent members of the screening committee. Brown, aware that she had applied for the principalship, suggested to her that she would in effect be accepting a demotion by becoming the resource teacher, since she had already been one, and the position she currently held as coordinator of the high school work-study program had district-wide responsibilities. He also told her that if she seriously wanted a position as principal, it would be wise to apply to other school districts in the vicinity.

Pennington, as we have seen, had been involved in planning the school at a variety of stages. He was young, friendly and energetic, had taught in Washingtonville for six years, and was currently a member of a teaching team in the new open-space addition to Oxford School. Brown characterized Pennington as a "young Turk" in the district, and selected him to be the resource teacher.

4. The Faculty

By February 1, 1975, the selection of fifteen faculty members had been completed; they were approved several weeks later by the Board of Education. It was a predominantly female staff, with only three males. As Brown initially expected, it was also a younger staff, with only three middle-aged teachers; the others were in their late twenties and early thirties. All had taught for at least one year in Washingtonville, and three had as much as ten or more years of experience in the district. The average teaching experience of all teachers was 5.5 years. Seven faculty members had tenure in Washingtonville, and eight were non-tenured. Eight faculty members had bachelor's degrees and seven master's. Eleven of the fifteen had received their training in colleges in the state. Only one teacher, the media center person, was hired from outside the district. Specialists in fields such as art, physical education, and music, and the nurse, were to be assigned by the district before the start of school in the fall. Chart 5.1 presents the staff listing as of February 1, 1975.

In spite of Brown's second criterion for selection (previous experience with team teaching) none of the teachers had actually team-taught before. One primary team, Priscilla Talbot, Wanda Molloy, and Dori Kraus, had classrooms close to each other in Fernwood School and had shared some materials and ideas. Similarly, the intermediate team of Norbert

---

*The basic responsibility of the resource teacher, a role not found in most school systems, is to facilitate teachers' realization of their instructional program. To some extent, the resource teacher aids the principal of the school in a similar way. Although the position sounds similar to that of a vice-principal, it is not administrative, but a teaching position with school-wide responsibilities.

CHART 5.1

INITIAL STAFF STRUCTURE OF LINCOLN ACRES SCHOOL
(February 1, 1975)

Sarah Fox Alice Houghton (½ time) Louise Hargrove*	Kindergarten team
Priscilla Talbot Wanda Molloy Dori Kraus	Primary team -- grades 1, 2, 3
Sally Candler Jane Baylor Katie Neustadt	Primary team -- grades 1, 2, 3
Alan Beretta Jeanne Browne	Intermediate -- grades 4, 5, 6
Norbert White Rebecca Barone Glenda Jacobs	Intermediate -- grades 4, 5, 6
Regina Hanley	Media Center
Sam Pennington	Resource Teacher
Ellis Brown	Principal
Monica Selwin	Secretary

*Louise Hargrove was actually hired a month and one-half after the other teachers, because of increased enrollment in the kindergarten.

White, Rebecca Barone and Glenda Jacobs also had classrooms close to each other in Fernwood School and shared materials, but did not team teach. Katie Neustadt and Sally Candler taught in the same school and knew each other, but were not on the same floor and had not collaborated. The other teachers were all from different schools in the district.

5. Faculty Expectations and Experience

To help the reader understand the selection process and its results more clearly, we present data from two questions on the first extensive questionnaire we administered to teachers on December 8, 1975. The first question gives us a retrospective glimpse into the teachers' motivation for joining the Lincoln Acres staff, and the second gives us a partial view of the teaching skills that they brought to Lincoln Acres. We asked: "Why did you choose to come to teach at this school?" The results are shown in Table 5.1. The prospects of teaching in open space and of participating in a new, innovative school are clearly the two most important reasons. The write-in answers emphasize the opportunity for team teaching, colleagueship and professional growth.

The second question provided data on the teachers' past educational practice and thus the "fit" between their experiences and the role demands they would probably face in their new positions. Teachers were asked if they had used a number of educational practices before coming to Lincoln Acres school (Table 5.2, p. 78).

These data indicate that the teachers had previously used most of the techniques intended for the new school. We have noted above that no teachers had taught in a team; that eight indicated they had team taught is probably the result of definitional difficulties. At least six had shared resources and ideas with other teachers. The definition used in the questionnaire was: "An arrangement in which two or more teachers plan and execute together the instructional program for a number of pupils, generally in the same or adjoining rooms."

At the second faculty meeting, on February 19, 1975, the teachers were asked via questionnaire about their hopes and expectations for the school. Here are the results (N=11).

1. "As briefly as possible, describe some of the aspects of being on the staff of the Lincoln Acres school that you are looking forward to."

All mentioned some aspect of the staff as important. Five teachers mentioned improved learning opportunities for students, and four specifically mentioned working in teams. Other responses ranged from looking forward to working with a new principal to an opportunity for professional growth. Sample responses:

Chance to help create a school without problems of a given structure.
Opportunity to work with a staff with an esprit de corps.
Chance to change jobs without going out of the L.A. area.
Opportunity to work with Ellis Brown.

TABLE 5.1

REASONS GIVEN BY TEACHERS FOR COMING TO TEACH AT
LINCOLN ACRES SCHOOL

10   Open space aspects of school

2   Quality of students

5   School's physical site and location

14   Prospect of participating in a new, innovative school

8   Other (written in):

- the chance to work more closely with my team members

- to team teach and grow professionally

- team teach

- teaming; multigrading

- to work with a team to maximize learning and personal growth

- the development of a close faculty feeling of trust and support among friends and professionals

- opportunity to learn professionally

- wanted to be full time

- cut back in staffing at previous school -- where I was quite happy

Sharing parts of my life with a group of committed stimulated people -- sharing my life with children who are allowed to explore and discover their potentials and themselves.

2.   "What do you expect the new school to be like?"

The most frequent answer (5) mentioned making education enjoyable, followed by flexibility (3), educational growth (2), and a community-like environment (2). One teacher was not sure what the school would be like. Some representative answers:

I hope L.A. to have flexible scheduling, without any lock-step programming. The open space is conducive to a sense of community within and between the students and staff.

Lots of energy -- openness between kids-teachers, teacher-teacher, Prin-kids-teacher-community. Warm-accepting-intellectually alive-well structured-constructive, forward looking, open to changes-flexible.

An educational utopia for students and instructors.

TABLE 5.2

TEACHERS' PAST EXPERIENCE WITH EDUCATIONAL PRACTICES*

	Have you used it?		
	YES	?	NO
A. Independent study	13	0	3
B. Nongraded classes	10	0	6
C. Multigraded classes	12	0	4
D. Team teaching	8	1	6
E. Teacher aides	9	1	5
F. Programmed instruction	8	0	5
G. Flexible scheduling	12	0	3
H. Student record-keeping system	11	0	5
I. Parental participation	16	0	0
J. Videotape	8	0	8
K. Outdoor education	12	0	4
L. Administrators performing classroom teaching	6	0	9
M. Computer	6	0	10

*Each practice was described briefly to provide a common definition.

---

3. "Do you have any concerns or worries about what life will be like in the new school? If so, what are they?"

For this question, answers were somewhat less homogeneous than for the two above. A kindergarten teacher whose class was self-contained was concerned with being cut off from the rest of the school; one teacher found the building ugly and without enough windows; a third was worried about the disruptive effects of noise and other possible distractions as a result of open space. Three teachers voiced some concern over the parents and community ("Parental ignorance of education values").

Three others expressed some concern with the actual operation of the school, or the related matter of adequate planning and preparation for the opening of school.

Team teaching offers a great challenge and demands understanding and cooperation among all involved. Problems may arise in coordinating, scheduling, and as in any new school, the first year may present problems of equipment, etc.

I hope we have enough time to get our program planned out so that I can feel comfortable and confident in helping my students make the transition into the new program.

Finally, three people, including the principal, indicated that they had no worries or concerns. One teacher wrote:

I have complete confidence in Ellis and Sam. I know that my concerns will be dealt with sensitively.

4. "Considering your own teaching, what would you like to do in the new school that you are not doing now?"

The responses fell into three broadly-defined categories: team teaching (3), meeting student needs (6), and professional growth (4). Some examples of replies are:

Teach with a group of congenial teachers -- sharing the planning, teaching responsibilities and experiences. I hope for a more open and supportive administrator than my current boss.

Be able to turn my full attention to a child or a group without worrying about supervising the rest of the class.

5. "As briefly as possible, describe what you would consider to be the ideal state of education taking place in the Lincoln Acres school five years from now."

Again, several teachers gave multiple answers. Five indicated that individual instruction would be ideal, two wanted community and parental participation, four wished to see the environment of the school open and informal, and two had no answer. It should be mentioned that two teachers wrote "see number 2" ("What do you expect the new school to be like?"). Taken literally, and assuming no misunderstanding of the question, this seems to mean that they expected the school to open with its entire program operational.

Representative answers to this question are:

After the model of British informal education I hope L.A. will become a lively, spontaneous place, where complete use is made of the physical plant and surrounding environment, where students are actively involved in their education, and all enjoy and are proud of being a part of this learning environment.

A resource of learning centers for students' interests -- to research and formulate ideas, with direction if needed from instructors. Education intrinsically motivated.

6. "How do you feel about being part of the planning committee for the Lincoln Acres school?"

Everyone answered that being part of the planning team was an important experience. Several mentioned that it created a sense of ownership of the school, and that it gave them a sense of responsibility. For example, one teacher wrote:

I feel good because I feel that our ideas are really being listened to (usually).

7. "What personal or professional goals do you have that you hope to realize in the Lincoln Acres school?"

The most frequently mentioned goal was to become a better, more effective, teacher and experience professional growth.

I hope to develop a better understanding of children and how they develop and learn by looking closely at them, growing with them in my ability to provide alternative educational experiences for them.

Several themes appear in the responses. First, most teachers wanted the school to have individualized instruction. Second, they viewed team teaching as an appropriate means for achieving individualization; along with this, they desired an informal organizational structure. Third, they stated a preference -- as one might expect -- for a social climate in the community and school that would be supportive of teacher and student efforts. A fourth theme is that the teachers wanted an opportunity for professional growth, and expected it would occur as a result of their experiences in the new school. Finally, enthusiasm for the new undertaking was clearly evident.

These themes fit both Brown's and Biddle's early visions of the school rather well. In fact, there are no major differences between the administration and teachers in their expectations for what the school would be like, or for the major goals of the school. One major feature in both Biddle's and Brown's visions had been the idea that the faculty would fill in the details of their general plans. Permeating the teachers' responses is a sense that they wanted and expected to have the opportunity to actively shape the new school's program. Thus, in this important aspect, there is substantial congruence between the administration's vision and the desires of the teachers.

E. BROWN MEETS THE COMMUNITY

During January, besides selecting the faculty, Brown worked on the district budget with the other principals, finalized the Lincoln Acres budget, approved the installation of equipment in the otherwise empty school building, and began examining projected enrollment and staffing. He also met with the community.

1. The LAHA Meeting

During the first week in January, Barbara Berger, the head of the LAHA education committee, met with Brown. She wanted to know what his plans for the school were, and if he would be willing to talk about them before the general membership of LAHA. Brown, whose ambivalent attitude toward community participation in planning has already been discussed, delayed making a commitment to speak with the homeowners' association. Reflecting on the request in a talk with the researcher, he said:

> In a mass meeting nothing useful would transpire. I might yet go door-to-door. I don't know what kind of relationship I want to initiate yet. I'm concerned about starting a dialogue too early. Sam Pennington and Bob Biddle have met with LAHA several times and I'll be guided by them in dealing with LAHA. LAHA raised hell with the builder and they asked about demountable partitions in the school. They want to close it up.

About a week later, Brown agreed to meet before the general membership of LAHA and other interested residents of Lincoln Acres on January 20, 1975.

The LAHA meeting was held at 8:00 p.m. in a multi-purpose room in a parochial school opposite the Lincoln Acres development. By 8:30, after the business meeting had ended, there were approximately 275 people in the

room, many of whom had to stand. Pennington and several other teachers
-- whose appointment had not yet been announced -- sat near the front.

Barbara Berger introduced Ellis, saying that the community had
waited a long time for the school to actually open. Brown then spoke for
fifteen minutes about what he thought the school would try to accomplish
with youngsters. He emphasized flexibility, individualization of instruction
and the advantages of open space education over traditional, self-contained
classrooms. In a crisp, strong voice, he then asked if the audience, which
had listened in absolute silence, had any questions. Questions from the
audience lasted for an hour and a half.

The questions were of three types: those dealing with operational
aspects of the school; those concerned with the benefits of open education
and its possible costs; and those concerned specifically with Brown and what
he intended to do as the new principal. In all three of these areas, the
questions ranged from asking for statements of fact to speculation about
anticipated problems. Many questions were posed in terms of prior
unsuccessful experiences children had had in open education schools;
questioners wondered how the program to be put into Lincoln Acres would
differ. Here are some typical questions and responses.

Operational aspects of the school:

Q: Will the school be equipped by September 1?
A: Yes, if the budget passes. We need support for it in
numbers. I know that Lincoln Acres is for it but we have
to make sure that the rest of Washingtonville is.

Q: What facilities will there be in the school, for example, a
lunch program?
A: There will be hot lunches provided. /Several women were
delighted by this./

Q: Will there be bus service? We live far away.
A: That is a Board matter.

Q: You indicated that you doubt you will have full control in
staffing. Do you think you will have control of the
school?
A: I think so. /From the back of the room a woman yelled in
a harsh voice, "Don't count on it."/

Q: Who is going to run the school, you or the superintendent?
A: I think I can handle it. I don't intend to be anybody's
marionette. /Applause from about three-quarters of the
audience followed this./

Q: Concerning the removable partitions: would you have
redesigned the school or do you accept it as is?
A: I probably would have made other recommendations. The
walls are really not that movable. The building design

was done before I came, but it's all right as it is.

Benefits and possible costs of open education:

Q: What about noise in the building and openness?
A: Openness will probably create less noise; people will have to consider others. I used to teach next to a shop room. All kinds of noise came out of it. I wished there was no wall between us, because if the shop teacher could have seen the pain he caused us, he would have been quieter.

Q: I don't want openness to fall on its face after six months. Are we ready for this?
A: Yes. I wish that I had pictures of my last school. It worked well there. Of course, we'll have growth.

Q: When my child entered an open classroom from a regular one she developed troubles. After a long time of investigation we found that she couldn't handle so many different teachers. Now she's in a self-contained room doing well again. How would you handle a child like this?
A: We can create structure for this type of child and individual attention.

Q: Are you being too idealistic? Are you that committed to your system or can you have alternatives to begin with?
A: There have to be alternatives. You can't learn to swim by being thrown in the water. We will start with where people are and work from there.

Q: What about discipline in the open classroom? Won't there be more problems?
A: Discipline is better in open space. In closed classrooms the kid only has to get behind one teacher's back. In open space he has to get out of sight of several teachers. [laughter]

Questions about Ellis Brown as the new principal:

Q: How many years of actual teaching do you have?
A: I taught science in Vermont for two years. I worked in Boston part time in a special education program and I was a principal in New Hampshire, where I started the school.

Q: How long were you principal in New Hampshire?
A: One and a half years.

Q: Can we expect you to be here longer?
A: I plan to be here a while and I'm dedicated to educating the youngsters of Washingtonville.

Q: Do you plan to teach here as you did in New Hampshire?
A: This is a larger school and I'll have more administrative duties, but I plan to teach as much as possible.

Some of the answers Brown gave in each area sounded like policy statements, as did his responses to questions concerning the role of parents in the school.

Q: Can we choose teachers as we do in Fernwood School?
A: Yes, when feasible. It could be a problem if there is too large a selection of a particular teacher.

Q: Will we be able to see teachers in action and make a "value judgment" about them?
A: Yes, we will have an open school.

Q: How will you report student progress to parents?
A: I'm not sure yet. I would like to have comments from parents concerning what they would like to hear about, as well as input from teachers.

Q: Will you welcome parents into the school?
A: Yes. This was a selection criterion for teachers. We wanted those who have and could work with parents as volunteers in the classroom.

The meeting ended at 10:40 when the president of LAHA stood and said:

My knowledge of Lincoln Acres is that it is diverse. People hold a lot of different views, some for and some against. You'll get a hell of a lot of input, that's for sure.

The same woman who had yelled from the back of the room, "Don't count on it", in response to Ellis' answer that he would have full control of the school now yelled, "You'll get hell." The audience, somewhat startled, gradually rose from their seats and began to leave.

Immediately after the meeting, Ellis reflected on what had transpired and concluded that it wasn't a "bad crowd." He thought they had asked naive questions, easier to answer than the questions parents asked in New Hampshire; there they had made their questions personal and picked apart the principal's personality. According to Brown, the applause after the "marionette" answer came because:

Biddle doesn't give the community its way, and is too direct with them. Poor public relations. They think they will get their way more with me, but they are mistaken.

Reactions to the meeting were less positive from other staff members' perspectives. Several Lincoln Acres teachers (for example, Alice

Houghton and Sam Pennington) thought the questions Ellis was asked were highly personal and somewhat hostile. Barbara Berger, chairperson of the LAHA education committee which had invited Brown to speak, commented on the meeting a few days later:

> Frankly, I was embarrassed. The people gave him a hard time. Some were snide and sarcastic. But most people walked away with confidence in Ellis. He handled himself well. But for example, take report cards. He said he would work with the community in making a report card. They now say that he doesn't even know what kind of report card he wants.

Charles Frisch, a member of the Board of Education, said of the meeting:

> When Ellis was at LAHA they asked some tough questions and he came through pretty well. It was my feeling that they thought, "I may not like open education, but I trust the man."

Considering that few community members had met with Brown previously, and that the only other source of information was a brief article on the front page of the local newspaper that morning (it outlined his career and new duties), the people who asked questions seemed fairly knowledgeable about open education, and fairly probing in their questioning of Brown's personal ability. The tone of the meeting varied from being intently serious to jovial, and on several occasions reached a threatening tone. Two things clearly emerged from this initial encounter. First, the parents who attended had an active interest in finding out what type of education would take place in the new school. Second, many of them had doubts that the proposed program for the school was suitable for what they viewed as their children's educational needs.

2. Parents at the Synagogue

Eight days later, Brown appeared before a parent group at the local synagogue, at the invitation of the rabbi. There were approximately thirty people present, including one teacher, Sarah Fox, who was a member of the congregation.

After an introduction by the rabbi, Brown gave the same speech he had delivered at the LAHA meeting, and invited questions. Again, the questions dealt with problems individual students might have, such as motivation and discipline. Other areas of concern were evaluation procedures and the general benefits of open education. Only one questioner, a Spanish language teacher in another town, was highly skeptical; she doubted that students could learn "fundamentals" in the open classroom. One or two students present spoke in support of the experiences they had had in open education classes in Washingtonville. Generally, this audience was less openly challenging to most of what Brown said, and appeared more favorably inclined to try open education than the LAHA group. Brown's estimation of the meeting was:

They basically accepted what was being laid on them. This group was as ready to accept without rationale as LAHA is unwilling to accept <u>with</u> rationale.

F. THE BOARD OF EDUCATION ELECTION, 1975

In late February, candidates for the March election to the Board of Education began campaigning throughout the township. Since its formation, LAHA had annually allowed the candidates to use one of their meetings as a platform for presenting views and answering citizen's questions. On March 5, 1975, one hundred and fifty residents attended the meeting, as did Brown, Anthony Smith, and Alice Houghton, a kindergarten teacher at Lincoln Acres school.

1. The Candidates

The first speaker was Barbara Berger. She emphasized her participation on the principal screening committee for the Lincoln Acres school, the fact that she would like to see the school board take a more active role in setting policy, and that she had time to devote to being a school board member. Her primary reason for wanting the position was that her child was entering the Lincoln Acres school in the fall.

Robert Klahr, a middle-aged stockbroker from Allwood Green, made the next presentation. He talked about the need to watch the ways in which money was spent, and that the key concern of a Board member was "what happens to kids". He then talked about lack of communication between the people and their representatives, handed out a list of elected state officials, with phone numbers, and encouraged the audience to contact the officials if they had something to say about education.

The next candidate was Charles Frisch, a former superintendent of schools, and current director of the Right to Read program for the state. Frisch said that he and his family had moved to Washingtonville because the school system was good. He emphasized his background in education, and explained that as part of his job he worked with boards of education throughout the state in implementing curriculum changes in reading programs. He also mentioned that he had been active in LAHA, and for the last three months had been serving on the Board of Education as a replacement for a member who had resigned. Frisch lives in Lincoln Acres.

Following Frisch, Gerrie Holden, a resident of one of the rural areas of the township, stressed her previous activity in her children's schools, and her work in writing a proposal for pre-school education. She said she would represent the parents, and that parents should be listened to. In her view, the Board of Education was a "management team" for the township.

The last candidate to speak was Dorothy Aiello from Allwood Green. She gave a rambling address as she wandered about the front of the room. Her main point was "Let's try to see if public school kids get as good an education as snobby elites."

After each candidate's talk there was applause; Frisch received the strongest applause, and Aiello the least.

2. Issues and Responses

When the candidates' presentations were finished, the audience was permitted to ask questions. Following are some of the exchanges; they indicate what some of the issues concerning the new school were, and how the potential Board of Education members responded to them.

Q: Knowing about Barbara's views on open education, I'd like to know about others' views and if we have enough support in the community for a variety of alternatives to open space.

Moderator: I'd like to explain the situation to the candidates. We have a new school opening. Some parents don't like the open space concept and would like to know if they came to you what you would do about it.

Klahr: My daughter was in an open-space class and learned a lot there. For her it was ideal but I can understand why it might not work in other cases. I don't know why some open space /programs/ wouldn't work.

Q: You're not answering my question. You say you want input from parents -- will you respond to it?

Klahr: If I felt you were right, I'd support it.

Karalis: Would you support Lincoln Acres if they asked for an alternative program in the school?

Klahr: I can't answer that. The Board doesn't run the school. We hire professionals to do it.

Holden: Yes. I would support you. The superintendent doesn't have a right to force anything on you. There should definitely be an alternative system.

Frisch: There is a more crucial issue. People hold onto terms like "open education," etc., but do you know what they are? It seems as though the open space schools that are successful have this structure. When it first came down the pike I was worried, but when I heard the principal at LAHA I felt better. There should be an alternative in Lincoln Acres, but I hope that it won't become a trap. I feel that some people in the community are upset. If they came to the Board I would consider their requests.

Aiello: Open words in a small island. I would support you.

Frisch: I would like to say that we should give it time.

Berger: Go to Oxford or Eastland Junction and it is working nicely. Washingtonville trains teachers for open space; there are no problems in the other schools.

Q: How will you evaluate if the Lincoln Acres school is meeting the needs of students and how long a period of time is needed?

Klahr: The answer to that is hard. If after a year people pound on my door I will look at it.

Frisch: The Board will get a reading on where the kids are, including tests, check-sheets and teacher perceptions and attitudes toward education. The problem with innovation is that it improves the teacher/learner relationship and we tend to forget to teach the basics. The Board will have a procedure whereby they can have a readout on the state of things.

Berger: I'd like to see us give Lincoln Acres a fair chance. A year probably won't do.

Frisch: A year isn't really enough time. You need more time to make a judgement.

Other questions concerned the relationship the prospective Board members expected to develop with the superintendent, and what their position was with regard to the school budget. All candidates answered that they would make policy and assume a role that would be to some extent independent of the superintendent. Only Holden was critical of the school budget and urged its defeat.

Essentially, the themes concerning Lincoln Acres school at this meeting were the same as those raised on previous public occasions. The basic concern, however, was over actions the candidates would take if elected: would they be responsive to the desire for "alternative"* forms of education that many parents strongly wanted, or would they ignore them and continue the policies that Biddle preferred? The Board of Education was clearly viewed by many residents as a potential vehicle for direct action against the superintendent of schools, if he did not comply with their requests.

Brown's reactions. When Ellis spoke with the researcher after the meeting, his reactions to the candidates' presentations and the questioning were complex, but clear:

_____

*Note that the "alternative" rhetoric here refers to the presence of more traditional educational programs.

I have a number of feelings. First, emotional: how typical they are for people having a new school; they have all kinds of anxieties. Second, I give allowance for some of this, because they have been the object of a poor public relations campaign. Third, I'm sympathetic because the school has gone up so slowly and given them time to speculate. I'll ultimately run my own kind of school anyhow. Whatever is decided in the political arena doesn't matter. They will come out with a school that I can run; I can run an exemplary school in an outhouse if necessary. I shouldn't get too hung up about politics. I will do things the most efficient way that the people want things done. Open education is an efficiency device. The dispute was about if I can deliver what is expected by the means I choose.

3. The Board Election

The Washingtonville Courier endorsed candidates for the Board of Education for the first time that year. The editor recommended Dr. Charles Frisch as the first choice, writing:

Dr. Frisch is articulate, outspoken but cool and reasoned in his argument for a school system which links innovation with a sound knowledge of the basics -- reading, writing and 'rithmetic.

Dr. Frisch is head of the state "Right to Read" program, and brings with him experience as a teacher, principal, and state administrator. But he is not a passionate advocate of any single theory of education.

He is open to public criticism and suggestion. He realizes in this day of inflation and with the inequities of our tax system, a school board member must curb his lust for new programs in favor of fiscal restraint. As one community leader described him: "He is the picture of the rational man."

In the district-wide campaign, there was no heated debate over any particular set of educational issues. In fact, aside from the Lincoln Acres school, there were no issues, and for the most part the candidates agreed with each others' positions. The newspaper comments on the candidates seemed to acknowledge that there were few substantive reasons for choosing among them. Frisch was the only candidate with expertise in education; others had to be judged on the basis of their pledges to perform a public service.

In mid-March, Washingtonville Township elected Frisch to the Board of Education by the largest margin; he was followed by Holden and then Klahr. Berger came in fourth, and Aiello was a distant fifth. Lincoln Acres itself voted most heavily for Frisch and Berger, who were both residents of the development.

In the same balloting an $8.7 million budget was defeated. As in past years, in the rural areas the vote was clearly against it. With the exception of one suburban community, which defeated it by four votes, the suburban areas of the township passed the budget by small margins.

The budget was recast by the township council with some cuts, but it was clear that Lincoln Acres school was being launched in a community with only a modest majority favoring the administration's budgetary proposals.

A few weeks later, the school board reorganized and elected a new president. Three members voted for Estelle Hunter, a resident of a rural community and former organizer of CLEAN. The other members supported Irena Farrell, who was re-elected school board president. Sylvia Peabody, a black from Lincoln Acres, Holden, and Hunter formed the losing, conservative, faction. In terms of representation from Lincoln Acres, Peabody was a conservative and Frisch was considered a moderate-liberal.

G. THE FACULTY BEGINS WORK

Preparations for planning the school continued during this period. Brown investigated possibilities for faculty meetings before the summer, and drafted, with Pennington, a proposal for a month-long summer planning workshop. Brown was considering an informal house-to-house open-ended survey in the spring, with the intent of getting a general feeling of the community. He also considered our research project's offer of matching funds for outside consultants to work with organizing the faculty.

It should be mentioned that Brown was the only person working full-time on the preparations for the new school at this time. The teachers, media center person and resource teacher were all employed as teachers in other schools until the end of June. To avoid creating too many demands on the teachers, Brown decided to have faculty meetings relatively infrequently for the remainder of the school year, and then to meet daily for a month during the summer. Descriptions of the faculty meetings held during the spring of 1975 follow.

1. The First Faculty Meeting

In early February, before formal appointment by the Board of Education, the faculty had its first meeting, an informal gathering held at Brown's apartment. Everyone was introduced, the Center for Policy Research study was explained,* and there was a brief discussion of the idea of having a summer workshop for planning the program of the school. The

---

*It will be recalled that the initial working agreement between our research project and the school district, approved by Biddle and Brown, specified that the project would be explained and reviewed with teachers when they were hired. Ellis did this at the first faculty meeting; the researcher was not present.

teachers raised no objection to the idea of the research study, and their reaction to the idea of the summer workshop was highly favorable. After some refreshments, the faculty went to the school, and Ellis gave them a guided tour.

2. The Second Faculty Meeting

The summer proposal is confirmed. Sam and Ellis prepared a preliminary version of the summer proposal, and it was presented to the faculty for reactions at the second meeting on February 19, 1975. Whether or not it would be funded by the Board of Education was an issue of some concern, as was student participation. Several teachers felt the wording of objectives was not specific enough at some points. The major concern with the proposal, however, was with the role it described for parents, and when they would become involved directly with the school. This excerpt from the field notes captures the tone of the first discussion the faculty had on this topic.

Regina: I have doubts about bringing in parents so soon [as part of the summer workshop].

Ellis: So do I.

Regina: We had the experience in opening a new school where we brought in parents too soon. We were not ready for them.

Sarah: Do we need them a full week? [as proposed in the summer workshop schedule]

Ellis: Maybe only one or two of us could work with them, or a team.

Lindy: I don't think we can communicate with parents yet. They should be involved, but I don't see how yet.

Sarah: What about taking a nucleus of parents from Fernwood, and have them train other L.A. parents? I'm sure you won't have trouble finding them.

Ellis: Part of the summer program is to let them see the school. Last night at the budget meeting, they asked if they could see it. Some have already seen it and commented to me. They want to see the facilities. Maybe we could have some language revision in the proposal. We can make that decision later on.

Beyond these issues, there were no substantive additions to or alterations of the proposal. Ellis, concluding the discussion, said:

What I've heard are really small changes. Is there somebody greatly disappointed? /No/ Otherwise, I'll integrate the changes and cut down the length and that will be it. If there is something else let me know. O.K.?

Basically, the atmosphere of the meeting was informal and friendly. All the teachers were eager, and many participated in the discussion actively.

The first draft of the final version as submitted to and approved by the Washingtonville Instructional Council* are largely identical. For example, in spite of the fact that many teachers, and Ellis, had reservations about including parents in the summer workshop, no changes were made in the activities parents would participate in. If anything, there were additional duties projected for parents. For example, Charles Frisch, who was a parent as well as a Board member and reading expert, was to serve as an evaluator of reading checklists developed during the workshop. In fact, Ellis told the researcher, that "student and parent educational decision-making roles.....may be expanded to parent and student involvements beginning earlier in the year."

The proposal's substance. Since the summer proposal is the major planning document that Brown and Pennington, with the input and approval of the faculty, produced, it is worth examining fairly closely. We should also note that the summer proposal was the main means of linkage contemplated between the initial plans and implementation -- the actual structures and practices that would form the program of the school when it opened for students.

The objectives the proposal said would be reached by the end of the month-long summer workshop were:

1. written decision-making processes for each team and for whole-staff decisions;

2. team-member role descriptions, written by each team; librarian, principal and resource teacher roles, written by the whole staff;

3. written programmed series of basic skills objectives, Kindergarten through Grade 6;

4. physical division of space within the school, based upon educational rationale;

---

*In Washingtonville, proposals are submitted to the Instructional Council, which is composed of volunteer teachers from throughout the district. After their approval, which is usually pro forma, the proposal is recommended to the Board of Education for funding. The amount requested for the Lincoln Acres School Summer Workshop proposal was $17,000.

5. circulation of basic skills learning strategies, centralized through the library/resource center;

6. written student needs assessment system;

7. written program effectiveness evaluation systems; and

8. student and parent educational decison-making roles.

These were to be achieved in the order presented, at the rate of two during each week of the workshop. Objective #3 was begun during the faculty meetings preceding the workshop, since it was expected to require more than a half-week's work. Accomplishment of objective #4, Brown pointed out, depended on deliveries of furniture and materials to the school.

The document also provides a glimpse of the relationships that Brown hoped would develop among the faculty. Teaching teams, the basic unit of the school, were formulated as operating together in making decisions, ranging from furniture arrangements to the curriculum. Brown, Pennington and Regina Hanley, the media person, were viewed in the proposal as facilitators for the teams; they were not superordinate administrators, but rather resource people, of equal status with the teachers. In fact, the language of the proposal was:

> ...the librarian, resource teacher and principal see a need to develop descriptions of their roles through interaction with staff that will break from traditional interpretations of those titles.

Concerning decision-making, in most instances it was proposed that the teams would formulate their own policy. However, in several areas (for example, the role of parents in the school; the use of checklists), decisions and procedures would have to be school-wide.

In general, the model was one of decentralization of tasks and decision-making to the level of individual teaching teams. Indeed, the lack of positions -- vice-principal, team leaders, department heads -- reduced the possibility of creating a well-defined hierarchy of authority with power delimited by position, and centralized in the principal's office.

The summer proposal was also fairly explicit about the relationships that Brown would like the school to develop with its environment, particularly parents. Parents were to be given the opportunity to react to the plans made by the teachers, and would be included in the final week of the workshop, where they would collaborate on a report card, begin the parent aide programs, and design community use of the school.

A general objective underlying the eight listed above was that of creating a "personal sense of ownership" in those involved with the school; the proposal emphasized the importance of joint planning, and stated that

> ...the obvious alternatives of patterning the school after some other school, modeling it after some theoretical structure, or shaping it according to some administrator's or consultant's thinking were rejected.

Here again a desire for independence and autonomy is evident. This passage also implicitly reiterates the theme of reliance on internal resources.

Lastly, the proposal concluded with the intention of having Lincoln Acres school and its staff become models and resources for the rest of the elementary schools in the district.

> Students and parents of Washingtonville will be provided with a unique new educational setting by the end of the summer's program. Processes of decision making, checklist writing, student needs assessing, program evaluating and team-teaching in open schools will be available as process models to other schools in this district. This is an especially important contribution to a district committed to development of open and informal learning systems. Lincoln Acres School staff will be available to collaborate with other schools' staff developing parallel programs.

(Comments.) Generally, the proposal is fairly straightforward, and seems to cover most areas important for the opening of a new school. But if there is a problem with the proposal, it would be its ambitiousness for what could be accomplished in a month, even though work on several objectives (deciding on furniture, developing some objective lists, and starting team development) was to begin in the spring faculty meetings.

A related comment is that the proposal presents planning as a rationalistic process that moves in a straight line from faculty selection to a smoothly functioning school. No contingency plans are mentioned, and no criteria are stated for minimum acceptable achievement of goals. This optimistic projection of task completion may have been an artifact of proposal writing style, which usually aims to impress the funding agency that the enterprise is worthy, and is not an expression of what the writers think will actually occur. But in this case the audience was more "internal" than usual, and doubt concerning the proposal being funded was not strong. A plausible explanation of the optimism and rationality is that the new school -- and its new principal -- had to present a formidable, even dynamic, public image to secure a place in the school system.

This raises the problem of understanding educational rhetoric that we have encountered earlier. Given the fact that educators -- as well as members of other professions -- often make goal statements that are idealistic and far outrun anyone's ability to achieve them, is it fair to be critical about "implementation failure"? From a methodological point of view, we think it is not: simple comparison of later achievements with ideally-stated goals is insufficient. A careful analysis will need to look for reasons why hyperbolic goal statements are made in the first place, and how more reasonable ones are substituted as work proceeds.

And can we say that the researcher is in a better position than those studied to make judgements upon what is "rhetoric" (and thus unachievable) and what is not? We will try to point to the possibility that some goals may be rhetorical, as in this case, but resist taking the position that "we know better," even with the advantage of hindsight.

Other issues. At this meeting, the faculty also discussed the budget for the school, ordering of materials, and furniture design and delivery. They also raised other operational questions: whether there would be a lunch program, and whether it was possible to get special equipment for the kindergarten and developmental gym.

During the discussion of these questions,the issue of the role of the resource teacher was raised when someone wanted to know if Sam could help with ordering materials.

Wanda: Is that your role, Sam, or not?

Sam: It's not defined yet. That is part of the summer proposal. There is a language problem in using both "resource center" and "resource teacher". Don't lock me into a resource room. I plan to be around the school.

At another point Priscilla Talbot raised the question of whether they were planning for "informal education", in the British tradition. Ellis did not respond directly, but said:

It's too bad that we have to order materials now. We don't know each other's educational views yet. The calendar causes this bind. Try to feel each other out and order stuff that gives you a sense of /fitting your/ style.

After some comments by Regina Hanley, the librarian, on media center procedures, the meeting ended.

3. The Third Faculty Meeting

Three weeks later, the third faculty meeting was held after school at the Board of Education offices. Before the meeting formally began, a book salesman made a presentation to those teaches who were interested. Other instructional materials were passed around for teachers to look at and comment on, and arrangements were made for meetings with other publishers' representatives.

The main topic of the meeting was furniture for the school, including teaching stations, bookcases, and closets. On a cardboard display, Ellis presented drawings of the furniture that had been suggested by Sam Pennington and other teacher members of the original design-input committee formed by Biddle. The intention was that after further suggestions and revision of the basic models presented, the furniture would be built by Washingtonville maintenance workers in the quantities requested by teachers.

Brown also announced that he would soon have a mock-up of the floor plan of the teaching space prepared; it would allow each team to move the furniture around; they could experiment and discover what organization of furniture and space they preferred. The meeting then shifted to a warehouse about 100 feet from the Board offices, in which the furniture was stored.

In the warehouse, Bob Haines, head of the maintenance department, explained the intended use of each piece of furniture and modification of the original designs that he had made in the process of construction. Several teachers asked Haines why he had made the changes, which to them decreased the usefulness of the pieces involved. Pennington also became involved, saying to Haines, for instance, "A couple of teachers say that this is too deep." Haines did not respond.

Shortly after, Biddle came into the warehouse, ostensibly looking for Haines, but pulled Ellis to the side and privately told him that going over the properties of the furniture was not a productive process. The only way to revise the furniture meaningfully, in Biddle's view, would be to have some teachers use it. After more criticism of the design, rationale for various changes ("There can't be pull-out drawers, because it would tip over too easily then.") and unfocused discussion by teachers, Brown shepherded everyone out of the warehouse back to the Board offices by saying, "Well, we've seen enough. It's 4:30, we've got things to do." Haines, who defended his design changes on the basis of safety, said to a couple of teachers who were on their way back to the meeting, "Well, I can't make each one different."

Later in the meeting, Brown commented on the "ownership" that Haines had developed for the furniture he had built. He then commented on several features of the furniture that he disliked, and cut Sam short when he was reiterating that Haines had changed the designs, by saying "It doesn't matter who designed it or what it looks like now. If it doesn't look useful, say what <u>would</u> be useful." Furniture is a topic that we will return to shortly; it became part of the debate over what the educational program of the school should be.

This incident also exemplified an aspect of Brown's personal style: along with the air of aloofness we have mentioned, he could be brusque, even curt, when crossed or annoyed. To Ellis, Sam's apparent wish to defend the "original" design seemed simply irrelevant to the immediate task, judging from his abrupt comment.

The next agenda item concerned use of the April 17 staff development day. The main issue was whether it should be used by the new faculty or, if teachers preferred, for participating with the schools where they presently taught. Brown emphasized that he did not want to place teachers in a position of conflict with their present schools. There was more discussion and explanation of what was planned for that day at other schools, and what problems, if any, would be caused by missing those activities. No decision was reached, and the topic was left with Brown's promise to get more information from David Hauptmann, the principal of Fernwood, on what plans could be made for that day with the Lincoln Acres staff that would not interfere with his program.

The meeting concluded with a preliminary discussion of student placement for the next year. The main issue was whether the procedure used in Fernwood school in previous years, which gave parents an opportunity to request teachers, would be suitable for Lincoln Acres school. Brown said the issue was wide open, and that it should be thought about and discussed at the next meeting.

Finally, Sam made some short announcements about learning materials that would be available for teacher inspection. The meeting ended with an unsuccessful attempt to find a next meeting time. After some discussion, Sarah Fox suggested that the group meet at different open space schools. But no decision on a day to meet could be reached; Ellis said he would work on finding a suitable date. He then repeated that by the next meeting teams should look at the mock-up of the floor plan, and that everyone should consider student placement procedures.

Ellis' view of the teams. On the day after this meeting, Brown commented to the researcher on the way he saw the teams developing. According to him, Glenda, Rebecca and Norbert, one of the intermediate teams, were working hard at building a group; they were making "a conscious attempt at building a human system"; this group was taking more time getting ordering done than the other groups, but was otherwise, he felt, doing fine. In Brown's opinion the other groups were more task-oriented: as far as their development into a team they would have "natural development." It was Brown's view that:

There is a great deal of knowledge being revealed by their preferences; this shakes out their values. This was my intention: to give them tasks and in the process /they would/get to know each other. To create opportunities for team building, to happen at natural development points.

Specifically, he thought that Sarah and Alice, the kindergarten teachers, knew their differences and took an intellectual approach to resolving them. Alan and Jeanne, an intermediate team, were "accommodating people", as were Wanda, Priscilla and Dori, one of the primary teams; he thought both teams would experience "natural development." The other primary team, Jane, Sally and Katie, "got along easily with each other," but Brown reflected, "I don't know how profoundly together they are."

Generally, he seemed to be satisfied with the initial progress made toward forming a faculty.

4. The Fourth Faculty Meeting

One week later, on March 18, 1975, the fourth faculty meeting was held in the recently-completed open space addition to Eastland Junction school. The teaching area of the addition -- which the teachers inspected informally but closely -- had well-defined "classroom" spaces. Several wall-to-ceiling partitions, and the arrangement of bookcases and other furniture created a sense of separation among the instructional areas, as in self-contained classrooms. A central aspect of the building was its flexibility. For example, most furniture was on wheels, the floor was entirely carpeted, and the walls were demountable, though not easily moved. Most Lincoln Acres staff members felt that the arrangement of furniture and walls reduced the openness of the space; they were unable to see the point of "open space" used in such a way. Alan, Sally and Sarah said they were particularly puzzled by what the benefits of open-space were when it was used this way. (At one point later in the meeting, Brown asked if it would be useful to continue to meet in Eastland Junction so they could "poke around" in the open space, or in Oxford school. Jeanne asked, "Is it like this, or is it open?")

Once the group assembled, the first topic of the meeting was parental requests for placement of children in classes. The issue, as introduced in the last faculty meeting, was whether or not the same procedure used for parental requests by David Hauptmann, principal of Fernwood school, should be adopted at Lincoln Acres. The general staff reaction, including that of the teachers currently working at Fernwood, was that parental preference should be eliminated, because it might result in a variety of unnecessary problems. Furthermore, it was agreed that "most parents actually don't have a concern with where their children are placed", and that only a "vocal minority" do. But it was the vocal minority that could present a potential problem.

This conclusion led to a discussion of appropriate methods for informing parents of their children's assignment to teachers, and when they should be notified. At first Brown said this would be done in the spring when Fernwood re-assigned its population, but after discussion the group concluded that it would be better to wait and make student placements during the summer workshop. They feared that having parents make placement requests would set a precedent, and give them too much power. The following exchange illustrates this as well as Brown's projected strategy for handling parents:

> Sally: We want to develop certain attitudes at the beginning in the parents. At Wright school certain parents want to run the school. We have to draw a fine line where the parents are concerned. How are we going to handle parents?
>
> Brown: That's my political genius. If a parent comes in, and says she wants a teacher with certain characteristics, I just say, "That's wonderful, that's just the kind of teacher she has." I can go through that routine asleep.*

A second, more subtle, apprehension made the issue of teacher selection important; teachers were afraid they wouldn't be selected by parents, casting doubt on their ability as teachers. Norbert White, who wanted the practice of parental preference discontinued, had in previous years enjoyed waiting lists of parents who wanted their children in his class. Others on the faculty had also developed reputations in the district as being exemplary teachers, and had what amounted to a devoted following. Several teachers, however, because of their recent arrival in Washingtonville, had

---

*Ellis liked acting in amateur theater productions. His avocational interest was not wholly disconnected from his performance as a principal; there was sometimes the feeling that he was putting on an act for parents, the Board, or other audiences. Here he was acknowledging this directly.

not had the opportunity to develop a reputation -- or perhaps weren't deserving of one. At any rate, the underlying feeling was not only that parental selection of teachers might create a channel for parental power, but that parental requests could potentially differentiate highly-esteemed from non-esteemed teachers.

After this discussion, Brown reported that he had made arrangements with David Hauptmann about the April 17 instructional development day. The Fernwood teachers who had joined the Lincoln Acres faculty were released by Hauptmann so that a Lincoln Acres all-day faculty meeting could be held. Everyone was pleased.

Regina Hanley, the librarian, who was a long-time resident of Allwood Green, had suggested privately to Ellis that the faculty have a meal at her house after the meeting. He reported this, people liked the idea, and several offers were made to help Regina with the preparations.

Ellis then announced that the superintendent was going to close all budget accounts soon, creating a deadline for ordering materials. He emphasized:

> I'm going to try to operate from here on and forever more
> without arbitrary deadlines. But in this case we need the
> money.

A short discussion of the technicalities of ordering materials followed. When it was over, furniture, the primary focus of the last meeting, again became the topic of conversation.

Several teachers had complained earlier to Ellis that Bob Haines had redesigned the furniture. At this meeting, Brown said that he had talked with Biddle about the problem and that it had been "hammered out." He added that he saw no reason why the furniture couldn't have wheels and drawers as originally planned, since he had had no problems with that type of furniture in New Hampshire. Then, with the models of the furniture on display, the faculty, led by Ellis, proposed ways of altering the designs, and discussed which teams wanted particular pieces of furniture.

In response to suggestions for change, Brown explained the limitations imposed on them and suggested that in some cases changes might be too late, because certain pieces of furniture might already have been built. He then said:

> I was thinking about the furniture we saw the other day. Why
> bother with the way it got that way? I thought back to New
> Hampshire, which was more open than Lincoln Acres. The
> only furniture we had was some bookshelves, blackboards,
> teaching stations and some standing cabinets. There was
> nothing else there. We had none of this mess center, teaching
> center, game center, etc. All of the furniture was the same.
> One reason for being general is that if they are too specific
> you might want to change them and not be able to. I can tell
> Haines to make nine different pieces from what we have here.
> I would urge you to think in terms of general utility and not
> the specific pieces up here.

When the meeting ended, the teachers remained and several discussed furniture placement. Others planned to meet the following day at the school. Alice and Sarah, the kindergarten teachers, asked Ellis if he would meet with them in a few days at Sarah's Allwood Green home to discuss furniture ordering for the kindergarten. Other arrangements were made to continue materials ordering, and furniture design and placement planning outside of the formal faculty meetings. Several teams had been meeting on their own time since the faculty was selected.

(Comments.) This faculty meeting, as well as the ones that preceded it, was relatively informal, especially considering the tensions that usually accompany the beginning of new social relationships in work situations. Although Ellis tended to be the center of attention, the faculty was consulted on all major decisions; most teachers had sufficient opportunity to express their opinions. Of course, as in almost all human groups, several people sat without offering any comments on the proceedings.

In these early meetings, collegial relationships began developing among the faculty. For example, Ellis made it known in the second faculty meeting that he preferred to be identified by his first name. Several teachers commented on how unusual it was to call a principal by his first name; principals they had worked with for many years still expected to be called "Mr. So-and-So." Sarah commented, "I would never think to call Mr. Silver Joe!"

We should also note here that the central administration encouraged this kind of informality among faculty members. Biddle, the superintendent, could call every teacher by name, and often knew a fair amount about their personal lives. Teachers' relationships with Biddle were in many cases equally informal and personal. It was not unusual to hear a teacher yell, "Hey, Bob Biddle, how ya' doin'?"; this would begin a conversation that might range from discussion of the weather to the problems of children with perceptual handicaps.

Relationships among teachers were noticeably informal and becoming closer; teams were spending more and more time planning together, often at one team member's home. The teams had begun to have labels. For example, someone dubbed the primary team of Jane Baylor, Katie Neustadt, and Sally Candler "NBC", using their last initials. This idea spread, so that everyone began referring to teams this way, except in the case of the kindergarten. The MTK team was the primary team of Wanda Molloy, Priscilla Talbot, and Doris Kraus; the BJW team was the intermediate team of Norbert White, Rebecca Barone and Glenda Jacobs; and the BB team consisted of Alan Beretta and Jeanne Browne, the other intermediate teachers.

During this period, while the faculty was meeting in preparation for opening the new school, members of the community began active opposition to certain aspects of the plans. We now turn to these concerns.

H. COMMUNITY CONCERNS

Earlier, while the school was in the final stages of construction, a group of Lincoln Acres parents, whose children were scheduled to enter kindergarten when the school opened, had requested that the superintendent implement an academic program rather than a developmental program. They also requested an enclosed teaching space for the kindergarten. Biddle acceded to the latter; the kindergarten area was separated by a moveable, wall-to-ceiling partition from the rest of the instructional area.

During the remainder of the construction, parents (for the most part members of LAHA) had monitored the progress of the building. In the spring of 1974 -- the school had originally been scheduled to open in the fall of 1974 -- they discovered that demountable partitions, delivered to Lincoln Acres school for use there had been sent to, and installed, in the new open space addition at Oxford school. They became anxious over the possibility that the partitions would not be replaced -- thus eliminating the "alternative educational program" that had been presented in the bond issue literature. This concern was brought to the attention of the Board of Education. As a result, in the early summer of 1974, parents received a promise from Biddle that some type of partitions would be used in the school.

By the time Brown arrived in January, 1975, and serious planning of the educational program had begun, demountable partitions for the new school had still not arrived. Indeed, as we have seen, the educational program intended for the school as Brown described it at community meetings, although using furniture for partitions, was entirely open space, with the exception of the kindergarten area. The result of these announced intentions was reactivation of community concern.

In early March, Barbara Collins, a resident of Lincoln Acres, began circulating a petition throughout the neighborhood; it called for one classroom -- with four walls -- for each grade level in the school. In Collins' words, she wanted "A traditional classroom which stresses the basics and discipline."

On April 14, 1975, at a Board of Education meeting, Collins presented the petition, signed by 153 residents of Lincoln Acres. The argument of the signers was that open education was not the best form of education for all children, that other schools in the township had "traditional" classrooms as well as open classrooms, and that the "alternative" forms of education which had been provided for in the bond issue were no longer being honored.

At the Board meeting, Ellis Brown stated that decisions on where partitions would be placed and what kind of classrooms would be conducted were not yet final. Privately, Brown said to the researcher that the petition was an attempt to

> bring the superintendent to heel. School Board members want to make decisions. They want to reassert their role.

> This is not my decision at all. I don't want any part of it. We could set up pup tents on Cape Cod and still have a good school. They know that.

He also told the researcher he had met with a representative of the group that had petitioned the Board; both that person and others told Brown they were pleased with his performance, and with the staff's.

LAHA's resolution. Before she presented the petition to the Board of Education, Collins had sought additional support for it from LAHA. After deliberation, LAHA's executive committee declined because the wording was too strong; they decided to write their own resolution and present it to the Board. The LAHA resolution, prepared in early April, read:

> The Lincoln Acres Homeowners Association believes that there is no one best way for all people to learn or all people to teach. Therefore, we want provisions and options available in the Lincoln Acres School. Effective as of September 1975, we want to see alternative education on every grade level, for example, self-contained classrooms.

The difference between this resolution and the Collins petition is that while it asks for alternatives on every grade level, it suggests self-contained classrooms as an alternative and does not demand them. The LAHA resolution was not presented to the general membership, but was approved on May 8, 1975. It was not presented to the Board of Education until June 2, 1975.

I. THE INSTRUCTIONAL DEVELOPMENT DAY

The Lincoln Acres faculty met all day as planned on April 17, 1975, in Fernwood school, primarily to write mathematics objectives. Norbert began the meeting with a brief announcement about recent activities of the Washingtonville Education Association (WEA), the local teacher union, and asked if anyone would be willing to be the Lincoln Acres representative to it. There were no volunteers. The discussion of WEA activities continued for a while, then the focus gradually shifted to recent inquiries from parents about the new school:

> Dori Kraus: We're having parent conferences now and some of mine were bad -- the parents don't understand much about Lincoln Acres. Is there some way we can have open house for Lincoln Acres parents?

> Ellis: I don't want to take away time from Sam, but I have arranged with Joe Silver to have a meeting for Lincoln Acres on the evening of May 7. The staff will be presented and the format will be to have you talk about why you are going to Lincoln Acres, and then break into small groups for questions and answers.

> Norbert: Oh! That's inviting trouble! The mass meeting at the Board was chaotic last week. At LAHA it was a good mass meeting, but a lot of information didn't get across.

> Ellis: The suspicion is that people really don't want to work at Lincoln Acres. They don't think you went there with free choice. This meeting will be an introduction and not much more.

Norbert: Don't have it in Lincoln Acres. It's too open and hard to imagine what it will be like. It's better in Oxford. And don't let us get chewed out in a corner by individual parents.

Ellis: We'll have a meeting to prepare beforehand.

Attention then turned to writing mathematics objectives. Sam explained that the statement should be of the specificity of "the students will be able to add a column of three numbers", not "the students will be able to add." He then instructed the faculty to meet with members of their grade levels and "brainstorm" objectives without worrying about the form; Ellis and he would standardize the language and put the objectives into a systematic format.*

Intermediate teachers formed one large group, while the two primary teams, along with the kindergarten teachers, met separately. One primary group, Sally, Jane and Katie, more or less decided to adopt a list of objectives from a Title III program that they liked. The other primary group, Priscilla, Dori, Alice, and Wanda, divided up basic skill areas in mathematics, then went through various textbooks and compiled lists. The intermediate group, after some discussion, used a variety of sources to fashion their list; unlike those of the other teams, it was not finished by the end of the session.

When the group reformed and subgroups reported briefly on what had been accomplished, the only comment was a question by Priscilla about the use of the computer to monitor student progress in reaching the objectives. She feared that narrowly-defined and rigorously-monitored objectives would defeat their educational purposes. Ellis explained that to him the computer was a technocratic convenience and that it would enable them to have a single set of objectives for the entire school and a common language for describing the students.

Objective writing, which began in this meeting, would resume in the summer. It was an important activity: essentially, it was the mechanism through which the faculty formulated a curriculum for the school. The objectives also formed the basis upon which teachers would evaluate student progress. In addition, meeting objectives eventually became one of the criteria upon which teachers would be evaluated by both the school administration and members of the community.

---

*The list of mathematics objectives appeared on a record form three weeks later. Some examples are:

Given two single digit numbers, the student will correctly add them without using any physical aids.

Given a three digit number, the student will correctly identify the place value for each digit.

Objectives of similar specificity would eventually be developed for reading and language arts.

When the discussion on objective-writing was finished, Sam suggested that the faculty create a "yellow pages" of teacher skills to form a resource booklet for the entire school. He distributed mimeographed sheets with places to write any skills, talents or interests that teachers had and were willing to share.

Glenda then noted that in her opinion there were still problems with communication in the group. As an example, she pointed out that until this meeting several people had not known the names of everyone on the faculty. She then suggested that the group have a communications workshop for a weekend at Rolling Ridge, an outdoor education site frequently used by the Board of Education, so that the faculty could get to know each other better. Other teachers liked the idea, but at least one thought it would be difficult to take an entire weekend. Sam suggested making it one day, which seemed acceptable, if it were held somewhere away from the school setting. Ellis asked the group if this was the type of activity they would like as part of the summer workshop. There was little response, except from Sam, who said that he too was concerned with the issue Glenda had raised; he suggested that the group might want to start work on interpersonal communication at the next faculty meeting. The response to this idea was weak. Sally then suggested that the process of becoming more familiar with each other would probably begin that night at the party at Regina's house. For the time being, the "communication" suggestion was left without action.

Next, Ellis reminded the faculty that on May 7 they would be meeting with parents at Oxford school; he suggested that before that, "we should find a time to get our act together." Finding a common meeting time was not easy. It was eventually decided to have the intermediates meet on the following Tuesday; the primary meeting time would have to be settled on later.

The final discussion of this meeting concerned the Board of Education's decision of the previous week to eliminate the position of resource teacher in the school as a budget reduction measure. Norbert said that he was afraid of that action because "I feel I would like the help that a resource teacher can give, especially in a new situation."

Sam, the resource teacher, explained the situation further, after which Norbert asked:

> Do people feel the resource teacher is important to us as a new school? Do we sit back as individuals or act together? I was looking forward to Sam for help. Open space and team teaching is not my style.

Ellis said he had already written to the Board* in support of the resource

---

*In his letter, Ellis highly praised Sam's performance thus far, and claimed that he was indispensable, especially since the school was new. He also detailed, for the first time, the job description of the resource teacher in the Brunswick Acres school:

teacher, and that it would be useful for the faculty to do so also. Rebecca Barone was appointed by the faculty to write a letter that would represent their feelings.

The faculty eats together. That night most of the faculty met at Regina Hanley's house in Allwood Green for dinner. It was an informal evening, with only a few short conversations about the school. People told each other about their experiences with parent conferences, which had just finished. In the conferences, many parents had asked what the new school would be like. The teachers admitted to having had some difficulty answering, but all had stressed the high caliber of the faculty. In their conversations with parents, teachers also found some misconceptions of what the school would be like. For example, some parents thought the kindergarten would have 75 children in it at one time, and others thought teachers didn't want to teach in open space, but were being forced to by the administration.

Overall, the discussions were animated and mostly non-school oriented. As Sally had predicted earlier that day, the process of getting to know each other seemed to have begun; interaction among the teachers was frequent, and warm, supportive relationships seemed to be developing among them.

(Footnote cont'd)

> He /Sam Pennington/ is working with the strict guideline that he is not to take on clerical or administrative functions. He has direct access to our school's secretary for all clerical needs; I have passed on no administrative responsibility to him. He is an exemplary teacher. He will function as such.

Brown then further specified the resource teacher's duties as:

(a) teach as a member of a teaching team;
(b) develop important new programs;
(c) improve existing programs, especially basic skills instruction;
(d) help students with unusual needs;
(e) foster parent involvement.

J. PARENT-TEACHER NIGHT

On May 7, 1975, in the midst of the diverse community activity expressing dissatisfaction with the proposed educational program of the school, there was to be a meeting to acquaint parents with teachers. In preparation for the meeting, the intermediate teachers met with Ellis. They discussed the format of the presentation briefly, and checked with each other on key issues to find out each other's views, so they could give coherent answers that agreed with those of their team members. A few days later, the primary group gathered at Priscilla Talbot's house for the same purpose. This meeting became a social occasion and only secondarily included preparing for the meeting with parents.

1. The Meeting

The setting in which approximately 250 parents gathered to meet the teachers was the open space addition to Oxford elementary school. The instructional area of the addition contained numerous floor-to-ceiling partitions, bookcases and other furniture that created boundaries -- in effect, well-defined individual classrooms.*

For this occasion, the teachers were more formally dressed than usual and seemed to be fairly nervous as they sat together in the back of the room and waited for the meeting to begin.

After welcoming the parents, Ellis Brown introduced each teacher, who then made a short -- at several points nearly inaudible -- speech. Each teacher described his or her past teaching experience. Most emphasized that they were looking forward to teaching in Lincoln Acres, usually because of anticipated personal growth and challenge, but in one case because, "the Lincoln Acres parents had been so cooperative in the past." Brown then explained the teacher selection process, emphasizing that he had had more than enough candidates to choose from, and that "two teams had worked together" before coming to Lincoln Acres.#

Once introductions had been completed, Brown had the teams locate themselves in various parts of the instructional area, so they could talk with parents. A group of parents ranging from 15 to 40 assembled around each teaching team. In most cases the teachers explained their intended program, then answered questions from parents.

---

*In contrast, Lincoln Acres school, which had not yet received furniture, had at this time no partitions, other than eight ten-foot-high demountable panels jutting occasionally from the outer wall. With the exception of the kindergarten, the instructional area was one large open space.

#Here Ellis was, if not stretching, at least leaning on the truth a bit; though members of two teams (MTK and BJW) had occasionally shared tasks, they had not actually taught together as teams.

In the BB group, the essence of the presentation was that Lincoln Acres was not going to be a "real" open school: there would be a considerable amount of structure. The first question parents asked was: "Will there be partitions?" A teacher answered that there would be "no confining partitions." Michael Karalis then made a statement and asked a question:

> Most parents here are aware of what the school is going to look like. I'd like to get a reaction to my statement. A group of parents want to see an alternative. I was glad to hear what you said about structure. What do you think about parents who feel that way? They understand what open education is, yet feel strongly that they don't want it.

> Teacher: I'd like to be able to show you what we can do in our open education. We have a problem here with the word "open". I'd like you to see it. Our open education will be better than traditional education.

> Q: Does this apply to all teams -- the way you feel?

> Teacher: I don't know what the others are planning, but it's probably similar.

> Teacher: The benefit of Lincoln Acres is all of our coming at the same time. We have each other.

> Teacher: We want the structure. Other teams might have structure because they feel you want it.

Other groups, while basically expressing similar attitudes and expectations, emphasized the flexibility of the type of education they had planned, but somewhat less so than the BB teachers. They did not say, as Jeanne eventually did, that they would prefer to begin with walls, and change the educational program from that starting point.

The answer to one question raised frequently by parents -- whether noise in open classrooms would result in distraction -- was vividly illustrated, since conversations in one group could be heard by all others. This countered teacher claims that noise would not be a problem.

Generally, the questioning was aggressive, persistent and demanding. The questions were similar to those parents had raised at the LAHA and synagogue meetings. The topics of discipline, attention span, motivation, curriculum, evaluation, noise and alternatives to open space dominated the small group discussions. The teachers' responses tended to be general and reassuring. Basically, they asked for time to demonstrate that what they had planned would work, instead of attempting to convince the parents with their answers.

Afterward, most teachers thought the encounter with parents had been a positive experience. Several were surprised at the questions asked, feeling that some were hostile and that others showed parents did not understand what open education was about. Rebecca Barone, speaking for her team members, said that the parent hostility she detected made her want to work harder, so she could "show them that open education works."

2. The LAHA Resolution

On the following night, with attendance lower than usual for meetings with the new school as a topic, 27 LAHA members voted for and 17 against the resolution demanding "alternative" forms of education in Lincoln Acres school. According to the constitution of the association, a majority vote meant that a resolution had the endorsement of the entire membership.

K. BROWN'S REPLY TO THE CRITICS

Eight days after the Parent-Teacher Night at Oxford school, an article appeared on the front page of the Washingtonville Courier, in which Ellis Brown described his educational philosophy and objectives. The bold-type headline read: "Brown: 'Open School not Permissive.'"

The article, written by the editor of the newspaper, provided background on both Brown's career and the educational movement toward open space schools in the United States. Quotes from an interview with Brown show his effort to state his intentions precisely, and clear up what he believed were false impressions. For example:

> The open space concept has been linked in the press to free education -- a concept almost antithetical to open education. Unlike students in "free" schools, open space students are constantly monitored and always doing the things they need to do and should be doing. Open schools are simply more individualized. A child's individual curriculum is tailored to suit his or her needs.

> I'm a Northern New England Yankee. The idea of coming into a school after learning as much as I have about how to do things and then turning the school over to a seven-year-old is absurd.

The text of the article then states that Lincoln Acres school will have demountable partitions, and that students will be taught basic skills. It follows with a brief account of the recent petition for traditional classes in the school. There is a comment from Brown on what he considered parents' lack of trust in the ability of the teachers, and their reliance on rumors rather than on information directly sought from him. The article then continues:

> Mr. Brown says the failures of open education are due to programs forced on teachers without much input from the

teachers. "You are saying to teachers who are already working harder than those working the more traditional way that they must swallow some new program the administration has decided they should teach."

The article then points out that Brown and the teachers had already been working together on the program for the school, and that work would continue through the summer, particularly on curriculum objectives. Other topics would include teacher and student responsibilities and student discipline. The article ends with the following quote from Brown:

> I think if you analyzed the time spent teaching the basic skills in open schools you'd find skills are taught in less time with no loss in test scores. And you'd find that students have a greater sense of ownership in their schools, feel better about it, and have a greater motivation than do kids in conventional schools. Tests, statistics are averages. The kid who fails in a conventional school is balanced by the successes. But in open education the individual who fails cannot be forgotten. We must deal with him.

The basic message that Ellis Brown presented in this interview was that the claims of open education were not essentially different than those of "traditional" education. The operating difference was that more elaborate staffing arrangements permitted individualization of instruction, a more effective learning situation. He also made it clear that to a large extent the critics of open education -- at least the variety of it planned for Lincoln Acres school -- were not basing their opinions on what to him were "the facts".

L. BROWN AND BIDDLE MEET WITH PARENTS

Shortly after the article appeared, Ellis Brown and Biddle decided that it would be helpful to meet with parents in small groups to explain the school (according to Biddle, "Coffeeklatches are the best method; mass meetings don't work."). Between the end of May and mid-June, Brown met twice with groups of a dozen parents in Lincoln Acres residents' homes; at another such meeting, Biddle was also present.

Charles Frisch, the Board of Education member (and an influential community leader in educational matters), attended the first small parents' meeting. He commented afterward:

> I hope he gets to everybody. The community needs somebody that makes them think they're being listened to. Ellis Brown has that ability. They want to believe. I want to believe.

According to Brown, the one meeting that Biddle attended had been less critical of his policies than the other two. Brown's overall evaluation of the meetings was positive: "I was very pleased with them; they were effective exchanges." The day after the first meeting, he gave a reassuring report to the teachers: the community, he said, was not upset with them, but with Biddle and the Board of Education.

Just before these meetings began, Brown told the researcher that he had begun to have doubts about Biddle's power base in the community. He discovered that Bill Gerson, the principal of Valley Junior High School, had been actively campaigning for Biddle's job. He had also formed the opinion that Biddle didn't have much support from the Board of Education, noting that for the past few years the Board had not granted him an ordinarily routine salary increment.

Although Brown did not indicate what impact these doubts would have on his own political strategy, assuming that he had one, it was clear that he was beginning to reassess his relationship with Biddle, and the degree to which he could rely on him for support backed by a reliable constituency.

Biddle's attitudes toward the problems with Lincoln Acres school at this time are also revealing. In late May, he said privately to the researcher that he was not prepared to spend $15,000 on partitions for the school, since they would probably not be in use in three years. He attributed the cause of community dissatisfaction with the proposed educational program to the reasons families had moved to Washingtonville: in his opinion, they were "running from the city" and its problems. As he saw it, there were two camps in the community; those who wanted reading, writing and arithmetic, and those who viewed education as something more than the three R's. In his words: "Most of those involved /in the criticism/ are not self-actualizing people."

M. THE LAST FACULTY MEETING BEFORE THE SUMMER WORKSHOP

Combined with a picnic, the final faculty meeting before the summer workshop was held at Sam Pennington's house, on May 29, 1975. After collaborative food preparation, but before eating, there was a brief work session. Ellis reminded one primary team (Sally, Jane and Katie) that they had not yet given him their list of math objectives. Sam then reintroduced the idea of a residential communications workshop, which Glenda had first proposed at the April 17 meeting. He said that he had considered having it shortly after July 4 for two days at Rolling Ridge, a rustic outdoor education facility. Anticipating that some teachers might be reluctant to attend, he emphasized that the workshop would not be "heavy" (in the sense that people would be forced to reveal themselves in any deep, possibly threatening, way). Regina asked if it was necessary to spend time away from the school. Norbert answered that in his experience working away from the school setting was beneficial, because it permitted focusing energy on one task. Persuaded, Regina agreed, and said she thought the idea of the workshop was a good one. Jeanne then raised the question if Rolling Ridge was the most suitable place to have the workshop; she had had unpleasant experiences with rooms and food on recent trips there with students. Further discussion of a location for the workshop ended with the understanding that Sam would look into the possibility of other places. Finally, agreement was reached that the most productive time would be at the beginning of the summer workshop, since the training in communication could then influence the remainder of the summer's work.

Near the end of this short meeting, Norbert asked about the fate of the resource teacher position. Ellis explained that he had received assurances from the central administration that funds would be provided for Sam's position.

Ellis then told the faculty about his first meeting with a small group of parents, which had occurred the night before. He said he had found that the parents were impressed with the staff, and had nothing against either the teachers or himself. Their grievance, he said, was with Biddle and the Board of Education, who they felt had not delivered on the promise of partitions. It was his view that while some parents still wanted self-contained classrooms, most were willing to give the school as planned a chance. The teachers were relieved to hear this. The picnic began.

Ellis cooked hamburgers while Sam and Sally served side dishes. After dinner, the teachers sat in small groups on Sam's back lawn and discussed a variety of topics from Zen philosophy to methods for growing lush house plants. Occasionally, school-related topics surfaced, but there was no serious discussion of issues related to the new school. Ellis left earlier than the others, to attend an audition for a play sponsored by a nearby community group. Within two hours all of the teachers had left what was a relaxed, enjoyable, social occasion.

N. CONTINUED CONTROVERSY

June, a hectic month of restless children and endless paper work for teachers, had no meetings of the Lincoln Acres faculty. However, activity concerning the school did not cease.

1. Citizens Complain to the Board

On June 2, 1975, LAHA presented its resolution to the Board of Education. Barbara Collins, who was also at the meeting, told the Board that her petition was more specific than the LAHA resolution and should be acted on. Collins continued:

> The people of Lincoln Acres have great faith in Mr. Brown, but
> we want to know what happened to bond issue promises. None
> of the original plans are being followed through and we feel
> we've been lied to.

At this meeting, Brown told the Board that the teachers would decide where partitions should be placed, after consulting with parents and assessing student needs. Biddle said that neither he nor any other school official had ever stated specifically what kind of partitions would be placed in the school. He went on to say that there was the possibility of creating space with partitions of furniture and bookcases, which were being constructed locally.

Collins then approached the subject from another angle, claiming that teachers at Oxford school had told her they would like more partitions.*

Another Lincoln Acres resident, Rob Goldman, made the following statements at the June 2 meeting:

> The Superintendent and the school board's credibility is at stake. I was at a meeting where Dr. Biddle promised floor-to-ceiling partitions which would be nailed to the floor and could be moved in a weekend. Because he assured us of these partitions, I recommended that the Jaycees support the school bond issue.

He continued:

> The thing that bothers us so much is we're not listened to. Whether the parents like it or not we're having the open system and a multi-age first, second and third grade grouping. This is revolutionary, and yet we're getting no choice in the matter.

2. The Proposal For A Community Survey

About this time Charles Frisch told the researcher:

> At the next Board meeting we will try to get a "go, no-go" thing. If the community is that upset with the proposed type of school, then I think we should have a school that reflects their wishes. Ellis will find out what they want and report to the Board. Personally, from an educational point of view it doesn't matter whether it is closed or open. What I'm suggesting is, do what the community wants. Good education can be delivered in either situation. As of now there is a 5-4 vote on the Board to go with the community. I don't see what's so radical about doing what the community wants.

As Frisch understood the situation, some members of the community felt, somewhat justifiably, lied to concerning the partitions, because the administration had never been precise as to what they meant by the terms "partitions" and "alternatives." More importantly, he suspected that no one

---

*This comment resulted in a letter in the next edition of the Courier from the open space teachers in Oxford school, including Sam Pennington; it denied that they wanted more partitions, and claimed that none of them had ever spoken with Collins.

knew what the actual opinions of Lincoln Acres parents were. In an attempt to understand the spectrum of community opinion, he intended to propose to the Board at its next meeting that they survey the community, and decide by August 1 on the basis of that information whether or not to change the educational program of the school.

In the course of the conversation, Frisch made several predictions:

> Ellis has a crucial decision to make in the summer. If he comes up with the wrong decision he'll have some trouble: if he decides they want it open and they actually want it closed he'll have problems. If they would have a situation as at Oxford, then there would be little opposition. When you think about change you don't do it in one fell swoop.

> But I also think that once the school opens the community will settle down -- I have a lot of faith in Ellis. But if it doesn't, it will be years before [things stabilize].

The Board meeting. The Board asked Ellis Brown to attend their June 9, 1975 meeting to answer questions about the program for the school. He explained the proposed organization of the school as having a self-contained kindergarten, along with four instructional areas in the open space area, each with 75 children and a team of teachers.

Biddle, in response to a question from a Board member, said that the deadline for purchasing steel partitions had passed, and that even if ordered they would not arrive by September.

Frisch's suggestion for a survey was acted on: the Board asked Brown to survey the community on its attitude toward the new school, and report the results to them by July 15, 1975. The Board indicated they would not make a decision concerning the school until the information was examined.

Thirty residents of Lincoln Acres attended this meeting and tried to speak, but were denied permission by the Board president, who maintained, despite heated exchanges, that the public could only have time to talk if before the meeting they had requested space on the agenda. The parents abided by the ruling but did not accept it; they charged that the school board was indifferent to their requests.

Brown's plan for the survey. Brown was not clear on how the survey results would be used, but thought that the Board might use them as the basis for redesign of the school. It was his opinion, however, that for all practical purposes no changes in the school would be made by September. He did say to the researcher that he considered using the information from the questionnaires for his dissertation.*

---

*Brown was searching for a dissertation topic at this time, and had spent a week in Boston in mid-June consulting with his dissertation advisor.

The plan he developed following the Board meeting was to administer a thirty-minute semi-structured interview to all households with students scheduled to attend Lincoln Acres school in the fall. This would occur during the first week of the summer workshop, when the interview guide would be constructed and administered by teachers and parent volunteers. The plan was to recruit the parents through advertisements in the local newspaper.

3. Plans for the Summer Workshop

In April, approval of the summer workshop proposal was granted; the Board of Education provided funds equalling ten percent of each teacher's yearly salary. After further negotiations, Brown was able to obtain an additional week of salary, so that teachers could make up for the time lost conducting the community survey. The workshop was scheduled to begin on July 1, 1975 and continue until July 29, 1975. Near the beginning of the period, on July 7 and 8, a two-day residential communications workshop for the faculty had been scheduled.* All classroom teachers, the school secretary, the resource teacher and the principal were to participate in this first phase of intensive planning for the new school, which was to open in September, 1975.

Monica Selwin, the school secretary, and Sam Pennington called nearly 40 possible hotels, camps and other places for holding the communications workshop, but had difficulty finding a suitable site for early July. Finally, they made arrangements to have the workshop at a nearby Playboy Club Hotel.

4. The Conflict Continues

On June 30, 1975, the Board of Education held its weekly meeting, with the Lincoln Acres school as the major agenda item. Along with people from other sections of the township, 50 Lincoln Acres residents attended the meeting. Two teachers, Rebecca Barone and Glenda Jacobs, were the only members of the faculty present.

After regular Board business, Lincoln Acres school became the focus.

---

*Although Ellis had not yet taken advantage of the matching funds available from our research project to hire external consulting assistance, he asked whether funds might be used to support the communications workshop, even though it was to be designed and carried out by an internal person (Sam Pennington). The project director agreed that this use met the spirit of the matching funds' purposes (to facilitate effective planning and implementation) and consented to pay half the costs.

The arguments presented by parents were, for the most part, those that have already been presented. Collins and LAHA members along with some new antagonists, confronted Biddle and the Board. For example, quotes were read from the bond issue literature which stated that "most inside walls will be demountable partitions". Paul Elfenbein, president of LAHA, said at one point:

> I think you're jerking us around, Dr. Biddle. I agree in principle with open space, but you used the word partitions, not cabinets or woodwork.

Biddle argued that the staff of the school should be allowed to determine if they wanted to use partitions. This was unacceptable to many present, and one woman said, "I'm not all that interested in what the staff thinks. I want what's best for my child."

Marie Bonomi, a resident of Lincoln Acres, argued against multi-aged classes on the grounds that the academic and social differences between a fourth and a sixth grade student were too great for them to be in the same class together. She presented the Board with a letter requesting "alternatives", which was signed by 13 other parents. Another parent, Alex Georgiades, argued in vivid language that his son had been in an open space classroom the previous year and had "progressively regressed", until he was placed in a traditional classroom, where he once again became a good student.

Georgiades and others argued against the board-mandated survey of the community, claiming that the 1972 referendum had already indicated what the community wanted: partitions. Other community members, in many cases newly-arrived residents, urged that the survey should be conducted so that they could have an opportunity to influence plans for the school.

Sam Schwartz, who had been a member of the principal selection committee, accused Biddle of "double talk", and of acting both as an educator and as a politician. Then Sylvia Peabody, a Board member from Lincoln Acres who said she favored alternatives, charged that Biddle had hired only teachers and a principal interested in working in open space. Biddle denied any role in teacher selection. Estelle Hunter, another school board member, said, "I am strongly in favor of offering parents a choice, and believe the people in this room have been shafted."

Continuing the attack, Board member Gerrie Holden said:

> The children belong to parents and this administration has no right to jam something down their throats. I want to see the results of the survey, but I believe we should give parents a choice.

Biddle replied to Holden, saying:

> I never said the administration would force anything down their throats. But the staff in that school is good enough to

teach in a tent, and I'm concerned that we don't push anything on them before they've had the opportunity to work with the kids, the community and fellow staff members to determine what they need. After all they must work with the equipment every day.*

A request by the Board vice-president for parent volunteers to help conduct the survey of the Lincoln Acres community ended the tumultuous meeting.

It seems fair to say that throughout the period between February, 1975, when the opposition to the school began, and this June 30, 1975 meeting, Lincoln Acres parents had demonstrated almost no public support for open space education in the school. In fact, the only directly supportive statement was a letter to the editor of the Courier, on June 19, 1975. Either there was little actual support for totally open education, or its proponents did not view the visible opponents as a serious challenge, and so said little in public. It is also possible that community norms and the pressure generated by the petition and LAHA resolution made it difficult, if not impossible, for those favoring open education to support it actively.

O. (THE EMERGING ORGANIZATIONAL DESIGN)

A month before the beginning of intensive planning -- filling in the details of the original vision -- the major features of the school were substantially complete. Of course, the faculty was not entirely familiar with one another yet, nor had there been an opportunity to test or refine various proposed components of the system. Nevertheless, more than an outline of a school existed. The basic organizational properties developed thus far are discussed and commented on below.

1. Features Internal to the School

First, the school was staffed with actively interested volunteers, most of whom were experienced teachers (though they had had little or no team teaching experience). The principal's qualifications fit his new assignment very well. Along with the teachers, he was interested in producing an innovative form of education, at least in terms of the educational practices in Washingtonville.

---

*This is a direct quote from a Courier article on the meeting. Biddle's reported use of "equipment" implicitly seems to include the walls, partitions, furniture, etc.

Secondly, the technological core of the school, while not finished, was firmly established. The key component in the educational delivery system, teaching teams, had been formed: the teams, with varying degrees of effort, were building personal and working relationships. Open space education and multi-age grouping of students, two central aspects of the innovation, had been actively accepted by the faculty when they accepted a position at the school, and were considered in planning. Curriculum, in the form of highly-specific objectives, was being developed, along with a computer-based system to monitor accomplishment. Finally, underlying these technologies was a philosophical focus on individualization of instruction.

The administrative structure is a third dimension of the organization that had been formed by this time. Despite Brown's early intention to operate as a charismatic leader, he functioned more as a "first among equals." He consulted with the faculty on all major decisions, he avoided arbitrary deadlines, and he made specific gestures to the faculty to indicate that he was to be treated as a colleague, not primarily as a superior.

At times, however, there appeared to be tension between his apparently easy-going, non-directive leadership style and latent "charismatic" traits. This was frequently evident in a very concrete way: Brown's voice was flexible and capable of ranging in a short time span from low, mellow tones to crisp, impersonal, "bureaucratic" pitches. When he used the latter -- which in these early months was relatively infrequently -- it was clear to the teachers that the meeting should come to order, that a decision should be reached, or that something displeased him. This habit, a form of social control, resembled a technique teachers often use -- modulating their voices to gain the attention of a class of youngsters. At times this mannerism seemed to violate the egalitarian norms that were developing in the group.

During this period, it also appeared that teachers welcomed another role for Ellis: that of bufferer and negotiator with the outside world, primarily the central office, the Board and the community. We might comment that this role naturally bore the seeds of a further reduction of Ellis' egalitarian emphasis: the more he buffered, the more special information he would garner; the more he negotiated, the more tempted he might be to make decisions rather than share them.

Within the school, however, as had been the plan, Ellis, Sam and Regina Hanley acted as facilitators for the teachers' work. But though Sam Pennington's role was prescribed in a job description, the duties he could be expected to perform were still somewhat unclear to teachers. Consequently, his rank in the authority structure of the organization was vague; when teachers asked him to make a decision, he almost always referred them to Ellis. That was congruent with his job description, which specified that he was not to perform administrative tasks. But that teachers approached Sam expecting that he could actively make decisions reflected their ambiguous understanding of his role.

Within the teaching teams, there were no formal differentiations of rank. "Team leader" was not defined as a position, and the idea that one of the team members should in some way either represent the team or be responsible for its activities was never discussed. When aspects of the school that could possibly differentiate team members in an informal way were discussed, every effort was made to prevent or minimize them. An example is the faculty's rejecting parent selection of their children's teachers, a procedure which could have resulted in differential prestige among the teachers.

By this time, however, it was true that informal leaders were emerging in each team. In the kindergarten team, Sarah was more outspoken, and was often regarded as representing the others. Priscilla served the same purpose in the MTK team, as did Sally in the NBC team and Norbert in the BJW team. At this time, the researcher could see no differentiation in the power Alan and Jeanne exerted in the management of their BB team.

Seen as a whole, the decision-making process, the administrative apparatus, the decentralization of tasks, and the informal interpersonal relationships that had developed in the faculty suggest that the pattern of relationships in the school at this time was essentially collegial. In addition, the attempt to create ownership of the plans, coupled with the reward structure (implicitly based on the intrinsic satisfaction provided by planning and eventually teaching) helped create and reinforce a normative climate that might be labeled "egalitarian professionalism".

Though relatively little explicit attention had been paid in the planning to the normative climate of the school, it seemed true that -- channelled by the structural features we have outlined -- some informal standards for appropriate behavior had already emerged. These norms can perhaps best be described as a set of implicit sentences, which an observer could infer were serving as guides to appropriate behavior:

Everyone's ideas are OK.

We should respond to each other, not ignore people's contributions.

Speak up, say what's on your mind.

We are professionals, not employees.

We are friends, and shouldn't be formal with each other.

No one is out to get anyone else here in our group.

We decide things together.

We know better than the parents.

Norms epitomized by sentences of this sort, like most norms, were never very explicit. Yet they did already seem to be guiding teachers' behavior toward each other, toward Ellis and Sam, and toward the community.

2. Features Linking School to Environment

By this time, mechanisms for coordinating the activities of the school with the community during the early planning had been formulated; some were put into practice immediately, and others were earmarked for later implementation.

So far, a number of ad hoc meetings had been held between the administration and small parent groups, along with more-structured introductory meetings of the faculty with interested community members. The local weekly newspaper was also used by Brown, and on occasion by individual faculty members, as a medium for their messages. Less-direct influence on the community was exerted through the superintendent's support for the faculty.

However, no other "durable" environmental linking mechanisms were yet in place. The summer workshop proposal did contain several intended linkages: in the final week of the workshop, under objective 8, "educational decision-making roles" for parents and students were to be defined. In the language of the proposal:

> During the final week of the project, parents will be invited for several half-days to view the teaching space, collaborate in developing report cards and other communications routines, start parent aide programs and design community use of the school.

The proposal also contained provision for a temporary linkage that could potentially develop into a stable, long-term means of legitimation for the new educational program. Charles Frisch, the director of the state Right to Read program, a resident of Lincoln Acres and Board of Education member, was to evaluate the results of the summer workshop, especially the curriculum checklists. Additionally, the summer proposal alluded to the idea that parents would serve as volunteers in the school, providing another environmental linkage mechanism.

Another communication device, a house-to-house survey of the community, had been considered by Brown as early as January 10, 1975. It was his view that this type of survey would serve as a more effective communication device than would public mass meetings. The Board's decision in June meant that this type of linkage would be used at least once; whether it would be repeated was not clear.

It seems clear that a good deal of faculty ambivalence* toward the community was present during the creation of these environmental linkages

---

*The ambivalence was not "personal", but social in origin. Merton and Barber (1963) identify "sociological" ambivalence as something generated by social structure: "...incompatible normative expectations of attitudes, beliefs and behavior assigned to a status or to a set of statuses in a society." In this case, the incompatible expectations for the teachers had their source in the conflicting normative structures of democratic and professional values (see next section).

both the temporary ones and the more durable ones anticipated. We have characterized this in Chapter 2 as the dilemma of "environmental contact vs avoidance". At several Lincoln Acres faculty meetings, there was debate over whether to approach the community actively or delay meeting with them; over whether or not to be responsive to their demands; and finally, over the extent to which parents should be involved in planning and operation of the school. These dilemmas were often resolved by the flow of events as much as by explicit faculty decisions. For example, although Brown's initial reaction was to postpone his appearance before LAHA, the insistence of the education committee's chairperson persuaded him to meet with them sooner than he had wanted.

P. (ANALYSIS AND COMMENTARY)

1. Social-Architectural Design

Thus far, how good was the fit between the emerging organizational design and the original vision for the school? Broadly speaking, it seemed reasonably close: the team set-up, the individualized approach, the flexible use of space, multi-aged classes and, above all, the right of the faculty members to participate in designing their own educational environment were in place or on the way.

However, two areas of the original vision remained relatively underdeveloped: the idea of responsiveness to community needs, and the hope that the school would become a model for others in the district.

Teachers' ambivalent attitudes toward the parents have already been explored. It should be noted here that no permanent structure for parent influence, such as an advisory council, had been contemplated. Except for discussions during part of the last week of the summer workshop, the only regular contact with parents after the school opened would occur through report cards, parent conferences and the PTA.

At this point in planning, it was too early to estimate the impact, if any, that Lincoln Acres school might have on the educational practices of other schools in Washingtonville. But no structures were being developed to enable the school to be a resource, or model, in the district. Perhaps it was Brown's hope that the school would become a model by merely providing an exciting example. But examples need to be communicated, and there were no proposals for visits, documentation of practices, in-service days with other staff, Lincoln Acres teachers' serving as consultants to other schools, or the like.

2. Actualization

As when the planning began, the implicit strategy for linking plans with implementation was to have the operators -- that is, Brown and the teachers -- do the planning. The summer workshop proposal strengthened this approach, and outlined a fairly concrete set of outcomes anticipated to influence -- even constrain -- implementation. It constituted a public promise to the school district that certain implementation efforts would be undertaken.

From the beginning, Brown asked the teams to do much of the planning on their own. Besides increasing the teachers' investment in the school, this strategy created an extra social pressure: consensual group decisions are more likely to be actually carried out. This form of social control affected both the teams and Ellis. In the case of the teams, it would be difficult for members not to honor commitments they had shaped together. For Ellis, unilateral administrative decisions, especially those that could negate teacher decisions, would be more difficult to make and enforce.

3. Knowledge Utilization

It seems accurate to say that Ellis and the faculty used only modest amounts of outside expert knowledge during this planning period. Although they listened to book salesmen and drew lists of objectives from texts and others' prior practice, more often than not they simply relied on their own past experience. The research project's offer of external consulting help was converted into support for an internal facilitator. There were no suggestions that other open-space, team-taught, schools outside the district be visited.

Why should this be? We have already alluded to the norms of professionalism in the faculty. These norms have at least two sub-categories, autonomy and expertise, and some discussion of these in terms of particular events may be helpful. First, Biddle's actions in some instances (for example, his intervention in furniture design) were viewed by Brown as a hindrance. As we have seen, one of Brown's objectives, at least in rhetoric, was to be independent of the central office and to plan his own school with the faculty's assistance. Secondly, when Ellis and Sam rejected the idea of external consulting assistance to help with organizational planning and team-building, they said explicitly that internal expertise in those areas existed (in the person of Sam), and that building the capability of the faculty itself was important.

Were the claims to expertise justified? Sam Pennington's source of expertise was his seven years of experience as a teacher, several of which were in open classrooms, and his training and active interest in organizational development and group dynamics. Ellis Brown's claim to expertise was based on his experience as a planner and principal of an open space elementary school, and his graduate training in educational administration. Regina Hanley was a trained librarian and in the year prior to coming to Lincoln Acres school had set up the library in another new school. The teaching-team members had a wide range of abilities and experience in education and advanced academic degrees in many cases. There was, then, some reason for the faculty to consider their own resources adequately expert in relation to the task.

Finally, Brown's belief in "ownership" (investment, commitment) by teachers during the planning may have led him to think that use of outside experts would jeopardize this important quality. So, both the professional desire for autonomy and the need for ownership of the planning product increased reliance on available internal expertise.

4. Political Stabilization

As we have seen, durable linkages to the community were still largely in the planning stages. At this point, however, it seemed clear that significant numbers of parents opposed the proposed school design. Although the early political linkages (for example, those between the central office and the community) had enabled resource acquisition (money for the building and staffing of the school), it seemed clear that endorsement, environmental approval, was decidedly absent.* As we shall see, relations between the school and community were to become critical for the success of the innovation. How did this opposition develop over time?

Initiation of parent opposition. The primary source of community dissatisfaction seemed to be a sense that a public agreement had been violated. As the plans for the school developed, it became clear that the educational program would depart substantially from what the community had expected, and voted on. Instead of the 18 classrooms with moveable walls specified in the bond issue literature, the actual plans, as presented to the community by Brown at the LAHA meeting, included five open-space classroom areas, with moveable walls around only one, the kindergarten. This change in plans was particularly disturbing to those residents who had actively worked for passage of the bond issue: the planning actions were not viewed as legitimate. ("We have been shafted...lied to.")

Intensification of the controversy. In the early months of Brown's tenure, parent disapproval of the plans was brought to his attention. Parents also informed Biddle and the Board of Education of their criticism. But the Board, and especially Brown and Biddle, responded with statements that adhered to the original plan, designed to reassure the parents that the educational program would be flexible enough to accommodate any student's special needs.

Not assuaged -- indeed, more alienated -- the protesting parents took more direct and formal action to press for their demands. Barbara Collins presented the Board with her petition for one self-contained, traditional classroom for each grade, and LAHA presented its resolution calling for "alternatives." As Coleman (1957) suggests, community-wide

---

*Here we refer to endorsement from the community environment. Generally speaking, Brown appeared to have been relatively successful in obtaining both resources and endorsement from the bureaucratic environment of the school. The summer workshop proposal was easily approved, and he was able to get the types of furniture and other equipment needed for the school. He was also careful not to act in such a way as to reduce endorsement from other principals (for example, he arranged the instructional development day to both his and David Hauptmann's satisfaction).

voluntary organizations often serve to channel conflict to some extent and prevent it from becoming an unregulated, diffuse battle. LAHA acted in such a way during the early planning.

Early responses to the opposition. As the controversy increased, Brown and Biddle adopted a temporary strategy of meeting with community members in small coffeeklatches. Brown's impression from the first of these meetings, which he did not revise, was that community anger was not directed against himself and the faculty, but against Biddle and the Board, since they were supposedly the ones not fulfilling the promises made in the bond issue. Brown had also received private assurances from community leaders that he and the teachers were not the targets of complaints.

Throughout this period, the teachers obtained information about the controversy through newspaper articles in the local press, through their meeting with parents at Oxford school in May, and through Ellis Brown.

The major messages Ellis gave the faculty were that, in effect, he would act as a buffer between them and the community, and that he had discovered that the parental hostility was not directed at any member of the faculty but at the superintendent and the Board. For the most part, the teachers accepted this view of the conflict. But bewildered by the parents' attacks (and ambivalent toward them even before the controversy erupted), they tended to minimize direct contact with them. Recall the statements made by teachers:

> I have doubts about bringing in parents so soon...Do we need them a full week?....They should be involved, but I don't see how yet...We have to draw a fine line where parents are concerned...We're not ready yet.

General comments. Basically, the central issue raised by the protesting parents was the dubious legitimacy of the plans for the school. In their view, Biddle had evaded his responsibility to fulfill the specifications of the bond issue. From Biddle's perspective, this was not true: he stated that partitions, as requested by the faculty, would in fact be used in the school. More importantly, in his judgement and in the judgement of the faculty, the needs of all students would be met in the school. In other words, Biddle asked the community to trust his and the staff's expertise in educational matters.* At the core of the conflict, then, was a clash between two pervasive value complexes in our society: professionalism and democracy.

The readiness of the Board of Education to accept Frisch's proposal to survey the community as a basis for further plans can be seen as an effort to restore lost legitimacy -- to reassert the claims of democracy over the decisions of experts.

---

*Biddle felt after reading this that he had always stressed faculty-parent partnership, and that problems should be "worked out jointly within the school."

6

INTENSIVE PLANNING CONTINUES:
THE SUMMER WORKSHOP

A. THE SUMMER WORKSHOP BEGINS: THE COMMUNITY SURVEY

On July 1, the first day of the summer workshop, the Lincoln Acres
school faculty and 15 parent volunteers assembled at 9:00 a.m. in the empty
instructional area of the school. Teachers sat in one group and parents in
another.

1. Planning the Survey

Brown explained that the Board of Education had requested a survey
of parents of Lincoln Acres students, and that after considerable thought he
had decided that conducting the survey was up to parents and teachers.
Then he divided the group into smaller units by assigning several parents to
work with a team of teachers. The task each group had was to "brainstorm"
areas to be included in the questionnaire.

Each group settled into an area of the school to work. Before this,
however, most of the teachers -- out of view of the parents -- expressed
bewilderment over what they were supposed to be doing. Few had heard of
the survey before this meeting. Dori, Priscilla and Wanda, incensed by what
they considered an inappropriate task for teachers, were reluctant to
participate.

Eventually, feeling somewhat awkward in each other's presence, the
small groups of parents and teachers discussed recent events concerning the
school, and began to compile lists of questions they thought should be asked
of parents. These meetings were punctuated with questions from both
parents and teachers: "Who's going to interpret the results? Should the
entire community or only parents of students be asked? Will the results be
valid? What use will the results be put to?"

Forty-five minutes later, with their brainstormed lists, the groups
reconvened in the open space area. The questions were read by a member of
each small group and written on a chalkboard by Brown. The suggestions
ranged from asking if parents thought the school should have bicycle racks
to whether they had any fears about open education.

Barbara Collins, who had turned up as a parent volunteer, complained after the proposed question on bicycle racks that the Board didn't want to know that. It was her opinion that "they want to know whether or not we want partitions, if people are satisfied with the Lincoln Acres school as now planned." Ellis agreed, and reminded the group that a list of questions that could be asked in twenty minutes was needed.

Brown went through each list on the chalkboard crossing out those questions that he thought were not germane. He told the group their purpose was to tell him what should be included and to stop him if he eliminated areas they thought important. No clear rationale or method was evident for the questions and areas Brown selected. When he was asked why he crossed out a question about the way the controversy over the school had affected children, his answer was, "We can't code it." This ended the discussion, and he continued rejecting questions. Collins pushed for including a question about differences between the school as it currently was and what people had thought it would be; Brown accepted it. The session ended after Brown asked the group which of them wanted to be trained as interviewers at 1:00 p.m., and at 7:00 p.m. He did not propose activities for the time before the interview training, but in response to a question, he said that the questionnaires would be prepard by 1:00, and that "you can stay around if you want to contribute to their wording."

With the meeting over, teachers again began complaining among themselves about their involvement in the survey. Jeanne said, "I don't want to do this crap. We didn't even know about it." Bert, Glenda and Rebecca agreed with her. Another teacher experienced the situation as "confining", and thought that instead of conducting interviews the staff should meet privately with small groups of parents.

Ten minutes later, at 11:40 a.m., Ellis, Sam, Jane, Sally, Katie, and three parents, Barbara Collins, Rob Goldman and Mrs. Horn, met in the multi-purpose room to begin rewording questions and preparing the final version of the questionnaire. Just after this process began, the three teachers left, and Wanda and Priscilla arrived. Wanda told the group that she didn't want to do the survey and that the teachers were considering talking to the Board about it. Priscilla suggested that because of the survey teachers might not want to remain employed at the school. Ellis' response was minimal: he listened and nodded. Wanda and Priscilla left the room, and Ellis, Sam and the three parents continued working alone on the questionnaire.

At 1:00, the teachers -- who had boycotted the question revision session -- and half of the parent volunteers met again in the open space area for training in interviewing techniques. Brown distributed and briefly explained a training guide for interviewers, which covered topics such as beginning the interview, recording the responses, impartiality, and how to handle respondents not at home or refusing to be interviewed. He then reviewed the commitments teachers and parent volunteers had made: teachers would be paid for the days spent interviewing, and all completed interviews were to be left at the principal's office by July 9. He added that at 9:00 the following morning there would be an optional meeting for teachers to discuss a possible meeting with the Board of Education about the survey.

After these announcements, each interviewer selected eight names at random from a box containing all the names of parents of Lincoln Acres students. Questionnaires were distributed, after which Brown conducted a session that involved role playing in groups of three: one person acted as the interviewer, another as the interviewee and the third as an observer and critic.

The interview guide. The guide used to interview parents, after a page of standard demographic questions, consisted of 10 open-ended questions, some of which had follow-up questions. Chart 6.1 presents the open-ended questions. They are far-ranging in content and minimally structured. Thus they provided the opportunity for respondents to use the interview as a forum for almost anything on their minds concerning the Lincoln Acres school.

2. The Faculty's Opposition

At 9:00 a.m. the following day, the faculty met with Brown to discuss what, if any, action they should take concerning the survey. After recounting the Board meeting at which he had been mandated to conduct the survey, Brown said the Board had more or less indicated that they were more afraid of the community than they were of the teachers. He continued:

> I told them that the human costs would be great in terms of kids and us. I feel differently about things now. I would support a letter to the Board saying that certain things were promised to you, for example, open space. The Board is so scared at this point that they need to know there is another side to this, that the community isn't the only side. Biddle has offered us five weeks, but that doesn't matter much. This has come between us and the community and it's too bad. We were going along well. If it comes from you, the Board might fear being faced by angry teachers and might change their minds.

After a brief discussion, it was decided to send a letter to the Board. Someone also suggested that the teachers request a private meeting with the Board, on the grounds that personnel matters were involved. Brown then left the school building to keep an appointment.

Sam assumed the leadership of the meeting, and he carefully checked with everyone to see if writing a letter of protest to the Board was acceptable. No one objected. Gloom alternated with anger as the teachers discussed the recent events. Some proposed that they not do the survey, but others counseled that they were contractually obligated as Board employees to carry it out. Others argued that the interview was invalid, and that conducting it would be an endorsement of it. Still others worried about the use of the results. Priscilla, reflecting the mood of most teachers, said:

CHART 6.1

LINCOLN ACRES SCHOOL COMMUNITY INTERVIEW GUIDE

1. What do you know about the school?
   What have you read?
   What have you heard? From whom?
   What meetings have you gone to?
   What does open education mean to you? (Please give specific examples)

2. Give examples of things you like about Lincoln Acres School.

3. Give examples of things you don't like about Lincoln Acres School.

4. What different alternatives would you like in Lincoln Acres School?
   2 or 3 grade levels in one space.
   2 or 3 teachers working with same group of students.
   Partitions used to enclose space. How and what kind?
   Other

5. What are the most important things for your child to learn in school? Please give specific examples.

6. How would you like your child's progress reported? Please give examples of what information and form.

7. Would you like to be involved in your child's education? If yes, please give five specific examples of how.
   In school?
   At home?
   Other?

8. Do you believe your child has needs that cannot be met in open space? If yes, please give specific examples.

9. Please give examples of decisions that the following groups should properly make about school.
   Board of Education
   Administration
   Teachers
   Parents

10. Did you vote on the October 17, 1972 Bond Issue for Lincoln Acres School? If yes, how does your understanding of the present school set-up compare with your expectations when you voted?

> I don't want to see anything from the survey in the newspapers. It is their survey. None of the questions are of any value to me. I feel that I have been co-opted and coerced.

Yet others complained about the amount of negative publicity the school had already received in the local press; in their view, the publicity and the survey were adversely affecting staff morale. Sam said that he felt "lied to about open space", and a teacher pointed out that the Board had already surveyed the teachers to find out if they wanted partitions and received a negative reply. Many teachers were disappointed because they had written a proposal for planning the school and wanted to begin work on the educational program; instead, they found themselves conducting a survey of the community. Depressed and disgusted, the teachers left the meeting either to work in their teaching areas or begin surveying the families. Wanda, Priscilla and Dori volunteered to draft a letter to the Board; a faculty meeting was scheduled for 1:00 p.m. to discuss it.

The faculty's letter. Copies of the first draft of the letter to the Board of Education were distributed as the faculty assembled at 1:00. Sam chaired the meeting, since Ellis had not returned. Reactions to the letter were mainly positive. For instance, to Bert, the language appeared to be "a little strong," but he supported it, as did the others. After further discussion of the intent of the letter, changes were made in certain words and phrases.

In the final version of the letter, the passage concerning the survey read as follows:

> The survey itself suggests that you /the Board/ are considering reorganizing the school disregarding us, the teaching staff....
> We feel that the Board has shirked its responsibility by not taking a definitive stand and by failing to support its staff. By conducting a survey at this time you are continuing to generate dissent toward the proposed /school/ organization.

A difficult decision. More discussion of whether or not to conduct the survey followed. While many didn't want to do it, Bert was of the opinion that the Board could take punitive action against those who refused. It was a highly emotional meeting. At least one person cried, and said, "I'm feeling that I really don't want to work here."

After a brief lull, resentment against the Board, Biddle and Frisch continued to build. When a teacher asked: "If we can't take a stand on this, how will we react when they say they want partitions?" Sam suggested that they brainstorm options. The following list of possible courses of action was contributed to by most teachers and written on a chalkboard by Sam.

1. Refuse survey
2. Do survey under protest
3. Foot-drag on survey
4. All quit
5. Job action -- no extra effort

6. Tell community our position
7. Do nothing -- go along
8. Sabotage or bias the survey
9. Write a letter to the <u>Courier</u> about our professionalism
10. Make opinions public at Board meeting

With this list, the meeting reached its emotional peak. Sam then made a suggestion that seemed oddly out of phase with the rebellious spirit that had pervaded the faculty since they had been informed of the community survey.

He suggested the possibility of taking the partitions from the kindergarten and arranging them so they divided the instructional area into four equal-sized spaces. It would still be open space, he said, and "we would compromise; we would be the good guys." Priscilla agreed that it might satisfy many parents, but Jeanne warned, "If they quiet down about open space, then they might make an issue about multi-age grouping or something else." Sam concluded the short conversation by saying that acting on his suggestion would produce a Lincoln Acres spatial arrangement similar to the one at Oxford school, and that Charles Frisch was moving toward this as a solution. Most of the faculty looked gloomy and somewhat shocked as Sam explained the possible compromise. They decided to end the meeting and resume it when Ellis arrived.

When Ellis came, he read the letter; Sam informed him of the events since he had left that morning. Ellis said of the letter:

> There are some things here that are not the Board's fault but mine. I used the staff, I wasn't asked to. I mistrust citizen interviewers. I wanted the teachers to interview so that the two could be contrasted. There was no time or access to get to the staff when the decisions were made. If that was wrong, I'm sorry. This involved technical grounds of the survey: it can be argued either way, and I tried to minimize bias. Beyond that I guess that I sit with you on your reactions to various things. All these things have run through my mind too. We should include that we want a private meeting with the Board, and it would be good to show them our anger. It seems to be the kind of Board that reacts to anger.

On Ellis' advice, the teachers decided to do the survey -- excepting those few who still found it totally unacceptable -- because the Board could punish teachers as well as himself on grounds of insubordination if they all refused. Ellis suggested that if they desired, after doing "the damn thing" they could file a grievance against the Board.

Shortly before the meeting adjourned, Sally asked Ellis if he thought that at some point they would have to compromise. Ellis answered:

> I don't know. I think in a period of two years we can move into a situation where we have a good school. The question with me is trust with the Board: are you going to lie to us, can we trust you?

That evening and the following day teachers surveyed the community.

The next scheduled event of the summer workshop was the communications workshop, starting on Monday, July 7, 1975.

B. THE COMMUNICATIONS WORKSHOP*

The Playboy Club, a modern luxury hotel in the rolling farmland of the southern part of the state, was the site of the communications workshop. Business at the hotel had not been especially good in the last few years, and it was rumored that the management, along with other interests in the state, was involved in efforts to have gambling legalized statewide. Playboy -- the magazine, and its enterprises -- was by this time a marginal feature of the hotel. Indeed, the only evidence of Playboy and its philosophy, beyond the hotel's name, was pictures of semi-clad females on the walls of the bar, and the tight-fitting "bunny" costumes of the restaurant waitresses.

1. Workshop Goals

In a large, sparsely-furnished meeting room on the ground floor of the hotel, Sam gave a brief overview of the aims and structure of the workshop. He set six goals for the two-day session:

---

*The researcher's role during the communications workshop was substantially different than it had been at any other phase of the study; he participated actively, in all but one of the exercises. This shift was prompted by Sam's request that, because of an odd number of people attending the workshop, activities that called for pairs or trios might have to be supplemented with the researcher. Agreeing to this arrangement had several benefits: it enabled the researcher to experience the workshop to a greater extent in the ways other participants did; it provided an opportunity to maintain rapport with the faculty; and it eliminated what could have been an awkward set of circumstances for passive observation, the researcher's usual mode. At the same time, however, total participation created several problems. For one thing, the researcher's participation was less "real" than that of the teachers -- at least to the extent that he could not draw on experiences in the Washingtonville schools (he had been an elementary school teacher in an urban school, however). Along with this, his presence in small groups probably altered their behavior. Finally, not only did his participation in a specific group limit data collection from other groups, but because note-taking was difficult and inappropriate during the exercises, field notes were recorded only at the end of the workshop. Thus various activities and their products were not recorded in their entirety.

1. To increase awareness of communications processes.
2. To increase communications skills through practice.
3. To increase empathy among staff members.
4. To increase ability to resolve interpersonal conflict within the staff.
5. To foster a sense of mutual trust, support and safety within the staff.
6. To enjoy ourselves.

These goals, along with a schedule of activities, were on a mimeographed sheet in a folder Sam distributed to all participants. Also in the folder were several short articles titled: "Comments on Listening," "Leveling with Others on the Job," and "The Case of the Hidden Agenda," and a sheet with suggestions for giving and receiving constructive feedback.

2. The First Day's Activities

Sam formed groups of six, and explained that the first exercise was for each group to brainstorm and record on newsprint a list of hindrances to communication. After 15 minutes of fairly serious brainstorming, Sam asked the groups to form a circle, and have each member talk to the group in turn without any of the other five's responding. Following this, he distributed a small sheet of paper with these directions:

Please answer the following questions as fully as possible:

a. How did it feel to make a statement and no one respond to it?
b. How did it feel to ignore a statement made by others?

Written answers to the questions were discussed in the small groups. When Sam reassembled the large group, he asked people to share the lists of blocks to communication. These lists were combined and a piece of newsprint with the essential hindrances was put on the wall for reference throughout the workshop. Examples of hindrances were: poor listening abilities, lack of respect for others' opinions, and inability to express feelings. Generally, the teachers seemed to take the tasks seriously. The tone of the discussion was even, not animated or excited.

Sam then asked each person to select a partner and locate themselves in separate parts of the room. The first exercise was for one of the pair to tell the other an incident that had occurred in school; the other partner then paraphrased the story without comment from the person who told it. Following this, each partner gave the other three sentences for paraphrasing without comment from the sender. Finally, the instructions were to send a message, have it paraphrased, and then negotiate the meaning of the message.

After some written response to the exercise and discussion by the pairs, Sam asked each pair to report on its experience to the entire gathering. For the most part they had taken the tasks seriously and gave thoughtful, honest, reactions. However, pairs seemed to feel a need to say something not already commented on by another pair; this created a mild tension, and there was not much of a feeling that new insights into the communication process had developed.

In the next exercise, groups of four discussed a topic, then abruptly changed to another topic, another, and so on. Then new reaction sheets were filled out. After discussion of the exercise, for the first time in the workshop, the faculty was asked to form groups with their teaching team members. Sam's instructions were for one member to talk to another, who would act as a sympathetic listener, while the third person observed and then commented on the conversation. The reaction sheet for this exercise included:

a. Did you always communicate what you intended to communicate?
b. Did you find the listener only responding to part of what you said?
c. Was it ever unclear what the speaker had in mind? What made it unclear?

At 4:30, a final discussion summarized blocks and hindrances to communication, and Sam said there was free time until supper at 7:00.

In this recreation period, several teachers played tennis, others took hikes around the hotel and the majority, including Ellis, played volley ball in the outdoor swimming pool. By this time most members of the faculty seemed to be fairly at ease with each other, and the opportunity to enjoy the facilities of the hotel -- a break in what several considered to be the artificiality of the exercises -- seemed to increase their familiarity with one another. After a leisurely dinner in the Playboy Club, the group met in the room they had occupied during the morning.

The only exercise of the evening was for each group of six to construct a self-standing, purposeful object with one moving part. This was to be fashioned from a Tinker Toy set, several balloons, drinking straws, pieces of wool, pipe cleaners and several pingpong balls. All but ten pieces had to be used. Sam announced that the products of the three groups would be voted on and the winning side awarded a prize.

The groups, which were pre-selected by Sam, set to work after initial hesitation, some pondering and considerable joking. One group developed a machine that broke balloons, which they called an "ego buster." Another group developed a gadget that looked like a windmill minus several critical parts. The third group's attempt was nondescript and considerably less elaborate than the products the other two groups had produced. When the construction finished, each group appointed a spokesman, who humorously described the product to the others. Voting resulted in a tie; the windmill won on the second vote. Sam presented a prize, a large bottle of Bardolino wine, which, after hesitant swigs, was passed from person to person, with many of the older female teachers abstaining.

Informal discussion. The teachers' expectations of glamorous night life were not fulfilled, and about half of them found their way to the Playboy bar, since it was the only attraction besides television. After a restless wait for service, the group decided to go to a drugstore in the hotel for ice cream sodas. In the meantime, however, a discussion began between Sally and Sam about what several members of the group perceived to be Glenda's, Rebecca's and especially Norbert's, negative attitudes toward the workshop. As evidence of this, they noted that instead of sharing his reflections with the group Norbert had often said he would rather "pass" than comment. He also showed little enthusiasm for the Tinker Toy exercise; he was a member of the group whose product was incomplete. Sam, concerned with these events, left to find Glenda, Rebecca and Norbert, and discuss the problems, if any, they were having.

In Sam's absence, the discussion of Norbert's reluctance to participate continued, led by Sally. The general tone of the conversation was that Norbert should have been able to adjust to this and other situations; several present had heard that he was upset because he thought the selection of the Playboy Club was improper and that he felt he should be at home with his wife and children. At one point in the discussion, Sally said she would bring the matter to the attention of the entire group during the first session in the morning.

Sam returned and reported that he had talked with Glenda and Rebecca, who said they were tired, and were watching television. Sam had also talked with Norbert, who told him that he did have some problems with staying at the Playboy Club, as well as with the workshop in general. He did not want to discuss the problems at length with Sam, though; he would try to work them through, possibly with the group's help, the following day. According to Sam, Norbert also planned to watch television in his room for the remainder of the night. This information ended the discussion of problems with the workshop, and the group talked about other, non-school, topics.

Soon after, the group worked its way to Regina's room where Ellis, Sarah, Monica and Regina were playing bridge. With this interruption, the card game ended. By 1:00 a.m. all had retired for the night.

3. The Second Day's Activities

The groups from the night before were reconstituted at 9:00 a.m. to discuss their products and the process they had used to create them. Sam briefly described an evaluation scheme, and the groups, following these guidelines, put their comments on newsprint. As on previous occasions, the groups were asked to share their comments with the others. All evaluations were positive: communication during the construction task had been good, and most felt that the task had been accomplished.

Although there was opportunity during this process to raise the issues discussed the night before concerning Norbert, Glenda and Rebecca's reactions to the workshop, no one did.

The major part of the morning was spent in exercises meant to increase awareness of others. Sam asked pairs to do a variety of things: stare at each other without saying anything, talk to the other person while he or she was continuously looking away, and sit back-to-back on the floor. Periodically, Sam asked for reports of these experiences to the entire group.

In some instances it took a while for a volunteer to emerge; when one did, the report was usually that the exercise was a useful learning device. After these exercises, the group ate lunch and checked out of their rooms.

Lunch and other business finished, the group met for the final time in the meeting room. As an aid to evaluation of the experiences they had gone through, Sam gave a brief lecture on transactional analysis. Afterward, he asked teaching teams to form, away from other groups, to brainstorm "caring" and "uncaring" behaviors in the educational setting. Norbert dominated his group; several others said they found his suggestions to be incisive. Reluctant to break with tradition, Sam had all groups report and discuss their lists.

4. Evaluation of the Workshop

Before the group left for home, Sam distributed an evaluation form for the workshop, which was to be returned to him the following day. Though Sam may have discussed the results with teachers, he did not make a final summary for them.

A review of the data shows that with the exception of concern over "Norbert's problem," and some discomfort over the choice of the Playboy Club, the faculty rated the workshop very highly, citing "feelings of support and safety" and "getting to know each other better." Sam's efforts and talents were praised, and almost all participants suggested that similar activities be conducted throughout the school year. Although there is reason to suspect that the evaluations may have been inflated -- the teachers' time investment, their ownership in the idea, and perhaps even their awareness of the fact that all their expenses had been paid probably increased the need to feel that something positive had been accomplished -- there were enough straightforwardly critical comments (ex: "Bert should have been given the option to be excused", "Timing seemed to be rushed.") to lend credibility to the sincerity of what they wrote.

In a short statement Ellis wrote for placement in Sam's permanent file, he recounted the arrangements for the workshop Sam had made, and noted that:

> From the evaluation by the staff, the workshop was entirely successful and done on a level equal with that done by many professional consultants in the field.

5. (Comments: What Happened at the Playboy Club)

The communications workshop was held at a crisis point in the life of the emerging organization; it provided temporary shelter from the problems the school was facing. Removed from the location of the difficulties, held in facilities designed and equipped for leisure activities, it gave the faculty an opportunity to experience one another in a relaxed setting and become acquainted with new aspects of each other's personalities. Nearly twenty-four hours of contact contributed to increased familiarity. To some extent, then, the fact of being together out of school for an extended period had an effect on relations within the group; it worked as a salve and presented an opportunity for people to re-group, re-think and feel more positively toward the school. In fact, negative sentiments toward the community, Board of Education and superintendent did not re-surface during the workshop. What had seemed a bleak future a few days before, now seen from a distance, took on an optimistic cast. So an unintended outcome of the workshop was relief from the problems of the school.

The intended outcomes of the workshop were probably only partially accomplished. Glenda, who had first suggested the idea of a retreat, and her two teammates, Rebecca and Norbert, were accused by several others of not having participated fully in the group learning activities. Norbert, an older faculty member, was singled out as having been particularly reluctant to contribute. Although Sam took preliminary steps to solve the "problems", and Sally considered bringing them to the attention of the entire group, as did Norbert, in the end the difficulties were simply ignored. Some teachers found interpersonal relationships with Ellis awkward. For instance, Jeanne and Dori commented privately to each other that they felt tense when they were Ellis' partners in the non-verbal communication exercises. Jeanne was particularly uncomfortable because Ellis had asked her if she was avoiding him: in fact, she was.

These incidents are interesting in two respects. First, they mark the first semi-public acknowledgement of difficulties within the organization; until now all problems supposedly had external sources. These problems were not openly shared with the entire faculty. Secondly, the incidents provide an insight into the effectiveness of the workshop, as well as into the dilemmas it created. Instead of using the complaints against others as occasions for "real" communications problems, the workshop continued with simulated communications exercises. Admittedly, using the actual problems would have involved risk: a minor problem could have become a serious crisis. Nonetheless, a situation that was likely to recur in the school situation was not confronted or used for instruction. Avoidance of the real communications problems that existed in the group -- among several faculty members and between the principal and faculty -- also made the exercises seem even more artificial. As it was, in the case of antagonism against Norbert and his team, the only contact between the two parties was through an intermediary. Face-to-face contact with the principal was avoided by some teachers, and others did not tell him of their discomfort in his presence. To paraphrase an old saying: what was preached wasn't practiced.

But the ideal of open, trusting communication in the school was certainly not abandoned. Indeed, if the workshop accomplished nothing else, it legitimated open communication as an ideal: the purpose of the workshop was clearly to improve communications. The inability to reach this goal fully during the workshop -- a situation which Sam recognized -- was perhaps not important. But the formulation of the ideal as attainable, though with much more work, placed a strain on the system in the form of high expectations that could not be easily fulfilled. In fact, as discussed above, the primary source of strain during the workshop was that some members questioned the sincerity of effort others were making.

The workshop had two other latent effects, ones presumably more beneficial for the organization. It demonstrated that faculty suggestions -- even expensive ones -- would be taken seriously. The idea of the workshop originated with a faculty member, and was approved by the principal and central administration, who provided funds for it. A closely-related effect was that the workshop probably increased each faculty member's personal investment in the new enterprise. Supplying time, energy, ideas and the willingness to examine one's own habits (with the implicit promise of attempting to change them) required -- and probably deepened -- commitment to the demanding role of being a teacher in a new, innovative school.

Finally, in the context of the conflict with the community, the decision to continue with the workshop, especially at the Playboy Club, puzzled -- even astonished -- the researcher at the time. It appeared to have been an avoidance or withdrawal from the problem, or a heedlessness of political realities. But, as has been pointed out above, a respite from the turmoil may have been just what the faculty needed. And though the action may be interpreted as inflexible, it can also be argued that the adherence to plans indicated self-confidence; Ellis and the faculty believed they controlled the situation with the community.

Later in the narrative we shall return to the communications workshop in an attempt to see what, if any, enduring effects it had on the faculty, particularly the teaching teams. The fact that so little time was spent during the workshop in actual team meetings suggested that its intended effects on teams were minimal, and that little actual team-building would ensue.

6. Pornography and the Politics of Planning

Two days later, in the local weekly Courier, a front-page headline read: "L.A. School Staff Meets at Playboy Club." In the article, Biddle defended the selection of the Playboy Club as having been the best and most reasonably priced of the facilities available. He also supported the concept of a residential communications workshop as an aid in planning for the new school.

According to the article, several Board of Education members did not know about the Playboy Club workshop, and would not have approved the site had they known. The article also described the Center for Policy Research study, which was correctly identified as the source for half the funds for the workshop; a Courier reporter had contacted the project director for information while the workshop was going on.

The article was stimulated by about 15 phone calls from Lincoln Acres residents to the editor, asking about the workshop; there were also several phone calls to Biddle complaining about the site. Beyond these, and in the article itself, little public mention was made of the workshop, possibly because the major critics of the school were away on vacation. Only one letter to the editor appeared, from a resident of a rural community. After questioning Biddle's qualifications to be superintendent, it continued:

Besides the obvious "fun and games" overtones, the trip to /the club/ wasted gasoline and time, and it cost money. It doesn't matter that half of the cost came from federal money (after all, who contributes to the federal coffers? the Martians?), the fact is that this is another flagrant case of mis-spent taxpayers' money -- in a time when this commodity appears to be in very tight supply. This is a typical case of lack of good common sense and a total disregard for the taxpayer. Also rather typical of the Washingtonville school system.

By the way, gang, how were the Bunnies?

Although it is difficult to determine how much damage selecting the Playboy Club did to the public image of the school, it probably did not improve relations with Lincoln Acres parents or the Board of Education. More likely, it reinforced or created a suspicion that the faculty did not know what it was doing. To a semi-outsider -- the researcher -- it seemed at the time to have been a potentially serious public relations blunder, a strategic error at a sensitive time that could easily have been avoided either by finding another place, delaying the meeting, or even cancelling it.

C. THE BOARD OF EDUCATION'S RESPONSE TO THE FACULTY LETTER

On Monday, July 7, 1975, while the faculty was working on the Tinker Toy construction task during the communications workshop, the Board of Education discussed and made public the letter the faculty had written the week before, complaining about the survey. School board member reaction was not favorable. According to the Courier, Estelle Hunter said:

> I am incensed. I really believe parents need a choice. The professionals are always espousing the need to stress individual differences, but it seems they're just paying lip service to the concept. If they recognize individual differences then they'll recognize the need for alternatives. I believed the survey was a chance to get input which might have offered alternatives. I am so angry with the staff. The utter gall. This is the most horrendous thing that has ever happened in this town.

Sylvia Peabody, a board member from Lincoln Acres, said that she too was upset by the tone of the letter. The Courier quoted her:

> It was as if they were putting us on notice that if we did not do such and such they'll go elsewhere. I agree with their charge that the Board is shirking its responsibilities in not coming down hard and strong one way or the other. I don't feel because teachers don't like what we do we should do what the teachers demand. There are some excellent teachers with no jobs. I know them. Instead of getting my sympathy the

> letter brings a negative reaction. I'm a teacher and I know a good teacher can adjust to many situations. If a closed situation hampers their ability then perhaps they should find another job.

And the _Courier_ quoted Gerrie Holden, a board member from one of the rural communities, as follows:

> I think they heard about the school board meeting last week and are running scared, feeling threatened. But I am not having a struggle with the community. I do not define listening to the community as struggling. They say it is an abhorrent manifestation of a breach of trust with them to conduct a survey. Well I do not consider listening as abhorrent. Sure the survey is invalid, if this is the attitude of those teachers helping to conduct it. I apologize to all those parents I called to arrange teas to hear Mr. Brown out, for now I do not believe he ever intended to listen.

Irena Farrell, the board president, sympathized with both the parents and teachers. The other two board members present remained silent on the issue. The Lincoln Acres parents present -- some of whom had participated in the survey -- were angry and surprised at the teachers' reactions to the survey.

Concerning the faculty request for a private meeting to discuss the school, the Board decided to have the meeting at the next session, but open to the public. As Sylvia Peabody viewed it: "This issue is not private. Sessions should be open, it's an open issue."

D. FACULTY PLANNING CONTINUES

1. Clarifying Decision Responsibilities

On the day after the communications workshop, the faculty resumed working in the school. Wednesday and Thursday were spent primarily in subcommittees, brainstorming lists of decision-making areas. Chart 6.2 is the brainstormed decision-making list produced by the subcommittee on teams.

Chart 6.3 is the brainstormed product of a subcommittee assigned to the topic of parent decision-making roles.

Finally, Chart 6.4 presents Ellis' decision-making areas, as he presented them to the faculty on Wednesday.

Each of these lists was discussed by the entire group. Ellis acted as the manager, and asked for suggestions or deletions to the lists. Several interesting suggestions were made when the principal's decision-making list was discussed. Priscilla asked if team members could share in hiring under the circumstance that a new member for their team were needed. Ellis said

CHART 6.2

BRAINSTORMED DECISION-MAKING AREAS FOR TEAMS

Intra-team
a. rules for unit space
b. sharing of materials and ideas
c. responsibilities
   scheduling
   attendance, clerical, etc.
   planning skills and activities
d. referrals for special services
e. conference (parent) planning
f. grouping kids according to ability

Inter-team
a. sharing material and ideas
b. kids as a resource
c. cooperative space arrangement
d. meetings
e. use of school facilities

CHART 6.3

BRAINSTORMED DECISION-MAKING AREAS FOR PARENTS

Parents' decision in cooperation with staff:

Retention   Reports of progress
Placement   Classroom participation
Enrichment or special activities   Outdoor activities
PTA   Fund raising
After-school use of facilities by kids

Parents not to be involved with:

Time   Methods
Space   Materials

CHART 6.4

THE PRINCIPAL'S DECISION-MAKING AREAS

Administrative

Hiring
Management (material and funds)
Shared evaluation
Use of building and equipment
Divide responsibilities among staff
Meetings

---

that they could, and added the word "shared" to hiring. Norbert suggested that Ellis add to his administrative list the responsibility of dealing with parent complaints; he didn't want parents coming in for a weekly session to "bitch, moan and groan" as some parents were prone to do. Norbert's recommendation was that the principal act as a filtering system, accepting information and communication from parents and the Board of Education, and passing on only what he considered important for teachers. Jeanne disagreed with the idea of information screening by the principal. It was her view that teachers should receive all information, both positive and negative. Ellis concluded the discussion by saying:

> What we're here to do is to find out what kind of things we can do -- and here is really a sort of middling course. Why don't we run it like the U.S. Post Office and the way they treat junk mail. You get one, and then you let me know if you don't want to get any more of that kind of communication.

The consensus of the group was that this was a feasible way to handle parent communication.

It should be noted that these lists were preserved, so they could be developed into a "kind of reference document."

2. Teachers Discuss the Courier Articles

On Friday morning, eight teachers gathered in the faculty room and read the Courier articles about the Playboy Club and the letter they had written to the Board of Education. Several teachers were surprised by the articles. Sally, in particular, was worried about the possibility of being fired or not rehired the next year, since she was non-tenured. Other teachers thought it was unlikely that they would be retaliated against for the positions they had taken. Another thought that both articles were "sensationalistic": the headline should have been "Teachers Attend

Communications Workshop", and the Playboy Club was of secondary importance. Other staff members had no objections to the headline.

3. A Furniture Decision

During these days furniture had begun to arrive and was being put into place by the teachers and filled with supplies. For the most part, the building was still unorganized and fairly empty; the furniture had not yet been arranged in functional patterns.

While the teachers were meeting in small groups to brainstorm decision-making policies for the school, Dr. Biddle had a piece of furniture sent to the school; it was placed in Alan and Jeanne's teaching area. It was a twenty-foot-long waist-high workbench made of heavy, varnished wood; it had steel pipe legs, and a large piece of peg-board attached on top, which increased its height to about six feet.

After several inquiries from teachers about the new piece of furniture, Ellis called an impromptu faculty meeting. He explained that the furniture was designed by the superintendent and was his compromise between openness and walls; Biddle would like to see each team use 15 of them in their space, if they were willing. The teachers' immediate reaction was suggestions for modifying the workbench-wall. When Ellis was asked what he thought of it, he demonstrated how easily it could be toppled over, claiming that many children in the school could do the same thing and that consequently it was unsafe.

Ellis communicated the faculty's dissatisfaction with the compromise piece of furniture to Biddle, and this scheme was abandoned.

4. The Meeting with the Board

During this faculty meeting, Ellis introduced a discussion of the July 14 Board of Education meeting at which the Lincoln Acres faculty were to be given time to discuss their problems in public (not privately, as they had requested). He suggested that the staff not attend, since there was no point in a public meeting, and that he had already told the Board everything. He mentioned that at the session in which a closed meeting had been denied, three Board members were absent; in his opinion, if a vote were to be taken again with all Board members present, their request for a private meeting would be granted. In addition, he said it would not be necessary to attend, because neither he nor any of the faculty had received an invitation. Thus his suggested strategy was to delay and hope for a more favorable ruling.

The meeting ended with an announcement by Sam that he had contacted the Washingtonville Education Association, the local teacher union, for advice on the problems with the Board. The association's opinion was that as soon as the Board of Education made a policy decision that in any way altered the original design of the school, the teachers would have the basis for a grievance, because they had been hired to teach in an open space school.

E. THE WORKSHOP'S THIRD WEEK: CONFLICT AND COMPROMISE

On Monday morning, Ellis told the faculty that he would spend the next few days tabulating the results of the survey, and asked for volunteers to help him, getting several. He said that the work for the day was for teams to sort out "what should be done by groups and what by individuals," to add to the role descriptions for teachers and for teams which had already been produced. These discussions began. Later that morning a film of an open-space kindergarten was shown for those interested.

1. The Board Looks at the Survey Results

Local flooding caused evacuation of the school at noon Monday, and the cancellation of the Tuesday workshop. It also cancelled the Monday, July 14, Board meeting which was to have the public discussion of the Lincoln Acres school.

However, the Board did meet the following night, and re-voted on the issue of whether or not to have a closed meeting for the Lincoln Acres faculty. This time a private meeting was approved. Peabody, Holden and Hunter voted against it. Most of the 15 Lincoln Acres parents present were angered by the decision, and argued that it was not a private matter. One parent supported the faculty, and suggested that the other Lincoln Acres residents at the meeting were "hung up on having partitions," a matter which he felt should be left to professionals to decide.

At this Board meeting, Ellis Brown gave a preliminary report on the results of the community survey. The basis of the report was a random sample of 92 respondents from the 193 completed questionnaires. The findings of most interest were:

Do you believe your child has needs that cannot be met in open space?

No	43%
Yes	34
Other responses	24

Did you vote on the October 17, 1972 referendum?

No	53%
Yes	43
Other responses	3

How should partitions be used?

Some openness and some closedness	37%
Closed-off single classrooms	18
All open	13

What do you want your child to learn in school?

Basic skills	67%
Learn how to learn: discipline: get along with others	60
He should work according to his own interests and abilities	10
Science	10
Physical education	4
Other responses	14

It is difficult to know what these results mean. For one thing, that the day after the survey two Board of Education members had complained that the demographic data collected could be discriminatory. They asked the superintendent to have that page removed, which he did, over Brown's protest. Aside from randomly selecting questionnaires out of a pile, then, there was no way of controlling for biases through the use of data such as occupation or sex of the respondent. Also, the results were coded in such a way that the "other responses" category is large in many cases. Several response categories are unclear. Brown was aware of these limitations, and presented the data to the Board with the caution that it was not entirely clear what the results meant.

This presented a dilemma for the Board; they weren't certain what they should do with the findings. Sylvia Peabody, who had requested that the demographic information be removed, helped the Board resolve the question. In the public meeting she said: "Without a survey of all parents, we can't use this to make a decision." The local newspaper, however, along with a report of the results of the survey and an article about the meeting in which they were presented, printed the headline: "Lincoln Acres School Survey Shows Parents Want Alternatives."

2. Partitions: The Conflict Continues

When the discussion of the survey was over, the Board asked Brown to propose an alternative organizational plan for the school. Brown said that he already had alternatives in mind, and proposed placement of the library at one end of the instructional area to create an enclosed area on either side for a primary and an intermediate classroom. In the same plan, three sets of partitions would be used to "visually and psychologically" separate another primary and intermediate classroom. According to Brown, this plan would create six separate walled-off areas. He also announced that the first grade teachers were planning on beginning the year with a high degree of structure, with the intention of increasing to openness gradually.

The proposed compromises did not satisfy many parents, who continued to object to 75 children with three teachers in a single classroom, which was still a feature of the revised plan. After the meeting, Barbara Collins wrote a letter, signed by 32 other Lincoln Acres residents, to the state commissioner of education. The letter recounted the history of the school, including the walls promised in the bond issue literature (which was enclosed with the letter), Biddle's refusal to honor the bond issue specifications, community petitions to have the school changed, and community activities at Board of Education meetings. The letter -- which was also sent to local state assemblymen, the Washingtonville Board of Education, the state board of education and the public information office of HEW in Washington -- closed with the following appeal:

> At this point in time, less than two months before the opening of school, the partitions we were supposed to have are not and, we fear, will not be forthcoming unless you, Commissioner Harris, help us.
>
> We beseech you for help!
>
> What else can we do to prove our total dissatisfaction for the present "airport hangar" concept forced upon our children as the sole learning environment available to them?

Later in the week the Washingtonville Courier, which seldom took strong stands on local issues, had an editorial titled: "Board Credibility Fades with Private Meeting." In its view:

> This week school board members forged another wedge between themselves and an already disenchanted public.
>
> In 1972 when a $3 million bond referendum was passed to build additions to other schools and to build the $1.5 million Lincoln Acres School, literature promoting the referendum promised floor to ceiling partitions in the school. Now the superintendent says the district hasn't the $15,000 it would take to buy such partitions, and the teachers will decide what, if any, partitions they will need.
>
> At school board meeting after meeting only school board members Gerrie Holden, Estelle Hunter and Sylvia Peabody have said they favor offering an alternative. Others have hedged on deciding whether or not to demand partitions as promised.

3. The Faculty Continues Planning

When the workshop resumed on Wednesday morning, the faculty met with Ellis at 9:00 a.m., as had been their custom. He told them that the Board had met last night and approved a private meeting with the faculty for the following Monday night. He urged all teachers to attend, and then continued:

> It seems as though we should bring a compromise proposal with us. They are afraid that some dimwit will submit a proposal and have it passed. They have been having trouble getting a

quorum. We can design a proposal tomorrow and submit it Monday night.

He then asked that the faculty meet again at 1:00 p.m. to work on objective-writing. After this he left for a district-wide administrative meeting which included a key topic: the distribution of secretarial time during the year. Ellis wanted to get as much clerical aid as possible for the school.

More furniture arrived, and the rest of the morning was spent arranging it and working on other aspects of the teaching spaces. The furniture was constructed without wheels and drawers, contrary to their requests, and the teachers complained privately about it.

Sarah Fox, a resident of Allwood Green, told several others that a parent had telephoned her the night before and asked if the teachers were going to the next Board meeting. Sarah answered that they were; the woman told her that she would bring several parents to the meeting who supported them. The teachers were relieved to hear that there was some community support for their position.

That afternoon the group met again and discussed objectives lists. Sam summarized which objectives lists had been produced (reading, math and part of science) and Ellis tried to get a sense from the group of how much objective-writing could be accomplished by the end of the workshop. After considerable discussion, it was decided to work on record-keeping July 17, and on social and emotional objectives on July 21. Ellis then answered questions concerning the furniture. After the meeting, teachers continued to work on arranging their teaching areas.

4. The Faculty Compromise Meeting

By 9:15 the following morning, July 17, the faculty had assembled in the instructional area to begin discussing possible compromise proposals. Ellis explained:

> I've talked to a number of people on the Board privately and they are willing to accept a proposal for a compromise. There is a solid bloc against us that attends the meetings regularly. There is some concern that one of them, or another community person, would propose something that can be voted on right away. This Monday night we should be able to get a proposal accepted. This is two months too late; it takes time out of planning.

After questions concerning money for the partitions and whether the school could physically have closed classrooms, Ellis went to a chalkboard and drew the diagram that appears on the next page.

The immediate faculty reaction was complaints about reduction in teaching space, especially by two groups, MTK and NBC, which had planned to have large areas without any furniture. The discussion, which was tense, continued as follows:

DIAGRAM II
PRINCIPAL'S PROPOSAL FOR PARTITIONS*

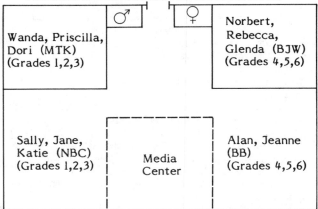

    *Solid lines are partitions. Dotted lines are the boundaries of the media center. Note that the kindergarten area is not shown: it is located to the left of the primary (1,2,3) groups.

    This diagram omits the kindergarten area, already closed off by partitions, and does not show the NBC area accurately (see simplified diagram below). However, it communicates Ellis' message accurately enough for his purposes: he wanted a partitioning plan that would satisfy the community and be acceptable to the teachers.

ACTUAL SITUATION PRIOR TO DIAGRAM II #

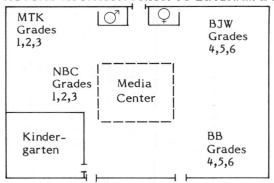

Furniture not shown. The reader will note that the diagram is turned from its position in the architect's plan; since teachers and students entered the area from the doors at the bottom, this position seemed most sensible to us (as it did to Ellis, evidently).

Jeanne: When these pods enclose us, will it be total, floor to ceiling?

Ellis: I'd like to treat that as a topic separately, but next.

Rebecca: I don't like it. [Some murmurs among the teachers]

Regina: Will this plan be acceptable?

Ellis: I think so. I've gotten assurances from three Board members.

Regina: We will change the walls but not the educational program?

[Ellis nodded "yes."]

Priscilla: I'd like to be firm with the Board. [The others agreed.]

Sarah: What about the survey? Are we taking account of the findings?

Ellis: Team teaching was good. There was concern about multi-age grouping, walls. The concern is mainly in the primary grades.

Dori: A lot of this seems firm. Unless I was naive, I didn't think all these decisions were made.

Ellis: They haven't been made. It's a plain harsh political reality. Last meeting left people angry. Some tried to say we couldn't have a private meeting with the Board, our employers. Some didn't like my finagling. There is talk of getting self-contained classrooms by the use of pickets, boycotts and lawsuits. I'd like to avoid this by making some changes. At least the psychological impression of change.

Alternative plans were offered, such as suggesting that parents who didn't like the school could have their children attend other schools in the district, and using folding walls with large doors in them, rather than partitions. About half of the teachers continued to complain about losing teaching space, and opposed the idea of a compromise. Ellis then said: "Do we want to let this sit? I feel that it's a bad time to ask for a consensus." The group silently agreed. Ellis suggested that they go back to their teaching areas, try to visualize the changes and meet at 12:30 for further discussion. Almost as an afterthought, he asked the primary group to meet with him immediately.

Ellis adds a compromise feature. Sitting on the floor in the instructional area, Ellis and the two primary teams (Dori, Priscilla and Wanda; Jane and Katie) discussed the compromise. The meeting began with the following conversation.

Dori: Don't you think we got the shaft?

Ellis: No. You have to keep it in perspective. We're two or three years ahead of the district and way ahead of the rest of the state. From what I've seen this state is backward.

Dori: Can you see us moving out of it in a few years?

Ellis: I don't see any Board member -- even the most committed -- keeping us as we are. We don't have a contract with them for partitions. Even after only one year with a fairly low profile, they can let us go our way. In a way you're buying a lot of valuable time. After this year a lot can happen. The Board has accepted open space within a pod. I'm not saying what you should do but think about going to a 1-2 and a 2-3 pod.* Think about what this would do proportionately. The numbers are good for that. It has other problems, materials is one.

The teachers, somewhat disoriented by Ellis' suggestion, began flitting from topic to topic: Board members, time problems that the suggestion would create, and statements of doubt about the need for compromise. Eventually two teachers voiced strong preference for retaining the original plan. However, more discussion followed, including attention to strategies for the Board meeting on Monday, and the possible alternatives were thoroughly debated. With the teachers still uncertain as to what they wanted to do, Ellis suggested that they talk about it for 45 minutes and then meet with him again. He left.

Near tears, Sally said, "I feel like crying." Jane, her team member, sighed and said, "I don't believe this." The others were equally unhappy with the events of the morning.

Without Ellis, the primary teachers moved to the faculty room and continued discussing the proposed change in plans. Disappointed and depressed, they had difficulty in reaching a decision; in a somewhat disorganized way, they re-examined the problem from a variety of perspectives. They debated at length whether or not to attempt to follow

---

*The significance of this proposed change is that instead of having two primary teams with grades 1,2,3 in each team, there would now be one primary team with grades 1 and 2, and another primary team with grades 2 and 3.

the results of the community survey. After they agreed that the survey had been poorly conducted, and that many parent responses demonstrated ignorance of educational practices, only Priscilla wanted the results to be followed. Her reasoning was, "I really have problems asking the community what they want and then completely ignoring them."

There did appear to be consensus in one area. Priscilla voiced it: "I don't think Ellis was telling us what to do, only telling us what was best." Debate continued, and there was little movement toward a decision. Eventually, after Dori made a suggestion to flip a coin to make the decision (not agreed to), Sally suggested that Ellis be asked to answer questions they had raised.

<u>The primary group accepts reluctantly.</u> Ellis arrived, and was immediately asked if proposals other than splitting the grades, such as only having walls, would be acceptable. He said that in his opinion it would not be, since a small group of parents, led by Rob Goldman, had objected to having three grades in the same primary classroom.

This appraisal prompted Wanda and others to devise elaborate schemes that would, in effect, leave the original plans intact. But they were quickly abandoned, because of a falseness about them that the group sensed would be easily detected. After more questions, the group acceded to the subtle pressures from Ellis; members of the group who had minor objections to the compromise said they would accept it with reservations. The remaining teachers then gradually changed their minds. It was clearly not their preference, and they offered justifications: "We can teach with any set-up", "We're doing it because of parent pressure, but it's against our judgment." Underlying these rationalizations was the hope that within a year the original plan could be restored.

Emotionally upset -- Wanda left the room in tears -- even after the decision was made, the teachers continued to question Ellis about the wisdom of the compromise.

Katie: I'm afraid we may be lousing things up that we haven't thought about. The Board might be, too.

Ellis: Yes, they know. The other side wants 18 classrooms or some other self-contained arrangement. I think the presentation that could be made is that we are doing incremental change, for the change to take place with input from the community and professional guidance. I think they could buy that easily, because that's something in the future and they always sell their future easily. That's why we're in trouble now.

Priscilla: I would be content if we could stave off a decision forcing us to do something.

Ellis: I think the quieter you make the first year, the better you can do the next year. You need to gain and build trust. The more trust you build now, the more you can do later.

Ellis left, and the teachers remained to decide which of them would teach the 1-2 and which the 2-3. Sally polled the group. With the exception of Dori, who wanted to teach a 2-3, and Katie, who wanted to teach a 1-2, the others said they had no preference. Several reiterated that they were not satisfied with the compromise, and would still like to have all three grades in both classrooms. On the question of whether the teams should remain intact or be re-formed, there was unanimous agreement that they should retain the same personnel. Indeed, several preferred that the teams remain intact even if it meant they would not be teaching the grades they desired.

Despite statements of trust in Ellis' political judgment by some, others continued to question the need for the compromise. They suggested that the community be informed that from an educational and professional standpoint, what they wanted was unsound. All of the teachers approved of this, but the majority sensed it was an unlikely course of action.

After more attempts to decide which team would teach which grade -- including a proposal that they draw straws -- they requested help from Ellis again. He happened to walk into the room at the time, and after Wanda explained the problem, he suggested that maybe the solution would be to break up teams. This was quickly put aside as undesirable by the teachers. After further discussion, Ellis recommended that the issue be put aside for the present time. Sally then asked:

What position should be taken in the Board meeting?

Ellis: I haven't heard any movement away from the 1-2, 2-3. The only problems are with who does it. Is the process O.K.?

Sally: We're leaving with what?

Ellis: 1-2, 2-3 and tell them we have a realignment problem.

Dori: I'm not sold on it. It's only fair for me to say so.

Ellis: None of us are.

With this conversation, the primary group meeting ended. Still disgruntled, they joined the rest of the faculty in the instructional area to discuss the compromise.

The whole faculty meets. The meeting began as Ellis reported to the faculty that he had met with the primary group, and with Bert, Glenda and Rebecca. He announced that Glenda, Bert, and Rebecca had agreed to take a reduction in square footage in order to keep their unique space. (This group had earlier spent over an hour working with the floor plan of the school and a calculator, to find ways to save an area of their teaching space that they had planned to have without furniture.)

Some teachers felt that in the process of saving the intermediate teams' space their own teaching space had been made less accessible, and traffic through their areas would be increased. Bert, annoyed by the charges, paced off the area that his team had proposed. This demonstration seemed to settle the major issues in the dispute. Other suggestions, such as moving the location of the media center, were made. These were unacceptable, because as Ellis pointed out, there would be difficulty in access to fire exits and other substantial traffic flow problems.

With the faculty depressed, many cursing frequently and on the verge of tears, Ellis ended the meeting by announcing that they would meet again Monday, when he would have a draft of the compromise proposal that could still be altered. As the faculty got up to leave, Glenda's laconic commentary on the compromise captured their mood: "Shit!"

5. Finalizing the Compromise

On Friday, the final detail of the proposed compromise -- which team would teach which primary grades -- was settled. Ellis suggested that since Priscilla Talbot had more experience with first grade than the others, her team should have the 1-2. Dori Kraus was not in school when the proposal was made, and Katie, who had wanted to teach the 1-2, reluctantly accepted. In Wanda's opinion, it would have been difficult for either Dori or Katie not to follow Ellis' suggestion: "When the principal says something like that you can't ignore it, you better do it." To the teachers then, Ellis' "suggestion" was regarded as a decision.

On Monday morning, the meeting to discuss the compromise was postponed until the afternoon, because Ellis had to attend a principals' meeting. Sam proposed that they work on affective objectives instead. After some debate, however, it was decided that psychologists had already formulated excellent lists of affective behaviors and that it would be more useful to work on social studies skills. The entire faculty sat in a large circle and brainstormed social studies objectives for the remainder of the morning. For example, a list of "map skills" included the ideas that the student should be able to identify the continents, understand longitude and latitude, and develop a grasp of distance.

The mood of the faculty this morning was lighthearted. When they mentioned the Board meeting to be held that night, they did it in a joking, somewhat sarcastic, way and showed no apparent sign of the tensions of the week before.

Deciding. Ellis began the 1:00 p.m. meeting, explaining:

I tried to come up this weekend with a statement that puts down the compromise we agreed on and some areas that were discussed but not agreed on. I think we have a plan that meets the needs of the kids as best we can in the circumstances. What we want is a commitment to this proposal that will let us expand later on. There are three points: (1) re-subdivision of space, it remedies the Kindergarten situation. I worked at it

and think it's O.K. It's the best I could do. (2) Change to a
1-2, 2-3. (3) Retooling -- specific costs of putting in
partitions and of getting more materials.

He distributed copies of the proposal to the faculty, and asked them to read
and comment on it. The few overall reactions complimented Ellis on the
tone of the document, and especially on his clear statement that in their
professional judgment the faculty did not think the compromise was the best
educational plan for the school. Except for a question about whether money
would be available to purchase the partitions needed for the compromise, all
questions concerned strategies toward the Board of Education, and ways of
responding to questions teachers might be asked at the meeting. The major
strategic issue to most teachers was whether or not a clear, definitive
answer was to be expected from the Board that evening. Ellis said that it
was his intention to get an immediate response. His advice on how to reply
to the Board was that they should avoid engaging in debate. He added:

> One thing I have told the Board is that the kids will recognize
> this as a familiar school. Change will be incremental from
> then on, and we haven't excluded any of our options here.
> They identified with things like noise. Theory and conceptual
> structure is beyond them.

Part of the strategy was to have as many teachers as possible attend
the meeting. Additionally, Ellis announced that he had contacted numerous
parents, and received assurances that they would support the teachers at the
meeting. When asked if the meeting would be private (only the faculty and
Board members present), Brown elaborated on some of the strategizing he
had done. He said:

> I have talked with Irena (Board president) about that. Sylvia
> Peabody talks to the press about all private matters. The
> press would then get the news from Sylvia Peabody, not us.
> What I would like to see is a public meeting with the public not
> able to speak, and then have the staff leave if there is any
> other business. I don't want you to be hassled afterward by
> parents. If that happens you can send them to me and I'll talk
> to them.

Lastly, Ellis informed the teachers that their attendance at the Board
meeting was semi-imperative: "It's in our best interest."

The compromise plan. The plan for reorganization of the school
presented to the Board of Education had a strident tone. Along with the
changes to be made and the rationale behind them, it included the following
passages:

> While the plan presented below is a sweeping change of the
> previous operating plans for Lincoln Acres School, our
> confidence in the original plan's worth as a process for

providing the optimum learning among the children of Lincoln Acres remains firm. It clearly capitalizes on the successes in organizational design both locally and in elementary schools throughout our culture: it strategically exploits the depth and breadth of each professional's expertise; it anticipates the individual and collective needs of children and parents of Lincoln Acres with remarkable sensitivity. We do not expect to lose these beliefs ever.

Nevertheless, our former plans for operation are now swept aside, because we want to be responsive to an aroused community and a concerned Board of Education. In order to respond, we have had to reassess our resources to determine how far from our former...optimal...organization we can go and still provide excellent professional service to Lincoln Acres' young people. We find we are able to be very flexible, which, coordinated with a little flexibility on the parts of the Board of Education and Lincoln Acres parents, will lead to a healthy and, we hope, noteworthy learning experience for the children.

Four reasons for the inappropriateness of self-contained classrooms were then provided in detail. Briefly, these were: (1) they were not clearly supported by the community; (2) construction of many walls by September would be impossible; (3) the number of self-contained classrooms required was unknown; (4) all furniture and walls would have to be removed from the building anyway at the end of the year for repair of the floor.* The text continued:

In addition to the above reasons, a change to self-contained classrooms would result in a disorganized, poorly-prepared opening of school in September, because it would shatter all plans made (primarily during voluntarily donated time of teachers) for the past half year. Great demoralization on the part of staff members would inevitably result.

Fortunately, there remains the option of self-contained teams. This gives substantial closeness beyond the present plan, yet allows for the team-teaching so strongly advocated both by the staff and the respondents to the survey.

After presenting a floor plan with the proposed changes (see Diagram III), and the cost of the changes, the proposal explained the alterations in the primary grades, repeating several times that the faculty did not think the changes were necessary and that they had caused problems. For example:

---

*The contractor had been successfully sued for having installed a rough, uneven floor under the carpeting.

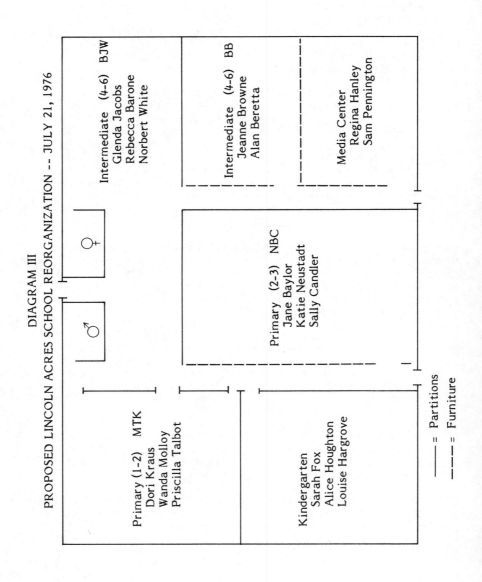

DIAGRAM III

PROPOSED LINCOLN ACRES SCHOOL REORGANIZATION -- JULY 21, 1976

Intermediate (4-6) BJW
Glenda Jacobs
Rebecca Barone
Norbert White

Intermediate (4-6) BB
Jeanne Browne
Alan Beretta

Media Center
Regina Hanley
Sam Pennington

Primary (1-2) MTK
Dori Kraus
Wanda Molloy
Priscilla Talbot

Primary (2-3) NBC
Jane Baylor
Katie Neustadt
Sally Candler

Kindergarten
Sarah Fox
Alice Houghton
Louise Hargrove

———— = Partitions
– – – – = Furniture

154

Words are not adequate to estimate the human cost of this change.

Multi-age grouping, according to the proposal, was not a problem in the 4,5,6 grades, and would remain in the plan.

The reorganization proposal ended with a strong statement about the desired future relationship between the faculty and community:

> The above proposal is made by the Lincoln Acres School in wholehearted desire for a peaceful, trustful rapport with the Board of Education and the Lincoln Acres community. The statement hardly measures the extent of change the staff has undergone; still, we hope some small portion of the flexibility in professional practice and sensitivity to our constituents comes through here. With matching flexibility and sensitivity from Lincoln Acres parents and the Board of Education, this proposal can be adopted, implemented and patiently allowed to bring forth its great potential for learning in the children of Lincoln Acres.

6. Reaching a Decision on Reorganization

That evening, the faculty, Board of Education and forty Lincoln Acres residents -- including several organizers of the protest groups -- met in the library of Valley School to discuss the reorganization of Lincoln Acres school. Irena Farrell, the Board president, announced that the first part of the meeting was private and asked the public to leave. During the ten-minute private meeting, Brown asked the Board what decisions would be made by them, and which ones by the faculty. Responses to his questions surfaced a lack of agreement on the decision-making or policy-setting role of the Board; some members wanted to take an active role in reorganizing the school, while others thought that was an internal school matter which never should have been brought to the Board. Throughout the private meeting, Biddle sat silently in his usual position at the center of the Board. With a vague assurance that the faculty's questions would be answered before the night was over, the public was permitted to return to the meeting.

Board president Farrell briefly explained the rules that would govern the public's right to speak: they would be allowed a thirty-minute period, with a limitation of three minutes for each speaker recognized by the chair. Since the proposal was not distributed to the public, Brown read the entire reorganization plan aloud.

The Board members began questioning the faculty. The first area of concern was the kindergarten. Since there were no walls between the two kindergarten areas, several Board members wanted to know how they would be separated. Alice Houghton explained that furniture would be used. Peabody then questioned the entire proposal:

The comment was made that this plan would limit the educational opportunities of the children. Are you saying that the other schools in the district are not doing a good job? Every other school in the district has small spaces and seems to have quite a few activities going on. Why is this plan limiting?

Ellis and then Sam answered that the original plan would permit flexible use of the space. They claimed that even demountable partitions would limit space use. Ellis finally commented:

I think your understanding is a little off. The change is not a handicap, but it is not what we would have chosen or what we have planned for. It is not our implication that this is bad.

Peabody responded that the staff was excellent, but she wanted to know why they had not considered starting off gradually instead of having entirely open space at the beginning. This query brought varied reactions from the faculty. Jeanne argued that walls were not the issue as much as the discussion of the walls, which had become detrimental to the planning of the school. Norbert, in a long, emotional speech, listed the advantages of open space and team teaching. From his perspective, the chief advantage was the opportunity to work in close contact with other teachers, who could provide support, professional criticism and advice. Peabody's reply was:

What you're saying is all well and good. I'm not getting at that. There seems to be some stigma attached to small classes. The kids in that class may be as good as one in an open space class.

Ellis and several faculty members denied that stigma was to be attached to children in self-contained classrooms. At this point Biddle entered the discussion, and asked Sam to describe his experiences as an open space teacher. Pennington again emphasized flexibility and the ability to meet each child's needs. Biddle then asked: "What can you do in an open space that you can't in a closed classroom?" Teachers answered that in an open classroom quiet children were less likely to be neglected because three teachers were present, and that sharing increased among students and faculty. Peabody reiterated that parents didn't want to eliminate open education entirely, but wanted an alternative to it. Farrell interrupted the discussion and asked that the Board consider the plan.

Board members compared the reorganization plan with features of other schools, asking if Oxford school offered alternatives to a 4,5,6. They disagreed among themselves over whether it did. In his response to this and other questions, Brown used the phrase, "incremental change" to describe what the faculty of Lincoln Acres school was going to attempt.

At this point, Board member Gerrie Holden, who had not yet spoken, asked:

In the reorganization you're not implying that you are offering alternatives?

Brown: What do you mean by alternatives?

Holden: /Laughing/ What the parents want. Really, I don't see the point because you haven't changed anything, the methodology is the same and so are the techniques. /The teachers collectively groaned./

Brown: What do you mean by technique?

Holden: I can't see that you have changed anything.

Glenda: It has entirely changed. We put up partitions!

Holden: But that doesn't really change anything.

Jeanne: I thought the issue was walls, not our teaching technique. I thought walls were what was being attacked.

Holden: I don't think so.

Grace Walters, a liberal Board member, then changed the subject and asked Ellis to describe the growth of a normal student in the school, with emphasis on who would be accountable for that student. Ellis did so.
After this, Harvey Stieglitz, another Board member with a liberal reputation, made the following statement:

I think that the staff has gone out of their way to meet community demands. I am aware that they haven't created self-contained classrooms. I'm aware that they wanted an open space school. I'm also aware of the skills and high quality of the staff. I join with Bob Klahr who last week, even before the compromise, said we should give this plan a chance. I realize the staff made a big compromise. I say give it a chance.

Walters then supported Stieglitz's statement. Klahr also agreed with Stieglitz, but raised the key question: how had the bond issue promise of 18 classrooms evolved into an open space school? Biddle gave the following response:

I wish I could remember four years back. I wish the architect hadn't put in the partitions pictured the way he did in the pamphlet. Grace Walters touched on part of the evolution. Four years ago we didn't have staff prepared for open space. My philosophy has been to allow teachers to work in the situation which they want. I have complete faith in the teachers. I think that the staff has made a tremendous compromise. If they are comfortable with it I support them, if not, I also support them.

Peabody repeated her view that alternatives to open space be provided. Then the public was allowed to comment.

Parent response was different in this meeting than in those that preceded it. Perhaps the most significant change was that several parents -- none representing an organized group -- actively supported the teachers. In all cases, they argued that the professionals should be permitted to do what they considered to be good educational practice. Several other parents, including Rob Goldman, viewed the reorganization proposal as having satisfied their demands, and asked for a spirit of cooperation between faculty and parents. And Sam Schwartz said:

> We have a school that's about to open. We have teachers that we didn't at the time of the bond issue. We have a school to open. I'm not pleased with what's gone on, but I think it is a big compromise for people who want airplane hangars. I'm annoyed with the Board and parents. They've been obnoxious. So have the teachers; I've seen their letter. We should try to cooperate.

Yet others argued that to keep the democratic system from deteriorating further, the bond issue should still be fully honored.

Generally, although some parents were still deeply dissatisfied with the compromise, opposition to the school seemed to have decreased considerably. The predominant community attitude turned to one of pleas for cooperation, tinged with a "we'll wait-and-see" posture.

Once the 30 minutes of public comment were over, Hunter reported the results of an analysis of the community survey data which she and Peabody had carried out independently. She began by accusing Brown of having biased the results he presented to the Board because he used predominantly teacher-conducted interviews, which according to her findings were more favorable to open space than those interviews conducted by parents. She had also discovered that 94 of the surveys contained demographic data, even though Biddle had ordered it removed. Despite these charges, the findings she presented were not significantly different than those presented by Brown. What did differ was the interpretation: Hunter and Peabody concluded that most parents wanted alternatives to open space. The discussion, with charges and countercharges, that followed the presentation of the survey findings was so confusing that Sam Schwartz commented publicly: "It sounds like a morass. You can't take little pieces from a survey and form a conclusion."

Farrell asked if the Board was ready to make a decision. Peabody, who until now had let Hunter present the survey results, said that she and Hunter had developed alternative plans based on the results of the survey. The proposals were fairly elaborate, complex schemes that would limit grades to two levels in each classroom, and also provide at least one self-contained classroom for each grade. As strategized earlier in the day by the teachers, Brown's response to these alternatives was that the staff would need a considerable amount of time to consider them; he reiterated that they were hoping to receive a decision that evening.

Holden asked that the alternatives formulated by Peabody and Hunter be considered. The other Board members restated their positions, and suggested that a consensus of the Board or a vote* be taken. More debate followed, until Holden, sensing defeat, and unhappy with the compromise, asked that "the Board take a vote on the original plan, because it costs $10,000 less and seems to me to be the same." Stieglitz's response was: "I would not like to do that because I think the staff has worked hard on the compromise, and it shouldn't just be put aside." Farrell then asked if there were other comments (there were none), announced her support of the faculty compromise, and then asked for a vote on it. The vote was five in favor and three (Holden, Peabody and Hunter), against, The absent Board member was Charles Frisch, on vacation.

Afterward. After the meeting, Biddle told one of the teachers that he was surprised they hadn't demanded the original plan; in his opinion, if they had, they probably would have prevailed. Most teachers were relieved that the issue had finally been resolved; they now knew what type of school to plan for the opening in September.

Later that week, under the front page headline: "Parents Win Partitions, Staff Compromise OK'd" the Washingtonville Courier reported:

> Parents won the battle for partitions in the new open Lincoln Acres Elementary School, Monday.

> But some parents who fought since April for a closed alternative to the new open school are still unhappy and say they may appeal the school board's decision to accept the staff's compromise plan.

A week after this Board meeting, Biddle was asked what he thought of the outcome. His reply was:

> Horseshit. The staff should have fought for what they wanted, but they didn't and they'll still be all right, they're good people. By January the community will like the school. It's just a matter of them seeing what happens there.

He continued:

> I didn't have much input into the compromise plan. The staff there is good. It's too bad they can't have the opportunity to use their professional judgment. We spent a lot of time on issues that had nothing to do with what is good for kids.

---

*The Board's custom was to avoid taking a vote whenever possible. Almost all actions were by consensus.

Brown's views a week after the Board meeting were somewhat similar to Biddle's. He stated that: "Biddle had no input. He thought that I worked out the plan out of necessity." He explained that Biddle had told him early in July that the Board was considering installation of some type of partitions. In response, Biddle had designed a partition -- the workbench-pegboard -- which was sent to the school and found unacceptable by the teachers. Brown recounted the events this way.

> I told him that in terms of process, the staff was upset and that in terms of the staff, having prototypes delivered to the school was a dangerous process. I think Biddle thought he was in the wrong place in terms of process and stayed out of it. At that point I met with Irena Farrell, the president of the Board, and Grace Walters, another Board member. Sam talked with Stieglitz. We had a fear that a whole redesign would come out if a school board member suggested one. This thing has been decided for the last six months. "The issue is how far we have to bend to shut up the community," that's how they put it. We gave the least to quiet them down.

Brown's comment to the researcher that "this thing has been decided for the last six months" was his first acknowledgement that he had not been as open with the teachers as he had presented himself to be. Assessing the results of the compromise and the planning of the summer, Brown sounded blaming, and less than exuberant. He said:

> I'm about the same as at the mid-June board meeting, the last one Frisch was at. I don't think it's proper for me to sound arrogant about it, but my experience is pretty unique. There aren't many planners willing to do what I can do. Washingtonville is not willing to do it. I was brought in under false pretenses. Now that I'm here I have an ethical responsibility to see what can be done. Washingtonville is back a few decades.

F. THE SUMMER WORKSHOP CONTINUES

1. Remaining Sessions

On Tuesday, the entire faculty brainstormed "affective" objectives, and teams worked in their teaching areas arranging furniture and materials. Because the BB team wanted more windows and access to a sink, they asked for and were granted permission to switch their teaching space with the space designated for the media center (see Diagram III).

Wednesday began with more entire-faculty brainstorming of affective and work-habits objectives, led by Sam. Work in teams filled the rest of the day.

Regina was unhappy with the reduction of space in the media center as a result of the compromise and the switch she had made with the BB team. Aware of the problem, Sam met with both intermediate groups, who agreed to give Regina several additional square feet. This solution left all involved pleased; it was one of the few genuinely cooperative efforts in recent weeks.

Teacher reactions to the reorganization were mixed:

Priscilla: I think that Ellis read the situation correctly and made the right compromises.

Jane: I like it.

Jeanne: I was bored with the Board meeting.

Wanda: I'm not pleased with walls and the 1-2, 2-3 but I can live with it.

Glenda: I'm not happy about it, but I would like to get down to planning and I'm glad it's over.

For the remainder of the workshop, almost all teacher energies went into unpacking instructional materials, storing them, and arranging furniture. To finish organizing their teaching areas, most teachers were planning to use the paid week following the workshop, volunteered time during August, and the two preparation days immediately before school was to open in early September.

2. Evaluation of the Workshop

In the faculty meeting. On July 29, the final day of the summer workshop, teams worked in their areas until 1:00, when the entire faculty met to evaluate the activities of the summer. Ellis made several announcements, including a decision not to have an open house for parents before school started, as Jeanne and other teachers had suggested. His reason was that the school would not be ready for parents to see. He then introduced the notion of evaluating the workshop; the Board and the Instructional Council wanted a report.

Quickly reading the objectives from the original proposal, Brown commented briefly on whether or not they had been reached. It was his opinion that: team decision-making had been accomplished; centralization of basic skills materials in the resource center hadn't been done; physical division of the space had been accomplished (not, of course, as the staff had intended); written student needs accounting had been worked on to some extent in teams but not in the entire group; methods for assessing program effectiveness had not been started ("we have not really decided how a program is working or not."). Finally, he left it vague whether the objective of clarifying student and parent decision-making roles had been achieved.

Brown then asked if there were additional things that teachers would like to put in the report. Dori wanted a statement on "how we were hassled about the walls and the readjustment of the classes and how it kept us from getting our act together." Most others agreed that the conflict with the community and the problems caused by the survey should be mentioned. Regina also suggested including comments on the problems the faculty had with communicating with the central administration, but that in addition, "something positive" be included "about the time given to us and that we did accomplish something."

After a reminder by Ellis to submit comments on the assessment program by the end of the day, his concluding comment to the faculty was: "I'd like to say you did a good job. We're ready to go." Teachers returned to their areas to continue adjusting furniture that had recently arrived. At 3:00 p.m. that day, the official summer workshop ended.

Brown's views. Privately, Ellis Brown admitted to having accomplished less during the summer workshop than he had hoped. He said to the researcher that the major area left unfinished was parent and student involvement, which, when it did occur during the summer, was not of the sort he or the faculty had intended. In terms of the faculty and its development over the summer, Brown had several observations. Faculty morale, he said, was:

> Not bad. They're naive. Part of that naivete is avoidance of what's going on politically. It's very easy for something to happen in the community that affects them. They give a passing glance at the Washingtonville Courier. Before long it's over with and they return to work, which isn't a bad way to handle it.

On the direction the staff would take in the coming year, he commented:

> The staff would have been very responsive to what I was doing. They have never been there before. Now I don't know. I did not select a group of people who are very tough. They don't fight for what they believe in. These are the kids who thought rationally about the Viet Nam war. Because they were logically right, they thought they should be listened to. They can't understand political realities.

In terms of what the faculty had actually developed into, Brown was more optimistic.

> Every team with the exception of NBC has had a real struggle to get together. NBC has had the least trouble in working out role relationships. They appear to be more together than everybody else. But everybody else is making satisfactory progress and that's fine.

Finally, he did not expect the partitions to arrive until October or November.

Teachers' views. Many teachers had also commented privately on the events of the summer. Below are some of the comments teachers made on the last day of the workshop.

Wanda and Priscilla felt that most of the goals of the workshop were met. But Wanda felt that the staff became "fractured" during the summer; she didn't know exactly what this meant, only that there had been a change. The BB team did not accomplish all that they had hoped to. In fact, they had lowered their expectations early in the summer and didn't reach even those. Jeanne said that Sam had given as much help as can be expected: "He's only one person. Ellis hasn't given any help. He's only shot down good ideas." Jane thought that little planning had been accomplished during the summer. Her teammates, Katie and Sally, disagreed and thought that although it wasn't on paper a great deal had been planned.

Later, after the school had been open for four months, we asked Ellis, Sam and the teachers on a questionnaire how they felt in retrospect about the summer workshop. The teacher responses on two questions asking for ratings of overall effects on the school as a whole were as follows:

Looking at the positive effects, do you feel...

<u>3</u>   1. It had a strong positive effect on the school

<u>6</u>   2. It had a moderately positive effect.

<u>9</u>   3. It had a small positive effect.

<u>0</u>   4. It had little or no positive effect.

And what do you feel about negative effects?

<u>3</u>   1. It had a strong negative effect on the school.

<u>5</u>   2. It had a moderately negative effect.

<u>3</u>   3. It had a small negative effect.

<u>4</u>   4. It had little or no negative effect.

Ellis answered that it had strong positive and strong negative effects; Sam's response was that it had a small positive effect. Ellis explained his answer by writing that the positive effect was, "team coordination, communication, planning" and that the negative effect was, "Board pressure for re-structure."

Another question asked: Now more specifically, how do you feel the summer planning affected your teaching team?

The teachers' answers were:

3   1. It had a strong positive effect on my group or team.

4   2. It had a moderately positive effect.

6   3. It had a small positive effect.

4   4. It had little or no positive effect.

And what do you feel about negative effects?

2   1. It had a strong negative effect on my subgroup or team.

6   2. It had a moderately negative effect.

3   3. It had a small negative effect.

5   4. It had little or no negative effect.

Considering both positive and negative influences together, the summer workshop was evaluated retrospectively as having had, on balance, a slightly more negative than positive effect on the school, although individual judgments varied widely.

Community views. A July 31 editorial in the Courier: "Whatever Happened to Summer?" offered commentary on a variety of subjects, among them the Lincoln Acres school.

What did we get this summer? Floods that caused $4.6 million in damage. A crisis over an open elementary school that sent parents who wanted a closed alternative into vicious battle with school board members and teachers. At least a dozen meetings over the issue.

Six months later, retrospective community responses to a questionnaire concerning the events of the summer indicate that it had not been a pleasant experience for parents (see Table 6.1). Though there was much diversity, certain themes are clear: the program did not have champions among parents as being "the best available"; there was practically universal agreement that unsolved school-community problems remained; and few people thought that the Board had well represented the interests of the parents.

It is also of interest to note that more parents felt an insufficient opportunity to influence than otherwise, and that more parents than not felt their suggestions had not been listened to and acted on. But only a small plurality (44% vs 36%) felt it had been hard to get answers about what the new school would be like. We can infer that for many parents, the answers were not what they wanted to hear.

However, we should emphasize again what had begun to be clear at

TABLE 6.1

PARENT OPINIONS ABOUT THE INTENSIVE PLANNING PERIOD

	Strongly Disagree	Disagree	Undecided	Agree	Strongly Agree
Parents had an opportunity to influence the planned educational program of the new school.	21%	31%	11%	23%	7%
Parents' suggestions were listened to and acted on.	16	33	23	19	3
School board members represented the interests of the Lincoln Acres community very well.	16	31	31	14	0
By the time school opened in the fall all problems between school personnel and community members had been settled.	52	34	6	2	1
The educational program of the school as planned represented the best available.	26	32	27	6	2
It was easy to get answers about what the new school would be like from school system staff.	20	24	14	33	3

the last Board meeting: the Lincoln Acres community was certainly not monolithically against the faculty's plans and hopes.

G. AUGUST WORK

In mid-August, the partitions that jutted from the outer wall were removed and combined to form several walls in the instructional area. Diagram IV shows the position of these partitions. The bulk of the partitions that were part of the compromise did not arrive in time for the opening of school in September.

During August, most teachers worked in the school for at least the five days for which they were to receive payment. Others contributed extra time. The major task was to finish organizing the teaching areas. Ellis and Sam supervised the delivery of large pieces of equipment for the kitchen, and helped workmen rearrange the partitions. By the end of August, the school was nearly ready for students.

H. (ANALYSIS AND COMMENTARY)

1. Key Decisions

During this intensive month several key decisions were made which had substantial potential influence on the school's shape and future.

The Board's decision to require the community survey seemed crucial; it sharpened school-community conflict in many respects, though it was designed to reduce it. The teachers' associated decision to carry out the survey, while protesting vigorously, both set the stage for continued conflict and signalled their reluctant willingness to have their vision influenced by outside pressure. With this decision, it began gradually to be clear that Ellis would manage, even manipulate faculty decisions as he buffered the school from, and negotiated with, the Board and community.

The tacit decisions to continue to hold the communications workshop, and to continue at the Playboy Club location, probably served to sharpen community conflict only slightly; they seemed more symbolic of the faculty's need to "get away" and its reluctance to be proactively "political" than anything else. At the workshop itself, the tacit decision by several key people (Bert, Sally, Ellis and Sam) not to surface and deal with genuine communications problems may well have set (or confirmed) a norm that problems in the system need not be dealt with directly.

The reconfirmed decision by teachers not to alter team composition, while it was natural, and reaffirmed team loyalty and cohesiveness, also reduced maneuvering flexibility during the period of the compromise discussion, and resulted in reduced ownership of the final plan.

The faculty's reluctant decision, engineered by Ellis, to accept the compromise partitioning plan and the 1-2, 2-3 grouping felt in many respects like a blow to the faculty's hopes, and perhaps to the community's sense of their professional expertise. It is ironic that more than one key figure in the conflict felt afterward that the compromise need never have been offered;

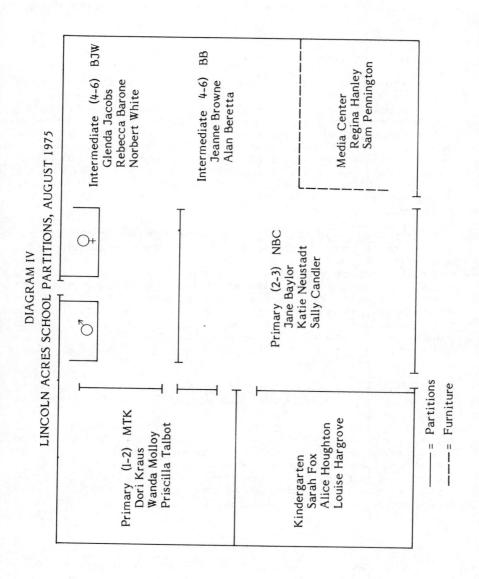

DIAGRAM IV
LINCOLN ACRES SCHOOL PARTITIONS, AUGUST 1975

Intermediate (4-6) BJW
Glenda Jacobs
Rebecca Barone
Norbert White

Intermediate 4-6) BB
Jeanne Browne
Alan Beretta

Media Center
Regina Hanley
Sam Pennington

Primary (1-2) MTK
Dori Kraus
Wanda Molloy
Priscilla Talbot

Primary (2-3) NBC
Jane Baylor
Katie Neustadt
Sally Candler

Kindergarten
Sarah Fox
Alice Houghton
Louise Hargrove

——— = Partitions
– – – = Furniture

167

the validity of that claim is of course unassessable. But it is clear that the process of reaching the compromise decision altered Lincoln Acres school as an organization, and indeed its relation to the community. We turn to these issues next.

2. Changes in the Emerging Organization

By the end of the busy and complex summer workshop, two critical changes had occurred in the emerging organization. First, the reorganization of the primary grades and the acceptance of partitions altered important aspects of the original design. Secondly, the social relationships within the faculty became more strained and less egalitarian; manipulative decision-making replaced collaborative decision-making, and authority became more centralized in the principal. Alteration of the design -- the compromise -- was a direct result of the conflict with the community. Changes in social relationships and the authority structure were an indirect result of the community conflict. What were the dynamics of the conflict?

Intensification of the conflict. In the last chapter, the conflict was analyzed as being between democratic values and professional values: the community felt that a school bond issue that implied a particular educational arrangement had been subverted by the superintendent of schools, who now claimed that another form of education was more effective. Charles Frisch, a Board member, proposed a survey of the community to find out its actual attitudes toward the school. But as a conflict resolution mechanism, the community survey had several unanticipated outcomes. It increased faculty opposition to the Board of Education because it threatened their professional judgment and autonomy; it created another "democratic" vehicle -- almost a plebiscite -- which made casting aside of the results difficult. We can speculate that Ellis may have been relieved to find that the demographic data had been removed; it gave him a good reason to claim the data were invalid, and thus obtain more maneuvering room.

In any case, the survey permitted the Board of Education and the educators to bypass the original issue of whether or not the plans for the school honored the original design.* The survey also brought charges from several Board members that the results were not tabulated or analyzed correctly and that their "true meaning" was not being followed. In general, it seems clear that the Board-mandated survey of the community did less to resolve the conflict than it did to increase it.

---

*This may have been an intended result of the survey. Many members of the Board of Education appeared not to want to make a decision.

Conflict resolution. Ellis and Sam played central roles in efforts to resolve the conflict between the school and community. Ellis served as a buffer between the faculty and community leaders. He cast himself in the role of politician and was accepted by the faculty as making politically wise decisions. As we have noted, many of these decisions, (for example, the reorganization plan, especially the division of grades 1,2,3) were manipulated or managed by Ellis. Perhaps unwittingly, Sam (who had affective leadership qualities Ellis lacked) helped Ellis manipulate or coopt the faculty. He was the first to suggest the possibility of a compromise, and presented it not as a defeat for the faculty but as a gesture to show the community that "we're the good guys," a form of power enhancement.

Overall, Sam and Ellis played mainly positive roles: they eased the faculty into a difficult -- and initially quite unacceptable -- decision which avoided intensification of the conflict, and eventually led to a partial resolution.

In the process of achieving the resolution, however, both men, but especially Ellis, created more differentiation in the authority structure of the organization. As principal, Ellis assumed a central role in the decision-making structure, since as Dori pointed out, the critical decisions had already been made and were in effect then sold to the faculty. Of course, Brown was not making these decisions under ideal circumstances; there was a considerable amount of pressure on him from the Board of Education, the community and probably Biddle to have the conflict resolved one way or another. He probably also felt pressure from the teachers; a successful resolution of the problem was needed to demonstrate his leadership abilities.

It was also clear at this time that although the early commitment had been to collegial decision-making by the faculty, their skill in delivering on this intention was insufficient. At several points of stress, their decision processes seemed wandering and unfocused. The fact that Ellis had usually led large-group decision-making in the past probably contributed to the faculty's lack of skill and made it easier for him to manipulate the compromise.

So the faculty had lost some power. The effect of this loss, however, was diffuse. Some felt they had not been treated fairly by Ellis, but the majority considered the real abuses to have been from the community and Board of Education. Biddle, even with his fairly inactive support for the faculty, was not viewed as having undermined their efforts as much as had the Board and community. By the end of the summer, the militancy the teachers had expressed in their letter to the Board about the community survey appeared once again in their contention that the compromise proposal was against their best professional judgment. But by the time of the compromise, a shift had occurred; they now felt that they could live with almost any arrangement, provided that it was not one of totally self-contained classrooms.

Overall, the relationships among the faculty, although clearly strained by the conflict with the community, remained collegial and professional. Perhaps more importantly, open, professional relationships with teammates and between the teachers and administration, as reaffirmed in the communications workshop, remained a goal at the end of the summer.

3. Political Stabilization

By the end of the workshop, the primary linkages of a durable sort between school and community were little different than before: Ellis and Biddle served as buffers and negotiators. The Board, more deeply involved than usual, served in its regular role of formal channel for citizen influence. The execution of the Board-mandated survey was a temporary school-community linkage; we have already discussed its effects.

But no new political linkages had yet been created, though the summer proposal had included this as an objective ("defining roles for parent involvement"). It seemed, too, that the teachers were ambivalent about how active, how environmentally confrontive, to be. Though they worded sharp objections in their letter to the Board and in the final compromise proposal, it took crisis to move them away from their natural preoccupation with the technical problems of planning the school. It seemed hard for them to realize that unless the political isues were dealt with, their technical efforts would come to little. Such a stance is not surprising: most teachers are naturally preoccupied with delivering teaching. And the fact that many of the teachers were non-tenured may have made them even more inclined to leave the hazards of politics to others.

Expertise vs. democracy. Throughout the controversy, a major theme was the role of expertise or professional judgment, as contrasted with the role of democratic norms in specifying the degree of community influence on decisions. Although in most cases the educators argued from the claim that they possessed expert knowledge, they were tempted at times to fall back on head-counting. For example, Ellis expected to have enough votes on the Board of Education to receive a private meeting. And many teachers wanted to be responsive to the community; several even suggested that the results of the community survey be closely followed.

There was also community ambivalence concerning expertise; some opponents attacked the violation of democratic norms and did not directly question the educators' expert judgment. Others, however, openly questioned not only the suitability of the plans, but the faculty's ability to implement them. And, late in the summer, still other parents fully supported the teachers' professionalism.

The compromise reflected the ambivalence toward expertise. While the faculty claim of expertise did not "win" the conflict, enough of the original plan was left intact to preserve this important aspect of professionalism. Democratic norms, the counter-norms of expertise, were also only partially satisfied; one minor demand, to eliminate three grades in the primary classrooms, was fully met. But the major issue in contention, the demand for self-contained classrooms, was only partially met by the agreement to install a few moveable walls. Indeed, the use of space was substantially unchanged from the original plans, as several Board members and parents noted.

In sum, the compromise avoided confronting the initial cause of the conflict -- that is, the basic question of the legitimacy of the plan for the new school. But the display of effort put into the compromise, along with the minor concessions, appeared to satisfy enough prominent community members so they could endorse the plan and call for cooperative relations with the school in the future.

4. Social-Architectural Design

How much slippage had occurred between the original vision, the faculty's goals for the school, and the emerging design? On the face of it, probably less than the pain over the compromise would have suggested. Though the faculty's intention to keep space use flexible was somewhat hampered, and the multi-age grouping range was narrowed in the primary teams from three to two years, it seemed as though many of the original goals were achievable within the emerging organization. It is also correct to say, however, that one of the original "process" goals -- the idea of collegial decision-making -- was beginning to be threatened by Ellis and Sam's engineering of consent.

5. Actualization

Finally, what we can note about the linkage between planning and implementation, and the factors that would promote or hinder actualization of the plans? The community conflict during the summer workshop diverted some of the faculty's time and energy from planning the school. Midway through the workshop, when the possibility of a compromise became evident, uncertainty over what kind of educational program they were planning for also slowed the teachers' efforts. Despite this, materials and furniture were arranged in teaching spaces so that they were nearly ready for students by the end of the summer. Objectives lists -- which actually constituted the curriculum -- were prepared for all academic areas, and were in progress for social and emotional areas.

Time was also spent on brainstorming lists of decision-making areas and role descriptions. Brainstormed products, however, were rarely taken much beyond the initial stages of listing of ideas by the group. In most cases, Sam was assigned to refine the lists, and they were eventually to serve as a reference work for the school. It appears that brainstorming mainly performed an investment-building function -- everyone's ideas were accepted and treated equally -- and did less to develop an intellectual framework or operational guide for the operation of the school. Since brainstorming was the only explicit faculty-wide method used in discussion of educational philosophy during the summer workshop, we might conclude that the consensus on educational views was not as deep or strong as the planners of new schools often hope for.

In general, the faculty's endorsement of Ellis' view that most summer workshop objectives were reached is technically correct, with the important exception of the goal of specifying parent and student roles in educational decision-making. But there is some question about the depth of overall goal achievement. Still, the most important link between planning and implementation remained the fact that those who had done the planning were about to become the operators of the new school.

7

SCHOOL OPENS: THE FIRST WEEKS

September arrived and the school opened. Teachers reported two days earlier than students to complete last-minute preparations. On both days, an early-morning faculty meeting focused on operational aspects of the school, from when lunch would be served to where teachers' cars should be parked. Ellis asked teachers to sign in and out every day, keys to closets and bathrooms were distributed, and the myriad details necessary for running a school were dealt with. In these preliminary days, speculation on what the school would be like was pushed aside for the practical business of setting rules and procedures.

A. THE PREPARATION DAYS

1. The First Day

On the first day, several important, non-routine, topics were discussed. Ellis requested that during the day each team take time to review their schedule and find a time when he could regularly join them to teach each week; the only day he could not teach was Wednesday, when the district principals met all day. Staff response to this request was slow; Brown had to repeat it the following day.

Another announcement concerned student interns from a local state college. After spending a few days at each elementary school in the district, the twelve interns would select schools they wanted to work in -- observing classes and aiding teachers -- until their semester ended at Christmas vacation.

Budget issues were also important. The voters had rejected the school budget in March, the township council had cut $125,000, and an additional $180,000 had been reduced in state aid. The Board of Education had devised ways of maintaining essential services, but also had to reduce some educational programs. Brown announced that the budget cuts would affect Lincoln Acres in the following ways: secretarial time would be limited, professional days for teachers would be decreased, vocal music and speech programs would be eliminated, and teachers leaving the district would not be replaced. To Brown, the most important loss was that in January computer terminals were to be removed from as-yet-undesignated elementary schools. He told the teachers:

> In order to keep ours we will have to document its use and show why we should have it. Other schools will not care, and others will fight us for it. We'll want to have ours. Whatever you do with the computer, let me know, so we can document it.

For Brown, the computer was the primary means of keeping track of student progress. Only a few teachers, however, had ever expressed interest in any application of the computer.

Perhaps the most important discussion of the first day concerned the proposed formation of the Parent-Teacher Association. Ellis announced that Sam was preparing a letter to inform parents on how they could participate in the school (for example, by donating household junk for use in art classes). Ellis intended to contact community people later in the week to begin formation of a PTA. He asked for teacher comments on the role they desired for the PTA. Essentially, the teachers said that they should be informed of PTA activities, because in past years, communication between parents and teachers had been poor. Thus many PTA programs, particularly fund-raising drives, were not successful. Ellis suggested that there be a teacher adviser on the PTA, to improve communication between the two groups and give the teachers influence in the association. He asked what types of activities teachers wanted the PTA to engage in. Several teachers suggested that the PTA pay for assemblies, a function it usually could perform well. Sam, an advocate of parent participation, said:

> I'd like to see it become significant so that teachers can participate. Fund raising is fine, but it should be something more. Parents and teachers should be involved. It can be a good communication device.

In reply, several teachers remarked that in their communities and in schools they previously taught in, the PTA had rarely been successful in involving both parents and teachers. Glenda responded, "One thing that would be useful would be some training or a workshop for parents." Others agreed, but were concerned whether a workshop could be meaningful; it was argued that if it wasn't, an entirely social PTA would be preferable. After the topic shifted slightly, Ellis ended the conversation on the PTA by saying:

> I can see some people are chomping at the bit to get a PTA going. We ought to get them involved and have some mea-ningful activity. I think I have something I can speak from now.

Parents, an irritant to the teachers during the summer, were to be actively included in the school as volunteers; only a few teachers, rather hesitantly, said they wanted a vigorous PTA. But as Glenda's suggestion for parent training suggests -- it had been her idea that the staff have a communications workshop -- some teachers did consider taking an active role in shaping the PTA.

2. The Second Preparation Day

On September 3, the second faculty preparation day, the first topic in the meeting was instructional objectives. Brown announced that one curriculum area a month would be added (for example, language in September, math in October, and so on). He also said he didn't want to see daily teacher plans, but that a record had to be kept by all teams of each child's work, so that he could "keep up" with what children were learning. Sam then explained the record-keeping system.

Several other issues were discussed: procedures for children's receiving free lunches, what to do with children who arrived early in the morning, problems with security in the building, and a time for weekly faculty meetings. Rebecca suggested that the faculty meet during lunch once a week. She reported that the result of an informal survey was that only person objected. The objection was from Jeanne, who explained that at her previous school, lunchtime faculty meetings often left her feeling upset and affected her teaching during the afternoon. After a short discussion, it was decided, more or less by Ellis alone, that they would meet once each week after school and that "the nuts and bolts of running this place" would be in written form, supplemented with occasional lunch-time meetings as needed.

The last item Ellis introduced for discussion was special instructional areas. Because of district-wide budget cuts, vocal music had been eliminated, and weekly allotments of art and physical education time were substantially diminished. Reduced special subjects meant that teachers would have less in-school time for planning during the week. Bert commented on this:

> I'm glad you brought that up. I went to a lot of open space schools in the state. The only one I saw and liked was Project A.B.C. in Meadows. The principal there gave teachers released time with specials.

Ellis said:

> You are in a better position than I am to get free time because the contract is being negotiated. Unless it is in there in black and white you'll never get it. You need planning time. The high school has it and it's about time we got it. But we don't even have anyone willing to be a building representative to WEA [the Washingtonville Education Association].

Someone suggested two other strategies for gaining planning time: writing a letter to, or making a public statement before the Board of Education.

Afraid that he might have been misunderstood, Ellis emphasized that the teachers needed planning time; he assured them that although the contract failed to specify released time he was looking for ways to create it. The meeting ended with Ellis' comment: "Well, I finally had a sign that it's really going to work. Last night I couldn't sleep."*

With their heads crammed with rules and regulations covering everything from where to park cars to the amount of milk money for a week, the teachers finished arranging their teaching areas for the last time before they would welcome the students. They worked quietly, and demonstrated no apprehension about the opening of school. It seems reasonable to speculate, though, that the faculty must have experienced some doubt over whether or not the conflict with parents would erupt again once school opened.

B. THE FIRST DAY OF SCHOOL#

When the school opened for students on September 4, 1975, all teaching areas were well prepared. Furniture was arranged in educationally-functional patterns; there were learning centers, and old sofas in "quiet areas," and most classrooms were elaborately decorated with bulletin boards, pictures and displays of books. Walls -- the symbol of the community's partial victory -- were only rearranged from those already in the building (see Diagram IV); several teaching spaces were separated with barriers of furniture. Overall, the impression the school gave was one of openness; it did not look like or have an atmosphere like that of a traditional school building, with long corridors and small classrooms on either side. Despite the few walls, when Lincoln Acres school opened for students, it was an open space school.

---

*This dry joke illustrates a characteristic aspect of Ellis' style: though he usually did not express warmth directly or easily, he did have an ironic sense of humor that often served well in his relationships with teachers.

#Once school opened for children, field work became more demanding; instead of a focused event (such as a meeting), the entire school was now the object of study. It was difficult to know where to look first, whether attempts at situational sampling were at all successful, and what issues should be selected for more-intensive data collection. Fortunately, even in the opened school, events such as faculty meetings, Board of Education meetings and informal meetings among teachers helped focus the research, since the topics of discussion indicated what was important to the participants. One key area, of course, was problems that students, teachers, and administrators faced, especially those that in some way -- either remotely or obviously -- tied the planning and its controversy to the actual operation of the school.

At 9:00 a.m. the doors were opened, and the crowd of students and parents that had been gathering since 8:30 a.m. poured into the school. Brown, Pennington and Regina Hanley greeted the students, directed them to their teachers and, in a few cases, when a child didn't know who his or her teacher was, found which class was the right one. Parents were allowed to enter the school, and many took the opportunity to inspect their children's classrooms. Michael Karalis was one of the few fathers to visit the school on this day. Visibly impressed, his evaluation was: "It looks like they did a good job. They really worked hard. It's always exciting to open a new school."

By 9:15 all children had been placed in classrooms, teachers were introducing themselves, and in some classes instruction had already begun. The kindergarten conducted twenty-minute orientation sessions for students and their parents; the teachers were busy explaining the program and answering questions the entire day. Before long, teachers -- each teacher had been asigned a "home-base" group of 25 children -- were escorting their students through the building. They explained the various rooms, and used the tour as an opportunity to instruct students in the rules and regulations of the school. The children were well behaved; many were already familiar with their teachers from experiences at Fernwood school in previous years.

By mid-morning, most of the faculty thought the day was going well. In Sam's view, "getting people in here today went more smoothly than it ever did at any other school, even the ones that were running for several years." Ellis was also surprised at how quickly the 350 students found their places. He commented sarcastically that the smooth entry was "part of the benefit of community involvement -- they know the teachers." Teachers, even though they experienced a little more tension than Sam and Ellis had, considered the first hours of school a success, for the most part. Dori Kraus commented that it was:

> A little rough in the beginning. Priscilla's children got out of hand. I couldn't talk with all of the noise so I went out in the hall. Now it's better. I need order: everybody doing things and none of this running around. I'll learn to relax a little and loosen up.

As she spoke, Dori looked around the teaching area. Priscilla and Wanda had taken their classes out-of-doors for recess, leaving her alone with her class; she was a little shocked by the implications of her statement. Rebecca Barone, while monitoring her class as they played a game, observed:

> At first I felt a little shaky. I didn't know what to do. Now it's all right. Compared to other first days, today is good. It's good to know you have support and are not alone in a classroom by yourself. I'm a lot looser because of that. Usually, on the first day I give the kids a lot of work to do.

Near the end of the session, which was a half day ending at 1:00 p.m., most of the classes were playing games, and the noise in the instructional area was increasing steadily. A few children were crawling on the floor, running around, or in general, not doing "school-like" activities. To the researcher, who was educated in a grim elementary school in a working-class neighborhood in the 1950's (which was probably the experience of many Lincoln Acres parents), the school was beginning to have a "permissive" quality. Just as the researcher had written the word "permissive" in his notebook, a parent passed by and said:

> It's so quiet here I can't believe it. My house is noisier. A lot of parents are going home after they take their kid to the kindergarten saying it's so quiet. They're ashamed of the big stink they caused. It's quieter than my house. At least it seems so.

Another aspect of the school that impressed the observer -- even before Rebecca's remark, "Usually, on the first day I give the kids a lot of work to do" -- was that in most cases, though time was spent going over rules and in academic work, substantial emphasis was placed on introducing the children to their classmates and teachers, and on "enjoyment" experiences, such as art, dancing and pleasure reading. As Rebecca's comment acknowledged, teachers ordinarily not only "lay down rules" but also, "let them know they're here to work" during the first days of school. The folk wisdom is that if this pattern isn't followed and the teacher is too lenient at the beginning of the year, later on it will be difficult to control the class. Rebecca implied that this practice was foregone because of support from other teachers, reducing the need for tight control. We can also speculate that it would have been difficult to behave sternly toward the students in front of other adults without undermining the humane, "caring" self-image the teachers desired.

School ended for the day at 1:00 p.m., and the children left quickly and as free of problems as when they had entered. Several teachers congregated in Sally's, Jane's and Katie's area, which was in the middle of the school, and had the following hurried exchange:

> Jane: The kids were together. It went well.

> Jeanne: Yeah, the work we did was worth it. The kids were good.

> Sam to Dori: Did you make it O.K.?

> Dori: It was the worst first day in six years, but I got through it.

> Sally: The kids were fine. My Wright school kids would have been all over the place.

> Wanda to Sally: How was your day?

> Sally: Much better than I expected, but not great. How was yours?

Wanda: Fine, but I don't know about my teammates. Dori /who had left the area/ is upset, and Priscilla got some wild kids.

Sally to Bert: How was your day?

Bert: It was neat. It was good. It was good to get back.

Sally: Ellis seemed pretty happy today.

Jane: Yeah, he did.

After cleaning up the teaching spaces, rearranging furniture, and hurriedly preparing for the next day, the teachers had a meeting in the teachers' lounge at 1:30. They were in a good mood, and joked mainly about non-school incidents. Ellis began the meeting by saying that he had not noticed many things wrong with the school; he suggested, however, that the bicycle racks should be moved to the side of the building, and that student entrance in the morning would probably be smoother if the intermediate children used a side door.

When Ellis asked if there was anything else to discuss, a variety of questions and requests surfaced. These included operational aspects of the school: whether pencil sharpeners were available, if broken glass in the playground could be removed, and what to do with children when it rained at lunch time. When Ellis couldn't answer a question (for instance, the one about attendance procedures), he called in a person who could (in this instance, Monica, the secretary). In this meeting there were no major complaints or difficulties mentioned, and the minor problems discussed seemed to have been satisfactorily solved. Ellis ended the first faculty meeting of the operating school with another cheerfully ironic comment: "Well, it all went so well today that we're planning to have school again tomorrow."

To the faculty, the first day of school was a success.

C. THE SECOND DAY

Nothing was significantly different on the second day; children entered the building quickly, classes began, and by 1:00 p.m. school was finished for the week, since it was Friday. As on the previous day, there was almost no team teaching; children reported to a "home-base" teacher, and remained with that teacher for the entire day. One slight exception was that, at one point in the morning, Bert's, Glenda's and Rebecca's classes were combined and Bert taught a math lesson to the entire group while the other two teachers observed. In Jane's, Sally's and Katie's classes the only hint of team teaching that day was a recess when the teachers jointly supervised all the children. During the recess the noise from this team reached a pitch that could be heard in Alan's and Jeanne's teaching area.

The delay in team teaching was the result of Ellis' request that for the first few days each teacher spend time only with the children assigned directly to him or her. The purpose was to assist student adjustment to a new situation, and to enable teachers to become familiar with the children as individuals. Even with this "traditional" teacher-pupil arrangement, the second day of school was relaxed. Children were engaged in a variety of activities, and although the noise level interfered with other classes at times, there were no serious behavior or operating problems.

In the course of the morning Sam and Ellis walked through the building several times. They stopped and talked with students, watched a lesson for a short time, or simply looked in on a class. Neither one intervened in the operation of classrooms.

D. THE FIRST FULL WEEK OF SCHOOL

1. Monday

Monday, September 8, was the first complete day of school; students arrived at 9:00 a.m. and left school at 3:00 p.m., with 11:30-12:30 for lunch and recess. During the course of the morning there was a wide range of activities in each classroom: testing, games, outdoor recreation, lectures on rules and behavior, and "bookkeeping" tasks (such as sorting those children who ate lunch in school from those who didn't). In several primary classrooms there were multiple activities at a single time (for example, work at different learning centers), while in others, mostly the intermediates, activities tended to be organized for an entire class. The cumulative noise of children talking occasionally interfered with more-focused activities in neighboring teaching areas (such as giving an oral phonics test).

That morning, Alex Georgiades, an active opponent of open space education during the summer, toured the school with Sam Pennington and appeared to be pleased with what he saw. As it happened, when he went into the intermediate classroom where his son was a student, the entire class was taking a test in a situation similar to that of a self-contained classroom. Another parent, Mrs. Charles Frisch, helped Regina Hanley organize the library. Mrs. Frisch had worked as a volunteer in the Fernwood library for several years.

Teacher evaluations of the morning varied. Sally felt as though it was going well, but too slowly:

> I just have to be patient. I want to get the whole show on the road too quickly. But I have to remember that the kids can't handle it all at once.

Regina, who except for Ellis was the only faculty member to have participated in the opening of a new open space elementary school, reflected:

> Last year at Janesville we had all kinds of pre-opening meetings and not much was accomplished. They worked out schedules for which classes would tour the building on the first day, etc. It was chaos. That wasn't so here, and we had no meetings.

For Jeanne, noise from nearby classes was a problem; several of her students mentioned the noise and asked when walls were coming. She continued:

> Some parents have come to me and said that the place still looks pretty open. One thing that I couldn't anticipate and still can't figure out is that at first we had a space in the middle with no furniture and we had all the kids meet there on the floor. They didn't like it and asked if they could sit on chairs. I thought it would be a big deal for them!

In Katie's view, events proceeded as planned, but "there are still some bugs." Rebecca Barone said:

> Things went well this morning, but a little disorganized. No, not disorganized -- unorganized, though. The kids don't seem to need order as much as we do.

> Laura, the intern, said that it went well. She said that she expected chaos. I asked her why and she said that a teacher in another school told her that kids were running around here and that it is in chaos. I don't know how the rumor got started. It must have been by someone who hasn't been here.

The rumor that the school was chaotic after only two half-days of operations is striking. It indicates that curiosity about the new school, as might be expected, was high.

After lunch, the activities in the teaching areas were similar to those in the morning. Toward the end of the day, the noise level in several areas, especially NBC's, increased considerably. This prompted a lecture on behavior for all the children in the NBC pod, shortly before school ended. As the children sat on the floor, Sally intoned:

> There are some rules that we all must learn. When you make noise it causes problem for others. In a school this size you have to work with us. If you disturb us you leave, it's that simple. You may not disturb your friends, or me, or Miss Baylor, or Miss Neustadt. That's a rule that's never broken. Do you want to talk over there? [Some children are talking -- Sally waits for quiet.]

> Katie: We let everybody go to an activity area today. At the Wendy house [a play house] people didn't clean up. They didn't at other areas also. These things are in the school but they don't have to be, we can give them to other classes. I don't want to stay after school to clean up. Tomorrow when we say clean up, clean up your area.

> Sally: I hate to end the day like this. I think we should sing a song before we go so I'm not grouchy. But there are some

rules we need. Do not disturb your friends. If you do you're out of the class. Does everybody think that's fair? [The children answer "yes" in unison.]

Katie: One other thing. I saw some people cleaning up when they didn't have to [reads a list of children who had cleaned up.] That was very good.

Sally: I liked when we came into school this morning and everybody sat down right away. What are some of the things you liked? [Kids raise their hands and tell about the things they liked (the rabbit, the Wendy house, etc.)]

Sally: What I like best is that we're sitting here like a happy family -- nobody's pushing or shouting. Do you have anything to say? [Jane answers "no."]

After a song, the class was dismissed.

Another team was finishing a similar rule-reinforcing session with their class. A teacher said to the students, "I felt as though I was teaching in Yankee Stadium." Sam, who observed this lecture along with the researcher, explained: "We found we had to lay down the law for two weeks last year before things really settled in." Earlier in the afternoon, Dori gave a similar lecture to her students.

So the first full day of school ended with some teachers assuming a more traditional, disciplinarian-like, role toward their students than they had desired. And adjustment to the architectural features of the school was more difficult than had been anticipated.

After dismissal, the faculty gathered in the teachers' lounge for the weekly meeting. Ellis presided, and began with an announcement that he would start reading student math objectives checklists (also known as profiles) by the end of the month. He also raised the related issue of report cards, saying: "I don't have any planned yet, and I'd like to hear suggestions from you." The first comment was from Priscilla, who asked what the results of the community survey had shown about parental preferences. Ellis said the findings were that parents were strongly against grades, that they wanted high teacher contact, and that they wanted immediate notification if something was wrong.* A lengthy debate began over how

---

*Ellis' main responses correctly reflected the findings he had presented to the Board of Education. The data, in response to the question, "How do you like to see your child's progress reported?" were:

"Some written system other than letter grades or numbers	72%
"Conferences with the teacher(s)"	54%
"Letter grades," or "Numbers"	10%
Other responses	11%

The data do not show, however, that parents "wanted immediate notification if something was wrong."

frequently report cards should be issued, and whether they should be supplemented with parent-teacher conferences. Brown asked if the teachers wanted to ask parents about frequency and type of reporting. The faculty's opinion was to delay involving parents. Brown suggested:

> One thing I'll throw out is -- when I throw out ideas don't pay them any abnormal respect -- when I worked in another school the teachers worked out their own report cards. Each had a different one. The only thing was that they had to be approved by the office mainly on clarity, and in some cases the teacher hadn't had enough experience and needed some guidance. I think we can do that team-wide, and I think Regina is right about having something to be able to use as a basis with parents.

Sam volunteered to aid anyone in designing a report card. Jeanne made the suggestion, which was agreed to by the faculty, that report cards be the same for an entire grade level to avoid parents' wondering: "how come she got a grade in a particular area and my child didn't?"

The meeting then turned to an announcement by Regina concerning films for classroom use, and Sam arranged a meeting for the following day for teams interested in having the college interns work with them. SWEP (a high school student work experience program) and the way it would be used in Lincoln Acres school was discussed briefly. Then Brown announced:

> I would like to get the parent-teacher group begun soon by having an open house next week. I checked on your medical records before and found there were no weak hearts.
>
> Bert: I just got one -- it's a little early for me. [Other faculty members make mock nasty comments about the parents.]

The open house activities were to include the presentation of a piano to the school by LAHA, and the formation of a PTA steering committee. The format of the open house was of paramount concern to the teachers. The alternative strategies proposed were to permit parents to wander through the building and ask questions, or to structure the evening by having teachers make presentations in their teaching areas. There was no clear preference for either plan. After more discussion, Ellis said that what he heard from the teachers was that they wanted to be able to tell parents what they were doing. With this the structured arrangement was settled on. When asked if more open houses would be planned, Brown said:

> I hope only once and then I'm out of the PTA planning. I would hope that the teachers involved are clever enough to work on the thing and guide them. They may want one again in the fall.

Problems with finding a mutually-agreeable day (by now typical) resulted in setting the open house for Thursday, September 18.

A fairly long and detailed discussion of lunch money collection procedures followed; it appeared to answer all questions. The meeting ended with Ellis' announcement that teacher interaction films would be arriving soon, and that the music teacher (who would be leaving the school system in a few weeks) would offer a Kodaly workshop for the faculty if they were interested. Arrangements were also made for Wanda to run a Cuisenaire workshop the Monday after the Kodaly workshop. It was Ellis' plan to conduct professional development workshops during the Monday meeting time, and to restrict procedural meetings to lunchtime. When the meeting ended at 4:40, teachers returned to their instructional areas to finish cleaning and preparing for the following day.

2. The First Week Continues

School routines for student entrance, exit, lunch, and discipline worked smoothly in most instances; the problems that did occur were easily and quickly solved. Instructional patterns remained stable too; the primary grades typically had more variety in instructional activities at any given time than the intermediate levels, which spent a substantial amount of time on written assessment tests.

Team teaching, an ill-defined concept, was still limited. By the end of the week, the only observable difference between teaching techniques at Lincoln Acres school and "traditional" self-contained classrooms was that on occasion the BJW and NBC teams had students rotate among teachers. For instance, Bert taught social studies, Rebecca math and Glenda language arts to a group of 25 students each. After a half-hour lesson, each teacher presented the same material to another group of students. In other teams, particularly in the primary grades, learning centers were spread throughout the area; they were supplied with self-instructional materials that required minimal monitoring from teachers.

Another instructional innovation began on Friday afternoon, when Ellis taught in a classroom. He spent nearly an hour explaining rudimentary science experiments to a group of MTK students. Brown sat on the floor with the ten children, many of whom were at first reluctant to join his class. During the lesson he never lectured to the group, but instead demonstrated and worked individually and with small groups. He seemed to enjoy himself, and after overcoming their initial fear, the children relaxed too.

College interns continued to observe classes in all schools in the district, including Lincoln Acres. (In the following week, they would be placed in the school where they would remain for the semester.) In addition, plans for the open house went forward; Barbara Berger, on Ellis' request, checked with parents and found that Thursday, September 18 was acceptable. And the president of the Board of Education, Irena Farrell, toured the school. She appeared to be pleased by what she observed.

Throughout the first full week of school, teachers arrived early in the morning and often stayed until 5:30 p.m. Several ate lunch at their desks, while they corrected student papers or planned activities for the afternoon. Others spent Saturdays in the school planning instructional activities. In general, the time teachers invested in preparation for daily school activities far exceeded what they were contractually obligated to spend.

E. PROBLEMS BEGIN DEVELOPING

Noise continued to be a problem in some areas of the school, especially for Alan and Jeanne. Another, more serious problem developed during the first week: Wanda, Priscilla and Dori had difficulty "team teaching."

Wanda, Priscilla and Dori, the MTK team, had taught for several years at Fernwood school, where they had shared materials and ideas. They requested that they come as a group to Lincoln Acres. (Among the other teams, only BJW had selected their teammates.)

By Tuesday of the first full week of school, however, relations among the members of the MTK team had deteriorated; they all felt that what they had planned wasn't working. According to Dori, the problem was differences in personality and educational philosophy, in particular, disagreement over what could be expected in the first days of school from first grade students (for example, in reading instruction). Another issue was differential amounts of time spent in evening preparation.

On Wednesday, the MTK team planned to remain after school to discuss the problems. Hesitant to involve Ellis, they invited Sam to join them, but he was unable to attend because of a graduate course. Instead they met alone until 5:15 that night. The meeting was tearful and uncomfortable. For the time being, though, the problems were at least partially resolved, and the team appeared to be willing to confront and manage them; they also decided to meet the following week with Ellis and Sam.

1. (Summarizing Comments)

Overall, during the first week many traditional interactions took place between teachers and students. In almost every team, teachers found themselves, at least once, either punishing or threatening punishment of the entire class. It did not appear that these reluctant departures from a "humanistic" approach to education permanently marred teacher-pupil interaction. Indeed, after the first week there were infrequent circumstances that required student "disciplining."

Children were not the only ones for whom rules were set; rules of behavior for the teachers were established. These included signing in, participation in faculty meetings, and the myriad rules regulating daily activities such as milk money collection, attendance and fire drills.

Finally, although some parents wandered through the building this week, they were not considered a problem by teachers, and plans were made to introduce the school to parents and to form a PTA. Negative feelings toward parents, while not eliminated, did not increase.

In sum, the first full week of school, while successful in most areas, also revealed some potential difficulties in the social system of the school. Noise levels were increasing, and one teaching team was experiencing interpersonal strains.

F. THE SECOND WEEK OF SCHOOL

1. New Personnel

A major event in the second week of school was the addition of new personnel to the school. Six interns from Reade State College had selected Lincoln Acres school to fulfill their student teaching requirements.* They were to work until Christmas vacation with teachers who requested them. Each member of NBC had an intern, BJW had two, and MTK had one. The BB team and the kindergarten teachers requested that they not be given an intern.

The other additional personnel were parent volunteers. Thirty-six had responded to a notice sent home by Regina requesting help in the media center. Somewhat surprised at the large turnout, Regina thought that many would have to be redistributed throughout other areas of the school (for example, the office, or possibly classrooms). These were not full-time volunteers, but mothers who were able to spend a few hours each week in the school.

2. The Teams

By Thursday of the second week, what had seemed like progress in solving the problems of the MTK team turned out not to have been. At lunch, the team met with Ellis and there seemed to be movement toward an understanding in at least one important area: who would teach reading to which groups. The team stayed until 5:30 that night, reorganizing their program. For example, they decided that Priscilla would teach reading to students from both of the other teachers' home-base groups. But this agreement did not last. Dori's view was that instead of doing team teaching they were actually three self-contained classrooms -- but without walls to eliminate noise.

All the other teams were gradually attempting to expand their use of team teaching. More use of combined classes (across both grade levels and teachers), less-confining supervision of students, and individualization of instruction were emerging. No serious problems were evident in any team other than MTK.

3. Student-Teacher Interaction

The ways most teachers dealt with students during the early weeks of school were similar. First, in these initial two weeks -- and later on --

---

*They accounted for half of the interns assigned to the district. They had spent several days in each elementary school before making a selection.

there was rarely any attempt by a teacher to segregate students according to sex. For instance, when children were organized to go to another room, or to leave the building, boys were not required to stand in one line and girls in another. A second similarity was that teachers did not require regimentation of students. Lining up (except for hot lunches), going to the lavatory as an entire group, sitting in straight rows and other student control devices were not present. As we shall see, absence of these traditional control mechanisms does not mean that discipline and pressure for conformity were not present.

A third similarity was that in all teams lecturing to the whole class, with the teacher as the sole focus of attention, was minimal. Even when the teacher was the point of attention, instruction was delivered on an individual or a small group level. It usually took the form of a dialogue between teachers and students, instead of being entirely directed from teacher to students.

There was also a school-wide practice of having groups of students work on a variety of activities at one time, often without assistance from a teacher. In fact, this aspect of the school -- which probably encouraged the tendency toward dialogue -- was, by the third week, one of the chief products of team teaching.

Teams controlled their students with generally similar techniques. The whole-class lectures of the first few days had given way to routine. During the course of the day, student behavior was mostly regulated by oral or written operating procedures ("Only three people leave the room at one time to go to the bathroom," "Five minutes before art period is over, clean-up time.") and so on. Initially, these were often put in the form of commands from the teachers, but they became so much a part of the school routine that after a short time -- and occasional reminders to individuals -- their meaning was not questioned by either students or teachers. Thus, many of the explicit rules of the classroom became un-noticed norms governing both student and teacher behavior.

Some aspects of overt discipline varied among teams, however, as well as among members of teams. Dori, Wanda and Priscilla (MTK) spent a considerable amount of time during the first weeks demonstrating the correct way to do a variety of things. The NBC team developed a more laissez faire posture toward behavior in the classroom than MTK's, although their children were slightly older, and they did not hesitate to punish individual children. In the intermediate teams, the men controlled their classes by the use of great amounts of energy in their teaching delivery: they were highly entertaining speakers, moving rapidly about the room, and in general, exuding enthusiasm. The female intermediate teachers were much more low-keyed than their male teammates, and exercised control by having established firm, and in some cases, non-verbal rules. Jeanne, in particular, seldom had to discipline a child: her mannerisms alone, including her facial expressions, were effective control mechanisms.

In several respects the patterns of student-teacher interaction in Lincoln Acres school were in sharp contrast with those in "traditional" classrooms, which place more emphasis on uniformity of behavior and tend to focus attention on the teacher. Clearly, there were no authoritarian teachers here.

4. Student Behavior

Somewhat surprisingly, the children adjusted to the new school almost immediately. Among the probable reasons were that most of them had attended Fernwood school and were familiar with education in Washingtonville, as well as with several of the teachers who had come from Fernwood. They also knew each other. (On the first day of school many children in an intermediate class changed the teacher's predesignated seating arrangement, so they could be near friends.)

The freedom of movement granted to students by teachers (and made possible by the open space) did not seem to be abused. During observations, there were few fights, running or other disruptive incidents. After the first weeks, it appeared that distractions from noise and movement in other classrooms did not affect students' behavior or ability to concentrate to any significant extent. Noise probably bothered the teachers more than it did the students.

In the kindergarten, often a difficult transition period for many children, the twenty-minute introductory sessions for students and parents appeared to have made life in school less threatening for many of the five-year-olds. There were few tearful incidents when they were separated from their mothers.

Overall, student behavior in the school was extremely good. This was probably as much a reflection on the socialization processes of the family and previous school experiences as anything the school personnel did or didn't do.

5. The First Open House

On Thursday, September 18, there was a lunchtime faculty meeting for dealing with administrative matters, and with preparation for that evening's open house. Brown began the meeting by reminding the teachers that Monday faculty meetings would be devoted to "professional growth" workshops. He also emphasized that teachers were responsible for reading posted administrative notices. Other announcements covered field trips, special services, problems with lunch money counts, a reminder that in the event of absence plans for substitutes should be available, and a request that teachers conduct an inventory of supplies.

After these items Ellis asked, "Does anybody want to know anything about tonight?" The sole question was: "What is the format?" Ellis explained that teachers would be introduced to parents in the gymnasium, where LAHA would make its presentation of a piano. Following this, the meeting would shift to the instructional area for teacher presentations. Then parents would return to the gym to begin organizing the PTA. He mentioned that it wouldn't bother him if teachers left after their presentations. He warned, however:

> In four or five months I don't want handwringing that the PTA isn't good. Get involved now and we should be able to have a good resource.

The meeting continued with an announcement about after-school volleyball for teachers, an unsuccessful attempt to find representatives to WEA, schedule-change information from special subject teachers, and sign-up procedures for use of the gym. Ellis reiterated several "nuts-and-bolts" procedures: lunch-counts should be sent to the office quickly, attendance should be in after lunch, several people had failed to sign in that morning. Finally, he asked if teachers had enough math profiles.

    With the parents. That night, Ellis Brown greeted the parents and introduced the teachers by having them stand as he called their names. He explained that in a short time parents could examine the teaching areas, until a bell rang for reassembly in the gymnasium. Then Barbara Berger, who substituted for the president of LAHA, presented a piano to the school. Immediately afterward, Ellis told the parents they were free to go to the instructional area.

    Once in the instructional area, there was some confusion; parents wandered from area to area looking for their child's teacher. At least one parent wondered if the school was "always this confused." Eventually, however, parents formed groups around their children's teachers, and listened to descriptions of the daily educational program.

    In the NBC team, Sally provided introductory remarks for her group, including an offer to answer any questions, because "there have been lots of fears about what the school was going to be like." Katie quickly explained the daily procedures, which essentially involved three hours devoted to academic instruction, during which children rotated among teachers for lessons in reading, arithmetic and language arts. Other periods during the day, she said, were spent in learning centers, where students worked by themselves on exercises designed to reinforce the earlier lessons.

    Parents' questions were mainly about the way rotation among teachers worked, and the methods used for teaching reading. After a more detailed explanation, rotation methods seemed understood satisfactorily. But even after Sally described the reading program -- an interaction method -- and said that the primary benefit was that children enjoyed it, parents still had questions. In reply to a parent's questions about the math program, the teachers said they were awaiting the arrival of textbooks from England, but in the meantime were teaching from other materials.

    One mother, in front of the entire group, asked Sally:

What has been going on all year [sic]? My child comes home
and says she's done nothing and comes home with nothing.

Sally suggested that they discuss it later in private. (This discussion, which was only semi-private, focused on misinformation the child had passed between Sally and the mother, mainly, that the family was moving soon. The mother couldn't understand how this could have happened. The conversation ended after Sally explained that the year had just begun, that things were still being sorted out, and that more work would be coming home soon.)

    At another point in the presentation, Sally, who acted as a spokesperson for her teammates, told the parents that the children used notebooks for their assignments. When parents looked through their children's notebooks, many found that nothing or very little had been written in them. Several asked the teachers what should have been in them. The answer was that work was just beginning, and that many children had not yet used their notebooks.

In the MTK team, each teacher (Priscilla, Wanda, Dori) met with the parents of the students in her own home-base group; they did not meet in a total group or present themselves as a team. As in the NBC team, a main area for questions was the reading program. The MTK teachers dealt with the questions somewhat more convincingly. Other questions ranged from concerns with milk money to playground supervision during recess. During the course of the evening, Wanda asked for assistance in the classroom, and 25 mothers volunteered. Dori and Priscilla also received numerous offers of parental help.

In the BJW team, Bert, in a highly animated style, explained his team's program to the parents as Rebecca listened (Glenda was not present). His presentation was so detailed that the bell signaling return to the gymnasium rang before he was two-thirds through. He quickly summarized, requested parent volunteers for the classroom, and invited parents to speak with him and with Rebecca (many did). Afterward Bert and Rebecca discussed how it had gone: they agreed it was successful, but that Bert ought to guard against becoming the spokesman for the team.

Parents drifted into the gymnasium, where coffee and cake were being served. The half hour provided for meeting with teachers had not been enough; many parents had remained in the instructional area to ask questions. Those parents in the gym -- about half -- conversed mainly about topics other than the school. One father, who attended most meetings and had earlier presented himself to Ellis as a representative of the Oriental community in Lincoln Acres, said he remained opposed to open space; he feared that too many children would not receive the attention they needed. Charles Frisch said he had not been able to get any information from his son on what was going on in school, so he wasn't certain what to think of it yet. He said, however, that from what he saw, the school "looked good." For the most part, with the exception of a few skeptical questions directed toward the NBC team, parents seemed to be pleased with their introduction to the actual operation of the new school.

At 9:40, Ellis ended the formal part of the open house with the following invitation:

> I encourage you to come back when the school is in session. I
> know that may not be convenient for a lot of you, but on a day
> off or some other time come by.

He then asked parents interested in joining the PTA steering committee to sign a pad, so they could be contacted when the group began to work, which would be soon. Until shortly after 10:00 p.m. parents continued to socialize in the school gym.

Teacher evaluation of the evening was positive. Most thought it went very well, though a few felt pressured. No teacher viewed the evening as unsuccessful. Jeanne, for example, thought that "the parents were

enthusiastic and said that their kids learned a lot and liked school."
Somewhat less positive was Jane's comment:

> I answered all questions affirmatively. I felt a little hassled.
> The parents have high expectations of the teachers and
> students -- they always do.

Sam elaborated on what he thought was a successful evening; in a discussion
with Bert and Rebecca, he noted that the school had already received good
reviews from Biddle and others such as David Hauptmann and Peter Rand,
both principals of schools in Washingtonville district. He continued, "If we
project a positive image we can help change the district." From the
teachers' perspective, their first encounter with parents in the open school
had been more positive than their contacts during the planning stages,
especially during the summer workshop.

G. (ANALYSIS AND COMMENTARY)

1. The State of the System

The first weeks of school went rather smoothly, as is often the case
when reasonably careful practical planning has taken place, and when all
stakeholders -- parents, students, administrators, and teachers -- are, for
the moment, suspending criticism and actively "willing" the new enterprise
to get off to a good start.

These background supports for the success of the launch were
augmented by a thorough and persistent "rule orientation" on the part of
both Ellis and the teachers. Procedures for everything from appropriate
entrances through lunch money collection, teacher sign-out, parking, record-
keeping, meeting times, and fire drills were put clearly in place. And in the
classroom, clear rules regulating noise-making, orderliness, disturbance of
others, and cleanliness were set forth by teachers and enforced.

It seemed clear, however, that the rules served primarily as a way to
ward off potentially chaotic situations, and not primarily as repressive
devices to maintain administrative or teacher power. The approach to
students seen in classes was predominantly non-regimented; a good deal of
variety was permitted within the general constraints of the rules. The
learning technologies used (small groups, self-paced learning materials as
often as large-group lecturing or demonstration) were keyed to the diverse
learning needs of individuals. The faculty had little uncertainty about their
colleagues' commitment to this style of teaching (probably because they
had spent more than a month working together), and they supported each
other in maintaining a humane approach to students that was congruent with
their initial vision for the school. Students, for their part, seemed to enjoy
the school and functioned well within it, after some initial minor
disruptiveness, which was rapidly absorbed by teacher rule-making.

Certain aspects of the teaching technology of the school at this point
are worth noting. First, the start-up was probably aided by the procedure of

teaching children as relatively self-contained groups for the first few days, before the methods involving teacher division of labor were used. More coherence for children probably resulted, and a faculty with little prior experience in team teaching could move into it gradually. Second, the emphasis on objectives in each major subject area, plus systematic record-keeping, offered several potential advantages: sustained individual attention to children, closer monitoring of instructional progress by Ellis and Sam, and justification of the program to parents. Third, the idea that each team could develop its own report card format supported not only diversity, but the idea of the team as the basic working unit of the school.

Most of the teams appeared to be functioning well, with one exception. In the MTK team, conflict, self-defined as occurring at the "personality" and the "philosophical" level (both, it can be noted, notoriously impervious to improvement efforts), was already sharp. Though the team worked on their conflicts, and received requested help from Ellis and Sam, the results were uneven; the difficulties tended to remain.

The early and natural problems of adjusting to open space (dealing with noise, primarily) did not seem to be major for either students or faculty.

The personal investment of the teachers was clearly high. Two faculty meetings weekly were seen as important. Teachers came early and often worked until 5:30, finishing the day's work and preparing for the next; some came in on Saturday. No one complained of overload, nor of exceeding contractual hours.

Ellis' administrative style at this point emphasized several things: detailed rule-making; continued sharing of information in faculty meetings (though not of major decisions, such as whether to have an open house, or a PTA, or to include interns); presentation of himself as actively interested in instructional matters (e.g., teaching several classes, as well as stressing the objectives and record-keeping); and continued treatment of the teams as the basic instructional unit (e.g., decentralizing the report card decision to them).

2. Actualization

Generally speaking, there did not seem to be any substantial slippages between the plans made during the summer and their early implementation. The way space was organized, the preliminary lesson plans, and the actual details of the start-up seemed congruent with what each team had developed: the model of "operators as planners" seemed to be working fairly well.

The communications workshop probably influenced the early implementation primarily by setting the norm that full internal communication was important (hence the acceptance of two weekly faculty meetings); it may also have made life in the MTK team more difficult by setting such high standards for cooperation and communication within teams that options such as letting individuals teach their own way were downplayed. It is of interest that the idea of a training workshop for parents was suggested; at least for Glenda, who proposed it, taking a "learning" orientation to parents' participation in the school was desirable.

3. Political Stabilization

Teachers still felt rather hesitant, perhaps naturally, about involvement of parents. Examples include Bert's comment about "having a weak heart", reservations about the PTA, resistance to involving parents in report card planning, and the fact that the faculty left it to Ellis to suggest what the format of the open house should be. Nevertheless, after Ellis' and Sam's initiative that informed parents on how they could participate in the school, teachers from several teams, and Regina for the media center, did actively invite parents to volunteer their assistance in the instructional program.

It appears that teachers still felt wary and potentially embattled, and wanted to avoid serious collaboration with parents. Their endorsing the idea of parent volunteers leads to our speculation that teachers also believed that having parents as aides would keep them subordinate to teacher expertise, and hoped that the parents' seeing the "reality" of the school would coopt them and change their negative attitudes.

On the parents' side, there seemed to be a reasonable positiveness, a wish to believe the best of the school as it started up, along with a continued motivation to ask hard questions of the teachers (which the teachers in turn tended to experience as "hassling").

Despite Ellis' encouragement to the teachers to become more active and demanding toward the district on the issue of protecting planning time, they did not do so. In fact, there continued to be difficulty in recruiting a faculty member to serve as representative to the district teachers' association, which had the prime role in negotiating such issues. Once again, the teachers seemed to prefer a non-political, environment-avoidant stance.

Generally, political issues in relation to other schools, or to the central office, seemed minimal at this point; Sam briefly reported positive reaction from these parts of the environment.

4. Knowledge Utilization

An illustrative incident in this domain involved the issue of reporting to parents. Although "report cards," parent conferences and other devices to handle parent-teacher interaction on matters of student progress appear in every school in America, and a good deal of knowledge and technology exists, no explicit suggestion was made that it should even be referred to, let alone borrowed or adapted. Instead, Ellis suggested that the teams develop their own methods, citing a previous experience of his. We might infer that Ellis was more preoccupied with building team ownership and acceptance of reporting methods than with the technical quality of what was used, or believed that internal resources were actually fully adequate to the task. It is possible, too, that he wanted to maintain an image of basing decision-making power with teams (and the faculty as a whole, who were tacitly being invited to approve the decentralized policy); note that he also said, "When I throw out ideas don't pay them any abnormal respect." He did protect a small place for the authority of position and expertise: "The only thing was that they had to be approved by the office, mainly on clarity, and in some cases the teacher hadn't had enough experience and needed some guidance." Though this is only one incident, it is not trivial; the problem of report cards is an important one for school-community contact, and much past knowledge exists.

5. Summary of Key Decisions

As suggested above, one of the key decisions during this period was that of decentralizing the report card issue to the teams.

The decision made by Ellis to launch the PTA, largely in conventional terms, and the associated decision to have an open house almost immediately, reversed the past tendency to avoid contact with the community until pressures mounted.

It is unclear whether an explicit, school-wide decision was ever made to invite parents to volunteer their services during school time. There are some relevant facts: willingness to work with volunteers was a selection criterion for teachers; the idea appeared in the summer workshop proposal; a question on this general topic appeared in the parent survey carried out at the beginning of the summer workshop; and Ellis reported at the last meeting before the opening of school that Sam was writing parents to explain how they could participate. Regina, and members of at least two teams, asked for parent volunteers, getting a "surprisingly" vigorous response. So it must have been clear at some point to the faculty that having parents directly involved during the school day was seen as desirable and legitimate. As we shall see, this tacit "decision" was to have far-reaching effects.

Finally, the decision to have two regular faculty meetings a week, one for administrative matters and one for professional growth, was important; it assured a continuing forum for faculty interaction and problem-solving efforts, and it dramatized Ellis' commitment to staff "learning" (that is, to professional matters, as contrasted with "nuts and bolts").

So, in general, the start-up of the Lincoln Acres school was reasonably smooth: the craft was off the runway and the journey begun. What next?

8

SCHOOL REORGANIZATION

Adjustments in a new organization, or, for that matter, in a mature organization, are to be expected. In any stage of organizational growth, change in social relations -- whether it is nearly imperceptible or total -- accompanies installation of new technical procedures, personnel realignments or other adjustments aimed at increasing goal attainment. Sources of organizational change may be either internal processes, or forces outside of the organization -- or their interaction.

This chapter provides a narrative of the changes in the social system of Lincoln Acres school that began shortly after the first open house for parents, and continued until Christmas vacation. (Actually, as we shall see in later chapters, the organization changed at a rapid rate throughout the entire year.) Our analysis will discuss the sources and pressures for change, and provide explanations.

A. THE THIRD WEEK OF SCHOOL

The week began with the same general instructional arrangements that had been used since school opened. Monday afternoon was the first faculty workshop, a presentation of Cuisenaire techniques for teaching mathematical concepts led by Wanda. Most teachers had already used Cuisenaire rods in their classes, but nevertheless found the workshop useful. Professional growth, a need that most teachers had hoped to fulfill, was the main aim of this and other after-school workshops.

1. Changes in the Teams' Work

The BB team. During the early part of the week, the BB teachers rearranged the furniture in their teaching area so that it formed a wall, varying from waist-high cabinets to seven-foot tall closets, between their space and the space occupied by the NBC team. The rearrangement was an attempt to reduce the visual distractions they had experienced from other areas. It also created a sense of privacy in their teaching area, though it did not reduce the noise level from other groups. Permanent library shelves also arrived during the week; they further reduced visibility between the media center and the BB and BJW teams. Overall, the new furniture arrangements had a minimal effect on teaching conditions; visual distractions were reduced but the problem of noise remained. Diagram V, next page, illustrates the new furniture arrangements.

The NBC team. In the NBC team, students were in small groups throughout the area, working on a wide variety of teacher-directed and self-guided learning activities. With the exception of some relocation of furniture and learning centers, no changes had been made in the area. However, the team was planning to begin a new program phase on the following Monday. Several parents had requested a more structured approach to reading; the change was made primarily to satisfy their requests. The new program involved dividing the children into three groups of 27, with a teacher and intern for each group. Within these heterogeneous groups, there would be small homogeneous groups for instruction in reading.* Eventually, it was planned, heterogeneity would be re-established; in Sally's opinion, "elitism is a bad thing." The teachers said they were "comfortable" with the parents' request, and felt that the program they had devised would be a good starting point, since parents could understand it easily.

Since school opened, numerous parents had visited the NBC pod# while teaching was underway. A frequent visitor in the early weeks was Marie Bonomi, who was also a parent aide in the library. During the third week of school, Sally complained to Sam that Mrs. Bonomi had spent time looking through notebooks and papers of children other than her own, without the permission of the teachers or the parents of the children involved. Sally also told Sam, "I feel like a monkey here with all these people looking at me." That day, in addition to Mrs. Bonomi, students from nearby State University were observing the school, which increased Sally's sensation of being under constant scrutiny. Sam suggested that the issue should not just be discussed privately, but should be put on the agenda for the next faculty meeting, and that a policy regarding visitors might have to be developed.

The MTK team. Team teaching in the MTK team was not flourishing despite attempts to solve problems the group had encountered. Toward the end of the third week, when the researcher asked Priscilla how everything was, she answered, "Good, all right, but they could be better." When asked,

---

*NBC had spent the better part of the previous week testing their children's reading ability to enable this grouping.

#The word "pod" was used by Ellis and the teachers to refer to teaching areas, even though they were not as structurally separated as "pods" often are in open-space schools.

DIAGRAM V

LINCOLN ACRES SCHOOL FLOOR ARRANGEMENT, SEPTEMBER 26, 1975

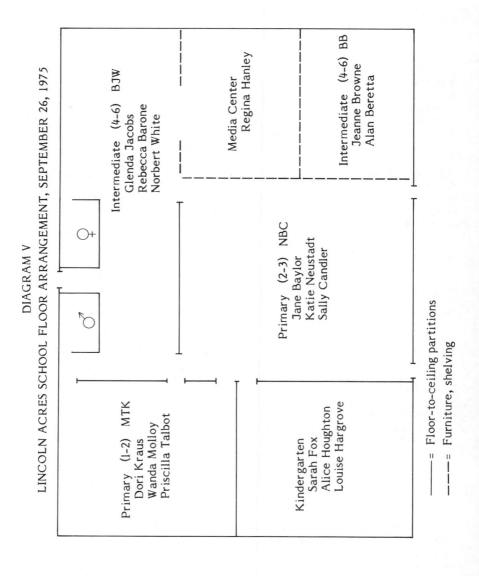

= Floor-to-ceiling partitions

—— = Furniture, shelving

Primary (1-2) MTK
Dori Kraus
Wanda Molloy
Priscilla Talbot

Kindergarten
Sarah Fox
Alice Houghton
Louise Hargrove

Primary (2-3) NBC
Jane Baylor
Katie Neustadt
Sally Candler

Intermediate (4-6) BJW
Glenda Jacobs
Rebecca Barone
Norbert White

Media Center
Regina Hanley

Intermediate (4-6) BB
Jeanne Browne
Alan Beretta

"How?" her succinct reply was: "If I wasn't here." Wanda, who wanted to avoid having the rest of the school involved in her team's affairs, explained that there was no team teaching in her group and that the problem was essentially Priscilla's uncooperativeness. Priscilla had indicated to her team members that she would consider team teaching -- later in the year. In the meantime, Dori and Wanda made plans to begin team teaching without Priscilla on the following Monday.

The other teams. BJW and the Kindergarten were experiencing no significant difficulties at this time. Occasionally, noise from BJW could be heard throughout the school. Regina had an introduction and short training session for about 35 mothers who had volunteered to work in the library.

In sum, three significant changes had taken place during the third week of school: the BB cluster had partially separated their teaching space from the rest of the school; NBC was to begin a new structure for their reading program; and team teaching in MTK would involve only two of the three teachers. One of the changes, the restructuring of the NBC reading program, was initiated by influences from outside of the school -- the parents. The other two changes resulted from processes within the social system of the school.

B. THE FOURTH WEEK OF SCHOOL

1. Faculty Meetings

Faculty meetings were the primary method of communication between the administration and the teachers, especially during the early part of the year. Even though the team structure made for more inter-teacher communication than is the case for traditional schools, and though the open space encouraged informal contact, the faculty meetings, whether aimed at "administrative" matters or instructional issues with emphasis on "professional growth", were the main method of communication for the school.

The vocal music teacher conducted a Kodaly workshop Monday afternoon, September 29, 1975, so that classroom teachers could continue to teach it while she was on maternity leave. The teachers' response to this workshop was positive; they enjoyed themselves while developing their musical skills.

Topics of a Tuesday lunch-time faculty meeting included announcements concerning field trips, inventory sheets, fire drills, the gym schedule and a report by Bert that he had found no one who wanted to represent Lincoln Acres school in the WEA. Sam told the faculty that he would run the next Monday workshop, which would demonstrate the use of videotape in the classroom.

Ellis also announced that the PTA Steering Committee was meeting that evening. He invited the teachers to attend and prodded them, as he had on other occasions:

> We need planners there. If we don't participate we'll be in no position to criticize them.

Ellis introduced another issue of some importance: earlier in the day a child had left school for home while school was in session. Ellis suggested that a sign-in and out procedure for students be installed to prevent that kind of incident. He added, "I'm not angry with you; I can understand the problems of keeping an eye on all the kids, but it's a public relations problem."

Another major item in the meeting was Sam's announcement that checklists for the writing and reading objectives would be ready by Thursday. Until now, only mathematics objectives lists were in use. Ellis continued with the topic of objectives lists by telling the faculty:

> I have had a number of parents question the program. I think we now have the tools to meet with an upset parent.

After other comments, including his mentioning that he would not be in town Thursday and Friday, Ellis said that since it was the last week in the month he would begin reading math profiles and start meeting with teams to discuss them. This prompted a teacher to ask what should be marked on the profile: only what had been taught to the student, or what the student actually knew? Ellis replied:

> Anything you know the kid can do. Don't let it bowl you over; you haven't done that much in September. The parents need some assurance that the kid is getting some kind of uniform individual attention. O.K.?

There were no further questions about profiles, and after a few more announcements the meeting ended.

2. The NBC Team Responds to Parents

The NBC team had spent substantial time in planning during the previous week, both after school and on Saturday. On Monday they implemented their new program. Besides reorganizing reading groups, they decided that Jane would be responsible for teaching mathematics the entire day. Sally would teach language arts, and Katie would be responsible for reading and independent study. The children were to rotate among the areas during the course of the day; each teacher instructed all the students in her specialized area every day.

Despite the new format, complaints from parents about the reading program continued. Mrs. Bonomi, an early critic, had spoken to Ellis about the NBC reading techniques, and told him she was going to spend time in

Sawyer school, where she could see a "regular" third grade reading program. Just before this she had observed Sally teaching a lesson in which the children were asked to compare a horse and a cow, and then write sentences on the differences between them. Mrs. Bonomi claimed that she could not understand how that exercise was a reading lesson. Both Katie and Sally viewed it as unbelievable that Mrs. Bonomi could fail to understand that reading was being taught in that lesson -- or indeed, to realize that most of the activities in school were actually teaching reading. Other indications of parent dissatisfaction with the reading program were less direct. For example, one student told her teacher that her parents had purchased reading and mathematics books, and gave her lessons at home. Ellis had spoken with Mrs. Bonomi and other parents, and told the teachers that he supported their efforts.

Along with restructuring their program, the NBC teachers decided to "brainwash" their students; they hoped that when parents asked if reading were taught during the day, the children would be able to say that reading was involved in all school activities, and provide examples. The mechanism of "brainwashing" -- a term the teachers freely used -- was compilation of lists (by students and teachers) of areas involving reading, followed by memorization. For instance, on Tuesday afternoon, an intern led all students in a recitation of the aspects of school that involved reading. These subject-matter areas were then put on a large piece of cardboard, and hung from the ceiling in the center of the teaching area; the students recited this list. Sally and Katie, the teachers primarily responsible for reading, planned to continue the "brainwashing" technique as long as necessary.

In the NBC team, reaction to criticism by parents was fairly quick. Restructuring the reading program within the first month of school was a responsive act. "Brainwashing", also part of the response, seems to have been an over-reaction; it was to a large extent, contrary to a central principle of the school: to promote individual differences among the students. Two anxiety-provoking sources may have led to the quick response: the criticism from parents during the summer, and possible feelings of low expertise, since all members of NBC had only taught one or two years prior to their coming to Lincoln Acres school.

3. Ellis' View

At this time, even with the problems in the MTK and NBC teams, Ellis Brown's evaluation of the school was positive. He was looking forward to seeing the results of the student profiles, and provided this general assessment:

> It feels as though something good is happening in the school but I don't know what yet. I hope that it's something real and not just a mask over the mistakes that have been made in the past.

From his point of view, except for a few complaints, there had been no real problems with parents -- the key factor in past problems -- and many had made positive comments since the school opened. Indeed, the PTA Steering Committee was to meet that evening to begin more active parent involvement in the school.

4. The PTA Steering Committee

Twenty parents had volunteered at the open house to work on the PTA Steering Committee. The first meeting was held on September 30, 1975, in the Lincoln Acres school media center. More than 20 parents attended, while Ellis and Regina Hanley were the only representatives of the school. Many of the parents present were those who had been active in earlier phases of the school's development, such as principal selection and passage of the bond issue. Some had been opponents of the emerging plan during the numerous summer meetings.

Those present were broken into smaller groups to brainstorm goals appropriate for the PTA. The following list of goals was produced by combining the individual brainstormed lists.

1. Get teachers involved
2. Find out what's going on in the school
3. Do some materials evaluation
4. Curriculum planning
5. Continuing education at home
6. Cultural arts
7. Tutoring program
8. Student progress reporting; report card study committee
9. Newsletter
10. Fund raising
11. Speakers and programs
12. Recreation: after school and evenings, children and adults
13. Fathers involved
14. By-laws and officers
15. Representative to Board meetings
16. Safety and health study
17. Landscaping of school property

As is evident, these goals place substantial emphasis on the actual process of education, not only on fund-raising and social activities. These parents viewed themselves as taking a fairly active role in instructional matters, though certainly not as supplanting teachers. In fact, an appeal was made that more teachers become involved in the PTA, particularly in the areas of materials evaluation, curriculum planning, cultural arts, tutoring, and student progress reporting.

It was decided that before organizing the association further, there should be a meeting on October 7 with presidents of nearby PTA's to obtain more information on fund raising, membership, and organization. The plan was that shortly after this meeting the PTA would be organized and committees formed. Then the program would be presented to the entire PTA membership and officers would be elected.

C. THE FIFTH WEEK OF SCHOOL

Although Brown was not present for the first three days of the fifth week of school,* everything went about as it had in previous weeks, with the exception of visits by a few parents. The faculty workshop, on the use of videotape in classrooms, was conducted by Sam.

1. The MTK Team

On October 8 at 7:30 p.m., the MTK team held a meeting for parent volunteers in their pod. The 25 mothers who attended were introduced to the programs and materials through simulation of a typical school day. The teachers thought the session went well.

The organization of the MTK team remained as it had been the week before; only Wanda and Dori were planning and team teaching together. Both of them talked infrequently during the day with Priscilla, and there were no plans to include all three in the team. Wanda's evaluation was:

> I feel good about things except for team teaching. The place looks good, the kids are starting to read.

2. The NBC Team Feels Pushed

"Brainwashing" continued in the NBC team throughout the week. According to Sally, the effort was only half successful: "The kids are learning when they are reading, but it's not working with the parents." On Wednesday afternoon Charles Frisch, whose son was a student in the pod, visited as a parent, not as a Board of Education member. He told the teachers that other parents were having difficulty understanding the reading program. Additionally, he said he disapproved of rotating children from teacher to teacher as an instructional technique, but accepted the teachers' rationale for it. He also said he would have preferred their beginning the year with activities such as phonics, and putting less early emphasis on reading for enjoyment. Perhaps his most important suggestion, or request, was that the team plan to meet with parents in the near future to explain their program. Mrs. Bonomi also visited the team on Wednesday, and requested a parents' meeting with the teachers.

Sally said the team was being "pushed into a more structured reading program." In her opinion she and her teammates realized the need for more

---

*Including two days in the fourth week and three days in the fifth week, Brown was out of town for five continuous days. He was in New Hampshire for an appointment with his dissertation adviser, and a visit to his former school. In his absence, Sam and Monica, the secretary, ran the school. If any policy decisions had to be made, they were instructed to consult with David Hauptmann, the principal of Fernwood School.

structure, but were taking their time with introducing it. Generally, the teachers felt upset and somewhat bewildered by the close parental scrutiny and criticism.

On Thursday morning, when Brown returned from five school days in New Hampshire, he met with the NBC team to discuss recent events. Ellis told them (somewhat abruptly, the teachers felt) that he too had noticed weaknesses in their reading program. Several decisions were made in this meeting: in approximately two weeks the team would have a parents' night to explain the reading program; on the following Monday they would begin phonics instruction; and Sam would meet with them that afternoon to offer suggestions for improving the reading program.

NBC reacts. Every Thursday afternoon the teachers in NBC had two hours for planning. On this Thursday, they were to meet with Sam. Before Sam arrived, they discussed Frisch. Sally called him a "creep". She also cast doubt on Frisch's expertise in reading by claiming that his own son read below grade level despite his attempts to help him.* The conversation then changed; the teachers agreed that "the place looks like a pigsty" and that they would clean it on Saturday. Eventually, the conversation returned to Frisch, who was reviled because he planned to visit the school on Monday despite the teachers' request that he wait. Their rationale for requesting the delay was that the program was new.

When Sam arrived at 1:20, he asked if the teachers needed any instructional materials. He then began suggesting elements of a phonics program, based, to a large extent, on what he had done when he was a classroom teacher. These included word games, charts, and brainstorming sessions. Sally, somewhat resistant, asked why the children should be taught things they didn't need to know. Sam's reply was: "I always use the rationale that they might need it later on in junior high school." Somewhat later, he justified his efforts by telling the teachers: "Be able to say something to the parents that they want to hear, isn't hurting the kids, and is honest."

Frisch and his criticism of the team became the subject of conversation. At first, Sam said Frisch should be listened to, but when others made uncomplimentary remarks about him, Sam agreed that Frisch was "uptight" and bothersome.

Offering a few more suggestions, Sam said:

Can I tell you my bias? I like the walls. I saw it at A.B.C. and at Oxford.# The walls give you a sense of place. The other walls should be arriving soon. I'm happy we changed to the 1-2, 2-3.

---

*Biddle's view after reading this was that Frisch never recognized or accepted the real problem with his son.

#A.B.C. is an open space school in Meadows, and Oxford is the school Sam had taught in.

Then Sam suggested a meeting Tuesday after school to make phonics games. This was agreed to, and the conversation returned to Frisch, Bonomi, other parents -- and to Ellis. The teachers complained to Sam that Ellis had been rough with them in their morning meeting. Sam defended Ellis, saying that he often found Ellis difficult to talk to early in the morning. Sam concluded,

> Ellis has piloted us through a lot of problems. I don't think that one of the other people we interviewed for principal could have done it.

After Katie said it was now time to support Ellis, Sally said that, nevertheless, she "felt put down this morning when he said we were missing something in our program." Sam, always looking for the positive aspects of situations, told the teachers he was glad they were in the middle of the building so everyone could see the good job they were doing.

(Comments). The role of the resource teacher throughout the school district was an ill-defined one:* it was neither an administrative position nor a teaching position. The resource teacher was to provide aid to teachers, but the problem centers on the meaning of "aid".

As the summary of the conversation reported above suggests, Sam performed ambivalently in the resource teacher role. He apparently did not know what his duties were -- or, if he did know what they were, he never found a way of successfully translating them into action. Depending on the circumstances, he either defended Ellis and became his apologist, accepted the parents' criticisms, or joined the teachers in their negative comments about parents and Ellis alike. Maintaining a credible performance under these conditions proved to be difficult for him by the end of the year.

The NBC team was not pleased with the way events had progressed in recent weeks. Alterations in their program appeared to be acceptable to them -- but not as a result of outside criticism. Nevertheless, they planned to take various measures to redesign their reading program to satisfy the critics. They also planned to have an open house, as requested by a few parents. We should note, though, that the first open house seemed to have left enough parents dissatisfied to have generated more parent visits and more criticism.

---

*Biddle's view, after reading this, was otherwise: he said the resource teacher role was generally defined as facilitative of teachers' work, but defined differently from school to school according to the principal's wishes. He pointed out that the "resource teacher" role was new to Ellis.

3. The School Board Sets Priorities

This week, the balance of Board membership was slightly altered, though not essentially shifted, by its election of a new member, Tom Hassfelt. (In late July, Michael Strassberg, a Board member who had supported the teachers during the reorganization meeting, had resigned.) Four of the six applicants for the position came from Lincoln Acres. In the final Board vote, at their meeting of October 6, Charles Frisch, Irena Farrell, and three other Board members supported Hassfelt; Sylvia Peabody, Estelle Hunter, and Gerrie Holden, who had earlier formed the Board opposition to the original Lincoln Acres school plan, supported Rob Goldman, who like Hassfelt was from Lincoln Acres. Thus the Board could not be said to have become more negative toward the hopes that Biddle, Ellis and the faculty held for the school.

At the same meeting, the Board endorsed a resolution that made the teaching of basic skills in the district's schools the highest priority. Basic skills as defined by the Board included: obtaining data, solving problems, thinking critically, and communicating effectively. The Board also decided to have math and language areas (reading, writing, speaking, listening) taught before other basic skills.

Part of the resolution asked the superintendent, with the assistance of teachers, to develop objectives in math and language arts, and a means of measuring whether or not these objectives were being reached. The plan was to be presented to the Board by November 3.

Frisch said that the basic skills emphasis would not supplant goals already established by teachers, but would show teachers what district priorities were. He said:

> We know there is a significant amount of basic skills training now in the system, but we're asking schools to list and evaluate the effectiveness of that training.

While this resolution did not develop a unified curriculum for the entire district -- something that Biddle had opposed since he came to Washingtonville -- it began laying the foundation for movement toward a standardized curriculum. In its weekly editorial the Courier proclaimed: "Basics are Back!" After lauding the Board's new policy, the editorial continued:

> It's about time in this and other districts. Teachers, students and parents have all complained that language arts skills are sadly lacking in many "bright" students who graduate from the local high school with top scores. Good high school age writers often don't know the difference between the use of the words "threw" and "through"; spelling among many high school students is atrocious. Parents of elementary age students complain their children's spelling is not corrected because teachers fear correction will stifle creativity.

> So now the pendulum swings back. The rote learning of the

past is called into the present to save the citizens of the future. Admittedly the swing could turn into a destructive backlash. The move of the 1960's toward meaningful, creative, relevant, innovative education should not be lost in this age of recession.

4. Frisch's Views

Though the NBC teachers wished to minimize Frisch's input, he certainly was not an ordinary parent. In addition to his statuses as Board of Education member, visiting professor of education in the graduate school of education at the State University, and father of a child taught by the NBC team, Charles Frisch was also the director of the Right to Read Program in the State Department of Education. One of his duties was that of cataloguing techniques of reading instruction. An article by Frisch, "Some practices in the teaching of reading in the state," a condensation of a book published by the State Department of Education, appeared in the October, 1975 issue of the state educational association's journal. At about the same time, Frisch became critical of the reading program in the NBC pod. Although the article is based on survey data from schools throughout the state, and does not deal with Washingtonville directly, it offers an opportunity to examine some of Charles Frisch's beliefs about appropriate reading instruction for elementary schools.

On the question of reading activities within the classroom, Frisch's data indicated that the traditional procedures of grouping within the classroom in the primary grades, and grouping within-and-between classes at the intermediate level, were the most common. Individualized instruction, homogeneous, ungraded and departmentalized approaches were used much less frequently. Frisch did not say whether he considered this beneficial or detrimental.

The article also noted:

> The predominant material used in most elementary classrooms to teach reading is one basal /reader/. Use of multiple basals supplemented with workbooks was significantly less frequent.

Somewhat surprising to Frisch was the finding that less than two percent of teachers used phonics materials as the principal instructional method, "even with the recent resurgence of interest in phonics instruction."

Frisch said reading instruction "should include definite emphasis on the application of reading skills to content subjects, starting at least in fourth grade." He found this purpose not being accomplished in two thirds of the schools in the state. In Frisch's view, this was a "definite area of weakness in the elementary reading program."

Frisch summarized his findings:

> While a wide diversity does exist within the state, clusters of similar responses occur quite frequently in each area reported. Generally these clustered responses indicate a reliance upon

classroom procedures that have been developed over the years and found to be effective in teaching reading. This is not to say that the newer ideas or techniques recently suggested by the literature are not being used. It is just that they are not as widely used as are those practices which teachers have been using for years in the classroom.

As in other parts of the report, Frisch did not comment on this conclusion. But while he did not support the "traditional" emphasis in reading instruction that he found, he did not criticize it either. He did criticize underutilization of phonics, and inadequate emphasis on the application of reading skills to other subject matter areas. Frisch's failure to criticize traditional practices tempts one to conclude that he found nothing unsound about them, though he fell short of outright endorsement.

5. The Faculty Meeting

At lunch-time Thursday there was a faculty meeting. Ellis, who had just returned from New Hampshire, began by explaining the budget for the coming year; he asked teachers to give him, in writing, any supply or equipment requests they had. Then he turned to recounting the events of the PTA Steering Committee meeting, and the list of goals parents had generated. When Ellis finished reading the list Priscilla asked, "This was their list?" Ellis replied:

This was brainstormed by them. This is a first list. Some of them are taking a pretty close focus on kids and program. Frankly, I felt a little embarrassed being the only staff member there.

Priscilla: Frankly, I didn't want to go. I was busy and they have given us a rough time in the past.

Ellis: We had people there from the state and county PTA's as outsiders. They are young and aggressive and have to be taught that they can make us uptight.

Regina: I saw a lot of change in the two meetings. In the first one they were very hostile and in the second they said they have to get everybody involved. The more involved they are the less hostile they become.

Ellis: I found that when I went to the teas. When there was no Board member there, they were very hostile. When the Board members were there it turned to "what can we do to help?" They stopped saying things like: "I hope so and so meets with a bad accident." When I was there at the PTA, it was less hostile.

Priscilla: Maybe we can rotate going to the PTA?

Ellis: Well, I had a feeling and I have the right to share that feeling. I felt embarrassed.

Linda: Do they have the right to deal with curriculum?

Ellis: I feel it's legitimate for them to have input, but not to make decisions.

A long silence followed. It was broken by a teacher's speculation that teachers did not attend because the meeting was held at night. Ellis said, "It could have been that -- but most likely not in 17 cases." The meeting turned to other topics.

D. THE SIXTH WEEK OF SCHOOL

1. Teaching/Learning Overview

Except for the changes in the NBC team, instructional activities had remained largely unchanged since school opened. There was a moderate amount of pupil control effort in several teams; it was not repressive or continuous, and seemed effective. In the intermediate areas several activities were usually going on at one time: up to now multiple activities had been typical only in the primary areas. Student-teacher interaction was frequent; teachers were usually actively engaged in teaching a group of students, not grading papers or doing clerical work while the class did seatwork. The self-directed exercises used were usually aimed at reinforcing material presented in teacher-directed lessons. Materials were well used; so was equipment, like the videotape machine. Interns, SWEP students and parent volunteers worked alongside teachers throughout the school. Overall, the school was fairly well organized, but somewhat noisy.

This was a week, however, when parent visits and criticism increased a good deal, and when several teams began encountering more difficulties in their work.

2. NBC Under Scrutiny

As expected, Frisch, along with other parents, visited the school on Monday, October 13, 1975. The furniture in the NBC teaching area had been rearranged over the weekend so that it was more clustered, producing small, well-defined instructional areas. Attached to each area was a sign explaining its use (for example, as a reading center or a science center).

Frisch asked the teachers why certain objectives did not appear in the student profiles they were using. The teachers answered that it was an oversight (and in fact met later in the week with Ellis to discuss adding the objectives). Sally, who was the most vocal member of the team, was somewhat puzzled by Frisch's visit. She said: "I don't know where he's coming from," but added:

> We've changed our program and we're pleased with it; the changes were needed. Ellis is familiar with our program and supports it fully.

But other parents also registered complaints about the NBC reading program during the week. The most serious one was a charge that a child had been placed in the incorrect reading book -- one that she was in by Christmas time the previous year. The child's mother said that an eighth of the year had already passed, and claimed that her daughter had not learned anything. The NBC teachers regarded this parent as being overly alarmed, particularly since they felt the past weeks were not that critical.

Influenced, however, by the parental criticism, the NBC team decided that instead of holding a parents' night as originally planned, they would produce a pamphlet explaining their program, and send it home with students. This was done, apparently, to avoid more face-to-face contact with parents, and to limit further criticism.

3. The Faculty Works on Report Cards

Monday's workshop was for constructing a system for reporting to parents. Ellis reminded the group that they had agreed during the summer to split the primary and intermediate groups for planning. It was decided that the product by the end of the workshop would be a preliminary specification of information to be contained in the report card. Priscilla asked, as she had in the early days of school, what the results of the community survey had been on report cards. Ellis couldn't remember the percentages, but reported that few people wanted numbers or grades, that no one had mentioned "pass/fail" and that there was no "overwhelming" percent who wanted a narrative form of report.* The faculty then split into two groups; the intermediate one was led by Sam and the primary by Ellis.

The group led by Sam had a wide-ranging, somewhat disorganized discussion. There was some uncertainty on what they wanted to report to parents, and a high degree of uncertainty on how it should be reported. Sam pushed fairly persistently for an objectives checklist, similar to one he had used in Oxford school. There was a lengthy discussion of whether grades such as "satisfactory," "unsatisfactory," and "outstanding" should be used, as versus a narrative approach.

---

*The latter conclusion is not at all supported by the parent data; see section D.1 of Chapter 7.

The primary group generated a list of topics to be covered in the report card, which included work habits, reading and social attitudes. Ellis proposed that categories such as "at grade level," "less than grade level," and "more than grade level" be used. The teachers sat passively during much of Ellis' presentation, but Priscilla, Dori, and Wanda were more vocal than the members of the NBC team. At one point, Priscilla asked Sally how she felt with the discussion. Sally responded that she was basically uncomfortable with the grading system, since one of its consequences for the students was that parents would take ownership of the child's learning. Ellis commented that what Sally said was "tragic," because it implied she would never be happy with any reporting system. Sally responded: "I see we have to do it, but the whole experience is uncomfortable." More discussion of Ellis' proposal followed until about 4:45. As with Sam's role in the intermediate group, it appeared that Ellis exercised the dominant influence, had decided before the meeting on the general outline of the report card, and elicited subject areas and suggestions from the teachers in an attempt to involve them.

Overall, the discussion reflected ambivalence between making a "professional" response to the grading problem and the desire not to get into excessive amounts of work. The solutions discussed to the grading problem were not particularly innovative, even though the discussion drew on sources such as a state commission report and practices at other schools.

4. MTK Problems Continue

Early that week, Ellis thought he might take advantage of the Center for Policy Research offer of matching funds to provide consulting help for the MTK team. In his view, the team had delivered instruction fairly well, but there were a number of innovative techniques they could have been using. The main obstacle, as he viewed it, was Priscilla's unproductive interaction with Dori and Wanda. By now he had had four meetings with the team to try to solve their problems. He felt these had been of limited help, and that Sam's efforts had produced little change. There were only two recent changes in MTK's operations: parents were working as aides, and Priscilla, who was still having problems with noise, had begun wearing ear plugs in school. No movement toward increased team teaching or joint planning had occurred.

5. Stress in the BB Team

Toward the end of the week, Jeanne complained privately to the researcher that she had a "vague feeling of discomfort" in the school. She was uncertain about its causes: perhaps the newness, or the openness of the school as well. She attributed part of her discomfort to the fact that she and other teachers felt the community had high but unclear expectations; it was difficult to know whether or not the teachers were meeting them. She explained:

> I feel as though I'm on a merry-go-round and can't get off. I'm here from 7:15 to 4:40 every day and do work at home, but it still seems like there is more to be done. I'm getting tired of it and my husband wants me to stop it. But I don't feel confident.

She said she had spoken with Bert, Rebecca and Glenda, and that they felt the same pressures.

When asked if the BB team had taken any steps to solve their problems, she answered that they had not. She said she had confidence in Sam and liked him, but for some reason unknown to her would not approach him with the problem. Nor would she consider bringing her problem to Ellis' attention, because "he doesn't care, wouldn't know what to do and is satisfied as long as too many parents don't see him." So communication within the BB team, and between them and the administration, was not particularly good. Even though the team seemed to be one of the more successful in the school, with no complaints from parents, they were experiencing strain. It was not surprising that they decided to turn to parents for rewards. They scheduled an open house for Thursday of this week for parents of children in their area, hoping to get some positive feedback to reinforce their efforts.

6. Sol Levinsky Consults with BJW

During the latter part of this week, Dr. Sol Levinsky, a professor of education at Reade State College, a supervisor of three of the student interns in Lincoln Acres school and a consultant to the Washingtonville school district since 1967,* met with the BJW team and interns at their request. The team had asked him to provide feedback on whether they were meeting the needs of individual students. Levinsky's technique was to observe their work for the day, videotape an interview he conducted with several students, and then discuss his observations with the teachers.

Levinsky's view of the team was that they were meeting their (and Biddle's) objectives of providing individualized instruction. However, he preferred to see more children working in groups. The team's responses to this and to several other observations -- which stayed close to the theme of individualization -- were somewhat defensive:

> Levinsky: One of the things I saw missing for me -- if I look at this as a culture -- was a unifying theme for this thing bringing it together. A unified purpose or identity. I admit that this is a highly personal thing.

---

*Levinsky was also a friend of the research project director's, and one of the consultants used by the Social Architecture project in other schools. He did not act as a project consultant in Lincoln Acres school, feeling that his past and current work with Washingtonville would preclude it.

Bert: You came on a bad day. The fourth grades don't go to the nurse for Human Growth and Development because of state law. This made them stand out as a group.

As we shall vividly see later, Levinsky's observation that the group lacked a purpose was incisive; when criticism from parents increased, the rationale for the program the BJW team had developed did not prove convincing.

The BJW team spent time discussing the videotape, what Levinsky's role could be in the future, and philosophies of learning (for example, whether children learn best in groups or individually). On this topic, there was disagreement; Bert thought learning was an individual act, and Levinsky argued that it could also take place in groups. Arrangements were made for Levinsky to meet again with the interns to probe further into the teaching problems they experienced. The meeting ended with all involved declaring that it had been a worthwhile and fruitful exercise.

During the course of the day, Levinsky made several other observations to the researcher. He seemed surprised that Ellis and Sam were considering using a consultant to help the MTK team. It was his impression that they wanted to "run their own ship". In relation to this, Levinsky commented:

Biddle is a nice guy but he gives with one hand and takes with the other. He gives autonomy to the principals but no one really takes it. Ellis is young and cocky enough to take Biddle seriously and run his own school; the others don't.

7. The Faculty Meeting

By mid-week, many parents had visited the school. They had observed the NBC and BJW teams; some parents claimed their children could not learn in an open space setting. Scheduled and spur-of-the-moment conferences were held with Ellis to discuss problems parents had perceived. Several parents had also requested appointments with teachers. On Thursday morning alone, four parents visited the school to talk, and to examine their child's cumulative school record folder.

At the Thursday lunch-time faculty meeting, after a brief discussion of fire-drill procedures, Ellis introduced the topic of visitors in the school.

Ellis: One of the things I want to discuss is the huge number of visitors we're having in the building. There are three things: Should we have a form that a lot of schools have, that is, "How to be a good visitor"? There has been a problem in at least one pod. What about others?

Regina: Bad visitors don't follow guidelines anyway.

Ellis: The other thing is would it be useful to have a particular day to come to school?

Wanda: A limited number of people. I think they would all take advantage of it.

Ellis: We wouldn't broadcast it.

Priscilla: I like Wanda's suggestion. Some schools have a father's day on vacations that we don't have.

Bert: One day a week will have us responding differently. I always do when an evaluator comes. You might also have the community thinking we're having them come only on a "show" day.

Priscilla: Do we have a general rule that visitors go to the office?

Ellis: Yes, it's a Board policy.

Bert: The other day, Barry's boss /Miles, the research project director/ was here and I felt awkward with this man taking notes. I didn't know what to say. Or, Mrs. d'Onofrio today. I didn't know if she had been to the office. With Barry's boss I looked at him and thought it was all right.

Several sub-group discussions concerning parents erupted in the group. Then the group refocused and the discussion continued.

Sarah: Could we set up a sign and have them check into the office?

Ellis: That's what we'll do and they'll get a name tag at the office. If they don't have a name tag you can ask them if they've been at the office.

Jane: Are we still going to have rules for visitors?

Dori: The other day I had some parents come in and I kept teaching. I felt a little awkward, though, and I didn't know if I should stop and talk to them. I didn't. I hope they didn't go away with the wrong impression, and it would help if there is a clear rule that says teachers are to continue teaching.

Jeanne: I was in a school once where visitors had to fill out a form when they left.

Ellis: That's Board policy and we'll start to do it.

The conversation concerning visitors and appropriate ways to control them ended here, as Ellis abruptly changed the topic to cleaning matters. He told the teachers that there were problems with cleaning the school; another custodian had quit the night before. He continued:

> I've looked at the areas and they are messy. I don't think it's good training for the kids to leave the place so dirty. There are lots of large things left on the floor. Would you want your vacuum cleaner to try to pick up crayons and erasers? A general rule should be that if not, it should be picked up by hand.

Eventually, the matter of cleanliness in the school would become a major issue dividing -- or used to divide -- the teachers and administration.

The meeting continued with routine announcements about physical education equipment, and relocation of bicycle racks from the front of the building to the side. After these, the subject of parents recurred. Jeanne explained that Mrs. Maggio, a parent of one of her students, had asked her to talk to the teachers about the PTA. Mrs. Maggio's message was that she and other parents would like to have the teachers participate in the PTA; they couldn't understand why teachers didn't attend. Jeanne reported that she answered that teachers "were tired of the hassle and of being cornered by parents and having to explain our programs." To this, Maggio had answered that not all of the people in the PTA were "activists"; she suggested that even if teachers continued not to attend meetings, it would be useful to have a list of teacher concerns. Jeanne said that she would solicit teacher suggestions and give them to her. The teachers decided to give written suggestions for the PTA to Jeanne; they said that their previous contacts with Mrs. Maggio showed she was "a nice person". In an effort to promote further participation, Ellis reiterated an earlier position:

> Please don't be timid about the process. If a parent wants to have a conference with you, tell them this is a PTA and not a conference -- which can be arranged.

Ellis began to end the meeting, but teachers had other issues. Among them were theft of materials from the building, plans for Halloween parties, and a decision to have the regular faculty meeting at lunchtime on Thursday. Ellis also announced that there would be no workshop the following Monday.

8. BB Team Parents' Night

On Thursday evening, dressed more formally than during school hours, the BB teachers greeted parents as they arrived for the open house. Parents walked through the space, inspected student work on the walls, books and other instructional materials. For the most part, what they saw was displayed as it was during the typical school day.

When the flow of parents slowed -- 35 adults and 20 children were present -- Jeanne began the presentation. She announced that the sections of the program would include a description of a typical day, an explanation and organization of ways parents could work in the classroom, and finally, "honest" comments from parents about the learning activities. Jeanne finished by emphasizing the long hours and hard work that were spent on preparations for school.

Using charts and 25 slides, the teachers presented an abbreviated version of the typical day. With the overview completed, a spelling lesson was explained in depth. It was stressed that the spelling was coordinated with phonics and reading. Jeanne said that both teachers were responsible for all the students, and that they tried to see each child individually every day.

Index cards were distributed to parents, and they were asked to write their names and addresses, along with days they would be able to come to the school. A teacher said: "We'd like to have as many parents in our space as possible." On the reverse side of the card, parents were asked to indicate if they had any talents or abilities that they could use in leading "interest" groups during school hours. Then they were asked if there were any questions:

> Mother: I know about parent participation -- I've seen it before. What does it do for children?
>
> Teacher: We'd like parent input.
>
> Mother: /same one/ I wonder if it isn't time for them not to be with parents. I also don't like them being taught by parents. I taught in high school and don't feel qualified to teach young children. Maybe we need parents in here to clean up this junk and to do clerical jobs.
>
> Teacher: Maybe I wasn't clear. They can do a lot of chores, clerical work, etc.
>
> Mother: /same one/ I've been in situations where the kids say the "mommy" did this and that.
>
> Teacher: They can do the clerical work and other things.
>
> Mother: /same one/ Not many parents will want to do the dirty work.
>
> Teacher: The basic thing for us is to open up the class to parents.

After this exchange, for which several parents later privately apologized, Jeanne asked for questions about the program. There were only a few queries: about reading, the report card and the daily schedule. These were not hostile, and did not start any debate or discussion.

A teacher said that if there were any other questions they could be asked after the meeting.

> Right now we'd like to have your honest reactions. What do you think about our program? How do you feel? We need your reactions.

Parents' comments were:

Mother: I'd like to say that I'm grateful for the notes that come home. You always send thoughtful notes telling me what is going on in school. The kids like it and I like what you're doing.

Father: My boy is happy and seems well motivated. But I don't know how to evaluate what he's learning. But as for his adjustment here, I'm happy.

Mother: I'd like to say that all the kids I know are adapting very well. That means they must be learning.

These were the only public reactions to the teachers' efforts. When parents spoke among themselves after the presentation and to the teachers they made other positive comments. No parent, except for the one who was skeptical of parents in the classroom, was critical of the BB team's efforts. Both teachers were pleased with the parents' reactions.

E. THE SEVENTH WEEK OF SCHOOL

1. A Visit from the Superintendent

On Tuesday, October 21, while Ellis spent the day in Boston, Superintendent Biddle visited the school. He observed the NBC team and talked with its individual teachers. Afterward he commented that they were doing a good job, but had made a mistake in not meeting parents' needs first; many parents had called him to complain about deficiencies in the team's educational program. Sally, speaking for the team, countered Biddle's criticism, saying that she thought meeting students' needs came first. Jane's assessment was that the problems would be solved if parents simply had more information about the program.

The outcome of Biddle's visit was a recommendation by Ellis on the following day. He suggested that the NBC team supplement their current plan of sending a notice to parents explaining their program by reinstating the open house originally requested by Frisch and others. The team accepted this, and made plans to split the parents into two groups, attending on different nights. Ellis and Sam were to help the NBC teachers prepare a presentation, to include videotapes of classes. The NBC open houses were scheduled for Tuesday and Thursday of the following week.

2. The PTA Steering Committee

Spurred by Ellis' open criticism of the faculty for their non-participation in the PTA, and by personal invitations from parents, several teachers attended the next PTA Steering Committee meeting on October 21, 1975. Ellis had flown to Boston the day before; he had tickets for the World Series. Among the dozen parents present were Sy Golden, Sam Schwartz, Barbara Berger, Marie Bonomi and Sylvia Peabody.

At this early stage of the development of the Lincoln Acres PTA, many of the organizers were people formerly or still active in LAHA. For example, Barbara Berger had been the education committee co-chairperson at the time of Ellis' appointment. Golden was the second president of LAHA, and a co-author of the LAHA constitution. Once the school opened, the PTA replaced LAHA as the community organization with greatest interest in education.

Golden, who ran the meeting, introduced everyone and distributed copies of the proposed PTA by-laws. The next issue was nominations for offices in the PTA. Although several offices had multiple candidates, others were either without candidates or non-contested; some time was spent on ways to induce people to run for office. Golden said:

> Hopefully one of the members of the faculty -- or more -- will take a position on the executive board. This is a brand new school and we can make new tracks in the snow if we want. It's exciting.

This comment led to a lengthy exchange between Golden, who wanted to know what could be done to get teachers involved in the PTA, and the teachers. Sam Schwartz advised the parents that a possible way of getting teachers involved would be to have a PTA representative talk at a faculty meeting. After more discussion, Lee Whitmore, the P.E. teacher, said she would be willing to run for either president or vice-president. Bert then offered to contact teachers to tell them about PTA meetings.

Seeking assurances, a parent asked if more teachers would be at the next meeting; he was concerned that they might not have an opportunity to influence approval of the by-laws. Golden said that he thought there would be teachers present, and Bert volunteered to distribute copies of the by-laws to teachers for their reactions. The parents seemed to be satisfied with this arrangement.

When the meeting ended, several parents talked with teachers over coffee. The teachers listened politely and there was no apparent friction between the two groups.

After the meeting Regina told the researcher:

> I have seen a change in the Steering Committee since they began. They are now less militant, less concerned with curriculum and evaluation and /less/ into the technical aspects of setting up the organization. Also, at one meeting someone suggested that they wait for making policy decisions until the entire group gets together to give everybody input.

3. The Faculty Meeting

Upon returning from Boston, happy with the Red Sox victory, Ellis held the regularly scheduled Thursday lunch-time faculty meeting. The primary topic was parent-teacher conferences, scheduled for November 3, 4 and 5. These were half days for all schools in the district, when required conferences with parents would be held. Ellis asked the faculty to consider how the conferences should be organized. After some discussion, it was agreed that there would be 15-minute conferences with each parent. Other issues discussed were whether any teams intended to meet with parents as a team, and if the student profiles (student achievement forms) should be shown to parents during conferences. Ellis answered that they were to be used, and that for children with unusual problems he would discuss the case with the teacher before the parents arrived.

During the meeting, Glenda said she had had a problem with a parent aide from another team observing her that morning. She continued:

> This disturbed me. She asked who I was. She said she had permission from you.

Ellis replied:

> I wasn't in the building this morning. If they're going somewhere else they should check with the office. This is district policy.

In response to Dori's remark that some parents refused to obey the policy, Ellis said, "If there are problems I'll talk to them." Later in the meeting, another member of the BJW team, Bert, also made critical comments about parents. In reference to scheduling parents for conferences, he observed:

> In my dealing with the parents most have been really good but some are bitching and I don't want to go out of my way for them.

Toward the end of the meeting, Ellis repeated his message from the previous faculty meeting:

> A couple of areas of clean-up are just way out of line. I'm hiring and firing clean-up people weekly. If the piece of paper on the floor is large enough to pick up the children should do it. Books, erasers and other things are constantly found on the floor and shouldn't be. If they don't pick up before they leave, you are teaching them an awful habit. If you want to see it, go to the high school where it's really bad. They must learn to clean up.

> Another problem is the bathroom. They are running wild in there. They have too much time. I've had a couple of incidents in the boys' room that you just wouldn't believe.

Bert announced that he would leave a copy of the PTA constitution in the teachers' lounge so that changes in it, if any, could be made. Other issues discussed were tests to be administered by the school nurse, and Sarah's question if there were objections to the kindergarten's parading through the school for Halloween.

Several times during the meeting teachers talked among themselves; their attention was not on the topic under discussion. Ellis interrupted and regained their attention. On one of these occasions he said:

The rumor went around last Thursday that I was in a bad mood. I wasn't, but please stay with me. I come out of these meetings and find that people haven't been listening.

As this quote indicates, to Ellis these meetings were an important mechanism for running the school; they were the primary means of distributing information throughout the faculty. He viewed it as the teachers' responsibility to know what decisions had been reached. No public minutes or records were kept.

4. The MTK Team Situation Persists

The problems that had developed in the MTK team were still evident. After a period of relative harmony (Wanda and Dori were still planning their work separately from Priscilla's), the situation worsened. Ellis, who acknowledged that his early attempts at supporting Priscilla and her team had not been effective, did not think things could be improved, because he felt Priscilla could not acknowledge the problems.

Ellis decided not to use a consultant to help the MTK team. Instead, he intended to tell Priscilla that she was not meant for the Lincoln Acres type of education, and that she should look for another position for the following year. At the same time he told Wanda and Dori, Priscilla's teammates, that in the next year they would not have to be in a team with Priscilla.

5. Ellis' View of the School and Community

Situations like those in the MTK and NBC teams made Ellis feel, he said, as though he were "firefighting." He spent entire days from mid to late October talking on the phone to parents, and meeting with teaching teams and individual teachers who were having problems.

Chief among his concerns was the fact that Charles Frisch, who had been a supporter of the school, was now one of its most critical opponents. Ellis no longer knew what to think of Frisch by late October. He complained:

One minute I hear an ex-teacher talking, another an ex-administrator, another an ex-superintendent and then the Director of the state Right to Read program. At times he even sounds like a concerned and bewildered parent. At others like a Board member with a thousand hidden agendas.

Frisch, as we have seen, was one of the parents who had wanted NBC to have an open house. But in Ellis' view, by the time of the open house

"Frisch had given up on the school." This assessment was based on the fact that he had threatened to transfer his son to Fernwood school. Biddle persuaded him not to, but the threat of a transfer remained.

Brown felt that Frisch's demands on NBC were not harmful as such, but that he had rushed them and created a crisis atmosphere. He continued:

> I believe enough in democracy to let the community have a say
> in the school. If what they want is a mediocre education then
> that's what they'll get. They certainly are not getting the best
> education that we could give.

In general, Brown's view was that the community complaints created a feeling among the staff of being "fed up." The only teachers to receive any praise from the community were the BB team, who had asked for it: "they had to go begging." Reflecting on his own position at this time, Ellis said he was "taking steps to straighten out my personal life and see where I'm going." He wondered if the role of principal was the right one for him, and how long he would remain in Washingtonville. Apparently, he too, was becoming "fed up" with the community complaints.

F. THE EIGHTH WEEK OF SCHOOL

Along with the usual activities of the school, two teams held open houses for parents this week on three separate nights. NBC divided the parents of their students into two groups and met with them separately on Tuesday and Thursday. BJW met with the parents of their students on Wednesday night. Both teams held these meetings at the request of parents, who either felt they needed more information about the educational program their child was receiving, or frankly viewed the educational program as inadequate.

1. The First NBC Open House

By 8:00 p.m. Tuesday, October 28, 1975, approximately 40 parents were waiting in the media center for the NBC open house to begin. The teachers and interns sat on the right front side of the audience, and talked among themselves; before the meeting there was no contact between parents and teachers. After 15 more parents arrived, Ellis began the meeting.

He introduced the teachers and interns and presented an overview of the evening's activities, which would include description of the math, reading and language programs, simulation of the daily activities of the classroom, an opportunity to ask questions, and a videotape of classroom activities. Ellis concluded his introduction by saying:

> One thing we can't do tonight is discuss your individual child's
> progress. We don't have the time. Fortunately, next week we
> have teacher conferences. Notices will be sent home giving
> you the details.

The reason we're having this meeting tonight is that in the beginning of the year we received 78 kids. We have since become familiar with them and made changes to meet their needs. We have also had comments from parents and made changes to meet the suggestions made, many of which were good. We're pleased with our program, but we basically found that we need more emphasis on basic skills: reading, math and language skills.

Using an overhead projector, Ellis reviewed the structure of the math, reading and language programs, including objectives for each area. He elaborated on each area minimally and said almost the same thing that appeared in the printed material given to each parent. Chart 8.1 shows the section on reading from the mimeographed pamphlet parents received.

CHART 8.1
DESCRIPTION OF READING PROGRAM, NBC TEAM
2-3 Pod Reading Program, October 28, 1975

The Reading Program, together with the Language Program and Spelling, contributes to a rounded experience in reading and language growth for the students. While reading is discussed separately here, it must be understood as a part of the whole program which includes vital parts of reading growth in the areas of language and spelling, rather than all of it just in reading alone.

The 2-3 pod includes readers who are just learning how to read all the way up through students who read easily and independently above the 3rd grade level. To cope with this range of reading performance, a variety of basal readers are used to give students at each level challenging experiences in comprehension and vocabulary. The daily lesson includes reading with a teacher and a follow-up (independent or sometimes teacher-led) activity that reinforces the content, vocabulary or some other aspect of the day's lesson. Formal handwriting practice is worked into the follow-up.

Besides the basal readers, many books are available for the children to choose to read on their own that have reading levels designated on them. (For example, a piece of tape of a certain color may be used to indicate books of approximately the same reading difficulty. Teachers and students become familiar with which color is suitable for each individual student to use in selecting material for independent reading.)

In his oral presentation, Ellis emphasized that each student read aloud to the teacher every day and that reading was actively taught to each student every day.

Ellis then divided the parents into three groups and assigned each to a teacher, who explained her teaching responsibilities when the group arrived in her section of the instructional area. Jane's specialty was math and science; Sally's and Katie's were reading and language arts. At predetermined times, the groups of parents were asked to move to the next teaching area, until each group had heard each teacher.

In these sessions, the teachers elaborated what had been said by Ellis. They also demonstrated or displayed materials used by the students. After their presentations they answered the few questions that time permitted. For the most part, these parents were not critical of the teachers. Noise was an issue, however, since even though only three people were talking at one time -- the teachers -- they could all be distinctly heard in any section of the teaching space. One parent asked Ellis if problems were created by noise, and was assured there were none.

Once all three groups had experienced each subject matter area, the parents were asked to return to the media center, where questions were invited. Here is a sample of questions and responses.

Mother: My concern is with the security of the building and grounds. In transition periods I'm afraid of kids leaving the building. Is there someone responsible for them?

Ellis: Oh, sure. The teachers always keep track of the students.

Father: In order to measure their learning will they be compared with others in the state?

Ellis: We already had the state assessment program. It is for the 4th, 8th and 12th grades. The district has standardized tests district-wide and they have national norms.

Same father: When these are scored can we see the results?

Ellis: Yes. You have the right to see them. The California test is given in May. It might take some time before the results reach us, but it should be before the next school year.

Father: Does this give you a true fix on how the school operated for the first year?

Ellis: No. The California is an achievement test. In a neighborhood like this they'll do well. It doesn't reflect the school. I've seen good schools in bad neighborhoods do poorly.

Father: What criteria will you use, then?

Ellis: The profile that the teachers use, which I read for every child every month. They have specific criteria on them. For example, can the child multiply by two digits? Maybe there is a problem with the child or the program. This is checked every month.

Mother: I find a problem with the lack of work that comes home. I can't follow the child. I'm a working mother and I can't come to school during the day to find out what is going on.

Sally: Mrs. Kelly, we have an abundance of papers now and we'll be sending things home. We didn't understand this at first as a parent need, but now we do.

Ellis: This is the kind of thing you can get at parent conferences.

Father: Why was so much time spent on testing the children when you have the test results from Fernwood last year? I can understand one week /of testing/ and then moving on.

Katie: We found a large discrepancy between the Fernwood information and our own.

Ellis: Achievement tests are not always accurate. They are not good for placement purposes. What we got from Fernwood was where they left off. After two months children forget things. I will agree that it took a long time, and we hope to make it shorter in the future.

The question period ended with what appeared to be the exhaustion of parental concern. Ellis announced that people could stay if they wanted and view a videotape of classroom activities. Most parents stayed and enjoyed what they saw, especially when their own child was on camera.

For the most part, the questions were not critical, nor did they directly concern the teachers' methods of instruction; instead, they focused on general school policy and gross measures of achievement. Katie, surprised that the questions asked "didn't relate to us," was somewhat relieved that the first open house was over. But she worried that the parents scheduled for the next one would be more critical. Sally was -pleased, and thought that some parents were beginning to understand the program. She too was not looking forward to the next one, because of the parents involved. Indeed, none of the parents who had become visible through their LAHA efforts, the petition, or recent complaints about the school had been present at this open house.

2. The Second NBC Open House

Anticipating a more critical group of parents for the second open house, the teachers prepared themselves in somewhat more depth. For instance, Katie read one of Charles Frisch's books on the teaching of reading and announced:

I'm going to use his terms. One thing I got from it is that he wants teachers to be highly organized. His book is heavy on detailed teacher planning, and he says plans should be made for two months in advance.

In fact, whether it was intended to serve as one or not, the first open house was a rehearsal for the second one.

The setting and organization of the second open house were the same as the first one's. The important difference was the presence of critical, influential parents, namely, Frisch, Peabody, and Bonomi. They, along with others, asked more probing questions of the teachers than had the first group of parents.

As before, Ellis gave a general overview of the program. Then he divided the parents into three groups for teacher lectures and demonstrations designed to explain the instructional areas.

In Sally's group, after she finished her presentation, which was the same she used at the first open house, there was time left for parents to ask questions.

Father: In this area how much time do you spend with individual children?

Sally: I'm not sure what you mean.

Frisch: Maybe it could help if you explain the daily schedule. They don't all come at one time?

Sally: Twenty-seven children at a time. They are divided up between Marcia, the intern, and me. Eventually it will be three groups. Some will work on follow-up /independent study/.

Father: You still haven't said how much time you spend with the children.

Sally: I would say it's a half hour.

Frisch: There are two basic areas here. Could you give us an idea of what happens in a week or a day? Do you work on both skills every day?

Sally: Monday through Wednesday we work on basic skills, Thursday and Friday on language. I work with Katie very closely.

Father: So that if you teach something, Katie reinforces it?

Sally: Yes.

Mother: I think the overall common concern of the community is that the children are "doing their own thing." I expect them to have some regimentation. They love the school and doing their own things. But I don't see the results. My daughter comes home and has no idea of what's going on.

Sally: There will be work going home now. We didn't understand that in the beginning. Every Tuesday you can expect a spelling list. We have a test on Friday.

Mother: Good.

Father: Do you feel the way you are teaching will work, that it's a valid approach and doesn't need to be changed?

Sally: Sure, but I'm always looking for ways to grow and change.

One father remained after the group switched to Katie's area, and questioned Sally further on her relationship with parents.

Mr. Kahn: You mentioned in your presentation that the homework was to appease the parents. Does it help learning?

Sally: Both.

Mr. Kahn: My concern is with the kids, not the parents.

Sally agreed with Kahn, but then explained the pressure from the parents.

I finally resolved myself to the fact that the children aren't going to learn if the parents aren't happy.

Mr. Kahn: It seems a little neurotic to me. Thank you.

After Katie's explanation of her part of the NBC instruction, the parents, led by Dr. and Mrs. Frisch, asked the same sort of questions they had posed to Sally. Frisch and others asked detailed questions about the methods Katie used to determine the appropriate level of reading instruction that each child received. Katie answered that placement was made on the basis of the child's previous work, and tests given at the beginning of the year.

The group re-formed in the media center for another opportunity to question the staff. The two basic areas of concern were the amount of instructional time each child received, and the methods used to evaluate teaching effectiveness. This exchange occurred near the end of the 15-minute meeting.

Father: How do you evaluate the program?

Ellis: I teach regularly and go over the individual profiles.

Frisch: How would the overall program be evaluated?

Ellis: Annual tests. They evaluate our record keeping. For example, state assessment tests and the California tests.

Frisch: Do I take it that there will be a California test at the end of the year?

Ellis: Yes, it's Board policy.

Frisch: Are you going to use it?

Ellis: Yes. But I value it less than a criterion-referenced test. A PRI and a PMI.

Schwartz: Wouldn't the California test be more useful when you've had two years of them?

Ellis: Yes, you're right, two would have more weight.

Mrs. Bonomi: What is a PMI and a PRI?

Ellis: I'm sorry. I used them because Charles /Frisch/ is a specialist and that's his language. A PRI is a Prescriptive Reading Inventory and a PMI is a Prescriptive Math Inventory.

Father: Can we see the results?

Ellis: Yes, it's essentially an audit system.

Mrs. Bonomi: So you're saying that an independent audit won't be made until the end of the year?

Ellis: Probably not.

In a short time the questions ended, and the group watched a videotape of class activities. Overall, this group of parents asked more specific questions about the activities in the team, and had more educational expertise than the first group. Many of these parents had actually spent a substantial amount of time in the school observing the class.

After the meeting the teachers seemed tense, but cautiously hopeful that some problems had been resolved. Jane received compliments from several parents about her teaching.

3. The BJW Open House

Between the two NBC open houses, BJW, one of the intermediate teams, held an open house for the parents of their students. The source of the open house was a mixture of parental pressure created by frequent visits to the school and the teachers' desire to quell parent concerns by explaining their program further.

Ellis was not present, and Bert presented an overview of the school day to 60 parents. He advised them, as had Ellis at the NBC open houses, that questions regarding individual children should be deferred until parent conferences, which were to be held the following week. Then the parents were divided into three groups, each one assigned to a teacher, for a simulation of the activities of a typical day. As in the NBC open house, the parent groups switched at a designated time to another teacher, for an explanation of another part of the program. As in NBC, the time after each of these sessions was short and permitted few, if any, questions.

When the "mini-day" or simulation was over, the group re-formed in the center of the teaching area and the teachers asked if there were any questions. The questioning that followed focused on the reading program and methods of evaluation and placement, much as it had in the NBC open house. Here, however, the tensions created between the parents and teachers were difficult to contain. At one point, on close questioning by parents Bert said he did not have to answer their questions, and threatened to leave the meeting. He was persuaded to stay.

The level of overt hostility in this meeting, compared with that in the NBC meetings, probably stemmed from the absence of Ellis or any other administrator. At the other open houses, Ellis had acted as a traffic manager and buffer between the parents and teachers.

Several parents told the researcher that the BJW open house had a negative effect on their relationships with the team members, and lowered their evaluation of the BJW educational program.

G. THE NINTH WEEK OF SCHOOL

The major activity of this week was parent-teacher conferences. On Monday, Tuesday and Wednesday, all teams scheduled 15-minute meetings with each set of parents during the afternoon and evening. Children were dismissed at 1:00 p.m.

1. BJW Problems with Parents Continue

At least one parent conference was not a positive experience. Mr. and Mrs. Golden found that, from their perspective, the BJW teachers did not know what progress their child was making. The student record sheets had only been used once -- the entry was for a few days before the conference -- and there was no work in spelling and language. The conference ended with Glenda's saying that other parents were waiting, but with the Goldens still unsatisfied. Mrs. Golden refused to leave even after Glenda left. Aware that there had been problems, Rebecca Barone spoke with the Goldens, and together they re-examined the child's work. After this experience, Golden said: "The rumors started to make sense. I'm a believing guy." Apparently, other parents had similar, though less severe, experiences in their conferences, causing them to raise further questions about the BJW team.

Later in the week, Golden met Bert at a LAHA-sponsored Halloween party. During their conversation Bert explained that large mass meetings like open houses were not the best way to communicate with parents. Golden asked if he thought small coffee-klatches with six people would be more useful. Bert said he did, and Golden invited him to speak at one he would arrange. A coffee-klatch was set up for the following Friday.

2. Ellis Confronts Priscilla

Early in the week, Ellis met with Priscilla and told her that he did not consider her to be fit to teach -- in effect, writing off her competence, though early in the year he had considered her one of the more valuable staff members. Priscilla, upset by this, consulted with an attorney to find out whether documenting her communications with Ellis would be necessary if either side wanted to take legal action.

3. Parents Request Transfers

During this week, several parents of children in the BJW and NBC teams requested that their children either be transferred to another class within the school, or (in the majority of NBC cases) to another school. It is not clear that the conferences directly caused the requests, but it is likely that they, along with the recent open houses in these two teams, were a contribution.

Ellis was successful in persuading parents not to transfer their children. But he dodged making a final decision in several instances by telling the BB team, to whose class many intermediate parents wanted to transfer their children, that they should meet with the parents to reach a decision. The BB team, however, felt uncomfortable, saying it was not their role to make such decisions.

H. THE TENTH WEEK OF SCHOOL

Ellis decided to take this week as a vacation from school to work on his dissertation. Only the first three days were involved, since school was closed for Thursday and Friday so teachers could attend the annual meeting of the state educational association. Nevertheless, he had chosen to be absent at a critical moment in the formative period of the school. Several of the teachers viewed his absence as avoidance of the difficulties facing him and the school; no steps had been taken to alleviate the pressures caused by the requests for student transfer.

1. Priscilla's Decision

By this time, Priscilla had evaluated her situation and announced to the researcher, "Maybe you should know that I'm job hunting." With a radiant smile, she explained that her decision was based on the conclusion that she had made a mistake in thinking that open space meant open education. As far as she was concerned, a self-contained classroom would be more suitable for open education; she didn't need the support of another adult in her classroom (a primary benefit of open education, as Ellis viewed it). She also complained that the noise created by other classes was a hindrance to effective teaching.

In her meeting with Ellis, Priscilla had suggested that for next year she team-teach with one other person, and that additional walls be erected. Ellis told her that her idea was unlikely to happen, in part because of the expense. From her point of view, Ellis was "talking out of both sides of his mouth," and denying problems. She felt the school was in disarray. If she found a suitable teaching position, it was her intention to leave Lincoln Acres as soon as possible.

Dori and Wanda enjoyed working with each other, had increased their team teaching (still at a relatively minimal level) and, overall, although disturbed by the state of affairs in the school, judged their own situation to be fairly good.

2. Transfer Requests Increase

By Wednesday, the last school day of the tenth school week, at least six parents in the NBC team had requested a transfer of their child to another school, and nearly 25 parents of children in the BJW team had asked for a transfer, either to the BB team or to another school. In the great majority of instances, the transfer request was for Fernwood, the school the children had attended the year before. Other transfer requests were for other public schools in the district, or for a nearby parochial school.

On Wednesday, Bob Biddle, the superintendent of schools, visited Lincoln Acres school. He commented:

> The parents are really uptight. It is probably because of the economic situation, but wouldn't you know it, they are doing just the wrong thing for their kids. When they should be loosening up they get tighter.

3. The State of the School

During the week, Sam confided to one teacher that he was uncertain about his role and duties; he didn't know if he was an administrator or a teacher. When the researcher asked Sam how things were going -- a question to which he had invariably responded with a cheery, smiling "Just fine, real great" -- he soberly answered: "So-so," shrugged his shoulders, and walked away. Similarly, Regina, who was ordinarily highly active and talkative, worked listlessly in the media center. Glenda, when asked how everything was, simply rolled her eyes and shrugged her shoulders.

In sum, by the tenth week of school, serious, persistent problems had arisen in almost all parts of the school. The teachers were depressed; many viewed Ellis as being inadequate to the task and, indeed, as avoiding his responsibilities. Furthermore, they did not see an end to the problems; their major strategy for controlling parent doubts and criticism, the open houses, had instead increased parental concerns and pressures for change. Certainly, the numerous requests for transfers were not a sign of community confidence in the school, or in the school's immediate future.

It should be noted that by this time an important change had taken place in the parents' criticism: during the spring and summer they feared what could <u>possibly</u> happen in the as yet unopened school. Now they were objecting to what they thought was <u>actually</u> happening in the classrooms. From a critique of the abstract concepts which formed a philosophy of open education, they had now moved to a critique of many daily practices in the school, based on close observation of classrooms.

A sense of inability to control events, coupled with disillusionment, spread among the faculty; the actualization of the initial vision of the social system of the school as it had been developed during the early planning proved to have serious defects. Jeanne said:

> A lot of the information in the school is from rumors. For instance, that point about children wanting to transfer started out as a rumor. Sam told Regina what Ellis had told him -- that's the way a lot of things happen in this school. We talked about being open and honest, but that's not the case. At the old school, I thought that nobody even pretended, nobody said they were going to be open and honest; everybody was closed and uptight and did their own thing, and I was more comfortable that way. At least you knew where you stood. Here there are lots of rumors.

4. The Coffee-klatch with BJW Parents

On Friday evening, the small meeting Sy Golden had arranged took place. Although the meeting was to have been a small one, close to 20 attended. Golden had invited Sam Schwartz, Tom Hassfelt (the new Board member), and several others, all of whom had children in the school.

Bert, the only member of the team present, tried to answer the parents' questions. For the most part, they were the same questions that had been asked at the open house. Sam Schwartz recalled it this way:

> There was food on the table but no one ate until the end. We heard some good answers but bad news. At one point things were so bad that everybody's stomachs started to growl and everybody reached for the food -- this is what I call "gastrointestinal reaction."

> Bert answered the questions but it was horrible: <u>he</u> /Bert/ said the answers were horrible. Our hearts went out to him, as an honest person he couldn't answer positively.

> The host asked us to stop talking at one point because he couldn't stand it. He wanted to change the topic.

Toward the end of the meeting the Board member present casually said, "How about report cards, are they coming out soon?" Bert said that he didn't know, and that "we can't get together on it." After this everybody started to eat again.

Reluctant to leave relations between the teachers and parents in such a poor state, Golden asked Bert to talk with the members of his team and contact him again on Monday to see if another meeting could be arranged. Bert, who was ill on Monday, called Golden later in the week and told him that he had spoken to Biddle and Ellis about the problems. Bert also told him that he thought the team was getting organized, and that he would discuss his conversation with them.

There were several other attempts to have another small meeting between parents and all of the teachers in the BJW team, but one never occurred. One contributing factor was that during the week of November 17 through 21 the entire BJW team and their students were at Rolling Ridge, an outdoor education center. But at one point, when a parent asked when there would be another meeting with parents, Bert replied that there would be one "when the team had something constructive to say." Not long afterward, Golden, Schwartz and several others approached Brown to ask for a transfer of their children out of the BJW team.

I. THE ELEVENTH WEEK OF SCHOOL

As in the weeks immediately preceding, stressful interaction between the school and the community continued; the conflict between the two groups intensified. The Board of Education, under pressure from the community -- and from several of its own members -- scheduled a meeting for December 1 (two weeks away) to discuss the problems with Lincoln Acres school. Strains within the school organization also increased.

1. Individual Faculty Members Meet with Ellis

Early in the week, Ellis asked that the teachers meet for private conferences with him by Thanksgiving vacation, which was to begin on November 26. The purpose of the conferences was unclear to many teachers. Several thought they were not needed,* but that a public faculty meeting to discuss school problems would be useful.

One of the teachers who felt this way, Dori, prepared a list of 36 problem areas she was willing to talk about with the entire faculty. The list, which she presented to Ellis, ranged from problems with bicycle racks to proposals for the arrangement of the school for the coming year. Some of the problems she identified were:

---

*In fact, Ellis did not meet with all teachers as proposed.

-- status of walls, school playground
-- idea that parents can transfer children whenever they choose
-- attitudes of "boss" displayed by secretary and janitor; wondering who's running the school?
-- lack of communication on this re: person in office to help teachers???
-- janitorial service -- usually poor
-- faculty meetings? 1-2 faculty meetings a week work load too much. Monday optional: if Monday no Thursday
-- lunch room atmosphere

For the following year she suggested:

-- no 1-2, suggest more coordination of K-1 programs
-- personally, for 50 children two teachers (2-3, 3-4)
-- better system for dispensing supplies, art, gym equipment

This list is fairly comprehensive. While it does not accurately reflect the concerns of some teachers, it does echo the general discontent that most were beginning to feel and express among themselves.

2. Virginia Vitelli's Letter

On November 17, 1975, Virginia Vitelli wrote a letter to Ellis that was critical of the school, and forwarded a copy to Bob Biddle. Vitelli, a graduate of a local elite women's college and former researcher at a large military installation, was also a former corresponding secretary of LAHA. She had applied, unsuccessfully, for the vacant Board of Education seat that Tom Hassfelt was appointed to in early October. The letter, because of its critical tone and its arrival in the midst of other problems, is reproduced in its entirety in Chart 8.2.

Ellis mimeographed the letter and placed a copy in each teacher's mailbox. No explanation or other commentary accompanied the letter when the teachers received it. In fact, the usual method of school-wide communication, the faculty meeting, was cancelled for both Monday and Thursday of that week, ostensibly because the entire BJW team was at Rolling Ridge. Teacher reaction to the letter varied along a continuum ranging from bewilderment to anger.

3. Board Members Visit the School

In the middle of the week Board members Tom Hassfelt and Gerrie Holden toured the school at separate times. Hassfelt, whose son attended the school, inspected the instructional area for some time before anyone inquired as to who he was or what he wanted. He talked to the teachers about the lack of control of outsiders entering the school.

During this week Charles Frisch commented to the researcher that there were, "all kinds of cross currents" concerning the school. Michael Karalis, who because of business obligations was unable to take an active

CHART 8.2
VIRGINIA VITELLI'S LETTER

Dear Mr. Brown:

It has been made clear to me during several visits to the Lincoln Acres School that my daughter Julie cannot survive either scholastically or physically in the present environment.

At Fernwood, which she attended for her first three years, she was considered by her teachers to be a very good student. At my recent conference with one of her teachers, Ms. Neustadt, I was told that she is average, working "on grade level." This is too drastic a change in scholastic ability to be accurate. A more probable explanation for her present level is that the teachers do not inspire, challenge or urge her to achievements she can make. Under circumstances of lack of control by the teachers, where there are no requirements and no expectations placed on the students most of them, if not all, are quite willing to absorb whatever they can as effortlessly as possible. I consider the school to have failed in this regard.

The school has also failed to provide a secure environment where the parents can feel confident the child will not be injured in any way. The condition of the playground, the Lincoln Acres Park, is well known. Very little has been said about the lack of security in the building itself. It is possible for an unauthorized person to enter the building at any time during the school day and cause harm to students or property. No one makes any attempt to stop intruders or question strangers. Also, I have seen children wandering around and out of the school building with no supervision.

The entire situation reflects mismanagement, poor organization and an overemphasis on experimentation. I am sure that these concerns are not mine alone.   There must be immediate and visible changes made to accommodate all the children adversely affected by the present situation. It is not my desire to transfer my daughter to another school, but to see these changes made in our neighborhood school.

Very truly yours,

Virginia Vitelli

---

role in community affairs, observed that the school "looks good now." Six months before, Karalis had been concerned about the school and expected it to fail; at that time Frisch had been optimistic.

During the week, Vitelli's letter, the visits from Board members and other problems were not discussed much among the faculty. Judging from their sparse comments and sluggishness in the classroom, Dori's succinct analysis of the school seemed accurate: "Morale in this place has hit the pits."

4. The First PTA Meeting

In the middle of this week, on Wednesday, November 19, the first general membership PTA meeting was held in the gymnasium of Lincoln Acres school. The main item on the agenda was the election of PTA officers. Along with this, Regina held a book fair in the media center, where parents could purchase inexpensive paperbacks for their children.

Approximately 175 parents, and 11 faculty members, attended the meeting. After Ellis greeted the group and gave a brief history of the PTA Steering Committee, he read the major sub-section headings of the proposed PTA constitution and asked if there were any suggestions for changes. One minor change was requested and incorporated; this was followed by a unanimous vote to adopt the constitution.

The next business of the meeting was the election of officers. Ellis read the rules governing PTA elections and asked for nominations from the floor. Listed on a chalkboard in front of the gymnasium were the names of candidates presented by the Steering Committee's nominating committee.

President:	Herman Burstein
	Sandra Waters
	Sy Golden
Vice-president:	Lee Whitmore
	Jim Peabody
Recording secretary:	Beth Johnson
	Jane Katz
Treasurer:	Bobbie Hoffman
	Anthony Bonomi
Corresponding secretary:	Leta Milstein
	Martha Joncey

Immediately before Ellis asked the candidates to speak, and before further nominations were accepted, Sandra Waters withdrew:

When I volunteereed, there were no others. Now, two well-qualified men have joined and I think we should have a man as president for the first year.

There were no other nominations for president.

Burstein, in his speech, emphasized that he had been a teacher in Hamilton, the largest city in the state, and was an attorney. He ended his short address by saying:

I know that some of the people here have gripes because of the way the school was put together. I don't personally, but I think they should be represented.

When Golden spoke, he stressed his position as the attorney for the Washingtonville Board of Education. He gave a long speech on how the school and community should cooperate, and claimed that parents in Lincoln Acres were eager to take an active role in the school. Finally, he mentioned that he had obtained professional landscaping plans for the grounds around the school and the atrium.

Nominations were requested for vice-president, and Sandra Waters was made a candidate for this position. Lee Whitmore was the first to give a campaign speech. She said only:

> If I am elected to this political office, I would be one teacher
> on the executive committee.

Then Jim Peabody (Sylvia Peabody's husband) stressed his experience as a former teacher, and his conviction that fathers should become involved in schools. Sandra Waters explained her previous experiences in PTA's.

No other candidates were nominated for the other positions. With the exception of the candidates for treasurer, who talked at some length about their experiences with handling other people's money, the campaign speeches were extremely short. After all candidates had presented themselves, Ellis asked the parents to vote. While the votes were being tabulated, coffee and cake were served.

Fifteen minutes later, Ellis announced that there was a tie between Jim Peabody and Lee Whitmore for vice-president; another vote would have to be taken. Ellis, annoyed that Lee, the only teacher to run for office, had not been elected, walked to the back of the gymnasium after making the announcement, and told several teachers, "These parents can't do a thing right. This will cost them dearly!"

A short time later, Ellis announced the final results of the election: the president was Sy Golden; vice-president was Jim Peabody; recording secretary was Beth Johnson; corresponding secretary was Leta Milstein, and treasurer was Anthony Bonomi.

J. THE TWELFTH WEEK OF SCHOOL

Transferring a child from one school to another in mid-year -- even from one class to another -- is a serious matter for both parent and child. The process is disruptive for the child: the daily routine is broken, friends may be lost, and a temporary decline in academic progress may occur. For parents, transfer is an inconvenience; new transportation arrangements must often be made, and bureaucratic procedures have to be followed. So for both parents and children, the process of making the decision to transfer to another school or class is emotion-laden, especially when it happens under circumstances of conflict like those at Lincoln Acres school.

On November 24, 1975, Charles Frisch, who had previously threatened to transfer his son from the NBC team to Fernwood school, but had been persuaded by Robert Biddle not to, turned his threat into a reality. Soon after, six other parents transferred their children from NBC to Fernwood school, and several parents in BJW asked for transfers. All this happened in a three-day period one week before the scheduled Board of Education meeting on the problems of Lincoln Acres school. Since Frisch had been a central figure in the school and school district, his reasons for transferring his child will be examined in some detail. We will also review the reasons other parents had for transferring their children.

1. Frisch's Reasons for Transfer

For Frisch, transferring his child to Fernwood school was the "second most difficult decision" he had ever had to make -- the first most difficult was choosing between two jobs -- and one that he delayed making because of his position as a Board member. The basic reason, he said, was "a feeling that the school wasn't going to get any better and that it didn't teach him." He continued:

> Every time you went up there you got a song and dance. I was an administrator, I can sympathize, but I'd get my tail in the classroom and you'd see change. We didn't see the changes. But they worked their tails off. I saw them there late at night. But maybe there was no leadership from the principal, resource teacher or superintendent. Probably a lack of leadership did it. Not having team leaders was a structural mistake.

From several visits to the school, both informally and during open houses, he concluded that there were things wrong; the complaints he and his wife had heard from neighbors were not without foundation. For example, at the NBC open house the teachers told the parents they were using a reading program called MOPPETS. Frisch had never heard of it, and checked with friends in the State Department of Education to find out if it was a "total" reading program. He was told it wasn't.

Frisch said many specific things influenced the decision: lack of continuity in homework; the "brainwashing" effort; absence of criterion-referenced testing; and their son's unhappiness and low productivity. Beyond these, Frisch said that in his view (and, he felt, in that of many other parents), the NBC team was "coming between us and our kids." Mrs. Frisch elaborated:

> I thought they had the wrong values. Right at open house they said "we want to be friends with your child." Chuck didn't need that. They should have started with where the kid was.

Overall, Frisch found that the teachers were not able to do what they said they were going to do; he did not disagree with their intentions, but could not accept their inability to realize them.

Mrs. Frisch had formed opinions of the school through direct observation as a result of volunteer work every Tuesday in the school library. She commented, "People might have thought I was a spy," and continued:

> You could see the difference between the BB team's class and
> NBC. One teacher was there doing things with the kids, very
> active. I couldn't figure out what Bert's team was doing.
> Parents said there were racial problems there between the
> orientals and whites. I would get depressed every Tuesday
> after working in the library. I couldn't see the kindergarten or
> the 1-2 because they are blocked off.

For Dr. and Mrs. Frisch, transferring their child from the Lincoln
Acres school resulted in the enmity of several neighbors. One neighbor,
once a good friend, insinuated that the Frisch's child wasn't "cutting it" in
the school and that was why they transferred him. Other parents verbally
assaulted Frisch. As we have noted, the decision was extremely difficult.
After recounting the agonies of another family that finally made the same
decision, Mrs. Frisch said:

> The real gut stuff never came out -- the real sob stories.
> There were so many little things going on. I don't think Mr.
> Brown understands what it means for a parent to take a child
> out of a neighborhood school. I liked him riding his bike. I like
> neighborhood schools. The community I went to school in had
> one. It's a very difficult decision. Mr. Brown could never
> understand.

2. Parents Requesting Transfer: An Overview

In a questionnaire sent in February, 1976 to all parents of Lincoln
Acres school students who were enrolled in September, 1975, we asked the
following question:

> Since the beginning of school this fall have you done any of the
> following things with any of your children who attend Lincoln
> Acres school? (Check all that apply)

Here are the categories, and percentages of parents saying they had carried
out the action involved:

6%   Transferred to Fernwood school or another
            Washingtonville public school.

0%   Transferred to another school (private or
            parochial).

4%   Transferred from one classroom to another within
            Lincoln Acres school.

27%   Considered transferring your child but didn't.

From these data it is evident that dissatisfaction with the school was
high; over one quarter of the parents answering the survey considered

transferring their children* and ten percent actually did.

Detailed reasons. Parents were also asked, "What were your major reasons for acting as you did?" Below are some of the answers.

These responses are all from parents who transferred their child to another school.

Transfers from NBC: After six weeks of trying to give the school a chance to organize, we could not continue due to no reading program, most assignments being oral with no written work, no math program (supplements on dittos being given). Lack of responsibility on the child's part towards his work, freedom to roam, play, etc. at will; three teaching periods a day, one of which was free play; and three discussion groups per day encouraging not communicating with parents if inclined to do so, expressing one's feelings at will.

After much soul-searching we transferred one of our children out of LA. After many weeks we could find no reading or math programs. There was utter confusion -- with my child feeling no sense of accomplishment. The class was run in a haphazard manner, no follow-up on assigned work, misplaced homework assignments, incorrect or incomplete grading of papers. There was no person to whom my child felt responsible.

We felt the teachers were not experienced, and the class was geared to 2nd grade. Our daughter in 3rd grade was learning nothing or reviewing. Everything was a game. She loved school but learned almost nothing. Her teacher at Fernwood said she was about 8 weeks behind. She transferred in early December.

There was no curriculum. Teachers didn't know how to teach. My daughter was put in 2 reading books above her level and below her level in math. In my opinion my daughter seemed to be regressing in her learning skills. Student teachers taught her 90% of the time and they seemed more competent than the teachers. My daughter was not learning. She was just getting confused.

Transfers from BJW: Child said he wasn't learning anything. Apparent lack of curriculum and lack of basic skill programs.

---

*The figure for "considered transferring" is probably inflated somewhat, since the question was retrospective. It should be noted that transfers began on November 24, and continued through approximately December 15.

Not enough teacher instruction and direction. Principal stated verbally he was not aware of daily classroom activity. Request to transfer from one class to another within the school was denied on 3 or 4 occasions.

I felt that my child was not getting the proper education that a child would normally be getting at his age. There were a lot of problems in the 4-5-6 group and I felt that the 3 teachers involved were not doing the kind of teaching that should be taught. There was no spelling, penmanship, social studies and many things that should be taught to a nine-year-old.

Transferred from NBC and BJW: Two children were not responding to their potential as they had done in Fernwood school. They were losing interest because of constant testing during first six to eight weeks of school. No review of prior learned skills was given at beginning of school. We felt teacher instruction was negligible and there was no follow-up of teacher direction with the little instruction given. These two children began to show signs of boredom and irritation. They were transferred back to Fernwood. The third child (grade 1-2 level) is still attending LA school because we feel he has an excellent, experienced teacher.

The following are the responses of parents who transferred their child to another classroom within Lincoln Acres.

Transfers from BJW: Disgust with BJW, E. Brown. BJW individually fair to good, teaching equals 2-3, inexperienced but learning. Brown a disappointment, no follow through. Very poor manager.

Plans had been made to place child in Fernwood, but principal at LA school asked us to consider other 4,5,6 class (BB group). New class observed and decision made to keep child at LA school. Personal observation of BJW group revealed to me what I had suspected after 3 weeks of school. There were absolutely no records kept of any kind by these three teachers the 1st nine weeks. All teachers were supposed to complete profile sheets on each of their students during 9 wk period. These teachers had no records of the progress made on any of their students. No papers were sent home of any work being done at school in any of the basic skills. Parents were told by these teachers at a special meeting after 6 wks of school that all papers were being saved for conference time. At conference time no papers were available in the students' folders. There was absolutely no teaching of spelling in this group and no language arts and a pitiful reading program. 1) no basics taught; 2) attitude of 3 teachers; 3) total program poor; actions of teachers incompetent.

We had no confidence in BJW to get down to teaching basics in an orderly fashion within a reasonable time.

Finally, below is a sample of responses from parents who considered transferring their child but didn't.

There should be a standard for each grade which every student should try to meet instead of different levels (two or three) for different students even in the same grade.

I felt my daughter in the 2-3 class was not getting the proper instruction and was not learning her school work. I decided not to transfer her because that would not solve my problem, as I had other children coming into that class within the next few years. The class has now straightened itself out and I am much happier with it.

My son must learn to make the best of most situations in life and deal with the problems those situations represent, so I decided to give him the opportunity now.

Considering LA school is new, I will give them a chance.

My nine-year old has a problem in that he does not like school and does not work. I felt Fernwood got more out of him.

I did not feel the child was working up to his potential and I don't think the teachers know my child and his capabilities. I feel there was a lack of discipline, instruction, and follow-up on child's school work. My child didn't seem to know what was expected of him nor did there seem to be any clear cut curriculum, or goals for him.

I don't act hastily. I prefer to keep things simple and keep the children in their local school; I feel things would get better at LA.

I am not happy with his progress in this class. I am now considering requesting a transfer although other parents have told me their requests have been denied.

It seems clear from the responses that the complaints of parents who carried out transfer requests emphasized teacher incompetence (disorganization, lack of record-keeping, inexperience) as much as or more than they did programmatic inadequacies (lack of particular subjects, misplacement of students). As might be expected, those who considered a transfer but did not carry it out had less biting criticisms, contented themselves with more general complaints (claims of student non-learning, non-uniform standards, lack of basics) and were willing to give the school a chance to improve; a few even entertained the possibility that the child was to blame.

K. THE THIRTEENTH WEEK OF SCHOOL

The number thirteen has mystical properties in our culture: it means bad luck. At Lincoln Acres school this week, although things had certainly been turbulent before -- and luck could not be wholly blamed -- it was as if the heavy weight of the number thirteen had fallen directly on the entire school.

At the Board of Education meeting Mary Hertz summarized many parents' frustrated feelings about the school:

> Will it take another 13 weeks now that you've started a crash program in spelling, grammar and reading? Why did you let 13 weeks go by before you began to realize the problem? Why does it take 13 weeks for experienced teachers to recognize a problem? Where was the supervision? Recognition of problems was precipitated by a meeting with the parents. Must I go up to the school every two weeks -- as I have been doing -- to get any action?

1. Administrative Intervention

On Monday, Dr. Biddle, reacting to parent complaints, assigned Harriet Stein, a learning consultant in the district, and Astrid Little, his assistant, to begin work with the NBC team immediately. Their purpose was to aid in strengthening the educational program. At the same time, Sam Pennington, the school's resource teacher, was assigned to help resolve problems in the BJW team. Additionally, Dr. Robert Marowitz, a State University reading specialist, who had been observing educational programs in the school for the previous two weeks, was now assigned to report on these two teams' programs.

2. The December 1 Board of Education Meeting

That evening, the only issue on the agenda of the Board's regular meeting was the Lincoln Acres school.

Biddle's report. The 60 Lincoln Acres residents present, along with 30 people from other parts of the township, and one Lincoln Acres teacher,* heard Biddle give an opening summary of his evaluation of the school, based on recent visits. He noted that one of the problems in the BJW team had been that there was no spelling program, but that now there was "a very good one." In Biddle's assessment, there were also problems in reading and

---

*Lindy Braun, the part-time art teacher, was the only faculty member present besides Ellis.

math instruction in this team. He announced that he had assigned Stein and Little to work in the school. He also said that Ellis Brown had asked Sam Pennington to work with the BJW group, and that a preliminary report had already been made by Dr. Marowitz. He explained:

> One of the things they will be doing is help tighten up. I was in there today and saw some good changes but not everything is changed. There is a communications problem with many parents and teachers. I sometimes feel that they want the same things. I'm also very much aware that the morale of the teachers is not the greatest at this point. They are feeling pressured and [are] having a difficult time with what they have set out to do. They are feeling that lack of communication.

> By the end of this week there should be a schedule of the 4,5,6 [BJW]and a rather marked shift in the way kids see things. There are good things in the school. We called in Bob Marowitz from the State University. We haven't gotten his entire report, but Mr. Brown and I have talked to him today and his assessment was that the kids are learning.

Parents' reactions. Following this brief assessment -- Biddle did not mention the NBC team except to say that Stein and Little would work with them -- Irena Farrell, the president of the Board of Education, opened the meeting for public questions. Needless to say, the parents' questions were critical. Generally, they focused on what parents perceived to be a prolonged period of testing, absence of curriculum in certain areas, poor monitoring of student progress and failure to take corrective measures. Here are some of the exchanges during this portion of the meeting.

> Sam Schwartz: Testing, testing. Every time we raised a question on the kids' education we were told they were being tested. Are you now going to start testing again? If we go under the assumption that the kids haven't been learning and we're now going to try to make it up, I think it's more like half a year lost than 13 weeks. Are we looking at a lost year here? I'd like Dr. Biddle to respond to that.

> Biddle: I'm not willing to say that no learning has been going on. The idea was to bring in some diagnostic instruments to get some benchmark data on these kids. I'm not responding to your statement because I don't agree. I don't think either that now we should have some way to be able to say to you, "Here's where your youngster stands and what we're going to do -- by January 15 this is where we expect him to be." In the event that we did not measure up, a number of things could be wrong: the background data or the prescription. We're not at that point, but we're working toward it.

Sam Schwartz: We were told that the kids in the 4,5,6 were being tested. No magic happened.

Biddle: There is no magic.

Sam Schwartz: I know there isn't. Now you're saying we're going to start again with testing.

Frisch: That's what you did say.

Biddle: I'm sorry. There was testing, but not as detailed as I'd like to see. There is all kinds of data available: observation, testing, kids' products. I'm not saying begin again, but let's form significant benchmark data that everyone can agree on. I'm talking about a set of information on all kids.

A fairly detailed discussion of types of tests and their uses followed. Besides Ellis and Biddle, several Board members, including Charles Frisch, contributed to the debate. When it was over there was still tension between the ideas of testing to monitor student progress, and excessive testing that supplanted instruction.

One father wanted to know what would happen when the three interns working with NBC left in December. Biddle, admitting that he didn't know, turned the question over to Ellis, who said they were additional personnel, not a planned part of the program, and would not be missed. The questioner responded: "The teachers themselves say that they are an important part of the classroom." Biddle then asked Astrid Little if more interns would be coming from the college. Little said they would not be. The meeting continued with Sy Golden's questions.

Golden: I'm the president of the Lincoln Acres PTA and Board of Education attorney. I want to ask a hard question of Bob and Ellis. For the 4,5,6 what day will there be a full reading and language program? Why has there been an interminable delay with these programs, and spelling that began last week? Lastly, who bears responsibility? I don't mean to push anyone to the wall. I understand there could be problems beyond personnel. If we can't get an answer tonight, I think we should get one soon.

Biddle: Ellis, what can you say about it?

Ellis: We had a specialist in today who said that the program was good. The teachers feel bad about the delay in starting the programs. There is no shirking of responsibility.

Farrell: Did you get an answer?

Golden: I didn't hear when the program starts. Are you saying we already have the tests?

Ellis: Yes. We don't need more tests immediately. We hope we have some external acceptable measurements to show the community and Board.

Farrell: Do you feel it was answered?

Golden: Not about the delay.

Biddle: I met with Ellis, Sam and some teachers last week and they expressed these concerns. They felt that the priorities that they had established were the ones they had to work on first. There was quite a lot of youngsters who were together for the first time this year. They spent a good deal of time doing two things. First, working on creating a cohesive unit, and second, getting motivated into learning processes. We can question their priorities, but this is what they chose and did quite well. They gave examples of things kids could now do, for example, listening.

Golden: The only thing I'm concerned about is that SRA and silent reading is not a reading program. Having one child question another is not a reading program. That's what I hear from the ground floor, from my daughter.

Ellis: A lot of what you heard was not from today. That's when these things started.*

The audience collectively gasped: Today!!

Rob Goldman: Dr. Biddle referred to a communication gap. I think there is one bigger -- between teachers and administrators and other schools. There are no complaints with the 1-2 /applause/. Some people with kids in both are only complaining about the 4,5,6. Parents are taking kids to Fernwood. They must be doing something parents like.

Marie Bonomi: I'd like to answer Rob Goldman's question. The 1-2 teachers have taken 25 children to themselves -- it is barricaded -- it might as well be an individual classroom. The 4,5,6 /pod/ in which it is working /the BB team/ is highly structured and barricaded, and has 50 kids. If you look at the two pods that are working, they are nearly self-contained.

---

*Several new programs had begun that morning in BJW, including spelling and more structured reading.

In this meeting, criticism of the kindergarten program was voiced for the first time in public since the school opened. Barbara Berger asked if there were educational objectives for the kindergarten, and continued:

> I feel there is a lack of substance and discipline; self directed and teacher directed. I feel that many of the children have regressed after two years of nursery school. There is no time for follow-up, and they learn incorrect things. I think this is the story of the school.

Two other parents, both Berger's friends, also criticized the kindergarten program.

During the course of the meeting, Sam Schwartz and Mike Perciatelli said that it was no longer a question of whether or not they would take their children out of the school, but only a matter of <u>when</u> they would transfer them. Several parents asked if the Board <u>had</u> the power to fire administrators and teachers. When the Board claimed that they did not, parents persisted in recommending that such steps be taken. The discussion then turned to how problems in the school should be handled.

> Biddle: This is not a criticism but a procedural comment. One of the problems is that a school can't deal with problems when they don't know what the problems are. They /parents/ often go right to the Board. People often don't want to talk to school people because they think it will be taken out on their kid. The line of communication we have to have is to talk first to the people who are directly involved.
>
> Farrell: It was my impression that parents had gone to teachers first.
>
> Frisch: I think you're giving the wrong impression. I think some stayed away to give it a chance. Many have talked to teachers. When the 2-3 problem came up it was settled. Now we have the same problem in the 4,5,6. Who takes responsibility? I can't answer that.
>
> Peabody: Three of us have kids in Lincoln Acres. We have talked to you, and many others have talked to teachers.
>
> Frisch: Are you implying that before this there were no problems?
>
> Biddle: No. All I mean is that problems are usually solved better at the operational level.

<u>Action steps</u>. The final part of the meeting concerned actions to be taken to correct the situation in the school. Golden wanted to know if there would be reports from Marowitz, Little and Stein. Farrell answered that the Board would receive a report, but not the public. Golden then requested a

meeting to check that progress was being made. Ellis replied that in a short time, notices would be sent to parents to arrange meetings with teachers. Finally, Frisch asked if a report to the Board in January on the status of the BJW team was acceptable; by consensus the Board agreed to require a report on the state of the school in January. With this action, the tumultuous meeting ended.

3. A Note on Who Was Protesting

That week the front-page headline of the Washingtonville Courier read: "Acreites Blast Policy, Teaching at School." In recounting the events of the Board meeting, the paper noted correctly:

> Many of the parents who protested at Monday's meeting were among the moderates in the Lincoln Acres community. This summer they had wanted to give openness a try.

Golden, Frisch, Berger, and Schwartz, among others, had been involved in the pre-opening stages of the school, and had at that time supported open education. Even after they transferred their children, Frisch, Golden and Schwartz regretted that the open space aspects of the school had not worked.

It is important to note here again that though the summer opponents had in effect been arguing against a phantom -- an unopened school -- the present "converted" opponents had had the opportunity to see the school in actual operation, and to compare their observations with what the teachers claimed to be doing. All the active opponents at this time had attended the open houses and the parent conferences, and had spoken several times with the teachers or Brown.

Other parents (for example, Mrs. Bonomi and Rob Goldman) had opposed aspects of the school from the beginning, and continued to, even though Goldman had been successful in getting a major concession before the school opened (the reorganization of the primary groups).

Another important change had occurred by now: those who had initially opposed the school because it violated the bond issue no longer argued from that perspective. Indeed, many of these people (for example, Barbara Collins and Alex Georgiades) were fairly well satisfied with the school.

Supporters of the school -- it seems reasonable to assume that more than a few parents approved of the education their children were receiving* -- did not come to the teachers' aid at the meeting. It is likely that community norms, the rapidity of the charges against the school, and perhaps unwillingness to get involved contributed to their silence.

---

*At later meetings, numerous parents did demonstrate support for the school as it was originally planned and operated through December. Survey data collected in February also lend weight to the idea that more supporters existed than was evident from public behavior.

In sum, opposition to the school was now led by a different group than in the summer, and was based on direct observation of classes, and on contact with the teachers and administration. Additionally, the most vocal dissenters -- Frisch, Golden, Berger and Schwartz -- were all prominent members of the community, and relative "insiders" in the educational system of Washingtonville. Frisch, besides being a reading expert, was also a member of the Board of Education; Golden was the Board attorney; Berger was the chairperson of the LAHA education committee; Schwartz had formerly held that position. These statuses provided credibility to the criticisms; the protesters were no longer a fringe group arguing about a historical event such as the bond issue, or an as yet unopened school.

These shifts in the protesting group intensified the conflict and increased the pressure on the school to change.

4. The PTA Executive Committee Begins Work

On Wednesday evening, the Executive Committee of the Lincoln Acres PTA held its first meeting, to form subcommittees and discuss fund-raising techniques. Sy Golden, the recently-elected PTA president, did not notify Ellis of the meeting. Ellis' reaction was:

> Shit. Golden started the PTA without me. I'll have to get on the phone and chew him out. According to the by-laws I'm a member of the executive committee. It makes common sense to tell the principal about a meeting.

It is not clear if Golden's act was intentional or merely an ommission. It does seem unusual, however, that so central a person as the principal could be overlooked, especially for such a key meeting of the new organization.

5. The Reorganization of BJW

Glenda, Bert and Rebecca, who had been the target of much of the recent parent criticism, began working with Sam Pennington on Monday, December 1, 1975. Sam's aim was to give the BJW program "more structure and make it more visible." Basically, he worked to help them organize more effectively; by late in the week they had produced a schedule of their daily activities and an outline of a curriculum. On Friday, December 5, a five-page report on the status of the reorganized BJW team was sent to every parent of students in the class. The report contained the weekly schedule, inlcuding activities of each day, and a description of the curriculum in reading, math, language, science and social science. An accompanying letter, written by Ellis, explained the program and invited parents to make an appointment if they wanted to discuss anything, but asked parents "not to come to the school to talk to the teachers during the school day (9 a.m. to 3 p.m.), since this kind of conference takes the teachers away from their students." The letter also explained the origin of the new program:

A great deal of the instruction outlined in this report has been started recently. I would like to explain how these new additions came into being. As a group of students proceed through the year, they make progress that requires some change in schedule and program; in a new school the adjustment period for some youngsters can be rather long and require rather large scale programming when it is over. As teachers proceed through the year they perceive better ways of delivering services to their students; again, these better ways can be more numerous and significant in a new school. A most important source of the changes, however, is parent input. I hope you will find whatever concerns you have been kind enough to mention to the teachers or to me responded to in this report.

Along with the report, all BJW students took packets of homework assignments home for the weekend. These were to be signed by parents, and returned to the school on Monday by the students.

Team teaching was not affected by any of the recent changes in the instructional program.

After working with the BJW team for a week, Sam's evaluation, expressed to the researcher, was:

I have confidence in BJW. They have more experience than NBC. These teachers were all in the system before. The Board, however, has to develop policies that are clear and that are the same for all schools in the district. For example, we can't test unless they give us the tests.

What I have done in BJW is to work on cleaning up their administrative procedures. Now they don't have to spend time on scheduling during the day, but can meet and plan for children.

The teachers in the BJW team were not happy with the course of events. But for the most part, they did not express their displeasure to Sam or Ellis at the time. As we shall see in detail later, they objected to Sam's intervention, and to the way Ellis had managed the reorganization. Their delayed criticism also focused on parents' role in determining the educational program; essentially, they felt the parents had interfered with what they were attempting.

6. The Non-reorganized Teams

During the reorganization of the BJW team and the NBC team (which we will describe shortly) the other teams in the school continued to change as a result of internal and external events. By the end of the week, most teachers had read the Washingtonville Courier account of the December 1 Board of Education meeting. They thought several statements attributed to

Ellis in the article were non-supportive of the school; teacher morale dropped even further.

The kindergarten team. As a result of the criticism by Barbara Berger and her friends at the Board meeting, the administration asked the kindergarten team to hold an open house for parents. All the kindergarten teachers, Alice, Sarah and Louise, thought the open house was unnecessary, and that it was unwise to respond in such a way to the complaints of three parents. Indeed, to Louise it seemed particularly unnecessary, since all three of the complaining parents had children in Sarah's class; the entire kindergarten program was not being questioned, only a particular segment of it. Louise and the others thought that the parents' actions were unfair on another basis; they had approached the Board of Education before talking with the teachers about the problems.

The MTK team. No changes in the structure of teaching had occurred in the MTK team during the past weeks. During this week, however, Dori's attitude toward Priscilla had begun to change. She now admired Priscilla because "she knows how to handle herself." And since the meeting when Ellis told Priscilla she was "unfit to teach," there had been no further interpersonal problems in the team. As for Priscilla, she viewed the current situation in the school as being "out-of-whack." She said she was going to put only a "minimal effort" into school, because "there are other things in my life -- I want to learn French."

The BB team. Jeanne said she felt tense in school, and wondered who was actually running it (she thought that Monica, the secretary, managed things most of the time). She also felt morale throughout the school was "down." In terms of activities in the classroom, Jeanne said she and the other BB teacher were, for all practical purposes, working in separate, self-contained classrooms. In some areas, however, they continued to switch students, but they planned instructional activities separately.

Jeanne noted another source of tension: Bert would often visit her and make semi-joking comments, such as "you're the team that's doing well, how do you do it?" She wished for better communication with other teams. For example, noise from NBC bothered her, but she felt unable to talk with them about the problem, because they had enough troubles already. Her solution to these problems was similar to Priscilla's: she decided to "wear blinders" when in school, avoiding attention to the activities of others.

7. The Reorganization of NBC

Astrid Little and Harriet Stein began working with the teachers and interns in the NBC team on Monday, as ordered by Biddle. Astrid and Harriet assessed the placement of children in reading programs, discussed reading techniques with the teachers, and re-examined the purposes of the current instructional program. By Wednesday, with consultation from Harriet and Astrid -- particularly Astrid -- the teachers reached an important decision: their program would be strengthened if they abandoned team teaching, and formed three self-contained classrooms. The new program was scheduled to begin on the following Monday, December 8, 1975.

Sally claimed that she and her teammates were looking forward to the change, mainly because all three of them had been feeling "overwhelmed," and that the move to self-contained classrooms would relieve this pressure. In her opinion the problem was that they had "bitten off too much." She felt, however, that the problems were aggravated by the removal that week of additional pupils from NBC to Fernwood school; on Tuesday Perciatelli and others removed their children. Sylvia Peabody, a Board of Education member, threatened to remove her son, but decided not to because of difficulties with transporting him to another school.* It was Sally's view that Frisch's transfer of his child the week before had begun the current trend.

Despite her claim that she and her team members were looking forward to the change, Sally spent time on Wednesday sobbing in Ellis' office. Ellis told her that he understood her feelings, but that he couldn't give her constant support; she should develop enough internal strength to be able to deal with criticism. Sally said that she accepted this response, and retained respect for Ellis. It had helped her understand Ellis' attitude when she saw the quotations from Monday's Board meeting he had posted on the bulletin board -- including the parent comments that asked when his contract ended.

Jane and Katie, the other members of the NBC team, were unusually quiet, and appeared to be depressed. Two weeks later, Jane, who had never had her abilities questioned, said:

> My program was fine. It was the other two that didn't work. I
> wish they had done better.

Biddle monitored the situation through conversations with Astrid Little during the week. He appreciated the job that his assistant was doing with NBC, and on at least one occasion, gave her a hug. At mid-week, Biddle visited the school and talked with the teachers in the NBC team. He left them somewhat puzzled: he told them that he supported them, but thought they didn't know what they were doing.

On Thursday afternoon, the team met with Harriet and Astrid to work on plans for creating self-contained classrooms. To aid the redesign, they intended to model themselves after MTK, and to borrow ideas from the BB team as well. That afternoon, they wrote a letter to parents to explain the new educational program; the teachers felt that this message was urgent, because it might prevent more transfers.

Ellis moves to fire Katie. On Friday afternoon Ellis asked Katie Neustadt either to resign or be fired, and requested that she not inform others of this action until Monday. His reason for this action:

---

*David Hauptmann, the principal of Fernwood school, had a child in the NBC team, but never complained about the education she was receiving, at least not publicly.

She is incompetent. She was responsible for the NBC reading program and had misplaced kids in reading levels by as much as a year-and-a-half. That's not so bad in the higher grades, but it's disastrous in the lower ones. We found kids reading in second grade books who should have been in fourth grade ones.

NBC reorganization planning continues. To prepare for the transition to self-contained classrooms to begin on Monday, December 8, Astrid Little called a meeting of the NBC team and interns for Sunday, December 7, 1975. She also invited Ellis to the meeting, which was to be held at her home. At first Ellis resisted, but after Little insisted, he came.

The all-day meeting was primarily a training session in how to teach reading. Also, because of the need for additional placement testing, it was decided to postpone the change to self-contained classrooms until later in the week. During the day, Ellis said practically nothing. Katie, who Little felt had been antagonistic toward her during the previous week, was now, in Little's phrase, "suddenly sweet and pleasant."*

Overall, Little was appalled by the lack of information that teachers had on student progress, and by the absence of data on teacher performance, a responsibility of Ellis'. At this time, Astrid viewed Ellis as having abdicated. Indeed, Sol Levinsky said to the researcher that, in effect, the faculty felt Astrid was now the principal.

It should be recalled that Astrid Little had been a candidate for the principalship of Lincoln Acres school, and was disappointed when she did not get the job. Now, with Biddle's support, she found herself reorganizing the most embattled part of the school, and thought that the principal had stepped aside. It is possible that she viewed herself as the person actually running the school.# But from the teachers' standpoint, it is probably more accurate to say that they felt no one was running the school. To them, it was "out-of-whack", as Priscilla put it, or run by the secretary, as Jeanne thought. The dominant feeling on the part of teachers was clearly that the school was drifting, rather than being controlled.

Katie decides to contest her firing. Despite Ellis' request that Katie not notify other faculty members of her dismissal until Monday, she did contact several teachers over the weekend. After talking with the president of the Washingtonville Education Association (WEA) and an official of the county teachers' association, she telephoned Bert White and Dori Kraus. On the advice of the Association, she asked Bert and Dori for advice, and whether one of them would be willing to attend a meeting with Biddle and Ellis as her representatives from WEA (since the teacher contract stipulated that in such circumstances a WEA member could act as a third party to ensure due process). Katie had previously discussed various problems in her

---

*At the time of this meeting, Little and the teachers present were unaware that Katie had been fired.

#After reading the study, Biddle disagreed with this supposition, and said that Little's participation had been agreed to by Brown, as had been Stein's help for the teachers.

team with Dori. In addition, both teachers were tenured and therefore less vulnerable than others on the faculty. Dori agreed to represent Katie.

After the Sunday meeting at Astrid Little's house, Katie telephoned Jane and Sally, her teammates, to inform them of the events that had taken place since Friday.

L. THE FOURTEENTH WEEK OF SCHOOL

On Monday morning, December 8, 1975, the president of the Washingtonville Education Association and an officer of the county teachers' association visited the school. They discussed the situation with Ellis, informed him that Katie had decided to contest her dismissal, and suggested that a meeting be held to discuss the matter further. A meeting with Biddle, Little, Brown, Katie and Dori was arranged for 3:00 p.m. that day.

The faculty was shocked by the recent events. Sally and Jane were especially depressed; they were afraid they would be the next to be fired. As it turned out, during the day Ellis reassured them and others that their jobs were not in danger. Sally said she looked forward to self-contained classrooms even more than before, and concluded, "I wouldn't even experiment next year unless I was sure I had full support from the parents."

1. The Faculty Discusses Katie's Firing

On Monday afternoon at 3:00 p.m. the teachers assembled in the MTK area, without Ellis or Katie, to discuss Katie's firing.

Somewhat bewildered and unorganized, the meeting jumped from topic to topic. The sequence of events that week -- the hostile Board meeting followed by the newspaper account of it -- suggested to the teachers that Katie's firing was not coincidental, but had been caused by these events. There were strong suspicions that Katie was being used by the administration as a scapegoat.

Bert talked about the need to insure that correct procedures were followed to protect Katie, and suggested that another faculty member be with her at all times to insure this. The teachers then elected Dori WEA representative so she could represent Katie. Regina, who was non-tenured, was elected to be the other WEA representative.

Jeanne expressed her sympathy for the non-tenured teachers in an emotional speech. She said: "I don't see how you can work in an atmosphere with this kind of pressure." Priscilla elaborated this view, and said the teachers were "caught in the middle: the Board hasn't acted responsibly." The others nodded agreement with both statements.

Bert recommended that the faculty keep information concerning the firing within the school. But Wanda said she had already heard that rumors about a teacher being fired in Lincoln Acres school were spreading throughout the district. Bert suggested that they obtain more information (for example, they didn't know exactly what Ellis had told Katie on Friday, or how much evidence had to be produced by the administration to show that a teacher was incompetent).

Someone asked if it would be appropriate to write a letter to the editor of the Washingtonville Courier and the Board of Education. After discussion, the teachers decided it would be a self-defeating course of action to have the "battle fought in the Washingtonville Courier." Rebecca Barone said:

> The Washingtonville Courier editor cuts up letters and meeting notes and distorts them. The Board meeting I was at once came out distorted and sounding more angry than it [really]was.

Sam said, "I have known Bob Biddle for a long time and I can't believe that he would use scapegoats." Most agreed with this assessment, but Priscilla noted that "Ellis tried to fire me. Maybe this is standard operating procedure with him."

This comment led Sally to say that it was not fair for only Katie to be fired, because she was part of a team. Prompted by this remark, other teachers asked Sally and Jane whether they had noticed any evidence that Katie had not performed her duties. Their answer was that she had done as much as they had -- possibly more -- and that they were stunned by what had happened. Others agreed, noting that they had seen Katie working in school late at night and on weekends.

The conversation then rambled: the Washingtonville Courier article was re-discussed; others noted the "lack of trust" between the faculty and Ellis; and there was further discussion of Katie's rights. Priscilla said that as she remembered it, Ellis made the decision during the summer workshop to have Katie teach the 2-3 class. Dori, she recalled, had wanted to teach the third grade, and Katie the first. But Ellis wanted Priscilla to remain a first-grade teacher and suggested that it would be bad to break up teams. She concluded, "The problem really isn't Katie's."

Comments were becoming sparse; the mood was sombre. Bert summarized by saying that they should get more information, and that they should support Katie in every possible way. At this point Sam was notified over the intercom to report to the principal's office. When he returned a few minutes later he announced, "Ellis has asked that we give time to Barry's questionnaire now."*

2. The Meeting Katie Requested

While the faculty was meeting, Bob Biddle, Ellis, Katie, Astrid Little and Dori Kraus met in Ellis' office to discuss Katie's dismissal. Dori attended the meeting as a representative of the WEA, and Astrid Little was present because her evaluation of Katie's teaching during the previous week had influenced, to some extent, Ellis' decision to fire Katie.

Near the beginning of the meeting, Biddle said he did not like Katie's having contacted the WEA. He said that when the WEA became involved in an issue the teachers never won. He also indicated that he didn't favor Dori's presence as a representative of the WEA.

---

*Several weeks prior to this we had made arrangements with Ellis to administer a general questionnaire assessing "the state of the school", during a faculty meeting. At that time the next faculty meeting without a scheduled activity was December 8, 1975; Ellis agreed that the

Biddle then questioned Katie on a variety of teaching methods. The questions were difficult and involved substantive knowledge of subject areas, as well as of educational practice and methods. For example, Biddle asked questions about young children with perceptual handicaps, which was one of his favorite areas, and thus one about which he knew a great deal. According to one knowledgeable observer, Katie answered the questions very competently.

When Biddle asked Ellis what Katie had done to deserve dismissal, Ellis produced a notebook, with a record of all the meetings he had had during the course of the year that involved Katie. He noted that in a meeting on October 7, 1975 it was decided that Katie would install certain practices and subject matter in the reading program. He said that these actions had not yet been carried out; he could claim no responsibility for this situation. Similarly, he noted instances when other decisions had been made, and who had the responsibility for implementing them.

At one point in the meeting, Ellis introduced the matter of Katie's having told other faculty members about the action he took against her on Friday. He pointed out that he had asked her to keep their conversation confidential. Katie claimed that she could not recall that part of the conversation, in part because she was disoriented during the meeting. She then apologized to Ellis for having told other faculty members. Not finding the apology acceptable, Ellis said that her action had turned the faculty against him, so that

> The hatred in here today was so thick you could cut it with a knife. I would rather have to suffer all year long with the kind of complaints I've received from the community than endure resentment from the staff.

During the meeting, Astrid and Dori said very little; the main actors were Biddle, Ellis and Katie. Toward the end of the meeting Biddle asked Ellis if he still thought Katie should be fired. After a long silence, Ellis answered that he did. Then Biddle asked all to leave with the exception of Katie.

As the others waited outside the office, Biddle offered a compromise to Katie; he said that she could be a substitute teacher in the district. Katie accepted this offer.

(footnote cont'd) questionnaire would be administered then. Needless to say, December 8 proved not to be a typical day. Here is a quote from the researcher's field notes, written that night:

> I was having difficulty in this situation -- I wanted to give the questionnaire, but felt it was a bad time. They didn't seem to be in the mood to take it; they were at their lowest point and our questionnaire seemed relatively unimportant to the organization in this context. I felt like not giving it. On the other hand, I felt as though we put a lot of work into it and needed the information; I wasn't sure that the atmosphere would be improved in a week, anyway. As it turned out, Ellis made the decision for me.

3. December 8, 1975 Ends at Lincoln Acres School

For the next hour, the teachers diligently filled in responses to the research questionnaire. At 4:45, Katie -- visibly pleased -- walked into the room where most teachers were working. She told Wanda and Sam the outcome of her meeting with Biddle, as other teachers continued with the questionnaire. Approximately ten minutes later Ellis entered the room, took a questionnaire, sat down next to Lee, and began to answer the questions. He joked with Lee, and seemed highly animated. No teacher acknowledged his presence. Shortly afterward, he joked that "This [the questionnaire] is for the football game tonight," and left. The remaining teachers finished the questionnaire, then talked briefly with Katie and left.

For Lincoln Acres school, the most turbulent day in its short history was over.

4. The Kindergarten Open House

The day following all of this activity was relatively quiet. In the evening, as requested by several parents, the kindergarten held an open house. Seventy-five parents attended. As at other open houses, they had the opportunity to inspect the teaching area and ask questions of teachers. The overwhelming majority of parents said they were pleased with the kindergarten program; many told the teachers they were unable to comprehend what some parents were complaining about. Understandably, the teachers were pleased and relieved to hear positive comments from parents.

5. Biddle's and Brown's Assessments of the Situation

On Thursday, Biddle reflected on recent events involving the Lincoln Acres school, and concluded that "the heat is almost out of it now." It was his opinion that the school was "on an upswing," since two weeks ago it had "hit bottom." He also commented that "stirring up the pot" was undesirable, and said cryptically that newspaper reporters had been doing interviews that he wished they wouldn't.

Ellis also viewed things as having improved in the school, but not as much as Biddle thought. He said that things were "very messy -- it's not clear what's going on." He added that he didn't know

> whether the blood-letting was aimed at Bob Biddle's head or mine. I think that the teacher dismissal might cool off things -- or arouse the blood lust even more.

In terms of his own situation, discussions concerning the following year's budget were beginning, and the district was looking for ways to make cuts totaling a million dollars. One of the possibilities was closing one of the rural elementary schools. If this were done, Ellis, as the junior administrator in the district, would be out of a job -- at least out of a job in administration.   He had discussed his future in the Washingtonville educational system with Biddle the day before, and said that they had "settled the issue." In Ellis' view, Biddle

> understood that I'd like to stay here and that I'm not going to preside over my own funeral. He accepted that. I feel that he understands and accepts what I'm doing, and there are no absolute implications, one way or the other.

He added that he thought Biddle was supportive of him, and that "I don't feel like letting go of something that I took a year and a half to plan."

6. Ellis Goes Public

Biddle's comment about an interview that he would rather not have seen conducted apparently referred to an interview Ellis had granted to the Washingtonville Courier. Later that day the boldest headline on the front page read: "Brown: 'Limits on Being Bull's Eye in Target.'"

The article begins with a summary of the history of the school. Following this, there is an extensive interview with Brown, who is identified by the newspaper as being "at the center of the controversy."   Before beginning the interview, the reporter wrote:

> Some parents say Mr. Brown is arrogant and unresponsive to their children's needs.   More moderate observers say he lacks the administrative know-how to monitor teaching methods in the open school and correct teaching problems. His supporters praise him for his hard work, his disciplinary action against unruly students and his efforts to correct teaching problems he has perceived.

Since this interview is Brown's response to his critics, an illumination of his state of mind, an assessment of the year thus far and a plan for the future, it is reproduced here with only minor deletions. The questioner was Linda Shaughnessy, the managing editor of the Washingtonville Courier.

> Q: Please specify the exact problems teachers in grades four through six and grades two through three are having.

> Mr. Brown: The two involve two different kinds of problems. Teachers of the grades four through six pod /BJW/ knew from the outset what was best for the students, what parents wanted and what programs were needed.   They were going about achieving all these things gradually.   But their values were not congruent with those of the parents. The children in their classes came from several local elementary classrooms, from a wide range of programs both structured and open, so teachers tried to clarify with kids what processes were going on and to give them a choice. They tried to trust the student

to make some decisions about his or her program and to allow him or her to work independently and responsibly whenever possible.

The teachers knew they needed a spelling program (one was started last week) and they knew they needed a beefed-up reading program but though they had started a formal reading program in September it was not strong enough. They waited until midyear to strengthen it.

Q: What about the problems in the grade two-three group? /NBC/

Mr. Brown: Teachers in that group began a program which was too ambitious. It was not a poor concept, nor was it poorly planned. Had it been, I would not have approved it. But teachers were trying to treat many needs of the student besides intellectual needs. They had a broad view of what they wanted to do for each student and a strong sense of the weaknesses of many of the more conventional methods of teaching. They were developing alternative ways of teaching while trying to do too much. I perceived a problem and on October 7 met with the teachers. I told them their program needed more coherence and that what I saw of their program didn't meet the reading and language arts needs of the students.

The students were doing a lot of different kinds of language arts programs and learning to love school, but the program was weak in reading and vocabulary skills.

During the first part of October the teachers reorganized their program to put more emphasis on intellectual needs and basic skills. They reorganized their schedule, spending more time on these skills. They began using the workbooks and other conventional material. They reported to parents on this October 28 and October 30 at our open house. I've seen a great deal of progress in this group.

Q: At the December 1 school board meeting Superintendent Bob Biddle promised testing as a diagnostic instrument to show parents what level their children have attained. Have you started this diagnostic testing?

Mr. Brown: We started testing students in September and recently have been testing where it seems appropriate. We are trying to test so /as/ not to interrupt the class schedule or to call off work to hold full-scale tests. The tests serve to validate groups of children and to change grouping of children if tests prove the grouping to be wrong. The kind of testing we are doing now -- criterion-referenced testing -- offers a statement of what a student can do. That is, it tests specific skills, i.e., if a student can locate Africa on the map of the world. It defines those things the child has mastered, has not mastered, and has mastered in part. It is prescriptive in the sense that it shows teachers what to work on with the student.

The kind of testing the layman is most familiar with is the norm-referenced tests which show the quantity of things a child knows and ranks him or her according to grade level. But this test doesn't tell anything about how a teacher should manage his or her student day to day. It can show a child is a fifth grade reader. But that same child might have an eighth grade vocabulary but be third grade level in comprehension. The teacher could discover these deficiencies with the criterion test.

Resource teachers, not the regular teachers, are doing the testing, and it is being done in grades four through six /BJW/where there are widespread concerns.

Q: Last week a parent said the other groups of classes which parents have not complained about are successful because they are more structured. Is this true?

Mr. Brown: These pods offer team teaching though perhaps a different type of team teaching. But the basic difference between those pods parents have complained about and those they are happy with, is not a question of structure, but of priorities. In the two "successful" pods intellectual training dominates during the teaching day to a greater extent than in the 2-3 /NBC/ and one of the 4,5,6 groups /BJW/.

Q: You tread a tightrope between supporting your staff and being responsive to parents. Is there any middle ground between the two?

Mr. Brown: No. Parents express their concerns and some criticize me saying I listen but don't hear them. I talk to my staff but when I hear parents I also try to make parents understand why teachers are doing what they are doing. I take note of parents' complaints, many of which are valid, and I follow up on the complaints, but many involve personnel issues which I can't discuss with parents. They say they don't see anything happening after they complain. But often I can't come back to parents and discuss personnel problems. It isn't professional. What I can and have discussed with parents is program, materials use, placement of students. And we've held more public meetings in this schools' first three months' operation than any other school I know about.

Q: Could this controversy happen in any town given the recent back-to-basics movements that is sweeping this nation?

Mr. Brown: There are lots of ways of opening a school [other]than the way this one was opened. Many parents moved into this area long after the school's planning had begun. It was difficult to measure those newcomers' desires. If someone applied the same scrutiny to any school in this or any other district, they would come up with many gripes about the way the school is run. Schools don't orient themselves toward accountability because they are not billing for their services or using their services as the basis for research. This school has spent more time on accountability than it might have done four or five years ago because of the recent push for school accountability. I sympathize with parents who came here after the school was developed and feel disenfranchised because either they weren't here when decisions about the school were being made or they did not know how to make themselves heard.

Q: You are only 27, a new principal in a new school with a new concept that has never been tried. Do you feel bitter about being thrust into controversy?

Mr. Brown: I feel I was brought here blindly. I arrived around January 1 and was told I had to choose a staff in 20 working days.* I worked from a list of volunteer transfer requests when I had anticipated being able to work first with transfers, but to choose from outside the district too. All the teachers here taught elsewhere in Washingtonville. On the interviews I had with the lay committee choosing the Lincoln Acres school principal, I was led to believe I was hired because they liked what I was doing in New Hampshire. I believed I was hired because of my school; otherwise why would four people drive 400 miles to see and compliment my school? I thought I would build a conservative model of what I had in New Hampshire here in Washingtonville. I was making commitments to teachers who wanted to teach in this situation. In 20 days upon my arrival here I had no chance to validate these assumptions with public opinion. Even among the district's professional staff members the opinion was circulated before I came here that Lincoln Acres would be an entirely open school. The hiring, architecture and choice of teachers was geared in that direction. Within the next few months public opinion showed that was the opposite of what many people wanted. Those who chose me knew where I was coming from when they brought me here.

---

*Biddle's comment is, "Nonsense."

But whatever bitterness I may feel about the confused pretenses upon which I was brought here, whatever anger parents may feel over their lack of input in the school architecture or program or hiring, here we are. We've got the kids. We've a school. What are we going to do with them? We must move forward. By midyear parents will know teachers better and teachers will know parents better. Both will have a clearer understanding of what each wants. In my own and my staff's proposals on how to set up the school next year, there will be more alternatives in staffing, programs and use of the architecture. Parents want and deserve alternatives and they will get them.

Right now I feel I'm 27 going on 81. I feel proud of the work I've done here. I feel I've taken and acted upon criticism well. I feel I've taken some criticism that might properly be directed elsewhere. I haven't evaded criticism. I've worked hard to resolve the problems. I think the kids here are generally pleased and the education we've provided here is excellent. I am a part of some things that should be continued and I want to see them continued.

There are for me and for the entire staff human limits to how much longer we can continue being the bull's eye of a target. I'll only be 27 once. I have wondered if I want to spend the year like this. I could not indefinitely put in this much effort with this little satisfaction. But I feel we've been through the crunch or we are going through the crunch -- the school morale is low now -- but I'm sure the job satisfaction for all of us will be greater in the future.

I would ask of parents that they be as quick to support us if they feel we are doing something well as some have been to criticize us. Some parents have voiced strong criticism and equally strong support. These parents are listened to because the staff knows they are not just here to attack.

(Comments.) For the most part, the majority of Brown's answers appear to be simply elaboration on previous events, or can possibly be viewed as a well-calculated public relations campaign. From the latter standpoint, it could be argued that Brown tried to placate the community critics, disassociate himself from various problems in the school and, in a sense, cast himself as having risen above the controversy, by stressing the need to get down now to serious work. Additionally, the interview has a quality of personal honesty; he admits to deficiencies and the feeling that he's "going on 81."

But beyond this, two themes Brown mentioned seem to be especially important. The first is that Brown felt he was appointed as principal for a type of school that the community did not in fact want. Secondly, he made the claim that he had taken some criticism that "might properly be directed elsewhere" -- that is, toward Biddle and the Board of Education. Both of these themes were to be elaborated by Brown in the following weeks.

7. NBC Becomes Three Classes

On Thursday, December 11, 1975, the NBC team switched from team teaching to three self-contained classrooms, as they had planned with Astrid Little the preceding week. The teaching area they had used as a team was now partitioned by furniture into three discrete classrooms (see Diagram VI).

Friday was to be Katie's last day in the school; a notice announcing the new teacher was placed on the bulletin board in the office, and sent to the parents and Katie's students:

> Miss Katie Neustadt will be leaving Lincoln Acres school today.... Mrs. Jan Holden will be assuming Miss Neustadt's class Monday, December 15th.

> Mrs. Holden comes to Lincoln Acres with five years of full-time teaching experience. A mother of two children and resident of Allwood Green, Mrs. Holden has most recently distinguished herself as a substitute teacher, particularly in the open space classrooms of Oxford school.

An open house was planned for Wednesday, December 17, to introduce the new teacher and acquaint parents with the new educational program in the second and third grades.

For the teachers, Katie's departure was an emotional experience. At lunch several congregated in the NBC teaching space and commiserated with her. Lindy, the art teacher, seems to have expressed what the others felt: "It was too bad that Katie had to be a sacrificial lamb." Near tears, the teachers had difficulty finding things to say. Sarah circulated a card that wished Katie well, and all of the teachers signed it. The mood of the school was one of depression.

Many of the children in Katie's class were also deeply affected by her imminent departure. They cried, and questioned why she had to leave; several told Katie they were going to ask their parents to contact the principal to protest her leaving.

M. THE FIFTEENTH WEEK OF SCHOOL

1. The Faculty Meeting

After school on Monday, the first faculty meeting in several weeks was held. Ellis put two topics on the agenda: formation of reorganization committees for the next year and open discussion. The teachers were quiet as Ellis explained that he wanted them to begin considering plans for next

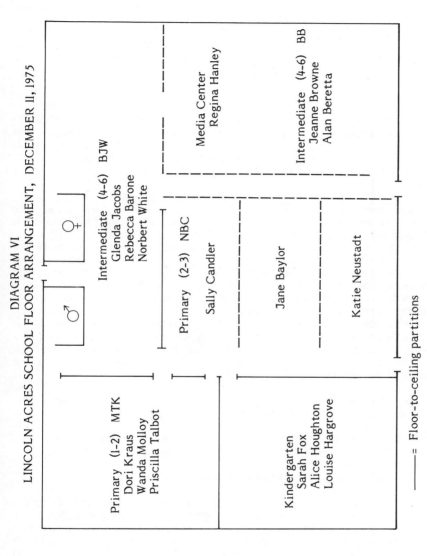

DIAGRAM VI

LINCOLN ACRES SCHOOL FLOOR ARRANGEMENT, DECEMBER 11, 1975

Intermediate (4-6) BJW
Glenda Jacobs
Rebecca Barone
Norbert White

Media Center
Regina Hanley

Intermediate (4-6) BB
Jeanne Browne
Alan Beretta

Primary (2-3) NBC

Sally Candler

Jane Baylor

Katie Neustadt

Primary (1-2) MTK
Dori Kraus
Wanda Molloy
Priscilla Talbot

Kindergarten
Sarah Fox
Alice Houghton
Louise Hargrove

———— = Floor-to-ceiling partitions

– – – – = Shelving or furniture arranged to form a barrier

261

year, what committees they thought were necessary, and which ones they would like to be on. There was little teacher response to Ellis' comments; when it was time for "open discussion" nothing was said. According to Wanda, everyone walked out of the meeting saying, "We wish we had discussed Katie."

Compared with the previous week, the first days of this week were subdued: the main business of the school was education, not politics. Remaining from the previous week, however, was a widespread gloom among the faculty.

2. The Open Houses

As promised at the December 1 Board meeting, the school made attempts to inform parents of changes in the instructional program. The first of these was an open house for the reorganized and reconstituted 2-3 grades on December 17, 1975. And on the following day the BJW team held an open house to inform parents of recent changes they had made.

The 2-3 open house. Fifty-five parents gathered in the media center along with the three teachers, and Biddle, Brown, and Little. Among the parents were several of the persistent critics who had decided to leave their children in the class: Peabody, Schwartz, Johnson, and Bonomi.

Ellis welcomed the parents, introduced the teachers, and described the new teaching arrangement, emphasizing that "we have a situation now of 25 students with an individual teacher." The teachers quickly described their daily schedule of classroom activities. In all cases it was highly structured: for instance, each class had three reading groups that met in the morning for a half-hour each with the teacher.

With the by-now-standard admonition that parents couldn't ask about individual students, Ellis opened the meeting for questions. Parent questions fell into five large areas: methods of dividing the classes, student profiles, reading instruction, testing, and progress reports. Below are some of the exchanges between parents and educators.

Mr. Johnson: Is this program being done now? Last time we heard a great program that wasn't being carried out.

Ellis: We have a third party here who can answer that. Astrid, is what has been described being done?

Astrid Little: Yes. It began last Thursday.

At several points during the session, Ellis referred questions to Astrid Little in this manner. Astrid's answers were always short and appeared to be accepted by the parents. Astrid viewed herself as a central figure in this meeting; she expected to be asked to comment on the state of the school. A dilemma that she expressed (in talking to Levinsky before the meeting) concerned what she should say about Ellis; she didn't want to "throw him to the wolves." She resolved the conflict by giving minimal, informational and non-accusatory answers.

Following questions about the placement procedure for reading groups, Mr. Jones asked a series of questions about the use of testing in the school. He concluded by saying:

The move you've made has been good. It's too bad it wasn't sooner. It has had an effect on the kids. They are upset with losing a teacher.

Mrs. Manning: You can't complain now! They made the changes you want. This is getting ridiculous. Let's get on with education. [About one-third of the parents applauded this.]

Manning's comment marked the first time since the beginning of the conflict that a parent had publicly defended the school. As we shall see below, other parents began to feel that the changes made, especially in the 2-3 grades, were not positive. The meeting continued with further queries concerning the day-to-day operation of the school, and with complaints from several parents that they were not being informed about their child's progress. Toward the end of the meeting, Sam Schwartz asked:

Where do you see the 2-3 going?

Ellis: It will be the same for a while.

Schwartz: Where would you like to see it going?

Ellis: I can't prophesize and say what's going to happen. We have to accommodate the students, teachers and parents. We have to find a way for finding the best way the kids can learn. I'm comfortable with what I see now and I think the teachers are. There are limitations that maybe we'll find out about.

Schwartz: I think that there were good things about the 2-3.

Ellis: Maybe in a year we'll go back.

Manning: If it wasn't for the parents could the open space 2-3 have functioned as it did elsewhere? Could that 2-3 space be operating today if it wasn't for the parents' pressure?

Ellis: You're putting me in a tough spot. I can't answer. I'm here to work with the parents.

Manning: Dr.Biddle?

Biddle: You're putting me on the spot now. I'll answer as honestly as I can. I think there were some good things done. I would like to see them working with each other again, but [at]the point we were at last week there was no choice. It was also not all parent pressure.

Peabody: You mean the teachers realized it?

Biddle: Yes.

The meeting ended with Biddle saying:

> The whole school can be an absolutely magnificent place for
> kids. I have listened to the parents and I don't hear anybody
> say we're not willing to work together. I think we have a good
> beginning.

A smaller meeting. When the meeting ended, groups of parents
formed and talked, mainly about the depressing impact that Katie's
departure had had on their children. One group formed around Sally, and
several parents told her they regretted what had happened, and wished that
parents had been more understanding. Biddle joined this group, and when
Manning asked him what he thought about the situation he said that he
would like to take some time to talk about it. He led the group, which
included Sally, Manning, and several other parents, away from the rest.
Ellis joined the group a few minutes later.

Sitting on the floor in Jan Holden's classroom, Biddle began the
following exchange:

> Biddle: I think if Sally will level with you, there were things
> that had to be done.
>
> Sally: Sure. But I would like to add that with Ellis' help and
> Sam's help it could have been worked on.
>
> Mother: In the beginning, at the Oxford School meeting, I said
> I was willing to give up two years. A normal child can catch
> up.
>
> Manning: This was a very exciting concept and you've lost it.
>
> Biddle: You haven't.
>
> Manning: I thought if it was having problems some changes
> should have been made, but not this.
>
> Biddle: Let me say this. I have said this to Sally and others
> and I wish I had in July. It didn't have an open space concept.
> It was departmentalization. We threw that out 40 years ago.
> /There seemed to be some agreement in the group that this
> was the case./ My ground rule for a new teacher would be to
> lay down the rules. Let me give you an example. In /my
> previous district/ many years ago we had a teacher who lost
> the class in two weeks. She came from Bank Street, a good
> school. She wanted to resign. I said that I would accept her
> resignation if she got another job. She got a job in /another

district/ and became an excellent teacher, she got it together. Here's what you do. You say here's a kid who has a problem, can you teach him math? Not departments.

Mother: How should they have started?

Biddle: As they are now, and then they could have flowed out.

Sally: I agree.

Biddle: /to Sally/ Someday I'd like to sit down with you and some others and really discuss the needs of kids.

Manning: Don't you think the teachers have gone through a lot? If I were a teacher in this school I'd be screaming like hell.

Biddle: I would too. I happen to be with your group.

Mother: The parents were against the school before it opened.

Biddle: I know they were.

Mother: In Fernwood there were no complaints. Here every parent seems to want to be an educator.

Biddle: I'm in conflict with myself on that. I think they have a right to voice what they think. But sometimes what they think isn't what should be done. In this country we're doing things that are oppressive.

Mother: Did you see the article in Newsweek, "Why Johnny Can't Write?" /several nodded/

Manning: My husband hires people from around the country and from the best schools and he finds people from Harvard who can't spell.

Biddle: It is a problem. We'll have Harvey Marsh come in -- it's a perceptual problem.

Mother: Let's hope this signals a period of cooperation between parents and teachers.

With this, the small, private meeting ended. Ellis, who said nothing during it, told the researcher immediately after it ended, "I'm fed up." A few minutes later Biddle repeated his earlier evaluation that three weeks ago the school had hit bottom, and that it was now on the way up. He continued: "When you get complaints that you've changed too much, gone too far, then it's time to stop."

In this meeting, and in the public one preceding it, Biddle seemed to acknowledge that there had been problems with the NBC team, but he never was specific. At the same time, he told the small group that he supported the teachers, and never directly criticized them. Instead, he said they had not actually been team teaching. It may have been that from his perspective the school was about to stabilize, and there was thus no reason to upset either parents or teachers further. But Biddle was often vague and sometimes evasive; he relied on a fairly large repertoire of gestures and facial expressions to convey his messages, rather than on precisely-worded statements.* At any rate, his message this evening seemed to be that the school had been changed in ways that the majority of parents desired, even though he and the teachers tended to dissent.

The BJW open house. The setting and atmosphere for this open house were the same as for the one the night before. Sixty parents sat in the media center. In the front of the room were Ellis, Sam Pennington, Rebecca Barone, Glenda Jacobs and Jim Jernowicz, an intern in the BJW team. Bert White, the third teacher in the team, was home ill. In the back of the room were Bob Biddle, Astrid Little, Priscilla Talbot, Wanda Molloy and Laura Bano, an intern in the MTK team.

After Ellis introduced the teachers, Rebecca read the team's instructional schedule, which was the same as the one delivered to parents at the end of the previous week. Parents were then permitted to ask questions. The questions fell into four areas: the use of student profiles, individual study, instructional practices and whether there were plans for a structure similar to the one in the 2-3 classrooms. As in the 2-3 open house, several parents supported the school. For example:

> Father: I don't see the problem. I think this school has more parent-teacher interaction than most others. When I get a paper at home and it has two wrong out of 100, I think the parent can judge what that means. I don't see what you are trying to get out of this. I'm very satisfied and we have two children here.

At this open house, too, Ellis used an "outsider" to support his assertions. In this case the outsider was Sam Pennington, who had worked with the BJW team during their reorganization.

One important difference between this meeting and the one preceding it concerned the attitudes of the teachers in the audience. Indeed, at the first meeting the only teachers present had been those in the classes under question. The following exchange illustrates the role of teachers from other classes in this meeting.

---

*Biddle's comment is:
This is a value judgment out of context. I was in an observer role, not a participant that night.

Mr. Lieberman: I still don't understand and others don't. I hear at LAHA meetings that the school isn't trusted, and also in the Washingtonville _Courier_.

Priscilla Talbot: I think you should speak for yourself.

Library aide: My son had Glenda Jacobs for two years before this and he's here because she came here. He has learned as much as any kid in this district.

Mr. Lieberman: But many feel...

Priscilla Talbot: Please speak for yourself. [Priscilla was sitting near the man and was more or less shouting this at him. He looked embarrassed and stopped talking. The audience seemed tense.]

Father: This meeting is not a personal debate. I think he can say whatever he wants to. It is his right. I agree with him. [He stood to say this and was forceful and somewhat emotional. The questioning continued.]

The meeting ended with a statement from Wanda Molloy. Standing in the back of the room, near Biddle, she said:

I'd like to say a lot of things. I hear a lot of confusion. You wanted papers and now you don't know what the marks mean. Your children are growing up and they have to see themselves that they are becoming responsible. Lincoln Acres is a new school and we're working hard and listening to you. Nobody moves in and furnishes a house in four months. You can't expect us to do the equivalent here.

After the meeting, the teachers answered further parent questions in private. The members of the MTK team present talked with Mrs. Wanamaker, who had written a letter supportive of the school to the editor of the Washingtonville _Courier_. They had difficulty believing what they thought to be the "picky" nature of the parents' questions, and concluded that the parents didn't understand the essence of education. They also agreed that a major problem with the school had been too much parent access: according to Wanda, "They used to line up to watch NBC."

Priscilla explained to the superintendent and the researcher that her actions at the meeting and the attendance of other teachers had been to make certain that what happened to the NBC team would not happen to the BJW team.

3. The WEA Meeting

The teachers were also beginning to resist further changes in the school through more formal means. That afternoon, at the regular meeting of the Washingtonville Education Association, Dori and Regina, the recently elected representatives, presented the situation as they saw it at Lincoln Acres school. Discussion lasted for an hour and a half, with the officers of the association interpreting what they heard as the basis for several possible grievances. Indeed, they wondered why the Lincoln Acres teachers had taken so long to ask for advice. It was agreed that another meeting of teachers, excluding Ellis, should be held at Regina Hanley's home on January 5, 1976, the first day after Christmas vacation, to discuss the situation in the school.

4. Teachers' Reactions

Reactions in the 2-3 group. On Friday, Jane said she felt as though the situation had improved, but that she would have liked to continue with the original program, even though her job was easier in a self-contained classroom. She continued:

> My program was fine, it was the other two that didn't work. I wish they had done better.

Sally, Jane's former teammate, felt differently. Ellis had recently observed her teaching; afterward, they had a conference. Sally asked if she was in any danger of being fired, and Ellis replied that he had not made a decision to dismiss her, and that there were two more evaluations to be made. During the conference Sally made several discoveries.

> I didn't know that how I related with parents, record keeping and the testing that I messed up were all going to be held against me.

She continued:

> My feeling is I'm fighting for my position. He said he's lost faith in me. He said I was the only one on the staff who he doesn't know where I'm coming from. It seems as though he looks at me with contempt. He doesn't trust me any more. We used to have a good relationship. The person I trust the most is Dr. Biddle. He's more of a humanist and has more feeling than Ellis. Most people believe Biddle is trustworthy. Katie still trusts Biddle.

Sally did think that things in her classroom had improved, but went on to say:

> We don't have a resource teacher anymore. Sam's with BJW all of the time. We've got Astrid Little instead who doesn't give me any help, nothing she does is any good. We see her two times a week. I told Ellis that I need help in organization, and I got Astrid Little, she's no help.

In the BB team. For Jeanne, things were "going well," but she said she couldn't wait for the year to end. The one bright spot she did see was that the Christmas vacation might provide time for attitudes to change. Additionally, she was pleased that during vacation the school, which in her opinion was filthy, was to be cleaned.*

In the other teacher's view, the problems of the school could be traced to the fact that at the beginning of the year there had been no discussion of "open education" or "open space" by the entire faculty, and that they had simply gone ahead with each team's making its own arrangements. He also thought that the lack of unity of purpose increased because there was no support from Ellis as the year progressed.

It should be remembered that teachers and community members alike regarded the BB team as the most successful teachers in the school; they were never criticized and found themselves the recipients of many children of parents who were dissatisfied with the BJW team.

5. Ellis Reflects

In a lengthy, tape-recorded interview with the researcher on Friday, December 19, 1975, Ellis offered his opinions and interpretations on recent events in the school, and discussed his plans for the future.

Concerning the conflict between the school and the community, Ellis' view was:

> What's happened is that a number of people in the community
> have just gotten to the end of what they were willing to
> endure on things they didn't like in the school, and started
> organizing support for where they were at. They went to the
> Board meeting [December 1] and did their thing. Those
> flames have partly been fanned by teachers being unable to be
> responsive on a one-to-one basis -- the only way that satisfies
> parents. In those two pods that are completely filled with
> teachers that do not respond well to direct, one-to-one irate
> conflict, there's a problem. One kind of parent comes in
> steamed up -- those teachers aren't the kind of people that
> know how to deal with that. In the other pods, we have
> teachers who have tempers of their own that the parents learn
> to respect before the parents push them too far. And the
> other piece that made it worse is some people said, "I've had
> it. I'm taking my kid out of here to Fernwood." And people
> started saying, "What's wrong with the school? People are
> doing this extreme, drastic act."

---

*The vacation time would also be used for the erection of floor-to-ceiling partitions -- the ones promised in the compromise plan of the summer.

Brown also had decisive opinions about teachers' functioning, as this excerpt from the interview shows:

> Researcher: Was there anything about those pods besides the personalities?
>
> Brown: They weren't delivering. I have felt really annoyed at some staff members because, for instance, in the 2-3 /NBC/things were set up in a viable way and it just wasn't followed, it just wasn't followed. If it was convenient to skip over something, like spelling, handwriting -- various things that were of big value to the parents -- because something was running on, then it got skipped over. And that cost. The schedule was not adhered to with much of any determination at all, and things were just being left out. Record keeping continued to be a mess and nobody really knew the kids on a really personal basis. It wasn't good.
>
> Researcher: Was this the parents' complaint?
>
> Brown: Not too many of them saw it exactly that way. Usually they had something that was a smaller thing, a paper that came home that didn't make any sense to them, or the kid was upset about something. There was usually a very specific focus, but taken together, that's what was going on. That's what I was seeing, too. So, I had had it. I got rid of the weak sister in that pod, and that has had real ramifications all around. A lot of teachers in the school, without openly saying to me, "Are you after my head?" have tightened up their acts. For example, people I've had trouble getting profiles from on time before, got them done and done well. Also, parents in the community who like things about the school, have started to come in and say that, and say it in public meetings. I think part of it is because they're afraid more people and things can get chopped out of the school until they start standing up in support of something.
>
> In the 4,5,6 /BJW/ there have been some problems that they couldn't face each other to handle. I think all three of them have been in some ways disappointed with the other two and didn't know how to approach that without treading on personal friendships, and they've put the personal friendships ahead of professional ethics even, during the school day. They can't have their school day relationships and their other personal friendships, and separate the day into segments or let them co-exist or anything, so they failed to criticize each other adequately to get things done. For example, one teacher was supposed to bring in a reading program to supplant the SRA kit that started the year and it never happened and nobody ever mentioned it to her.

Researcher: What was the critical difference between NBC and BJW, if there was one?

Brown: You mean why I chose to go one way rather than the other?

Researcher: Exactly.

Brown: Well, I did not feel that NBC had learned anything about teaming from September to November.

Researcher: What were they doing?

Brown: Well, they were team teaching, but they weren't doing it effectively. They had not learned to do it so effectively that they would do that better than the self-contained thing. I believe the BJW does know how to team better than they know how to do the self-contained thing, and I've seen them in both situations. As well as the fact that the personnel in the 2-3 /NBC/ were looking for the security of something simple, and I think were a little nervous about depending on their teammates for their own job security, whereas the people in BJW looked to their teammates to be supportive, because they are very personally supportive of each other, and do know how to team.

The whole hang-up is personal. It really is. They've got some kind of phony impression that to be friendly with somebody means you're nice to them, so never point out to them that they fucked up on something. I'm meeting so many touchy-feely folks around here -- maybe that's the way. But where I came from, people often had the expression, "I like him because he cares enough to get mad at me." They don't like each other enough to get mad -- they don't value anything enough to take that risk. And they knew that's how they got in trouble.

I'm being asked to deliver, I am delivering. I make assumptions about what's being delivered, and I turn around and look and see that those assumptions aren't there. Will somebody tell me that my assumptions are wrong! Somebody tell me it's wrong to assume the kids won't do SRA all year long, that it's wrong to assume they will study handwriting, they will study grammar, and spelling, and then document to me that you did it. And they didn't, and they know they didn't. They back off but they're still kind of pissed off, and I'm trying right now the approach of, "I don't want to read your goddam lesson plans every week, I don't want to keep reading your day-to-day record keeping systems -- it adds a lot of time and is making this job even less pleasant than it already is. But I've got to develop a feeling of security that you are delivering a program, or I know about it, one or the other."

An example came up last night. I was under the impression that SRA would be taken from total program to supplemental status. That is, one or two assignments in SRA a week, kind of a maintenance dosage of that kind of instruction. It was wiped out for two weeks. I turned to Sam and said, "What the hell is going on?" and he said, "There's just too much to do." I said, "Horseshit -- the communication is screwed up! I should have known about it!" And there I am hanging again. I will have to keep up this kind of obnoxious monitoring until that's over with, because I've been caught too many times with that kind of stuff.

Ellis' assessment of the other three teams was that there were "substantial interpersonal problems" in each of them, but he did not elaborate.

Later in the interview, he reiterated his view that he had inherited many of the current problems because of Biddle's and the Board's early mistakes in planning the school.

Maybe I'm copping out on some things that are rightly my own responsibility, but I honestly feel that most of my hassles have been cleaning up somebody else's mess.

He recounted the Board's role from the planning steps to the present.

That was a period of time when people were starting to give up working on the Board, and the reactionaries we've got in there now started coming into the Board. And Bob started losing control over the Board. So at that point, I don't know, maybe the Board's responsible, since they were hell bent and determined to do the major administrative decisions as a Board function. Maybe if they were being the grassroots rebellion that they claimed to be, they would have picked up on some of this and cleaned it up earlier. I don't know. So I got that mess, and lately I've had to do some things for teachers that I really shouldn't have had to do. This business of bulling through a schedule and bulling through a program description for those two pods that have been in trouble -- that never should have happened. But, I figure part of my function is to be a target.

Researcher: Is that a role description?

Brown: Well, it ought to be, because when things are tough there's got to be somebody to blame, which is why I make the disclaimer. I don't know whether my being annoyed that I'm cleaning up other people's messes is really accurate. I don't know whether I'm not doing just the same thing. I would kind of feel bad if that were revealed to me; if I were to discover that about myself I would feel angry toward Ellis -- so I don't really know. To some extent that has paralyzed me from confronting staff and Board members and Biddle, and saying, "What the hell are you doing to me?"

From their point of view, I hit them with things that the teachers who have been having trouble accept as their hassle -- things that they have brought upon themselves. But they usually come back with, "Well, if the parents had been more trusting we would have worked it out and there would have been no harm done," which is true. So I don't know whether implied in that, they're saying, "Had you kept the parents off our backs like you were supposed to as principal, there would have been no harm done," or "Had you helped me do what I had to do like you were supposed to, there would have been no harm done." I don't know whether that feeling is there or not.

Another theme in the interview was Brown's perception that problems in the district were widespread; he said at least two other principals shared his view. Thomas Flint, the principal of the high school, was confronted with problems such as an inadequate building that antedated his appointment, and was deeply dissatisfied with the Board's policies. Brown then compared his own attitude toward the school board with those of another district elementary school principal.

Mal Portnoy is concerned for the same reason I am. He doesn't want to be principal here. He doesn't want any part of open space. He has established himself where he is with his community, which is very different from Lincoln Acres, over at Sawyer school. He is also an idealistic kind of person, a nice guy, not like me, and sits back and looks dispassionately at the Board and doesn't feel they're the kind of Board he can work with -- in a very different way than I would say that. I get to the point where I can't put up with those sons-of-bitches any more, but he would just say he believes in different things and his values are different, and some kind of horseshit like that, you know. He's just extremely sincere.

Brown then evaluated the administration in the school district.

That's one thing that hit me last night while I was lying awake -- what happens if I really get this particular school put together?

I would ultimately get back to confronting the administrative team I work on, more and more than I am now. I would have more and more time to be thinking about the general administrative problems of the district that I participate in, and would become more and more disenchanted on the basis of working with a bunch of idiots.

Brown also predicted what he thought the next few years would be like in Washingtonville, and placed his current position within that framework.

> The problem with having this budget thing happen where maybe I won't have this job in another six months, is you start looking around at the whole thing and you get a wider perspective, and you start to appreciate the magnitude of some of this stuff. You say, "Hey, are you a missionary? Do you want to commit yourself to this thing, and that's what you're going to do instead of relaxing evenings for the next 15-20 years of your life, or not?" I can't do it. I can see just as wild and hectic a year next year as this year on new problems, not necessarily in this school but in the district. Part of my responsibility is part of the administrative team. If I'm going to do the excellence in education trip, I wouldn't be able to overlook it. I couldn't sit here and get fat like the rest of the guys.
>
> So that reinforces the thing -- how long do you hang around a situation that is ultimately not viable? That's a bad place to get to, because then little things bother you. If you're tired at 5 p.m. you say "What right do they have to work me this hard?" and say "Fuck it," and go home.
>
> It's funny, Lee Whitmore told me last week that she perceived I'd given up two weeks previous to that, and I knew I'd felt differently for the previous two weeks, but I hadn't thought of it in that way. But she picked up something. I've decided that I'm not going to sit through the administrative restructuring rehabilitation of this district -- I'm not going to do it. I'm willing to put this school together because it's no big thing -- we've been through the worst, but the hope of being able to last several years until I'm 30 to make a significant jump upward is past.

Brown compared Washingtonville with the school district in New Hampshire where he had been a principal.

> I just can't imagine what kind of incredible things people /could/ get done in New Hampshire with the resources that are spent /here/. It's just so completely out of line it's ridiculous. Teachers in this school make more money than the assistant superintendent did there. As a first year elementary principal I make more than the superintendent did there. We spend more money per pupil for the art program here in terms of supplies than we do for the supply budget in the entire program in all subjects there.

And he said:

> A problem with this state is that you don't feel significant. I
> felt significant where I was. I was a central figure in the
> town. I knew the Commissioner of Education for the state. I
> knew most of the state structure. My mother has the
> governor's son in school. It's closely knit. Not now. I feel you
> could take or leave an entire district in this state and make
> absolutely no difference.

Overall, the comparisons he made have a definite tone: Brown viewed
himself as being in an alien world. There is a strong sense of anomie;
suburban America is normless, while deep-rooted values and associations in
rural areas give life coherence.

At several points in this interview, Ellis said he was thinking of
leaving; in fact, he was already looking for another job. His decision to
leave was not public knowledge; the faculty and the central administration
were unaware of his intention. One of the influences on him, Brown
claimed, was the possibility that an elementary school in the district might
close, and that as the junior administrator in the district he would lose his
principalship. If this happened, Biddle had said to him recently, he would try
to find him another position. Ellis commented on this:

> I believe he /Biddle/ wants me to remain with the district, and
> where I'm at, there's far too much work to be done and the
> satisfaction is so distantly delayed, that I don't know what I'd
> need at this point to feel secure -- but I'd have to have a hell
> of a lot more than what I have now!

But even if his job were not eliminated, he wasn't certain what turn
his personal career would take.

> I'm all confused. There is a particular teaching opportunity I
> have in mind. To teach in the same school with a person who
> is, in my mind, the best open space teacher I've ever seen.
> That would have been hard to resist under any circumstances
> that were financially feasible.

Again reflecting on his career, later in the interview, Brown
observed:

> Many people have not given one thought to administration
> when they were 27 and it's been another five years before they
> got into it and had fine careers. What I'm very fearful of is
> that I could become one of these precocious people who
> becomes an administrator when he's 35 and doesn't have the
> good sense to get out before 65. I don't think there would be
> enough of my life other than work for those 30 years that I
> would do anything much. What would be left? So that's where
> education's at for me.

At no point in the conversation (or for that matter, during the year thus far) did Ellis say that he had performed poorly in the position of principal, or that he was tired of being an educator. He did say, however, that his feeling about the situation in the school was: "I'm sick of it."

6. The Christmas Spirit

In early December, Monica and Dori organized a faculty Christmas party. It was to be held in a local restaurant at a fairly substantial cost for each person. By mid-December, it had become clear that few teachers were interested in participating, and the party was cancelled. Most faculty members attributed this to their low morale.

Members of the community became aware of the difficulty the faculty was having in organizing a party, and to show her appreciation one parent invited the entire faculty to her home for December 22, 1975. Shortly afterward, the PTA hurriedly arranged a Christmas party for the faculty to be held on December 23.

As it turned out, the private party was cancelled. Teachers had heard that the PTA discouraged it, on the grounds that the PTA party on the following day would be more appropriate. Many teachers thought the PTA action was unwarranted.

The PTA Christmas party was held in the school cafeteria. Since the PTA had only been formed recently, the treasury balance was minimal; only sandwiches and soft drinks could be afforded. Most teachers thought the party was a disaster. Sally's view is representative:

> It was like come on in and sit with your friends, your camp, people who share your philosophy, and leave. The camps were those who have been struggling and those who have not been. It wasn't hostile, but there was no camaraderie at the party. Ellis sat with Monica as he usually does, and things were just polite.

With the faculty Christmas party, school recessed until January 5, 1976.

9

THE DYNAMICS OF REORGANIZATION

The reader may well feel adrift in the sea of events described in the preceding chapter, at a loss for satisfactory explanations. The Lincoln Acres faculty, and the researcher, had the same difficulty as the events unfolded. The teachers often felt overwhelmed, were anxious, increasingly upset. Frequently, they could not understand what was happening. For some, things became so confusing and disturbing that they abandoned their efforts to make sense of the events in and around the school; they withdrew, were insulating themselves from their surroundings. The researchers were often puzzled and amazed by a new development; the phrase "What next?" often appeared in research project staff meetings when Lincoln Acres was on the agenda.

In this chapter we seek to make sense of the changes in the school which took place between the first open house and Christmas vacation. To aid the reader in understanding the flow of events, and our efforts to provide coherent explanations, Chart 9.1 provides a chronological summary of the most salient events described in Chapter 8.

A. THE STATE OF THE SYSTEM

1. Changes in the School

By mid-December, several important changes had been made in the structure of the school. Priscilla was teaching independently, and Dori and Wanda functioned only minimally together. The BB team no longer attempted team teaching, and had isolated themselves from the rest of the school by building a wall of furniture. The BJW team, with Sam's help, had reorganized their educational program. After Katie's firing, her former NBC teammates and her replacement had switched to self-contained classrooms. Finally, student interns and parent volunteers had supplemented teachers in many classrooms.

These organizational changes had two fairly distinct sources: internal social processes and external conflict. In the cases of the MTK and BB teams, the movement from team teaching to practically self-contained classrooms was primarily a result of interpersonal processes within the teams. We have seen that the problem in MTK was described as being over "personalities" and "philosophies." This team sought assistance from Ellis and Sam that, for a variety of reasons, was not successful. In the BB cluster, one sensed an incompatibility of preferred teaching styles. But the BB teachers did not seem to consider either Sam or Ellis to be useful sources of help. Neither the MTK or BB groups experienced conflicts with the parents, so we conclude that they did not succeed in implementing team teaching because of reasons internal to the school.

CHART 9.1
CHRONOLOGY OF DECISIONS AND CRITICAL EVENTS
AFTER LINCOLN ACRES SCHOOL OPENED

Week

3   BB cluster delimits area with furniture
        NBC changes to homogeneous reading groups
        MTK changes to 2-team and 1 teaching alone (Priscilla)

4   NBC tries "brainwashing" parents
        Volunteers program implemented in library, and MTK
        PTA Steering Committee organizes
        Ellis away for 2 days
        Parent volunteers begin work

5   Ellis away for 3 days
        Frisch visits and criticizes
        Board pushes basic skills emphasis

6   NBC begins phonics program
        Parent visits increase

7   Ellis away for 3 days
        Ellis considers suspending Priscilla

8   NBC has 2 open houses
        BJW has open house (upsetting, Ellis absent)

9   Parent conferences
        Ellis says Priscilla is unfit to teach
        Transfer requests begin

10   Ellis away for entire week
        Transfer requests increase
        Faculty is depressed, dissatisfied
        Norbert holds coffeeklatsch, with negative results

11   Vitelli letter criticizes school and NBC
        Board members visit school

12   Frisch transfers his child; 6 other NBC transfers

13   Biddle intervenes - sends in Little and Stein
        Tumultuous Board meeting
        Golden and Schwartz transfer their children
        BJW restructures their work with Sam's help
        NBC reorganization plan (with Little) to self-contained teaching
        Ellis announces intention to fire Katie

14   Katie contests; WEA representatives meet with Biddle and Ellis;
        Katie reassigned
        Faculty begins mobilizing for support
        NBC begins self-contained teaching
        Katie leaves

15   2-3 (formerly NBC) holds open house; first signs of parent positive
        emphasis
        BJW has open house; other teachers defend BJW, attack parents
        WEA decides to hold January meeting to consider grievances
        Ellis has started looking for another job

On the other hand, changes in the NBC and BJW teams were initiated primarily by sources external to the school. Increasing parent pressure resulted in Biddle's radical intervention: assigning Astrid Little and Harriet Stein to reorganize NBC, and Sam Pennington to reorganize BJW. Ellis' removal of Katie was also driven by parent complaints. In these instances, although the pressure for change was initiated by parents, the school's internal social relationships were weak enough that it proved difficult to resist the demands effectively. Basically, there was an inability to solve problems.

2. Sources of Problem-Solving Inadequacy

Difficulties with problem-solving grew in large part from a structural weakness: the absence of team leaders. The team leader position was never created, apparently because the teachers wanted egalitarian relationships among themselves; a team leader would be a position with higher rank than that of the other team members. But without team leaders -- who could have met and worked regularly with Ellis -- communication, inter-team coordination, assignment of responsibility, problem-solving, decision-making and follow-through were all extremely difficult.

It quickly became apparent that maintaining egalitarian relationships within teams was difficult; there was a continual conflict between affective and instrumental norms. There were several examples where team members did not confront their peers with their failures. An accountable team leader could probably have been more direct.

Many problem-solving efforts turned out to exacerbate the conditions they were trying to resolve. For example, the idea of using parent volunteers, a strategy for coopting critical parents, boomeranged as parents collected more and more information with which to attack the school. Several of the open houses, aimed at "explaining" the program and improving relationships with parents, simply created more confusion, doubt and hostility.*

Biddle's intervention, a response to what appeared to be internal difficulty in solving problems and making adjustments, severely limited the autonomy of the faculty and led eventually to more conflict. Ellis' authority, already declining because of his inability to manage a variety of situations effectively, was further undercut when Biddle, in effect, took over the leadership of the school by ordering Little, Stein and Pennington to reorganize its troubled parts.# By this time, the teachers were no longer in a position to influence decisions in any significant way either. The sense of powerlessness and depression became pervasive.

Mistrust of Ellis also grew, and his authority was eroded further because the norms of the group no longer supported it (Blau, 1964). This was especially true after the teachers learned he had fired Katie. Then teachers themselves began to take measures that would reestablish their authority.

In general, during the process of trying to adjust to external demands, the social structure of the organization changed substantially. The major difficulty in the social system of the school was its inability to adjust to its environment without radically altering central features of the innovations being attempted.

3. Actualization

Linkages between planning and implementation weakened as the conflict between the school and community progressed. Faculty meetings were held less frequently, and in general communication within teams, among teams and between the teachers and administration decreased. As we have noted, trust between the teachers and administration also decreased.

---

*In the 10th week, for example, Bert not only failed to explain and defend the BJW program, but actually cast doubt on the competence of the team's work.

#Biddle's comment is:
/The paragraph is/ a value laden statement. I was criticized for not doing it long before. It was /also/ by agreement with Brown.

In addition, the objectives lists (profiles) in several teams were not ready until several weeks into the school year, and even then were not routinely used by teachers. Similarly, no mention was made of the brainstormed lists of team roles and decision-making areas developed during the summer. The objectives and role-description lists were not only potential linkages between planning and implementation, but also coordination mechanisms; their infrequent use indicates that the school was not well coordinated -- the school was, in fact, drifting.

Further evidence of drift, lack of coordination and thus failure to couple planning and implementation can be noted in the behavior of the administrators. Ellis, often absent, felt as though he spent much of his time "fire-fighting." Sam was uncertain what his role was, until he was assigned to work directly with the BJW team. Biddle essentially took a laissez-faire approach to the situation* until Lincoln Acres problems were substantial enough to threaten the operation of other schools in the district as a result of transferred students. While these behaviors were in part responsive to conditions in the organization, they also inadvertently contributed to problem-intensification.

B. IMPLEMENTATION SUCCESS

In terms of the first three criteria of implementation success presented in Chapter 1, the Lincoln Acres school had experienced little, if any, success by December 23, 1975. It will be recalled that these criteria include goal congruence, problem-coping ability, and stakeholder satisfaction.

Few of the original goals survived. As we have already noted, team teaching (except for BJW), open space education, and shared decision-making were no longer part of the school. Individualization of instruction was partially achieved. To a large extent, the original goals were replaced with the single goal of simply surviving for the rest of the year.

The weak problem-solving ability noted above was a primary cause of the loss of the original vision. Of course, the problems the school faced were considerable, and in many instances complex. The important point, however, is that the adjustments made to "solve" the problems substantially altered the original vision.

---

*Biddle disputed this conclusion, and the "laissez-faire" label very strongly, saying "Not so, absolutely not so." He explained that he had repeatedly given very specific help to Ellis without results. In any case, he emphasized, a superintendent cannot "rescue" a principal, without, in effect, destroying him. He acknowledged that he had been immersed in many other problems, and had also misread the community, based on his contact with the earlier residents of Lincoln Acres. "But laissez-faire, no way."

Satisfaction for teachers diminished as the year progressed, and increased almost inversely for parents. In other words, as the original, teacher-formulated vision of the school eroded, causing lowered teacher morale and loss of energy, the community demands were being increasingly satisfied. It can be argued that despite the abandonment of most goals, one of the major unachieved goals of the summer workshop -- responsively-oriented involvement of parents in education -- had been accomplished to a considerable extent (partly unintentionally) after four months of operation. So for one set of stakeholders, the teachers, the enterprise was a disaster. For another set of stakeholders, the parents (at least a sizable number of them), satisfaction was eventually considerable. Chart 9.2 illustrates the parents' increased satisfaction with the school. Unfortunately, no comparable quantitative data are available for teachers, but it is clear that their satisfaction decreased as the year progressed. Our hunch is that data for teachers would be similar to the dotted line on Chart 9.2.

C. POLITICAL STABILIZATION

One of the central questions raised by the preceding chapter is: Why did parents react to the school as they did? The answer is complex. We believe it involves (1) elements of the summer conflict that remained once the school opened; (2) the charge of teacher incompetence; and (3) characteristics of the community.

1. Residual Conflict

Responding to our survey, 86 percent of the parents disagreed with the statement: "By the time school opened in the fall, all problems between school personnel and community members had been settled." This percentage may be inflated somewhat, since the question was answered in February, after the conflict had heightened considerably. But it was clear that after the summer compromise many parents were still not satisfied, or only partially pleased, with the plans for the school. Perhaps more importantly, the conflict over the summer signalled to the community that without constant monitoring, the educators would be likely to implement their own plans. (Such suspicions were not entirely unfounded; note that the walls which were part of the summer compromise were not in fact installed until January.) In general, the community did not have a high level of trust in the educators. The political base of the school was substantially reduced as a result of the first episodes in the conflict; the tension between democratic and professional values remained.

It seems probable that the parents' lack of trust in the school increased their desire to observe classrooms in action. Though Ellis and the teachers were at best ambivalent about parent contact with the school, Ellis did invite parents to visit the school during the day, and few controls were instituted on visiting, in spite of repeated teacher complaints. The volunteer program moved ahead actively. Open houses and parent conferences were held. In brief, any parent who wanted to could observe

CHART 9.2

PARENT RETROSPECTIVE RATINGS OF SCHOOL PERFORMANCE*

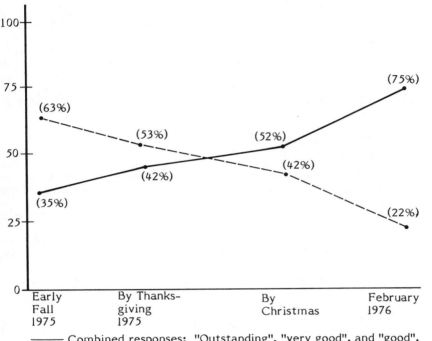

——— Combined responses: "Outstanding", "very good", and "good".
— — — Combined responses: "Fair", "rather poor", and "extremely poor".

* The questionnaire items, answered in February, were as follows:

"There are often rapid changes in new organizations. We would like to know your attitude toward the Lincoln Acres School at various times.
a. What kind of job do you think the school did in the first weeks that it was open in the fall of 1975?" (response mode: outstanding, very good, good, fair, rather poor, extremely poor)
Items b through d repeated the question in relation to these time periods: "by about Thanksgiving"; "the period shortly before Christmas"; "right now" (Feb.).

teachers directly in their role performance. High teacher observability was facilitated by the architecture of the school. (Recall that Mrs. Frisch, who volunteered for work in the media center, said that from there she could see all of the teams at work except for MTK and the kindergarten, who were behind walls.)

The following data from the parent questionnaire indicate the frequency of contact parents said they had had with the school. Table 9.1 represents the respondents' "best estimate /February/ of the number of contacts you or a member of your family have had this year with the school since it opened." We see, for example, that 108 parents, or 92% of those replying, had attended one or more school-wide parent-teacher conferences; 84% came to one or more open houses; and 75% had had special conferences with their child's teacher.

Why were these visits made? Table 9.2 presents the data from another questionnaire item: "If you or your husband have had direct visits to the school, please check those items which describe the reasons for the visits."

It should be apparent from both tables that for a period of five months* parents visited the school frequently. Naturally, most parents (90%) went to discuss their child's achievement. But particularly important is the high number of parents who acted as volunteers in the classroom (63 parents, or 53% of respondents); media center (9%); or other parts of the school (14%). Beyond this, 58% visited to "see how your child's class was running," and 45% to "see how the school was running in general." Multiple visits were frequent, and parents had the opportunity to see the school under a variety of conditions (not only on open house night), and in many cases once or more each week. This brings us to consideration of teacher competence; a major charge of parents was that members of the NBC and BJW teams were incompetent.

2. Teacher Competence

Judging teacher competence is not a straightforward matter. In most current educational practice, the tendency is to rely on "objective" -- or at least observable -- markers such as academic credentials, the teacher's "control" over a class, or the physical condition of the classroom, at least as much as on student output measures such as standardized test scores. Teaching-process measures, such as student time on task, plan books, report cards with teachers' evaluations of students, and judgments of interpersonal competence are less frequently invoked. And it is quite rare to make any

---

*Since the questionnaire was administered in February, data for January were also included. In most instances, parental contact with the school either ended or was minimal after December. For example, there were no open houses after December.

TABLE 9.1

PARENTS' CONTACT WITH THE SCHOOL SINCE IT OPENED

	Number of Contacts Reported (N=118 parents)						Total contacting	
	0	1	2	3	4	5+		
School-wide teacher-parent conferences	10	52	31	13	10	2	108	(92%)
Special conferences with the teacher excluding school-wide teacher-parent conferences	29	39	28	12	7	3	89	(75%)
School-wide open house	19	70	18	10	1	0	99	(84%)
Contacted by telephone to discuss behavior, school work, etc.	69	21	14	5	3	6	49	(42%)
School organization meeting, such as PTA, parents' associations, etc.	32	49	27	6	0	4	86	(73%)
After-school activities, such as adult education classes, recreation programs, committee meetings, etc.	88	11	11	1	1	6	30	(25%)
Sent notes to school	48	20	23	9	10	8	70	(59%)
A teacher visited your home	111	5	1	1	0	0	7	(06%)
Casual or accidental contact, just happening to be in the same place as teacher	66	16	18	4	5	9	52	(44%)

TABLE 9.2

REASONS FOR VISITS TO THE SCHOOL SINCE IT OPENED

Number of Visits (N=118 parents)

	0	1	2	3	4	5+	Totals	
Helping out in the classroom	55	6	11	9	5	32	63	(53%)
Helping out in the media center	107	3	0	1	0	7	11	(09%)
Helping out in some other part of the school	102	4	0	1	1	10	16	(14%)
Attending some of the children's activities (plays, concerts, sports)	83	26	6	1	0	2	35	(30%)
To discuss your child's academic and social achievement	12	30	34	19	13	10	106	(90%)
To see how your child's class was running	49	32	24	4	0	9	69	(58%)
To see how the school was running in general	65	30	16	0	1	6	53	(45%)
To talk to a teacher about something of immediate importance (without an appointment	74	21	21	6	1	4	44	(37%)

direct test of the teacher's knowledge of subject matter or techniques, once he or she has left college or university.*

Ambiguity about the best way to assess teacher competence certainly appeared at Lincoln Acres. But it was considerably reduced by the fact that parent educational expertise was high. Frisch, a major critic of NBC, was an acknowledged expert in reading. And fully 29% of parents who answered our questionnaire indicated they had been teachers at one time or another. Thus the questions parents directed to teachers were not general and vague ones, but highly specific questions which demanded specific answers# that were in turn further questioned if they were found inadequate. Given high observability and high expertise, the parents' scrutiny of teachers was intense; at one meeting, Board member Robert Klahr doubted if any other school in the district could survive the close monitoring that had occurred at Lincoln Acres. We suspect that few schools anywhere could be held as "accountable" as Lincoln Acres was without serious deficiencies' appearing in the process.

By pointing this out, we do not mean to imply that the Lincoln Acres teachers were entirely competent; it is certainly possible that they could have been more effective, in spite of their colleagues' strong claims of teaching effectiveness. (The teacher questionnaires asked, "On the basis of your experience and information, how would you rate the quality of teaching that the students generally receive from this school?" The responses were: 4 (17%) outstanding; 15 (62%) very good; 4 (17%) good; 1 (4%) fair. The responses, "rather poor" and "extremely poor" received no answers.)

Clearly, substantial differences existed between teacher and parent evaluations of the ability of teachers in Lincoln Acres school. To understand this discrepancy, we need to look at the conditions under which teacher "competence" was being defined.

---

*In fact, administrators -- department chairmen, principals, superintendents -- are also relatively immune from any systematic evaluation of what they know, or the way they actually perform their duties. Educational organizations are typically "loosely coupled" (Weick, 1976); as Miles (1981a) notes, low interdependence, low surveillance and control, and teacher isolation are usual. Such features are probably caused, he suggests, by schools' need to maintain "legitimacy" (lack of inspection implies trust on the part of administrators and citizens), and by the need to buffer conflict among the political, managerial and instructional "domains" making up the school. As we have seen, legitimacy breakdown, and failures to buffer conflict were at the heart of the Lincoln Acres situation.

#Notice the detail of the responses in Ellis' interview in the Washingtonville Courier on December 11, and the comments made in the December 1 Board meeting.

Recall, first, that for all practical purposes, the MTK team never functioned as a team. Similarly, the BB team had begun functioning essentially as self-contained classrooms by about the middle of October. Neither of these teams experienced the conflict with parents that the NBC and BJW teams did. In fact, by December, parents were asking why NBC and BJW hadn't patterned themselves after these two "teams," because parents were satisfied with them, and they appeared to have no problems. Furthermore, when NBC was reorganized with Astrid Little's assistance, the teachers decided to borrow elements of MTK and BB's work in the shift from team teaching to three self-contained classrooms.

This set of circumstances offers a partial explanation of the conflict that NBC and BJW had with parents -- and a deep irony. The explanation is that these teams were the innovative teams in the school -- the others had not even partially implemented the innovations -- and, although less-than-perfect teacher competence, some mismanagement and other variables intervened, the basic cause of parent reaction was the nature of the innovations being attempted. The irony is that by their rapid failure to implement the innovations, the MTK and BB teams provided a form of education that the parents could not only identify with, but considered successful. The non-implementing teams created this unanticipated outcome by providing a well-controlled educational situation that served as a backdrop against which the difficulties to be expected in the implementation of an educational innovation stood out in sharp relief. The MTK and BB teams made whatever innovations NBC and BJW succeeded in implementing look much more chaotic than would have been the case if all teams were trying to innovate. Evaluation is a comparative process; the innovative teams were being compared to the "traditional" ones, and were found wanting.

The idea that dissatisfaction with the innovations was a strong contributing cause of the opposition to the school is further supported by the fact that once the reorganizations were made, opposition ceased. Of course, many parents had transferred their children to other schools or other classes, thereby reducing their continued need to criticize the school. But as we have seen, most of the parents who considered transferring their children decided not to; all of the classes in Lincoln Acres school from the middle of December through June were self-contained, with slight variations. As we shall see -- except for some problems between the school and the executive committee of the PTA -- there were no conflicts with the community for the remainder of the year, and no teacher was accused of being incompetent.

3. Community Variables

In the early stages of the conflict, the central issue was the legitimacy of the plans for the school. The specifications of the bond issue had not been honored, many citizens felt; petitions and public meetings suggested a consensus that democratic values should prevail over professional values. Barbara Collins and members of the LAHA executive committee were among the educational opinion leaders of the community at the time.

Once the school opened, although the issue of the role of democratic versus professional values was still present, it was surpassed by conflict between two sets of experts: those within the school and those who were community members. The change in the community's power base (toward expertise), which was evident in their detailed criticisms, directly challenged and diluted the teachers' ability to claim that they were the experts. The community opinion leaders were now educational experts like Frisch, and "quasi-insiders" in the local educational system (like Golden, Schwartz and Berger). And many parents had claims to educational expertise as a result of teaching experience.

The influence of the community educational experts and others was extensive. Several Lincoln Acres residents told the resercher that events in the new school were a continuous topic at cocktail parties, in the local supermarket and on the streets. Rumors spread quickly, and the opportunity to witness the school first-hand -- either to confirm or disconfirm rumors -- was great. LAHA meetings, Board of Education meetings and the local newspaper also supplied information, and amplified the sense that there were problems in the school. Ellis recognized this communication pattern when he commented:

> And the other piece that made it worse is some people said, "I've had it. I'm taking my kid out of here to Fernwood." And people started saying, "What's wrong with the school? People are doing this extreme, drastic act."

Although it is difficult to measure the impact of parent transfer requests -- in particular Dr. and Mrs. Frisch's -- they did seem to influence other parents to take a closer look at their child's class, and in many cases to take similar actions.

Another possible explanation of the parents' aggressiveness toward the school is that they simply wanted to assert their presence. There are some indications that this occurred early in Lincoln Acres history, when LAHA aggressively sought political power. However, recent studies of new suburban communities (Berger, 1960; Gans, 1967) have indicated that most behavior does not change substantially with a change in residence from an urban to a suburban community. Social class and life cycle variables provide more powerful explanations than residential location (Gans, 1962).

The majority of heads of households in Lincoln Acres were professional or managerial-level employees. Additionally, 19% of the fathers of families responding to our questionnaire had some college training, 31% were college graduates and 37% had some post-graduate education. For mothers, 25% had some college, 31% were college graduates and 9% had done post-graduate work. If we juxtapose these data with those on the purchase price of homes in Lincoln Acres, (which in 1975 sold for between $50,000 and $70,000) it is clear that most of these families were stable middle-class, and not new to this socio-economic stratum.

Along with the high educational attainment and occupational status of these families was the fact that they were young. Some were still involved in the early phases of child rearing (children not yet in school); others' children were in elementary school or about to attend junior high school. To middle class families in this stage of the life cycle, schooling is an important aspect of life. Additionally, substantial numbers of Oriental and Jewish families lived in Lincoln Acres, two groups with high educational aspirations (Coleman, 1966). We conclude that commitment to educational attainment, as a function of family life cycle stage -- and in some cases ethnicity -- was more salient than sheer community newness or residential location in heightening parents' preoccupation with the quality of education their children were receiving.

So several variables were influencing community interest in the school and critical reactions to it: distrust in the educators remaining from the summer conflict; expertise among the community members; positions of authority that several members held (Peabody and Frisch on the Board of Education and Golden as Board attorney); easy opportunities to visit the school; and the social class and life cycle stage of most families.

It should be noted, however, that the community was not monolithic: not all residents were opposed to the school, and not all of those who opposed it did so for the same reasons. However, those residents whose opposition to the school had the largest impact -- that is, resulted in changes -- held substantially similar views. In the first wave of the conflict, they formed a coalition around the demand for alternatives to open education, and enforcement of the bond issue specifications. In the second wave of the conflict, once the school opened, a temporary coalition was formed around the issue of teacher and administrative incompetence. It should also be noted that for the most part the teachers perceived those members of the community opposed to their efforts as somewhat more organized and like-minded than they actually were. That was understandable, since it wasn't until major changes in the school had been made that parent support for the innovations became visible.

D. CONCLUDING COMMENTS

The pattern of relationships between the school and community (and subsequently within the school) during this period was increasingly one of force and force threat. Essentially, the school attempted to deal with threats from the community(e.g., student transfer) by making minor adjustments (reorganizing the NBC reading program and staging open houses). Unsuccessful in these attempts -- in effect, forced to make further changes to prevent more transfers -- the administration of the school (Biddle and Brown) reorganized the school unilaterally, without the collaboration of the teachers. As a symbol to both the community and the faculty of the depth of the changes, a teacher was charged with imcompetence and forcibly removed from her position. This symbolic action ended the conflict.

But social processes go on. As we shall see in the next chapter, the use of force within the school created a counterforce; the teachers mobilized in opposition to the administration in an attempt to re-establish professional privilege.

10

THE REMAINDER OF THE FIRST YEAR

Following the resolution of the conflict between the school and community, the accumulated tensions within the school resulted in a conflict between the teachers and the administration. This shift in conflict focus was primarily the result of the teachers' reaction to the way Brown had managed the community conflict, and the consequences of his actions for the school.

A. THE TEACHERS ASSERT THEMSELVES

On the first day of school after Christmas vacation, the faculty, minus Ellis and Sam,* met semi-secretly at Regina Hanley's house to discuss actions to be taken to improve their situation. Also present was Rita Colazzi, the president of WEA (which had urged that the teachers initiate a grievance against Brown.

A wide variety of topics was discussed: the BJW and NBC reorganization, the recent behavior of Ellis and Sam; how to deal with parents in the future; and how the original plans for the school had been abandoned.

In brief, it was the teachers' consensus that the school had been reorganized in reaction to unjustified complaints by parents, without a fair attempt to correct the situation in other ways. They saw Ellis, not themselves, as responsible for the problems. Biddle was viewed as being

---

*At first, Sam was to be excluded from the meeting, because he was an administrator and had sided with Ellis in the reorganization of the BJW team. But after further discussion, the teachers decided to explain their attitudes to him, and present him with the options of attending the meeting or not. As it turned out, Sam defined himself as an administrator and decided not to attend the meeting. This episode further illustrates the resource teacher's role ambiguity.

without blame; his role was minimized because, in the teachers' view, Ellis had not informed him of the difficulties in the school. Indeed, Biddle was viewed as a supporter of the teachers, since he had refused to fire Katie as Ellis desired. Concerning Sam, there was agreement that he had become ineffective, due to the confusion over whether he was really an administrator and thus an evaluator, or a genuine resource to aid teachers.

The teachers also wondered what had happened to the role descriptions and other plans they had formulated during the summer workshop. They concluded that Ellis had ignored them because he did not want to be constrained by them.

1. Actions against Ellis

Several actions were discussed and agreed on. The first was that a grievance would be filed against Brown on the basis that his inability to maintain a clean building indicated his poor administrative qualities.* With the guidance of the WEA president, the teachers reviewed the procedures for filing a grievance, and decided to follow them meticulously, to insure success.

After a discussion of the increased paper-work demands that Ellis was now making on teachers (for example, daily submission of lesson plans), someone observed that he routinely produced three copies of all paper-work and kept one for his files. In turn, the teachers decided to keep careful records of all of Ellis' activities, in the event that documentary proof were needed.

Another complaint was that there had been no opportunity to discuss the problems of the school with Ellis. Teachers pointed out that in pre-Christmas faculty meetings, Ellis had ignored agenda items submitted by teachers. Rita Colazzi told the teachers that according to their contract they were permitted time to present their concerns during faculty meetings. If they wanted to, she said, this could be the basis of another grievance. The group decided, however, that instead, Jeanne, Priscilla, and Dori would ask Ellis the following morning for a faculty meeting for the following Monday, with a teacher-generated agenda. Following from the decision to maintain documentation of all transactions between Ellis and teachers, they also decided that at least one witness and one secretary should be present at all meetings between Ellis and any teacher.

In response to a lengthy discussion of Ellis' failure to control parents' access to the school, Rita Colazzi suggested that the teachers hold talks with groups of parents in their homes. She explained that WEA had recently

---

*Cleanliness was not, of course, at the heart of the teachers' complaint, but was chosen because of its concreteness. The history of cleanliness in the school was a long one; it reached back to the first faculty meetings in the fall.

held a communications workshop for developing coffee-klatch skills, to enable teachers to build support among parents for the upcoming bond issue. The same training could be put to the use of informing parents of the problems with the school, persuading them of the soundness of the present educational programs, and, if necessary, enlisting their support in seeking Ellis' removal. After some prodding by Colazzi, the teachers agreed to the idea, and a verbal skills communication workshop was arranged for January 29 at Regina Hanley's house.

Another strategy discussed for registering displeasure with Ellis was that teachers could make requests for transfers to other schools. No one actually made this commitment in the meeting, but Bert and Priscilla said they were considering it seriously. Several teachers were astonished to learn that one of the BB teachers -- who up to now had been apparently satisfied and productive -- had already requested a transfer.

In sum, the teachers' anger and intent to take actions to improve their situation increased over the Christmas recess. Their solidarity was based on the perception that the administration or the parents -- at any time, for any reason -- could vociferously question the way teachers carried out their responsibilities. To decrease their individual vulnerability, they evolved the basic tactic of enforcing the rules available to control Brown's behavior; until now his administrative style had lacked a predictable pattern. Along with this controlling function, the rules were to serve as instruments of harrassment and punishment; many in the group desired to create an atmosphere uncomfortable enough to force Brown to consider whether he wanted to remain principal of Lincoln Acres school.*

2. The Teachers Arrange a Faculty Meeting

On Tuesday, January 6, Dori, accompanied by Jeanne and Priscilla (who both took notes), met with Ellis. Acting as spokesperson for the faculty, she informed Brown that a grievance was being filed against him for the custodial condition of the school, and that he had until Monday, January 12, to respond to it (otherwise, further action would be taken).

Dori also told him that the teachers wanted to itemize issues for a faculty meeting on January 12. Disturbed by this, Brown claimed that it was his prerogative to set the agenda. Countering, Dori said that the contract specified that teachers were permitted to influence the agenda. Brown acquiesced; later that week he was presented with an 11-item agenda generated by the teachers. It appeared on the bulletin board as follows:

---

*Brown's interest in seeking another job was unknown to teachers at this time.

*****

Given to Ellis 1/6/76 3:30 before posting or distribution.

Faculty meeting agenda for January 12, 1976

1. Policy on lesson plans
2. Policy on profiles
3. Parent visitation policy
4. Evaluation process
5. Definitions we decided on as our roles (summer report -- we need a copy of the "handbook").
6. Discussion of proper procedure for dealing with parent concerns
7. Role of resource teacher
8. P.T.A. -- faculty role
9. Recording minutes of meetings
10. Report going to Board concerning school
11. WEA report of meetings

*****

During the week, in an attempt to reduce the tension in the school, Ellis wrote notes to a few teachers, saying he hoped their relationship with him would not be weakened because of recent events. He also announced that January 16, a day reserved for all schools in the district to work on math objectives, would be used instead by the Lincoln Acres faculty to work on unspecified "school business."

B. WALLS ARRIVE

The walls that had been part of the July compromise were installed in the instructional area on January 12, 1976 (see Diagram VII). They changed the atmosphere of the school considerably; it was now much more difficult to observe the classes.

Several people still considered the walls unnecessary, while others were relieved that they had arrived. For example, Sam said that although the walls were ugly, they were needed, because:

Teachers haven't taught the kids how to talk in an appropriate voice. That is necessary if the space is going to be open. We spent a lot of time on that in Oxford school.

Sally accepted the walls with resignation and relief. She said:

I don't mind them. I have some place to hang things now. If they had been up sooner we could have avoided a lot of our problems. Mrs. Frisch wouldn't have been able to see us from the library.

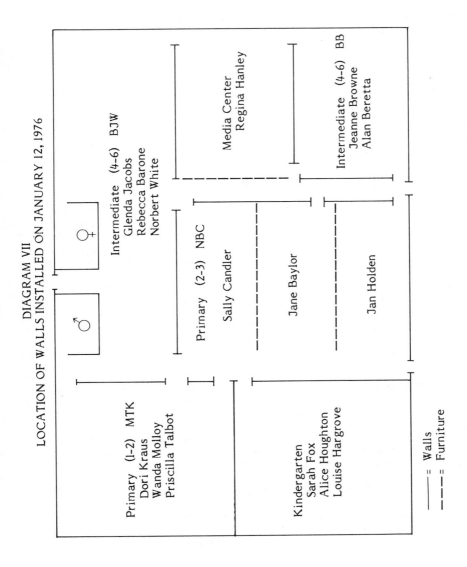

DIAGRAM VII
LOCATION OF WALLS INSTALLED ON JANUARY 12, 1976

Primary (1-2) MTK
Dori Kraus
Wanda Molloy
Priscilla Talbot

Intermediate (4-6) BJW
Glenda Jacobs
Rebecca Barone
Norbert White

Media Center
Regina Hanley

Intermediate (4-6) BB
Jeanne Browne
Alan Beretta

Primary (2-3) NBC

Sally Candler

Jane Baylor

Jan Holden

Kindergarten
Sarah Fox
Alice Houghton
Louise Hargrove

——— = Walls
– – – = Furniture

295

C. THE FACULTY MEETS WITH ELLIS

With Alice Houghton appointed by the teachers as their secretary, the faculty meeting began. Ellis was more subdued than usual, and there was a sense of tension as he reviewed the agenda items.

The first item, lesson plans, developed into a discussion of the reorganization of the BJW team. The tone and content of the meeting are evoked in the following passages from the field notes.

> Bert: It seems like a question of if we want to lay down to power. I wasn't at the meeting [the second BJW open house]-- I was sick -- but it seems that the people who are busting their backs are getting hit over the head. It seems not well planned and arbitrary. I've taught a lot and this is the worst it's been. The lesson plans are a symptom of what's going on. It seems like a classic case of the "squeaky wheel gets the grease." I'm tired of getting greased.

> Ellis: Well, er, er....We can deal with the squeaky wheel now; there may not be any reason to have lesson plans now. I've put in time in various areas of the school only to have a parent say at a Board meeting that it wasn't being done. It's a tough way. We need, like Glenda said, a way of communicating.

> Bert: I feel like it's being imposed and that's not good. It just seems like everything comes at a crisis point and nothing is evolved in a logical set of steps.

> Ellis: It's funny that we're agreeing, Bert. We're coming from the same place. I don't want another crisis in BJW -- not to single anyone out. If I can look and see what's going on on a weekly basis, then we're not going to go into another crisis. That's where I'm at.

> Bert: My problem is I don't know where we're at. I'm operating on blind trust. In BJW spelling was going on. The story coming out was that none was being done and the same with reading. It was being done less formally than now. When we walked into that meeting we were asked what basal [reader] do we want. I remember that we talked about a variety of ways to teach reading early.

> Ellis: Just to clarify. I've had no problem with the multi-test math you use and have told parents [that]. But when people ask me where kids are reading and I can't find out, that's bad. This is the state Right to Read head asking.

> Bert: There was no step in there where you could come to us and work with us instead of the crisis? I had no feeling that there was a crisis. Some things were wrong but we were

operating at our own level. If I heard things were that bad I wouldn't have gone to Rolling Ridge /the outdoor education camp/.

Ellis: I don't like to communicate hysteria.

Bert: Well, that _was_ hysteria. If this is only for my team, maybe we can meet later.

Sarah: I'd like to know what's going on. All we ever know about is through rumors.

Priscilla: I think there is a feeling that "it could happen to us." I think this discussion should continue.

The discussion did continue, with a recounting of the reorganization process of the BJW team, especially whether it had been "imposed" on the teachers, and what Sam's role had been. After an emotional series of charges and countercharges, the discussion on this item concluded:

Bert: I feel numb now -- at first it was shock. That piece was painful. If it's going to be that kind of aggravation, I'll pack my bags and go elsewhere.

Ellis: That's ditto for me. I don't want to walk around with it. That's why I'm here. I don't want to be an idiot administrator. I want a written program. I have to have something to stand up there with when I'm being shot at /by parents/. You can write it.

The next agenda item, student profiles, was discussed quickly with the resolution that they would continue to be used. The profiles would not only be checked by Ellis, but could be used as part of the evaluation of a teacher's performance.

The meeting then turned to the key issue of parent access to the school. Teachers proposed plans such as escorting parents through the school and having only certain times on specified days for parent visitation. Ellis resisted these proposals:

I want you to appreciate the impact -- this is a delicate moment. I think you're saying, "we don't trust you."

From the teachers' point of view, however, creating good will or trust with the parents was a secondary matter: they wanted to be protected from parent incursions. Though he was not in agreement with the teachers' strong demand for stringent controls, Ellis nonetheless agreed to draft a set of rules governing parent access to and behavior in the school.

The main problem that surfaced concerning teacher evaluation, the next item, was that the criteria were not clear. Several teachers also commented that they found Ellis' observations of them intrusive and disruptive of their instructional activities. The outcome was that evaluation procedures would be "improved", and that teachers would have an opportunity to influence the process. Because it was getting late, the remaining agenda items were put off until Friday afternoon, as were reorganization plans for the following year.

Finally, the grievance against Ellis was discussed. In accordance with the formal procedure requiring a progress report five days after the initiation of the grievance, Ellis explained that he had fired the custodian and taken steps to improve the appearance of the school. Several teachers indicated that they did see improvements, but the majority was still dissatisfied. After his report, Ellis left. The teachers then voted to continue the grievance, by formally initiating the second step (presentation of a written grievance to Ellis).

(Commentary)

This meeting marked the first faculty-wide attempt to discuss the disorganization of the past few months openly, and to find ways to prevent its recurrence. From the teachers' point of view, Ellis, the Board of Education and the parents had all disregarded their professional judgment and abilities, violated due process, and had, essentially, overreacted. Ellis stressed that he felt the teachers had not met their responsibilities: profiles were not properly kept, information was distorted, and teachers did not handle individual parents well. In general, although some concessions were made by both sides, the meeting was essentially an accusatory confrontation. Indeed, the tactics the teachers had devised to delimit Ellis' power -- and the power of the parents -- were already being used. Through confrontation, the role confusion that marked the first half of the year was being reduced; constraints were being applied on all participants' spheres of activity -- including those of the teachers.

For the first time, the teachers were employing force and threat of force. But they took a different approach than the parents and administration had: they selected rule enforcement as their primary method of coercion. In a short time, this changed the configuration of relationships within the school, and between the school and community, to a "conflict bureaucracy." Specifically, the conflict was now over rules designed to limit the power of the administration and the parents, and thus to increase the power of the teachers. With this shift, the arbitrariness of the preceding months was diminished: the administrative apparatus was becoming bureaucratic, based on rules governing the behavior of all members of the organization -- parents, the administration and teachers. Compared with the earlier force and force threat period just before Christmas, the conflict bureaucracy was highly stable; even the extent of the conflict and the punishment of Brown by the teachers was regulated by rules -- for example, the procedure for filing a grievance. But the bureaucratization of the school was an unintended consequence of the teachers' attempt to improve their situation by finding a mechanism for increasing their professional autonomy.*

In addition to increasing the teachers' distance from the community and controlling Brown's behavior, the establishment of the conflict bureaucracy protected the teachers from ineptness (Goode, 1967). Instead of feeling the weight of the consequences of Brown's mismanagement, or the inept classroom performances of their colleagues, the teachers were insulated by the bureaucratic procedures' prescription of standardized complaint procedures. Similarly, the inept were protected -- since they too were covered by the same rules that stressed uniform, systematic treatment, instead of the capricious "scapegoating" tactics of the administration during the reorganization of BJW and NBC.

D. COMMUNITY AND BOARD REACTIONS

1. Reports to the Board of Education

That evening, at a Board of Education meeting, the smallest audience in several months listened to Ellis summarize the content of a report he had submitted to the Board of Education on the current state of Lincoln Acres school. In addition, Astrid Little and Harriet Stein presented written accounts of their consulting efforts in the school, along with a detailed curriculum and schedule for the BJW team.

Although there was still some suspicion among Board members and parents, the changes in the school were generally viewed as favorable. In fact, it was suggested that other schools in the district be required to formulate curriculum guides as detailed as the one produced by BJW, and that other schools be evaluated as carefully as Lincoln Acres had been. The only negative consequence of the reorganization was pointed out by Biddle:

> Some of the things and excitement of a new school are gone.
> There are good teachers there. Some of them now have bad
> vibrations.

(Commentary)

In its second-page headline that week, the Washingtonville Courier announced: "Acres School Dispute Ends Quietly." Indeed, after considerable conflict, it had. The reorganization of the NBC and BJW teams, the certification of the programs through intervention by Little and Stein, and

---

*Collins (1975, p. 320) recognizes the process of bureaucratization presented above as a principle of organizational behavior. He writes: "The greater the pressure to disperse control equally and prevent personal long-term appropriation of authority, the greater the emphasis on bureaucratization."

the construction of a written curriculum all restored a sense of confidence in parents that the school had not only attempted to change, but actually succeeded. Finally, the installation of walls served as a conflict resolution symbol. At the same time, however, the walls were a further concrete confirmation that the community complaints had not been unfounded; after a struggle, the school now fit the parents' image of education, not the educators'. Of course, as we have already begun to see, though the conflict between the school and community was resolved for the most part, its legacy was conflict within the school.

3. Conservative Board Candidates Emerge

But even after its resolution, the school-community conflict was to have a lasting effect on the educational policies of the township. In early January, Anthony Bonomi, Rob Goldman, and Estelle Hunter, all Lincoln Acres residents and vocal critics of the Lincoln Acres school, announced their candidacy for the three vacant seats in the yearly Board of Education election. Bonomi and Goldman were sponsored by Sylvia Peabody, an incumbent Board member and resident of Lincoln Acres. Although they publicly denied it, their intention if elected was to form a conservative, anti-innovation coalition on the Board.

E. IMPROVEMENT AND PLANNING EFFORTS

1. Planning for Next Year Begins

The faculty spent the morning of January 16 on the construction of report cards; custodians were shampooing the carpet in the BB instructional area.

At 11:30, the entire faculty attended a voluntary meeting of the committee to propose reorganization plans for the following year. Ellis explained the purpose of the committee by saying:

> This is an advisory committee that will come up with recommendations for next year. There will /also/ be a committee of parents that I will meet with. At some point I hope the two committees will meet. With that preface I don't want to do anything more but be a notetaker and clarifier.

Among the topics discussed during this fairly friendly and relaxed meeting were the anticipated enrollment, the possibility of self-contained classrooms, whether there would be team teaching, student placement procedures, and the role of parents in the reorganization. At one point in the meeting, Ellis polled the teachers for their preference for the following year: a few wanted to have self-contained classrooms, others wanted slight modifications from the current arrangements, and one team (BJW) wanted to remain intact.

In Ellis' view, the parents would be satisfied with an arrangement that provided alternative teaching strategies; none would insist on all classrooms being self-contained. When asked who would choose the parents to participate on the reorganization committee, Ellis' answer was:

> Not me. I'm not so politically naive. I talked to the PTA steering committee last night and told them that I didn't want to be responsible for the selection.

With this the meeting ended.

2. Faculty Problem Identification Continues

At 1:20 p.m., the faculty re-gathered with Ellis in the teachers lounge to resume their march through the agenda items remaining from the last faculty meeting.

The first item, the role of the resource teacher, resulted in the following conversation, which captures the essential problems:

> Priscilla: Is his job administrative or evaluative?
>
> Ellis: By definition not either administrative or supervisory. The Board said that in the absence of the principal the resource teacher is an administrator and accountable. When the principal is present he is the only one accountable.
>
> Sam: I can be under administrative direction. I'm not an administrator but a vehicle for carrying out the administrative directive. That's very touchy, like walking on eggshells. I see myself working for two sets of people -- teachers and Ellis.
>
> Priscilla: Right now we see you working entirely for Ellis. Maybe you should do one or the other. We're uncomfortable with the situation.
>
> Sam: I am too. I'd like to hear what people would like me to do.

The conversation continued, with Sam repeatedly admitting that he did not know what his duties were. As he floundered, the teachers became increasingly critical of him, until Ellis re-entered the discussion.

> Ellis: I want to find out what you're going to do on your own initiative.
>
> Sam: I need help with that.

> Ellis: I feel I told you things that should have been your initiative. I feel I can't go to a budget meeting and tell them I want a $13,000 helping teacher, not a resource teacher. When the entire school is in need of help and Jeanne says she doesn't have the time [to use Sam], that is something the school needs -- it probably needs the resource teacher most now. That's what I heard.

At this point, in reaction to Ellis' intensification of the attack on Sam, the teachers quickly defended Sam by pointing to the positive contributions he had made to the school. Several teachers challenged Ellis for his dim view of Sam's performance. Shortly afterward, however, several teachers claimed that their "trust" in Sam was so low that they didn't think he could perform useful services for them any more. Eventually, after the main arguments had been rehashed several times, the discussion lost its focus, and teachers began talking among themselves.

Essentially, it was clear that all members of Sam's role-set, as well as Sam, were confused over his responsibilities. The only outcome was a vague promise by Sam to improve the situation and take more initiative in the future.

The final portion of the meeting was devoted to a wide-ranging discussion of parents. The teachers agreed that the Board of Education, and to some extent Biddle, had acted inappropriately in responding directly to parent complaints, rather than referring them to teachers, who thus felt powerless. In this conversation -- for the first and only time during this or the preceding meeting -- Ellis adopted a self-reflective attitude. He told the teachers:

> I'll share a decision with you -- I made it selflessly, I think, but it's hard to tell. It was clear to me at one point that I could stonewall the whole thing -- not talk to the Board or Biddle or the parents, which I felt very certain would have put me as the object of a witch hunt, and they would have gotten me. As I say, it's hard to know if it was selfish or not. At that point I was so shaken and numb it's hard to know. I could have been shut right out. I made that decision, and I don't honestly know how I would do it again, or how much more I'm willing to compromise for the stability of the school. I feel that in some ways Bob was protecting himself from being set up as a scapegoat. I don't know for sure; I didn't ask him. I hope this helps explain my actions.

The meeting ended without proposals for action, aside from the already-proposed formulation of rules governing parent access. When Ellis announced that Sy Golden, the president of the PTA, would make a presentation at the next faculty meeting, some teachers asked if he would be a good person to explain the problems with parents to. Ellis said he thought it would be useful to discuss parent-school communication with Golden.

(Commentary)

Overall, the discussions that took place when school resumed after the vacation did raise the central issues, and gave the faculty an opportunity to confront Ellis and each other -- but usually did not result in new understandings, or agreement over actions to be taken to avoid school-community conflicts in the future. The need to develop procedures to regulate parent behavior was forced on a reluctant Ellis by the teachers. But there were no real plans for alleviating the tensions and conflicts within the faculty, or for clarifying administrative roles. Differences of viewpoint, and assessment of past blame, were perhaps rooted enough in underlying values that steps toward improvement were unlikely. For example, it became apparent that the role of the principal in teacher evaluation as Brown perceived it was not congruent with the subordinate participation model that the teachers wanted. To change present procedures would have meant substantial redistribution in power of administrators and teachers, not something Brown welcomed. In addition, though the faculty had developed more solidarity and militancy, they had little experience so far in serious shared problem-solving efforts on the scale that serious corrective action would require: Ellis' actions inside and outside the school had increasingly pre-empted these functions until now, and the teachers had in effect acquiesced.

4. The PTA President Talks with the Teachers

At his request, Sy Golden, the recently elected president of the Lincoln Acres PTA, addressed the teachers at their regularly scheduled faculty meeting on January 19. His basic message was that the PTA wanted to develop more active participation in it by teachers. He asked for a teacher to join the executive board of the PTA, and invited teacher participation in fund raising, and their suggestions as to how the PTA could help raise teacher morale.

At various points, teachers asked pointedly hostile questions of Golden. When he asked for suggestions, few if any were offered. In general, the teachers viewed Golden as among those having caused them trouble and as continuing to threaten them. Accordingly, the teachers conveyed the clear message that they were not ready to cooperate with parents. In fact the atmosphere of the meeting was so antagonistic that soon after Golden strode out of the room Regina said, "I never saw such a hostile group in my life." As for Golden, he told the researcher, "They gave me the silent treatment -- I was really iced."

5. Attempts to Improve Communication

As we have seen, the working relationships between Brown and the teachers at this point were weak, at best. In an attempt to improve the situation, Brown wrote memos to several teachers. Below is an excerpt of a

January 20, 1976 memo from Brown to the BJW team. It was a pathetic plea.

> I am rather concerned with meetings. We've had a lot of trouble getting together for almost a month now. I view the meetings we have as helpful...they help me, they help you. They are not primarily information-giving meetings because we can write back and forth /on/ various things that keep our information stockpile up to date. In helping me get to a place where I can be more trustworthy and more helpful to you and helping you get to a place where I can work with you in a manner that is more pleasant for both of us, I think we need some meetings. I will leave it only at that, because if we are not mutually committed to the need for the purpose of meetings, we're just going to be wasting each other's time. Please contact me, set up meetings individually or as a team to work on these issues or any other issues. I really want us to get a lot more together than we are now.

The difficulty in communication was partly due to Brown's increasing lack of interest in the affairs of the school; more substantially it was a result of the teachers' distrust of him. This portion of the memo also shows how far the administration and operation of the school had developed into a conflict bureaucracy by January: it illustrates the need to rely on written communications rather than face-to-face contact.

6. The WEA Meets

In the middle of one of Brown's periodic trips to New England (this one began on Friday and ended the following Tuesday), the WEA chapter of Lincoln Acres school held a meeting to review various issues.

Dori announced that on Friday a formal written grievance had been presented to Ellis, and that as specified in the union contract he had three days to reply to it. She also announced that the WEA communications workshop for improving coffee-klatching skills would be held at Regina Hanley's that Thursday after school.

Another topic discussed in the meeting was the possibility of having a faculty member attend all executive PTA meetings to insure that the teachers' viewpoint was not distorted. This idea was acceptable, but no one volunteered to attend. There were also complaints that Brown had "dragged his feet" on sending out rules regarding parent access to the school, and that he still didn't have a sign on the front door directing visitors to the front office.

There was some dissatisfaction directed at the lack of participation by "three or four faculty members" in WEA meetings and other activities. This was the first indication that the faculty was less than fully united against Brown, and that factions might be forming within the teachers' ranks.

7. Rules for School-Community Contact

The students of Lincoln Acres school carried home three letters to their parents on January 26, 1976. The first one explained the school reorganization committee, and asked for volunteers. Besides specifying that the committee would be advisory, the letter clearly noted that Sy Golden would screen the applicants and make the final selections.

The second letter from Ellis presented a clarification of the communication procedure between parents and teachers. It read in part:

> Whenever a question or problem comes to your attention, please take it personally to the teacher closest to the situation. If you are unable to solve the problem with that teacher, please make arrangements to meet with me. I prefer to meet with you and the teacher together, but I can arrange individual meetings where appropriate. Only after we have made these attempts to help you, should you resort to communication with the Superintendent, Board of Education, or others.

The third letter specified the rules for parent visits to the school. The key paragraph read:

> All visits should be arranged in advance with the teacher(s) whose class you wish to visit. Visitors report to the office upon entering the building. While visiting a classroom, do not talk to the teacher beyond introducing yourself. The teacher is teaching at that time. Contact him/her away from the children to arrange a conference. A visit is not a conference. Before leaving the building, check back in the office. The secretary may ask you to complete one of our feedback questionnaires.

These procedures, which had been demanded by the teachers, had been reluctantly formulated by Brown.

8. A Faculty Meeting

The next faculty meeting was held on January 29 during lunch hour. A series of routine announcements began the meeting: a guest speaker on developmental gym who would talk to parents, field trip arrangements, problems with children running in the school, and so on.

Ellis then announced that a new sign-in sheet for parent visitors and volunteers would be in use beginning Monday. He emphasized:

> With the sign-in procedure we have to be careful. The first teacher who screws up will break the dam for the rest.

This led Dori to ask about the posting of a sign to direct visitors to the office. Ellis answered that it would be put up soon. He then turned the meeting over to Dori, who explained that the teachers had decided to have rotating pairs of teachers, determined alphabetically, attend PTA meetings. This announcement raised the issue of teacher participation in teacher-sponsored activities, and there was goading of those teachers who were notably absent from meetings. Dori concluded by asking Ellis if the agenda items for faculty meetings could be posted on a bulletin board designated for the exclusive use of the teachers. This led Ellis into the following speech.

> O.K. We'll rearrange the office. You'll get a board. O.K., the next item I have is about trust -- that I am surprised about. Teachers at this school have related to the community the details of our discussions at our reorganization meeting. This individual or individuals violated the process also by asking parents to solicit requests now for various teachers [for their children next fall]. This is pretty lousy stuff, folks. We can't work unless there is trust in these meetings. I wouldn't bring this up if I wasn't absolutely certain. I can't help you with that.

These comments brought gasps of surprise from several teachers. As with his admonition quoted above on the parent sign-in process, Ellis tried to shift some of the onus for the problems of the school onto the teachers. But, on balance, the atmosphere of this meeting was somewhat more relaxed than that of those immediately preceding it. It appeared that both Brown and the teachers had resigned themselves to the fact that mutual trust between them would not be restored.

Later in the day, when the researcher asked Brown how everything had been recently, he answered:

> All right. I've been cast in two shows, but haven't heard from the director yet.

> Researcher: I mean school life.

> Brown: O.K. But you can only take away so much of a man's motivation until he looks to other areas of his life.

The teachers' current attitudes were exemplified in the BJW team's plan -- which was to follow the schedule Sam had devised for them, to continue to write lesson plans, but on their own to return gradually to team teaching and the use of open space.

In other words, they decided that the wisest course was to conform to the superficial parts of the administrative reorganization, and to ignore those aspects that did not meet their needs. It was consistent with this plan that they did not respond to Ellis' offer of help in the memo on "meetings" quoted above.

9. Learning to Coffee-klatch Effectively

Later that afternoon, about half of the Lincoln Acres faculty attended the verbal communication skills training session at Regina Hanley's house in Allwood Green. A representative of the state education association led the group through a series of exercises designed to increase their ability to present a viewpoint convincingly to a group of parents. The teachers paid rapt attention to the presentation, and seemed seriously committed to improving their communicative abilities. Most wanted to use these skills to defend themselves to the community if necessary.

10. The Grievance Continues

Toward the end of the week, Ellis replied to the formal grievance in a four-page letter. He claimed that the grievance was not a school-wide one, and that he could ignore it because the proper procedures had not been followed. The teachers were surprised at his rebuttal; they initiated the second stage of the formal grievance procedure, by sending a copy of the complaint to the superintendent of schools.

11. The Weekly Faculty Meeting

At the regularly scheduled lunch-time faculty meeting, Dori reported on the PTA meeting she had been assigned to attend the previous night. Basically, Sy Golden was still looking for ways to bring parents and teachers together; he had suggested a wine and cheese party. The teachers' mood was now more conciliatory, but they took no clear steps toward improving relations with the PTA.

Next, the meeting focused on the school reorganization. It was suggested that Biddle be invited to talk with the teachers about the reorganization and the effect of possible sharp reductions in the school budget on educational programs. Ellis agreed to make arrangements for this meeting.

The other important announcement was that Ellis had fired a custodian, as part of his effort to meet the complaints in the grievance. Only one teacher commented publicly at the meeting that she thought he was a good custodian and would be missed. Others remarked privately that the firing was a scapegoating action, similar to the firing of Katie.

Again, although there was an underlying tension, the tone of the meeting was more or less one of business-as-usual. There was no discussion of the major issues raised and left unresolved at earlier meetings.

12. Sally Resigns

A week after being evaluated for the second time since school opened, Sally decided to resign as a Lincoln Acres teacher, effective

June, 1976. Her reasoning was that Ellis was not going to recommend her for rehiring, and that by resigning she could bargain with him for a positive recommendation to future employers, and collect unemployment benefits as well. Ellis did agree to write a favorable evaluation of her in return for her resignation. Needless to say, Sally did not wish Ellis well; she hoped that he would be fired by the end of the year.

13. Ellis' Report

In his mandated monthly report to the Board of Education, Brown discussed recent events, such as Golden's visit to the school and work on math objectives. He also wrote:

> I worked with the staff in problem-solving within the building. During periods of crisis, certain policies and roles became strained. We have now begun to reaffirm appropriate policies and roles for Lincoln Acres school internally and externally. Some of these discussions have resulted in communication with parents. Communication with parents has covered areas such as school visits, parent/teacher conferences, process for handling parent concerns and solicitation of parent feedback on our report card.

F. SCHOOL OPERATIONS AS OF MID-FEBRUARY

1. The State of the School

From several sustained observations of the school, it appeared that by mid-February classroom activities had stabilized. The addition of walls to various classrooms created a more "controlled" sense, as did the separation of the NBC team into three classes. There was also a detectable reduction in most teachers' energy level; they were clearly not as active as during the first months of the school. Many simply wanted the year to end, and others, as we have seen, were planning on leaving at the end of the year. Despite this drop in energy and morale, teachers appeared to continue delivering well-planned instruction to their students. As for the students, although it is clear they had not passed through the conflict unaffected, they seemed to adjust to new circumstances more easily than the teachers did.

Beyond the more subdued tone of the school, the most significant recent change was that of institutionalization of procedures. On a typical day, the bulletin board in the office had a sheet for teachers to put agenda items on, minutes of all faculty and PTA meetings, a letter from the PTA president either praising teachers for their efforts or cordially inviting them to participate in a PTA event, a parent visitation form filled in with positive comments, and a draft of a letter written by Ellis to the Board of Education or other group (posted so that teachers could offer revisions and approve it).

The few parents that might be in the building would have had to sign in, and wear name tags.

2. Reorganization Plans Continue

Twelve parents and Brown met in the second week of February to begin work on the reorganization of the school for the following year. Brown informed the parents clearly that their role was advisory, and that he would make final decisions. The task set for this meeting was generating a list of topics for discussion at future meetings. These included: number of students in a class, use of playground, physical structure of the interior of the school, the use of self-contained and team teaching approaches, criteria for grouping, and report cards.

At approximately the same time, the teachers and Ellis held their second reorganization meeting. A basic question raised was the degree of influence the teachers would actually have in the planning.

Jeanne: I don't feel like sitting here and doing this if you have the final decision and we don't know where you're coming from.

Ellis: I don't know yet. I haven't made any decisions. I have no hidden agenda and am not trying to coopt anybody. The groundwork for this school was never done previous to my coming. We have had to live with that. I found that we need more alternatives in the school. We should have a variety of options for parents who want them for various reasons.

Wanda: What happens if we get a situation like last summer with the survey? If we ask for input and don't listen to it, won't we have trouble?

Ellis: I have every right to refuse it, and yours as well.

Wanda: But that happened this summer with the survey.

Ellis: That was the Board's survey. I have to act. You can make the decision whether to participate or not, but I will make some decisions anyway without your input. We can't operate on the basis of knowing that 66% support something, nor can we afford to be philosophical.

The substance of the planning was not much different than that of the previous meeting: teachers were still trying to decide whether they wanted to team teach or use self-contained classrooms, and whether to have two or three age levels of children in a class. It was evident, however, that the trend was toward less-innovative arrangements than those the year had begun with; at least two teachers (Dori and Jeanne) were already firmly requesting self-contained classrooms, and only two others (Wanda and Alice) were certain that they wanted to form a team.

The teachers also asked Ellis what was happening in the parent reorganization committee. Brown said he thought there would be no problems with parents, and that he hoped to have them discuss "philosophical" questions, such as the benefits of having first and second grade children in the same classroom.

G. EVENTS IN THE SCHOOL: FEBRUARY THROUGH MID-APRIL

The pattern of social relationships within the school that had developed by February -- conflict bureaucracy -- fluctuated in intensity during the next months, but hostility between Brown and the teachers never diminished enough to permit steps toward collaboration. In the following pages, we summarize the events that sustained the conflict.

1. The Grievance

A new, more experienced custodian was hired, and by late February the building was noticeably cleaner. In early March, Biddle wrote to the WEA informing them that from his point of view the grievance had ended; the major problem was the former custodian, and the unsanitary conditions were now corrected. After a faculty meeting on March 8, the teachers once again discussed the grievance, with most of them finding the improvements acceptable. They voted to discontinue it. They also decided, however, to keep logs of the conditions in teaching areas, in the event they needed documentary support for another grievance.

2. The Structure of Faculty Meetings

The most significant change in faculty meetings was that teachers controlled the flow of discussion by designing the agenda around their concerns. Brown still acted as the chairman of the meetings and managed them, but not with as much ease as earlier in the year: joking, silence and frequently blunt remarks kept him from dominating the proceedings as he had previously. The teachers also physically isolated Brown; he often found himself the only one sitting on one of the several sofas that lined the walls of the teachers' lounge. In addition, the teachers kept minutes meticulously, and posted them after every meeting.

Brown repeatedly told the researcher privately that he had lost interest in running the school, and was actively seeking other employment. But when he presented himself to the faculty, in spite of occasional hints that he might leave the school, he behaved as though he were still in control of things and intended to remain for the next two years of his contract. For example, he retained power by either firing or threatening to fire teachers, and he guided the reorganization for the following year in such a way as to maximize his role.

3. Social Relations in the School

Underlying all interaction between the teachers and Ellis Brown was a sense of tension. Though both sides regarded trust as desirable, it was absent, and given the magnitude of the conflict, not likely to increase. The teachers' approach to the situation was to contain Brown's power; they did little to try to restore the collegial relationship of the early days. In fact, the teachers not only enforced rules and regulations throughout the school, but also met secretly, excluding Brown. In many respects, the conflict became independent of anyone's actions on either side; after the teachers acknowledged that Brown had corrected the custodial situation, they found other deficiencies. Eventually several teachers developed a deep dislike of Brown, not only as an administrator but as a person.

In March, Ellis Brown asked the teachers to provide him with feedback on various aspects of his job performance. The form containing the questions emphasized that the replies were optional and anonymous. A sample of the questions asked follows.

1. On what tasks do you see me spending the most time or effort?

2. On what tasks do you feel I spend too much or unwarranted time or effort?

3. What tasks of the principal are most important in your opinion?

4. What tasks do you feel I do best?

5. What tasks do you feel I do worst?

6. In what ways would you most want me to change?

Brown used the information on these forms for his own purposes; he did not discuss issues raised by them with the faculty (or with the researcher), and told the researcher that the main function of this feedback was to provide an emotional outlet for the teachers.

Throughout the conflict, solidarity among the teachers was surprisingly high. Even after various teachers were chided by others for non-participation, the feeling that any one of them could become the object of attack by the administration or parents pulled them tightly together. Indeed, the perception that "we are all in this boat together" united the teachers and kept them from collaboration with Brown. Brown was not among the "we."

4. Classroom Activities

Instructional activities did not change much from the time of the NBC and BJW reorganizations until the end of the year. The basic differences from the beginning of the year were that more attention was paid to formal reading instruction, the organization of instruction was less open, and little if any team teaching was done. Through the use of lesson plans and observation, the administration monitored instructional activities more closely. For example, Astrid Little periodically evaluated, worked with and instructed some teachers, primarily Sally and the BJW team. Part of Little's responsibility was to report on her interventions to Biddle. Here is a paragraph from her April 15, 1976 report.

> In summary, my observations this week indicate that a well-planned and comprehensive reading/language program is in progress in the BJW pod. The children are receiving instruction in all aspects of reading/language development, they are assuming responsibility for reading independently, they are writing and learning the skills of writing, and most importantly -- they seem to be enjoying the whole process.

This type of evaluation, coupled with the addition of walls and the changes noted above, served to substantially reduce parents' fears and complaints about what was being taught in the school.

Little's efforts were not appreciated by the teachers, however. In a meeting in April she tried to explain the source of her involvement in the Lincoln Acres school and what she was actually doing. In sharply-worded comments, the teachers accused her of being a secret evaluator, and of influencing personnel policies. Little failed to convince them that she was, in her words, an "objective observer" of activities in the school; after enduring a mixture of hostility and silence, she left the meeting. The teachers had treated Little as they had Golden when he attempted rapprochement earlier in the year.

5. Achievement Measures

In the spring, the results of the state assessment tests and the California Achievement Tests were released for the Washingtonville school district. On both tests, Lincoln Acres students scored higher than those in any elementary school in the district on reading. In mathematics Lincoln Acres students ranked highest in the district on the California Achievement Test and were a close second to Fernwood school on the state assessment tests. The schools that ranked lowest on both tests were the rural schools, which had students with the lowest socioeconomic background. Lincoln Acres, which had the highest socioeconomic student body in the township, ranked highest. It seems reasonable to assume, then, that the well-established influence of socioeconomic background on academic achievement was a factor; these test scores may have been produced independently of anything that occurred in Lincoln Acres school. On the positive side, we should note that the conflict, reorganization and defects in the educational program did not appear to have reduced the academic achievement of Lincoln Acres students.

H. SCHOOL-COMMUNITY RELATIONS: FEBRUARY THROUGH MID-APRIL

1. Parent Control

Although there were periodic problems with parents' arriving to observe a teacher unannounced, the problem of parental access to the school was generally solved by enforcing sign-in procedures and other rules. After a long delay, a sign was posted on the main entrance that read:

> All visitors MUST report to the principal's office upon entering the building.

The only major problem was that a parent had called Bert and complained bitterly about personal qualities that she disapproved of in his teammate, Glenda. The parent also complained to Brown, with the result that her child was transferred from Glenda's to Bert's class. This apparent lack of support from the administration prompted Glenda to request transfer to another school the following year. The incident reminded the teachers of earlier problems, and put them on alert to try to avoid further parental interference. As it turned out, in late March Biddle fired Glenda (effective in June), on the grounds that she was unable to communicate effectively with parents.

2. Relations with the PTA

Tensions between the teachers and community, although they were sharply reduced since the reorganization of the NBC and BJW teams, remained below the surface of all PTA activities. Eventually, there was an open conflict between the executive leadership of the PTA and the teachers.

Representatives of the faculty attended each PTA executive committee meeting, and reported on the proceedings to the rest of the faculty. At this time, the main interest of the PTA was fund-raising. Although this sort of activity was of peripheral interest to the teachers, they did cooperate in most fund-raising ventures. But when it came time to spend the money, although the PTA asked for suggestions from the faculty, the parents set their own priorities and ignored the teachers' advice.

The conflict between the teachers and the PTA crystallized over Golden's plans for the school atrium. As in proceeding instances, the teachers were not consulted on a project that directly affected them, using money they had helped raise. Brown became involved in this issue when he told the PTA executive committee that teachers really didn't care what went into the atrium. His comment was reported to the teachers by their representative, and created another confrontation between the faculty and Brown. In a letter sent to Golden, the teachers stated that they had never seen the final plans for the atrium. The letter continued:

> It is without a doubt that every member of our staff was embarrassed, bewildered and angered by Mr. Brown's remark

at the meeting of April 6 -- "Not one staff member came to the office to look at the plans -- that says something about staff involvement."

We strongly feel that we must have the right of final approval for any plans affecting the landscaping of our school.

This incident incensed some teachers so much that they considered contacting Biddle to ask him to outline the procedures for firing a principal.

The difficulties with the PTA were reduced somewhat with the election of Sandra Waters to the presidency. She has supported the teachers throughout most of the year. However, until almost the end of the year there was a struggle between the teachers and the PTA executive committee for control of a variety of activities within the school.

3. Reorganization Plans

Two more parent reorganization meetings were led by Sam. Almost all aspects of the school were discussed. For the following year, most parents wanted to see a variety of teaching styles for each grade level. They also wanted to find ways to improve relations between the school and community, and better ways for learning about student progress.

In parallel, the teachers continued to discuss their preferences for the following year. Because of possible transfers, resignations, the addition of new faculty members, uncertainty over enrollments, and problems caused by a delay in the state budget, little was accomplished in the way of concrete plans. It was clear, however, that the teachers were not intent on either team teaching or open space, but on moving toward some combination of open space, two-person teams, two-grade-level classes, and, in increasing numbers, self-contained classrooms.

On March 25, in a tense, highly formal meeting, the parent reorganization committee and the teachers discussed the plans for the following year. Because of Ellis' tight control of the meeting, there was little real discussion of the issues, so it appeared that the teachers and parents were in essential agreement. Both groups did want "alternative" learning environments (that is, the presence of more traditional teaching patterns along with the innovations tried this year), and better relations between parents and teachers. But several teachers were annoyed with Ellis' apparent attempt to gloss over problems, using the occasion to present a non-existent unity of purpose between teachers and parents.

4. The Board of Education Election

In contrast with previous Board of Education elections, this year's had several genuine issues: the most pre-eminent one was the Lincoln Acres crisis. All five of the candidates (there were three seats open) attacked

Biddle for his handling of the situation; Goldman and Bonomi -- two of the four Lincoln Acres resident running -- hinted strongly that they would work for Biddle's removal once they were elected.

As noted above, Sylvia Peabody, an incumbent Board member, sponsored Goldman's and Bonomi's campaigns, and intended to form a conservative coalition on the Board. Despite public protest over this (and over the fact that if they were elected four members of the nine-person Board would be from Lincoln Acres), Bonomi and Goldman were elected by the highest plurality. The other position was retained by Grace Walters, a liberal. Lincoln Acres was now represented by four "conservatives" on the Board of Education: Frisch, Peabody, Goldman and Bonomi. Hassfelt, a Lincoln Acres liberal, may have lost his seat because of his refusal to comment critically on Biddle's overall performance as superintendent of schools.*

5. Problems at Oxford School

In late winter and early spring, a group of Allwood Green residents scrutinized the open space instruction at Allwood Green school. They charged that many of the same deficiencies that had existed in Lincoln Acres were also present in Oxford, especially in the fifth and sixth grade classes. After several meetings, the conflict was resolved with the reorganization of part of the open space program, and the familiar promise that the school would contain more "alternative" types of education the following year.

To a large extent, the examination of open space in other schools in the district was influenced by the events at Lincoln Acres. Open space education had been an uncontroversial part of Oxford school for almost four years before Lincoln Acres opened.

6. Attempts to Oust Biddle

During the spring, there was another attempt (one of several in recent years) to have Biddle removed as superintendent of schools. It was organized by Charles Minetta, and most of its supporters were residents of the rural areas. Among the usual complaints were defects in the high school work-study program, the lack of curriculum in the district, Biddle's poor administration, and declining SAT scores. Added to these were the "experimentation" in Lincoln Acres school, and the inefficient handling of problems that arose from it.

---

*Biddle did not agree with this view, and cited deficiencies in Hassfelt's performance which led to his not being re-elected.

There were several heated Board meetings at which Biddle was charged with ineptitude. On June 7th, the Board received a petition with 1,100 signatures, calling for his removal. On July 1, the Board announced that it could not consider the petition, since Biddle could not be legally removed until the expiration of his contract.

7. State School Funding Crisis

In February, as plans were being made for the following year, it became apparent that the state legislature was having difficulty formulating and passing a state aid formula for public education. Even if the problems were quickly resolved, because of technicalities in the formula, Washingtonville was likely to suffer a substantial reduction in its budget. This, of course, had a considerable effect on planning. For example, one option the Board of Education discussed was closing one of the district's elementary schools.

Biddle visited the Lincoln Acres faculty to explain the funding problems and their possible implications for the district and the school. In his talk with the teachers, he connected the monetary difficulties with the larger social trends and the problems that had faced the school earlier in the year. He said:

> The state situation is 50 teachers per 1,000 students, and Washingtonville is 73 per 1,000, which is the source of Washingtonville per-pupil expenditures being two to three hundred dollars above most districts in the state. If people equate education with the basic skills, you can have 40 per 1,000 and do a good job. It isn't /just/ Washingtonville but the whole cotton-pickin' nation that's going back to basic skills -- every time a depression hits. You talk about wanting to humanize education -- it's going the other way. I wish I knew what basic skills were. I know that to some people it is equivalent to reading, writing and arithmetic. I know they're important.

The basic impact of the funding crisis on Lincoln Acres -- as in many districts around the state -- was to add another element of uncertainty and confusion to planning for the following year.

I. THE PRINCIPAL'S RESIGNATION AND SUCCESSION

1. Brown Resigns

On April 12, 1976, Ellis Brown told the faculty of his resignation. With characteristic understatement, he replied to a question from Dori asking if he might be leaving the school:

It is extremely likely that I'll get a number of jobs that are attractive, and I'm well qualified. I have to admit that I'm not sure what I want to do. I'm not happy with education in America and I'm not willing to take grief as a change agent. I think a change is in order for my own personal well being.

While several teachers were shocked by this announcement, others said that they had been expecting Ellis to leave; they sensed that he had been under severe strain in recent weeks.

In an interview with the researcher shortly after he announced his resignation, Brown reflected further on his experiences in Washingtonville.

Researcher: How would you summarize where the school is now?

Brown: I think the organizational format of the school on the micro level -- how each classroom is organized and conducted -- is close to what the parents can identify with. I believe in that -- I believe parents should have what they can accept and value. My function is only to lead them in a direction in which they are ready or interested in going, or to persuade them to do things that they can be persuaded to do. So we got into rather a conventional situation that doesn't interest me.

Researcher: How is that in educational terms?

Brown: Conventional. The kids are getting a tremendous amount of input in the cognitive domain, and there is systematic erosion of the psycho-motor and affective domain instruction.

Researcher: You don't see that as something that will change here?

Brown: I'm not that kind of a change agent. I'm not a revolutionary. I'm not an incendiary. I'm a practitioner. I know how to change. I know how to run good, creative programs, I think. But I don't do the PR for that kind of thing. I don't do the ground work. I'm not really a parent educator. I feel a little uncomfortable saying that, because parent relationships are important, but I'm not in the business of taking a parent from point A to point B in their awareness of children. I try to be responsive when the parent has a need, and I can either easily point that need out or they can find it themselves and initiate some self-education, but for people who think they know how to parent children, who do not have my interest and my values in children, we should just separate them.

Concerning his relationship with Biddle, Brown said:

Oh, bizarre. The man is falling apart.

Researcher: Why is that?

Brown: He's been under the same pressure I have, except magnified and for a longer number of years.

Researcher: District-wide?

Brown: Well, it's not district-wide, it's worst here. But there's not a compensatory area of support for him in the district. Everybody's got something to bitch at him for, throughout the district, and that's what's wrong.

Researcher: How has that affected how you've been able to operate?

Brown: He's been inconsistent, non-supportive, emotional, impulsive. I have no administrative support in this position at all. Zero.*

2. Later Events

A few weeks later Brown told the faculty that he would become the principal of a three-year-old open space elementary school on Cape Cod. He was to return to rural New England.

In early May, as a result of difficulties the state had in funding schools to meet constitutional requirements, the Board of Education "fired" all non-tenured teachers. This created additional uncertainty for the future of Lincoln Acres school, since over half of the teachers were non-tenured. It also created an atmosphere of crisis throughout the school district, because neighboring communities were affected in the same way by the funding problems, but had found other solutions. Eventually, the teachers were rehired, but the funding problem was not solved.

In early June, the teachers met with Biddle to discuss problems in the school. Chief among them was finding a suitable replacement for Ellis Brown for the following year. Biddle said that the faculty could draft a letter outlining qualifications for the next principal. Shortly after, with guidance from Ellis (relationships between him and the teachers had turned somewhat less abrasive, once he announced his resignation) they formulated a set of criteria for the next principal.

---

*Biddle's response to this characterization is unprintable. He also noted:

Ellis was supported far beyond anything reported [in the case]or by Ellis. Many, many conversations and planning sessions are not known to [the researcher].

Several of these meetings were restricted to teachers alone. In these meetings, teachers guessed that both Astrid Little and Sam Pennington would be candidates for the position. They strongly disliked Little (at one time several teachers had considered filing a grievance against her presence in the school), and though they were personally friendly with Sam, most disapproved of his performance in the school. Others found him unacceptable as a principal because they did not consider him strong enough to deal with parents. By June they had submitted a letter with their recommendations for the qualities a principal should have -- chief among them the ability to handle parents.

3. Succession

On June 8, at the regular Board of Education meeting, Biddle asked that Alberta Bard be named acting principal of Lincoln Acres school, immediately replacing Ellis Brown. The appointment was approved, and the next day Alberta Bard, an administrator at the Washingtonville junior high school and resident of Allwood Green, became acting principal of Lincoln Acres school. Although the teachers' input into the principal selection process had been limited, after some initial surprise they were extremely pleased with the new appointment. Mrs. Bard, a matter-of-fact, warm, person who exuded competence, also seemed to have the confidence of the parents who knew her.*

The year ended with several meetings organized by Alberta (as she was soon called) to discuss reorganization for the following year. Several teachers insisted on a self-contained classroom, and others wanted some form of self-contained space with the option of team teaching. Only two teachers, Alice and Wanda, wanted to team teach at this point.

With the exception of the two teachers who had been fired, the one voluntary transfer and the one who had resigned, all other teachers planned to return to Lincoln Acres the following year.

After two weeks in her new position, Alberta was beginning to form impressions of the school. In an interview, she said:

> I think the community perhaps sees the Lincoln Acres teachers as not wanting to teach basic skills. Therefore, if they are going to teach basic skills, they are going to have to be made to. And they would see that as my job. Well, I think the teachers are very willing to teach basic skills at this point. And I think they will find really great relief in not having to deal with the question of how you create really "meaningful" education. The original intent of this group of teachers was to

---

*The reader may remember that Bard was the runner-up in the principal selection advisory committee's initial recommendations to Biddle before the school opened.

do something better than they'd ever done in their previous schools, to create a unique, really meaningful situation. Well, in a way, I'm saying, and I think it makes sense, we'll back off from that just a little bit. Let's get our feet firmly on the ground and get the community convinced that we can do a good job with a traditional kind of education -- and then we'll be able to move into really improving it and coming up with something that's a bit better.

J. THE YEAR-END STATE OF THE SCHOOL AND COMMUNITY

The second half of the first year was as complex as the first half. Since commentary has been provided frequently throughout this chapter, this section will focus on the relations between the school and community in the period after the resolution of the conflict, and on the social relations within the school.

The second parent questionnaire was given in June. When asked retrospectively how good a job the school had been doing at educating their children, 56% said it was doing an "outstanding," "very good," or "good" job by Easter. If we recall that 75% had rated it this way in February, it seems possible that satisfaction with the changes that took place after the reorganization had declined, once the new program became familiar to parents. But satisfaction improved again: 70% of the parents gave equivalently high ratings to the school as of the end of the year.

Most significantly, in response to the question: "What kind of job do you think Lincoln Acres School is doing now compared with the beginning of the year?", 75% of parents answered that it was "much better," or "better." Only 18% of the parents thought the quality of education had remained the same, and 7% thought that it was "worse" than at the beginning of the year.

Undoubtedly, the increased year-end level of parent satisfaction came in part from the fact that the most dissatisfied parents had either transferred their children to another school, or to another class within Lincoln Acres. Mildly dissatisfied parents had also seen corrections in most of the defects they had observed in the school.

(Comments.) As we have noted, the conflict that remained after the school reorganization was between the teachers and a few members of the PTA executive committee -- not parents in general. The nature of this conflict was different than the ones that preceded it; the effectiveness of teacher classroom techniques was not being questioned. This reduced conflict was over the ability of the teachers to maintain and extend their control of the school, by deciding spending priorities.

As we have seen, relations within the faculty also changed after the school reorganization. Basically, the teachers united against the administration, with the result that the daily operation of the school became stabilized through the installation of bureaucratic procedures. At the same time, the teachers created boundaries between themselves and the parents. We have labeled this period a "conflict bureaucracy."

In sum, from the formation of the faculty in February, 1975 to June, 1976, there had been a progression from a professional (collegial) organization to one characterized by force and force threat, and finally, to a conflict bureaucracy. The social relationships, and with them, the social structure of the school (including the distribution and grouping of students) had gone through very substantial changes by the end of the first year of operation.

K. THE SUMMER

Teachers did not work in the school during the summer. Sam volunteered time to help Alberta organize the school for September; her work included hiring five new teachers, allocating teaching space, moving several walls, and cleaning the school. Late in the summer, after a search that the Board of Education took an active role in, Alberta Bard was appointed principal of the school.

It should be noted that during the summer the state school funding crisis led to the court-ordered closing of all schools in the state for several weeks. The effect of this was general disruption, like that in the spring when the teachers were "fired." For Lincoln Acres school, it meant further delay of planning for the second year.

L. PARTING SHOTS

In June, as he had been required to every month since the eruption of conflict in the school, Brown submitted a report to the Board of Education. This one he titled, "End-of-Year Report." A subsection titled "Programs" begins:

> The concern for "Basic Skills" instruction among Board of Education members and community members has been one of the most unfounded of all concerns over the new school. Nonetheless, since it has still not been put to rest, the accomplishments of the Lincoln Acres School staff in Basic Skills follow.

In a statement highly supportive of the teachers' efforts, Brown explained the rationale, assumptions and practice of the instructional program. He stressed the positive features of team teaching and open education. The following paragraph illustrates both his tone and what he considered the school's achievements.

> The output from the programming in Basic Skills as measured by state assessment tests and California Achievement Tests show that Board members and others who publicly stated periods of time up to half a year had been wasted at Lincoln Acres School were wrong. They were speaking without data

then; they are strangely silent now that their wild speculations have been swept aside by a tide of data.* A chance to regain some of the confidence of the Lincoln Acres staff and the Board awaits. The praise they have earned in this area should be made by the Board. The Board's current thrust of interest in the "Basics" requires praise for jobs well done in this area.

Brown then spent several paragraphs discussing the decision to build the school, and the implicit understanding in the bond issue that it was to be a neighborhood school. In his opinion, Lincoln Acres should have been a magnet school with open enrollment throughout the district for those parents desiring open space and team teaching for their children. He continued:

> The viability of Lincoln Acres school as a neighborhood school depended upon the community's investment in and ownership of the open school concept of education. The Lincoln Acres community never evidenced any more positive attitude towards the design of the school than a dubious "wait-and-see." The selling of the concept was unsuccessful. Responding to community input in the design phase was not done on any significant scale.

In another subsection, "Information Given to the New Principal," Brown recounts the principal selection process, the Board of Education's apparent endorsement of his educational practices, and what he termed, "the string of errors preceding my entrance into the situation." For example:

> During the interview process, I was told that I would have to consider teachers within the district or township first, but that I would then be free to go outside the district for staff. After I started the interviewing of Washingtonville candidates, I was denied outside candidates. The current staff members are not a problem: I raise the issue as another example of incomplete information furnished to me and failure to keep promises made to attract me to the job.

Concerning the Board of Education, Brown wrote:

> The Board of Education gave the staff at Lincoln Acres school no support. Insistence upon major changes in organizational format were required before one day's instruction had gone on.

---

*As noted above, Lincoln Acres children were of the highest socioeconomic level in the district, a fact which Brown chose not to mention.

That is <u>pre-judging</u> people. The etymological step from "pre-judge" to prejudice is a short one. That is, I believe hidden prejudices existed on the Board of Education. They should have informed us of their prejudices. Then, at least, we would have understood the source of their lack of support.

In response to the concerns of the community and the Board of Education, Lincoln Acres School has held two open houses and several meetings with Lincoln Acres parents and community members. Reports have been written for the superintendent and the Board of Education, and much written material has been passed along to parents. While the content of the curriculum never had to be changed, since good education proceeded from the beginning at Lincoln Acres School, the style and appearance of the programming was changed to accommodate Board of Education and community mind-set about education.

The report ends with cautious optimism on the future of the school.

A difficult year has passed at Lincoln Acres School, and an easier one can be expected next year. It is easier to be second than first. Also many of the problems inherited by the Lincoln Acres School administration and teachers have been alleviated somewhat. The extent to which the second year is easier than the first /will be/ dependent in my view upon the response to items in this report. The response is not needed from the community of Lincoln Acres or the staff so much as the Board of Education. Parents, students and teachers have many questions in their minds this summer besides the looming specter of collapse at the state level:

1. Will the Board of Education make the Lincoln Acres School building livable, educationally flexible and safe?

2. Will the Board of Education give the Lincoln Acres children the same break other Washingtonville elementary children have for textbooks and supplies?

3. Will the Board of Education give credit where it is due for Lincoln Acres School successes, and support for the development of a comprehensive modern educational program?

In this report, once again there is a denial that Brown was in any way responsible for the troubles that the school encountered. The only change in assigned responsibility is that the teachers are mildly praised and cast as unwitting victims. Another interesting aspect of the report is Brown's claim that the curriculum was never changed, but only formalized and presented differently to parents as a result of their pressure. (From the researcher's perspective this appears to be true; the changes made in curriculum and organization were, for the most part, cosmetic.)

The report accomplished two other things. First the teachers approved of it, and thus felt more supportive of Brown on the eve of his departure. That probably served to reduce some of the anxiety that several of them experienced after he announced his resignation; they were afraid they had punished him too severely. Secondly, the report gave the teachers an opportunity to tell the Board of Education, Biddle and the parents what they thought of them without taking direct responsibility.

M. LOOKING BACKWARD

1. Brown's Reflections

In an interview, Brown reflected on the events of the year. In his view, one of the major problems the school had faced was the socio-economic composition of the Lincoln Acres community. Thus, in his view, the complaints from the community:

> ...were directed at the non-conforming nature of the school. They were trying very hard to conform to a clear model of how you rise up from the city and make it to the suburbs. You really get concerned about discrepancies with the model, when the school is definitely a discrepancy from that model.

> Researcher: How, precisely?

> Brown: It's not lifting people up by the bootstraps and pushing them ahead with all kinds of arbitrary motivational devices to make them over-achieve and become CPA's. It really isn't.

On the behavior of teachers toward him, Brown said:

> I felt that I was misunderstood in some cases and not given a fair chance in some cases, but for the most part I felt that I was treated honestly. I don't have any real complaints. I haven't really described the feeling. I don't know just where I'm missing it. I like to think that I allowed myself to be a target when there needed to be a target. And I feel cheated that once in a while when I needed a target and I was foolish enough to let them be it, I sometimes was not given the same understanding that I felt I had for them. In simpler terms, maybe I forgot unpleasant things, flare-ups, anger, whatever. And I'm not sure they always did.

Finally, in response to a question focusing on what, if anything, he would have done differently during the year, Brown replied:

It's hard to second-guess yourself, you know. I would obviously do many things differently the second time around, but that's just the benefit of experience. And I'm not prepared to say that I was unprepared for the job, that I was incompetent for the job. I could say, yes, at this point I could do this kind of job much better a second time. But I can also tell you I will never take this kind of job again.

Researcher: This kind of job being specifically what?

Brown: A community that's at odds with the district or the township and is working it out in a political process essentially, but in the area of education. I'm too far into education and too far away from politics to belong to that kind of thing. So maybe I was the wrong guy to bring in here. I don't know, but that's not my responsibility, that's theirs. I certainly heeded every warning signal I got, and tested myself against what they were saying. And I far more than matched that. What I'm trying to do is to leave space for the conclusion that maybe somebody else could have done better. But it's pride and it's conceit, but I think it's also accurate that I don't think anybody could have. That's my honest opinion.

I'm not saying it's absolutely a fact that nobody could have done better, because that's a possibility. I just don't happen to know anybody I think could have done better, or that I'm sure could have done better -- with the exception of a few people who would never take this kind of work. There are probably people like me who have done it once and therefore would never do it again. And I suspect that this state has a lot of lousy jobs that are of the same type that lots of people do once.

Here Brown seems a bit bemused, not quite clear on "where I'm missing it," as he thinks back over the year. But we see again his view that the problems were generated almost solely by the community's pressures, and that, on balance, no one could have been expected to do any better than he did. In short, as might be expected of nearly anyone who has decided to leave a conflictful situation, he pays little attention to the possibility that his own actions may have contributed to the outcome.

2. Biddle's Reflections

At about the same time, Biddle was asked a similar set of questions by a researcher.

In response to a question asking for the main reasons why events unfolded the way they did, Biddle said:

You know, I really haven't given a great deal of thought to that, although off and on I do when I get a little bit of time to do it. Part of that problem was strictly mine. Back in September or October, not of last year but the preceding year, a few of the parents in Lincoln Acres began to complain about, bitch about, start rumors about, the kindergarten at Oxford school. And two or three other kinds of things. Prior to that time, some of the Lincoln Acres people had stood up on their hind legs and screamed and moaned and groaned about township matters, about their own personal matters, and this sort of thing. They were fighting internally, tremendous amount of in-fighting among LAHA, among residents of that particular group or that particular development. So it was a rather amorphous kind of situation, which I suppose, if we hadn't been involved in the construction projects and other kinds of things that were very demanding, we might have looked at a little more carefully -- I might have. Hindsight is always better than foresight.

Let me say this, had I really recognized how absolutely demanding some of the people would be, I would have forced myself to take the time to have gotten a little bit closer to it. I misread it from that point of view.

Concerning his role in the reorganization of the NBC and BJW teams, Biddle explained:

I wasn't getting pressure from the community directly. It was mentioned, I remember, at the Board of Education. But I had had some concerns about it myself and I had walked into the group. And I had expressed that at that point. But I thought that they could have been resolved rather readily. Oh, I don't know what all took place. It's very difficult to reconstruct. There was a series of meetings, as you well know, with parents. I deliberately stayed out of those for the simple reason that I did not want to give the impression that I was dictating what was going to take place in the school. I thought they could probably resolve it themselves. Hindsight, again, says, if I'd known that, I'd have been there from the very first meeting held.

Researcher: Being out of those meetings was a mistake?

Biddle: Yes, because I think probably I might have been able to say to the staff, hey, look, simply diagnostically, here's what you're doing, here is what's coming in, here's how it's coming across; you're doing this, you're saying that; this is the way you ought to be picking it up. That sort of thing. I did finally attend a couple of meetings with the BJW group, and the communication was just not there.

When asked whether the community's reaction to the school came in part because Lincoln Acres was perceived as "Biddle's dream school", and thus offered a vehicle for attacking him, Biddle stated:

> I don't know. It's a possibility. But what I tried to do from the very outset was to say, this is not my school, it shall be planned by the staff and by the people within that particular building. I mean, the community that it serves.

In retrospect, along with having taken a more active role in managing the community, Biddle said:

> I would like to have done what I have done with every other preceding principal in this school district: insist that that person become involved in organizational development work -- as a prerequisite to anything.

As far as Brown's performance was concerned, Biddle offered the following comments:

> Biddle: Oh, you know, I'd rather not even make any comment. Let me say that I think I could have done more than I did to be helpful to him.
>
> Researcher: You'd like to have been more helpful, so in part you're feeling you didn't supply as much assistance and support as he could have used.
>
> Biddle: Yes, that's partly true. You know, I don't really see this as my evaluation of him.
>
> Researcher: If he had wanted to stay, would you have accepted that?
>
> Biddle: He had a two-year contract.
>
> Researcher: So the decision to leave was essentially his.
>
> Biddle: With some encouragement.

Finally, Biddle's hope for the school for the next year was essentially that the original version would be recaptured.

> Well, for one, I have never been hung up on people having either open or closed space. I think that that is a professional decision that professionals need to make. I would hope that they could feel free enough -- and this is going to take some doing -- to trust each other, to work together as a team, start out with a very consistent pattern or somebody being responsible for a particular group of youngsters, branching out from that point as the needs of the youngsters indicate. In

terms of hope, I would just hope that they would begin to recoup the kind of enthusiasm that they went into that school with initially. That's going to take a long time. But it may not. I think it's contingent upon how well they get off the ground in September.

I think that it's entirely possible that the group of parents and the group of teachers can work constructively together. That's a foregone conclusion. That has to occur. That's not a hope. It's highest on the priority list. I think that's about all one can hope for. That's been a damned good school. The kids are amenable to working with adults, with each other. It has an absolutely magnificent mix of youngsters. It's one of those rare opportunities we should take full advantage of.

Here we see a superintendent acknowledging both the pressures of the surrounding community and to some degree his own fallibility, both in misdiagnosing the setting, and in not intervening even more vigorously than he had for support of the teachers and principal. His indirect acknowledgement of his doubts about Brown's performance is only a distant mirroring of Brown's feeling of complete lack of support. He closes with typically expansive optimism.

N. (COMMENTARY)

Strong leadership -- an ingredient that many theorists view as essential for successful innovation -- was present to some extent during the planning, but notably absent in the implementation process. Although Biddle regretted not having acted more decisively, his stated aim was to permit the principal, teachers and parents to form their own school with minimal guidance from him. To a large extent he succeeded in this. Brown's view of his own role was initially that of an active, "charismatic" leader. By the second month of school, however, his ability to assume such a role, he claimed, was diminished by inadequate planning before he arrived and lack of support from the superintendent and Board of Education.

At any rate, neither man acted over an extended period of time as a strong leader, one who could actively influence the actions of those around him in the desired direction without the use or threat of force. Erratic, uncertain and often seemingly irrational leadership behavior was undoubtedly one of the causes of the failure to implement the core features of the new school. It was not, however, either the central or single cause, as some theorists claim (see especially Gross, et al., 1971; Herriott and Gross, 1979).

In our view there is validity to both Brown's and Biddle's interpretations; they were enmeshed in a larger field of forces that affected their leadership behavior. Properties such as the goal diffuseness, weak knowledge base, permeability to the environment, and domestication of public education affected the range of behavior that was available to them. Strong, decisive behavior was frequently either inappropriate or not possible, given these constraints and the community context of the school. Failure to recognize these inherent and contextual constraints leads to a conceptualization of innovations as flourishing or withering because of the support of one person, the leader.

By stating that leadership -- either the absence of presence of it -- is not the central element in the degree of implementation, we do not mean to lift the entire burden of the errors in judgment and the faulty decisions made in the Lincoln Acres school by Biddle, and especially Brown. Each made numerous important mistakes. But as documented in the preceding analysis sections, leadership is only one variable that determines the results of the highly complex social process of organizational innovation.

11

THE SECOND YEAR: RECONSTRUCTION

The major research question posed for the second year of operation of the new school was: What, if any, parts of the original vision for the school would remain (or reappear) and be implemented? Corollaries to this question were: What lessons were learned from the previous year? What strategies would the new principal develop for managing the teachers and parents? What role would the community take during the second year? These questions are examined in this chapter, but in substantially less detail than in the preceding chapters.

A. THE BEGINNING OF SCHOOL

In September, 1976, the division of teaching spaces in the school was substantially different than for the year before. All classes were separated; one had four walls and several approached being self-contained. Over the summer Biddle had had 36 large wooden cabinets constructed; they were placed throughout the instructional area in the fall, forming walls about eight feet high, not reaching the ceiling. It was no longer possible to observe several classes from one location. The second-year spatial arrangement is presented in Diagram VIII.

Alberta Bard's planned strategy was to buffer the teachers from the community, and to take an incremental approach to reinstituting team teaching and the use of open space. This excerpt from an interview on September 8, 1976, illustrates her thinking at the beginning of the year.

> I plan to be fairly manipulative. Where I think they are really ready for it /team teaching/ to enrich their program, I shall encourage it, as with Wanda and Alice. Where I think, because of their personalities or some other reason, they'd rather not, I will drag my feet. I think it can enrich programs for kids and I'd like to see it happen, but I think it's fraught with dangers, I really do, particularly in a school where there have been some problems in the past. I don't think the wounds are really all healed by a long shot, and I'd rather not run the risk of

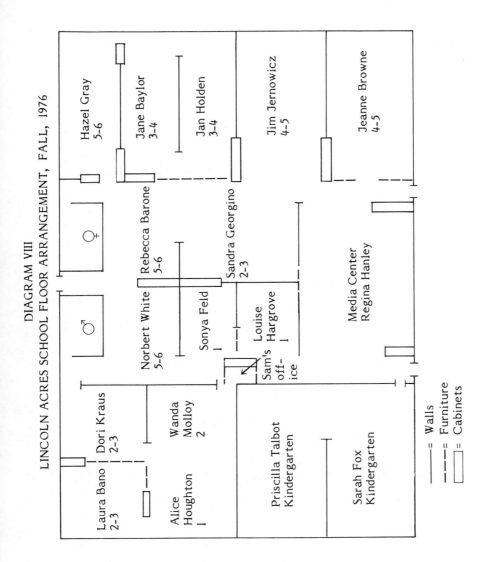

DIAGRAM VIII

LINCOLN ACRES SCHOOL FLOOR ARRANGEMENT, FALL, 1976

331

anybody getting into a situation of getting kids involved in a team teaching situation where they haven't really worked out their personal relationships with one another.

It is important to note that even though Alberta was well informed on the problems of the previous year, she did retain an innovative intent for the school. Several teachers were also committed to the original vision: after several weeks Wanda and Alice, and Jane and Jan Holden formed teaching teams. Several teachers used "open" teaching techniques in their self-contained classrooms. Other teachers, like Dori and Jeanne, preferred self-contained classrooms and made no effort to team teach.

In early faculty meetings Alberta told the teachers that she would make every effort to "keep parents off your backs" and establish positive school-community relations. And in the same interview excerpted above, she stated:

> I plan to involve the parents whenever a group is working toward teaming, to involve the parents by having them come in and listen, participate in discussions. I think I can size up the general tenor of the community by talking with, or listening to, several of these subgroups. I would expect to be able to find out whether it is the team teaching they are objecting to -- which I doubt, really -- or whether it's lack of planning. Or, as I think is largely responsible for what happened last year -- just poor communications, just not being able to explain and when parents challenged them, becoming very defensive and everybody stopping listening. I may be wrong, but I am convinced at this point that if parents believe that their kids are being taught to read and write and do arithmetic, and if their kids are happy, they don't really care how the teachers go about doing that.

B. EARLY SCHOOL OPERATIONS

In the early weeks of school, Alberta put an enormous amount of effort into the problem of cleanliness in the school. She made an especially pointed effort to inform the teachers of her awareness of the problem of keeping the school clean, and asked for their cooperation. In this particular area, she was greatly influenced by the experiences of her predecessor. Also in the early weeks, Alberta -- with substantial advice from the faculty -- formulated the basic operational rules and procedures for the school, including such detailed matters as lunchroom procedures, use of duplicating machines, and the collection of milk money. In general, it appeared that both Alberta and the teachers were working toward establishing a sense of "normalcy" in the school.

One of the noticeable differences between Ellis and Alberta was her conscious attempt to create a sense of belongingness and openness in the faculty. She had the teachers remove the tables from the faculty room for meetings and sit in a circle facing each other to facilitate communication. More fundamentally, from the beginning of the year Alberta always consulted with the teachers when making decisions. Even in cases when she had already made a decision, she would present her reasoning and ask for comments from the teachers. Teacher suggestions often resulted in altered policies. As another method of keeping teachers informed, Alberta distributed a weekly memo listing school activities and special events. Her objective of direct, open communication with the teachers was usually achieved.

C. RELATIONS WITH PARENTS

1. Managing Parents

A few individual parents entered the school and spoke with teachers or observed classes during the first week of school. As a result of careful monitoring by Sam and Alberta, after a few weeks parents learned that they could only visit a teacher or classroom with an appointment. The control of parents, a central issue the first year, remained a highly sensitive area during the first weeks of the second year, but was managed more effectively. It should be noted, of course, that eight of the highly critical parents from the first year had not returned their children to the Lincoln Acres school; thus most of the parents of children currently attending the school were interested in monitoring the school, but not in changing it.

2. Reinterpreting the Innovation

On September 16, for the first time in almost a year, the school received positive publicity in the Washingtonville Courier. The front page headline read: " 'Walls' Don't Slow Kids' Learning." Near the beginning of the article the author observed:

> The change, however, is primarily physical. There's been no change in the school's open education approach to learning.

Later in the article, Alberta elaborates on this; she is quoted as saying:

> Open education doesn't necessarily mean open space, though open space can facilitate open education.
>
> I think the question of rooms, partitions and walls became symbolic of the fact that some parents felt their children were not learning. They did not understand some of the programs their children were involved with, and it seemed to them that one of the main reasons that more learning was not taking place was because there was this open space and teachers couldn't conduct the kind of traditional classes they were used to. I think some extremely good teaching went on last year, but I'm not sure it was always explained adequately to the parents. I don't think that the teaching that goes on this year

is going to be substantially different, but I think that the new arrangement of partitions is going to help teachers maintain programs that are comprehensible to parents.

In other words, the reality of education in Lincoln Acres school wasn't going to change in the second year, only its appearance, and its "selling" to parents. In the previous year, the faculty had attempted, and failed, to re-socialize the parents into accepting the original innovation. This year the strategy was different: the educational program was slightly altered, and explained so that it fit comfortable images of education that parents could readily identify.

3. Open House

On September 29, the first open house of the year was held. Alberta structured it so that only 20 minutes would be spent by parents in their children's classrooms. Each teacher was responsible for his or her presentation to parents; Alberta only suggested that they not let parents simply wander through the classrooms. In all instances, the teachers prepared highly structured and fairly detailed presentations to explain their daily educational program. Parents were attentive and asked questions, but were not as hostile or probing as they had been the previous year. Most of the teachers thought the night went extremely well. One noted:

> Somebody said to me that I had a nice beard. Last year they would have walked up to me and pulled it out hair by hair.

4. Hints of Last Year

The only internal crisis of the school year occurred a few weeks after the open house, when a parent requested that her daughter be transferred from Bert's class to Fernwood School. Bert, it was claimed, did not provide the proper educational atmosphere for the child. Bert, who had experienced transfers the previous year, was deeply upset by what seemed to him an unjustified accusation. After several meetings with the parents, Bert and Alberta arranged to solve the problem by having the child transferred to Rebecca's class. The rest of the teachers watched these events eagerly, but exercised caution and tried not to aggravate the situation; they particularly wanted to avoid forming factions within the faculty, or between the teachers and administration. Their interest in the matter was natural: this incident could potentially create the same problems the NBC and BJW teams had experienced in the fall of last year.

During several faculty meetings, the history of the transfer was presented, and all of the teachers' questions were openly and satisfactorily answered both by Bert and Alberta. It was clear that the teachers thought that Alberta had managed the situation optimally, and had acted in the best interest of the people involved.

With the successful passage of her first crisis, Alberta's authority was enhanced among the faculty. In general, her candid, supportive -- near-maternal -- way of working with the faculty contributed greatly to problem-solving, coping ability and organizational stability all year.

D. SCHOOL LIFE: ROUTINIZATION

By November, the daily operation of the school was extremely smooth. The children had adjusted to the new spatial arrangements of the school, as had their parents. For the most part there was little change in teaching arrangements from those in place at the beginning of the year. Only two sets of teachers (Wanda and Alice; Jane and Jan) were team teaching, and then only periodically. No other teachers seemed interested in collaboration. The basic difference in the school was Alberta's ability to command the respect of the teachers.

Relations with the community during the first months of the second year were harmonious. Teacher attendance did not improve at PTA meetings, but a permanent representative was appointed, and Alberta and Sam attended most meetings. The PTA sponsored fund-raising activities and cultural events, and helped make arrangements for a playground that was to be constructed in the spring as a school-community project. In contrast with the situation last year, the PTA expressed no desire to influence internal, "professional" aspects of the school; its role became institutionalized as a social organization used to support school activities. This shift was probably a joint function of Alberta's careful attention, and the presence of a more moderate PTA president.

In addition, LAHA, now supplanted by the PTA, no longer played an active role in school affairs. It did not, however, abandon its role as an organization for community action; throughout the spring the homeowners opposed the construction of a shopping center bordering the newest section of the Lincoln Acres development. They used the same tactics that they had employed to oppose the educational program of the school: strenuous protests at planning board meetings, endorsing candidates for town council, and petitioning. An interesting addition to their strategy was the use of outside planning, architectural and legal experts; during the school dispute they had not called on expert testimony, apparently feeling they had enough internal resources to successfully demand alterations in the school program.

Relationships between the school and community had, in fact, improved so significantly that on November 7, the Daily Eagle, a regional newspaper, reported: "Lincoln Acres School Solves Parent Problem". The article credited Alberta's leadership and the alterations in the building for improving the situation. After recounting the events of the previous year, the article continued:

> Frisch now says the school has made significant strides towards improving its problems and added that next year, when his daughter starts school, she probably will go to Lincoln Acres.*

---

*This public change of heart undoubtedly had extra impact because Frisch had been elected Board president in October, after Estelle Hunter resigned.

With this article, former critics began publicly endorsing the new leadership and educational program of the school; relationships between the school and community stabilized.

E. THE STRIKE

The Board of Education and Superintendent Bob Biddle were relatively uninvolved with the Lincoln Acres school in its second year. The main problem they faced was that teachers and other personnel in the district had been without a contract for over a year; the Board hired a negotiator to work toward a settlement with the teachers' union and other employee associations.

On November 20, the Washingtonville teachers, school aides, clerks and custodians formed a coalition and demanded that the Board bargain with all of their associations at one time instead of separately. The Board responded that this arrangement was unacceptable. As a result, the coalition called a job action that began on December 1, 1976. Basically, the job action required that union members work only the hours specified in their old contracts. This meant, for example, that there could only be one faculty meeting a week in the Lincoln Acres school, and that teachers did not arrive early in the morning, nor stay after school.

Alberta, as an administrator, did not participate in the job action. She felt a slight tension between herself and the teachers, and was disappointed because the job action meant that several activities the faculty was going to work on -- including increased team teaching -- would have to be postponed.

The job action lasted until the Christmas vacation. During this time, although some concessions had been made, little progress appeared in negotiations. The Board claimed it was limited by a state-imposed restriction on spending, part of the effort to equalize educational opportunity by equalizing municipal educational expenditures. The coalition claimed there was money in the budget for salary increases, and that the Board should negotiate directly with the coalition instead of through the hired negotiator, who was paid large sums and in their opinion did an inferior job.

On January 2, 1977, the day before school was to resume after Christmas vacation, the coalition went on strike against the school district. Picketing was widespread -- Lincoln Acres was picketed -- but in the third week of the strike several classes in Oxford elementary school were opened, staffed by parent volunteers and substitute teachers. This and other actions increased the strain between the administration, community and teachers. After major concessions by the Board, the strike ended on January 24, 1977.

The strike did not damage relationships in the Lincoln Acres faculty. Teachers did not resent Alberta's non-participation. In fact, during the strike, Alberta and other administrators had urged that the Board grant concessions to the teachers. Among the teachers, the strike created a sense of camaraderie; although some resentment was expressed toward Priscilla, who did not participate, she was not punished afterward.

During the strike, the community's anger was directed toward all of the district's teachers, not specifically at the Lincoln Acres strikers. Only two community members -- Frisch in his role as Board president and Marie Bonomi, who crossed teacher picket lines to volunteer as a teacher -- were the targets of teacher hostility. Once school resumed, there were no apparent lingering strains between the school and its community.

An important consequence of the job action and strike was that planning time needed to move toward open space and team teaching was lost. Thus, by mid-November Alberta's plans to increase the degree of innovativeness were temporarily put aside. And after the lengthy strike it appeared even less feasible to attempt to innovate; once again there was a feeling that a return to "normalcy" was the wisest course to take. So the strike ended an already halting effort to re-implement parts of the original plans. But for most teachers and the administration, the innovative vision did remain intact.

By February, under the pressure of budget deadlines, plans for the third year of school were being made. Alberta hoped to be able to encourage team teaching; she began looking for ways to remove walls and create open space classrooms.

F. THE SPRING: A BRIEF SUMMARY

March was a quiet, uneventful month. Teachers, parents and students were well settled into the routines of school; there was scarcely a hint that a little over a month before there had been a district-wide school strike. There were no other attempts to change the already-established patterns of teacher and administrative behavior. The pervasive attitude was to "leave things well enough alone," and hope that the school year would end without further problems.

In early April, the long planned-for school-community project of building a playground for the school was realized. With the help of an outside consultant who organized and directed the construction, in two days the faculty and over 200 community volunteers erected an elaborate playground made from old tires and telephone poles. This was the most successful school-community venture to date; it served to prove to parents and teachers that they could work together constructively.

G. THE END OF THE SECOND YEAR

1. Brief Summary

Even with the extension of the school year through the end of June due to the days lost to the strike, the problems in the school remained minimal and were confined to the daily operational level; there were no further crises.

By the end of the year, Jeanne and Dori were on maternity leaves and Sam had sought and accepted a job as a teaching assistant-principal in a nearby progressive school district for the fall. All other teachers planned to return to the school.

By the end of the year, the plans for the third year (as begun in February) were to move incrementally toward more team teaching and use of open space techniques. Before school ended, three sets of teachers were already planning to team teach, and two other sets were seriously discussing it. Several teachers, however, were definitely going to continue with self-contained classrooms, and were not considering team teaching in the future. In other words, the school continued to move toward the original vision, but was significantly altered, since a variety of teaching strategies would probably always be present. This was what many parents had originally demanded -- and the teachers had learned to accept.

2. (Comments: The State of the School)

In general, although little had been accomplished in terms of the originally-planned innovations, the school was a substantially more satisfying work place for the teachers and administration by the end of the second year than at the close of the first year. Problem-solving capacities had increased, and a sense of unity and purpose began to emerge; the return to "normalcy" seemed a necessary process after the failures of the previous year. Much of this was the result of Alberta's administrative skills. In contrast to Brown, she provided a "rational", steady, uniform and "warm" approach, mixed with a sensitive reading of the events of the previous year which led her to treat both the teachers and parents with caution.

3. Community Attitudes

As we have seen, relationships between the school and community improved considerably during the second year (with the exception of the period during the teachers' strike). The harmonious relations that developed are reflected in the parents' rating of the school. When parents were retrospectively asked in June, 1977: "What kind of job did you think the school did in the first month or so it was open this fall?", 79% answered either "outstanding," "very good" or "good". By Christmas, 81% of the parents rated the school as performing positively. As of June, 85% rated the school as performing positively, including 8% who thought that Lincoln Acres school did an "outstanding" job. Finally, 75% thought that the school was doing a "much better" or "better" job compared with the same time (June) in the previous year. Twenty-three percent thought that the school did "about the same" job as in the previous year and only 2% thought that it was "worse".

These levels of satisfaction with the performance of the school were by far the highest at any point since the school opened. Interestingly, however, 32% of the parents thought that the teaching methods had not changed in the school from those used during the first year. Only 17% thought that the teaching methods had changed a "great deal". This suggests, then, that to a large extent the changes that increased parent satisfaction were of a non-instructional nature, and had more to do with the efforts that the faculty and administration made to improve the community's image of the school. This is apparent in the write-in responses to the question: "If there have been changes, could you describe them briefly?"

> Things settled down. Parents and teachers worked together. More openness between school and home.

> There is a strong feeling that all is well.

> The biggest changes have been in communications between the parents and teachers, and the warm feelings of interest and concern for parent feelings on the part of the principal.

Only 28 parents (28%) described changes as they saw them; of these, six simply mentioned the disappearance of team teaching for their children. Fourteen said the changes were in effect toward a more traditional program, citing "more stress on basics", "structured atmosphere and teaching method", "more phonics", "more homework", "concern with academic, not with social skills", "more teacher instruction". On the other hand, seven parents felt the changes were in directions usually labeled innovative: "more independent study", "shift in emphasis from school work to play", "more responsibilities on children", "teacher concern for social success", "more relaxed atmosphere". It is also of some interest that two parents who had just moved into Lincoln Acres from Louisiana and New York City saw the program as comparatively non-traditional, and as not emphasizing academic work sufficiently.

So while the shift to self-contained classrooms was evident, only half of those describing changes saw them as traditionally-oriented; the other half of those responding either mentioned the reduction of teaming, or saw new emphasis of a non-traditional sort. How many of these distinctions lay in the eyes of the beholders is not clear, but it is reasonable to guess that, on balance, the image of the instructional program changed more than the actual practices, with the exception of the shift away from team teaching.

H. IMPLEMENTATION SUCCESS

In sum, what can we say about the implementation of the Lincoln Acres vision, after two years of operation? Chapter 1 lists four criteria of "good" implementation. The first is reasonable goal congruence, presence of the core features of the original vision. Of course success varies according to whose vision we are talking about. The more sweeping aspects of Biddle's vision, including the ideas that the school should be "a situation where change is the main process" and education would be "redefined", were clearly not achieved. However, at a more modest level, his commitment to teaching teams, the importance of flexibility, the desirability of shared decision-making, and the notion of responsiveness to pupil and community needs were moderately realized. (The initial commitment to flexibility did permit, ironically, the erection of partitions that reduced flexibility; teaming was only partially present after two years, with promises of more to come. The other irony is that responsiveness to community needs resulted in a less-innovative educational setting.)

Ellis Brown's vision included the goals of high adaptiveness, an "open" educational program with a strong "individualization" thrust, team teaching in open space, and the hope that Lincoln Acres would be a "model" for others. The "model" aspect never received explicit attention. Both team teaching and the amount of actual "open space" were much less in evidence two years later than Ellis would have hoped. The implemented school did probably succeed reasonably well in individualizing the learning environment for students, though how "open" it was is clouded by much ambiguity around most participants' use of the term. And as above, "adaptiveness" had a flavor of bowing to community wishes.

The teachers' early vision stressed individualization, creative use of the open space, and teaming. The latter two -- which were clearly core hopes -- must be counted as only partially achieved. We have some quantitative data bearing on the teachers' endorsement of certain goals, and the degree to which they felt these goals were achieved at various points in time (See Table 11.1).

By the end of the summer planning period, teachers had a more differentiated idea of key goals. At that point they were committed to individualization (item A) and its associated goals of enhancing autonomy for students (B) in a trustful atmosphere (C). They were somewhat less committed to innovative space use (D), and only about two thirds had innovative, experimental hopes (F).* There was also commitment to three goals which have been recurrent issues in our account: teaching basic skills (G), providing for collegial policy influence by teachers (H), and developing good relations with the community (I).#

For the individualization goal (A), commitment stayed high, and rated achievement improved by the end of the second year. The same was true for the "climate" factors of autonomy for children (B) and adult-child trust (C).

The interest in innovative space use (D) dropped substantially during the first year, then recovered somewhat, though its achievement, as might be expected given the addition of walls, remained low.

---

*This finding, along with the fact that only 50% of the teachers thought that Lincoln Acres should have the goal of "being different from traditional schools", suggests less commitment to innovativeness as such than the early rhetoric suggested. Perhaps selective recruitment and resocialization (which we discuss further in Chapter 12) were less effective than the planners had hoped. And the seeds of movement toward a more traditional school were in part present within the faculty -- not just "out there" in the community.

#It should be recalled that December, 1975 represented a crisis point in our account, that June, 1976 saw the departure of the first principal and that June, 1977 was the end of the second full year of operation.

TABLE 11.1

TEACHERS' ENDORSEMENT AND RATED ACHIEVEMENT OF KEY GOALS

	Summer 1975 Endorsed*	December 1975 Endorsed/Achieved**	June 1976 Endorsed/Achieved	June 1977 Endorsed/Achieved
A. To provide personalized and individualized programming and instruction	100%	81%/67%	94%/65%	95%/74%
B. To increase the independence and autonomy of students	100	90/67	100/59	95/84
C. To foster an atmosphere of trust between adults and children	100	86/71	94/47	100/90
D. To try out innovative uses of space in the educational program	88	67/48	53/36	70/47
F. To increase "sharing" of teacher abilities, talents and skills	#	86/35	88/12	100/94
G. To experiment with new educational programs and structures	69	38/24	42/42	75/53
H. To teach students the basic skills	100	95/67	100/94	100/100
I. To give teachers a substantial role in setting policy	94	81/13	82/47	90/74
J. To develop good relations with the community	100	86/10	89/24	84/77
K. To have opportunities for professional growth	#	95/38	94/40	85/52

#Data not collected on this goal.
*"Endorsement" included answers of "agree" or "strongly agree" to the statement, "I think this is an important, valid and worthwhile goal for our school."
**"Achievement" included answers to "agree" or "strongly agree" to the statement, "Our school is achieving (or on its way to achieving) this goal.)

The commitment to "sharing" (an indirect expression of the teaming goal) remained high during the first year, but, as might be expected, was only weakly achieved. That almost all teachers thought this goal was realized by the end of the second year (in spite of limited teaming) may suggest a general improvement in climate, perhaps supported by the decisive upward shift in "teachers' role in setting policy" (H), which was at an all-time low in December, 1975.

We note too that commitment to maintaining community relations (H) stayed high as a goal, and its achievement was rated substantially higher at the end of the second year, following the abysmal achievement record in the first year.

Finally, many teachers cited the importance of their own professional growth (J) as an important goal, and the proportion who felt this was achieved rose somewhat by the end of the second year.

Meanwhile, the commitment to teaching basic skills (G) never wavered, and all teachers said this was being achieved by the end of the second year.

In general, then, we might conclude that (a) some goal succession occurred in relation to using the open space, but goal commitments were generally maintained; (b) by the end of the second year a decisive majority of teachers thought the goals of child autonomy, trust, teacher sharing, and basic skills were at least "on the way" to being achieved; (c) a sizable group thought that individualization, collegial decision-making, and good community relations were being achieved; and (d) only about half the teachers thought innovative space use, and educational experimentation more generally, were occurring, though the trend was upward.

We should note, however, that the typical achievement level was "agree" rather than "strongly agree" (with the exception of the basic skills and teacher sharing goals) so the picture is one of moderate accomplishment, especially if we allow for the idea that teachers might be inclined to give higher achievement ratings on goals for which they were held accountable (such as teaching basic skills).

On balance, looking at all the categories of planners and implementers, we conclude that the implemented school fell somewhat short of its planners' hopes. It was not notably and strongly congruent with the original goals, even when allowance is made for the fact that some initial hopes were perhaps too lofty to be achieved.

When implementation success is judged by stakeholders' satisfaction, Lincoln Acres looks better. Both parents and teachers, by the end of the second year, felt that the school was functioning well. And we never got any impression that students felt dissatisfied or upset by their life in the school. Parents' satisfaction probably came as much from the fact that they saw the school as, finally, responsive to their wishes as from any other aspect of goal achievement. For teachers, though they had had to give up or moderate their hopes for open space and teaming, satisfaction may well have stemmed from the increased stability, collegial decision-making, and freedom from the community pressure that had marked the first year.

Problem-coping ability, our third criterion of implementation success, appeared to be strong. No longer did the internal or external situation of the school threaten to be out of control, beyond the coping range of the principal and teachers.

Learning outcomes, our last criterion, seemed well achieved, though that fact is of course clouded by the high socio-economic status of Lincoln Acres children -- and by the fact that we do not have any measures available other than achievement tests. Seen in comparison to other elementary schools in the district (and, probably, to those in neighboring districts), Lincoln Acres was doing well.

In summary, though much was lost from the original vision, the school can be counted a moderately successful implementation by the second complete year. But the loss of core hopes is not minor. Producing a school that works well and satisfies its stakeholders is not the same thing as realizing an innovative dream.

I. (ANALYSIS AND COMMENTARY)

What might account for the degree of implementation success we noted? We shall have more to say about this in the following chapter: here we comment mainly on the primary planning/implementation tasks and how well they were carried out.

Considering the primary task of political stabilization, the school was functioning well. Many of the community complaints had been satisfied; there was no longer cause for worry over the new school. Secondly, the physical structure of the school did not permit the parents an opportunity to examine the teachers' work closely, in contrast to the situation during the first year. Third, parents' entry to the school was carefully controlled.

But there was also evidence that the faculty had heeded the lessons of the previous year: their actions toward the community were more deliberate and well-planned. The net effect was not only to create harmony, but to elicit constructive community action. We should also note that Biddle viewed Alberta favorably, and did not intervene in the school, so relations with the bureaucratic environment were also quite stable.

On the task of knowledge utilization, though matching consultant funds were still available, and Alberta considered drawing on them, she did not do so. One special workshop was held with an outside expert, but the pattern of relying on insiders' knowledge and skills continued. Given the consolidating, retrenching and stabilizing strategy being followed, it seems unlikely that increased use of expert assistance could have aided fuller implementation of the original hopes.

What occurred in relation to vision development? The second year of operation of the Lincoln Acres school retained elements of the original vision of the school: there was some team teaching and open space education. Alberta's plans for increasing implementation of the early hopes, however, were not realized. In part this was due to the job action and strike, and to the teachers' reluctance to collaborate after the failures of the previous year. But by the end of the year more teachers were planning to team teach. We conclude that although some of the innovations were discontinued, a significant portion of the mechanics were retained and the vision remained; the innovative effort did not end with the apparent failure of the first year. It did, however, decrease.

Actualization of the social-architectural design (which did not differ in any important respect from that of the previous year) was limited, and proceeded with reasonable effectiveness. The second year was primarily a period of consolidation.

The teachers and Alberta were careful in their relations with each other (as they were with the community). An example of this was Alberta's inclusion of the faculty in all important decisions. Although decision-making was more centralized than in the original vision, Alberta's model of consultation with the teachers created a professional or collegial organization, of the sort both teachers and administration had originally wanted.

The teachers' behavior during the strike also illustrates the increased thoughtfulness of their actions. They were careful not to create schisms within the faculty, even in a situation of extreme tension.

In general, it can be argued that the degree of actualization achieved was in important respects a function of the calming, stabilizing -- and active -- role played by the new principal. Although her exercise of the role took place in a setting with reduced community pressure and increased legitimacy, her personal style was also a factor. Though teachers (and the community) were clearly ready to accept her leadership (there was a certain amount of battle-weariness), it made a difference that she was politically skillful, collaborative, did not maintain social distance, and was proactive about problem-solving.

Finally, we should not overlook an obvious point. The second year of school did not have to contend with the problems associated with newness, especially innovative newness. Roles were simplified, clarified, and enforced; uncertainty was reduced, and teachers did not have to cope with the overload which is characteristic of new systems. In brief, institutionalization was well under way.

12

CONCLUSION: IMPLICATIONS
FOR EDUCATIONAL CHANGE

In the preceding chapters we have presented an ethnographic account of the planning, implementation and transformation of a complex, large-scale organizational innovation. Throughout the text our commentary and analysis has focused on accomplishment of the six primary planning tasks, and resolution of the associated dilemmas presented in Chapter 2. In this final chapter, we further examine the causes of change in the organization, and suggest several implications for theories of organizational innovation. We do not offer comprehensive or definitive interpretations, but our reflections on several forces that caused the school to change as it did. The reader is invited to construct his or her own explanations.

A. CHANGES IN ORGANIZATIONAL STRUCTURE

Over the course of the first year, the Lincoln Acres school changed from a quasi-collegial organization to a legal-rational bureaucracy. The basic changes in organizational structure were accompanied by re-definitions of the type of education offered by the school, which were primarily the product of the conflictful interactions between the school and the community.

1. Successive Organizational Types

Collegial organization. During the planning period and at early implementation* the faculty defined education as "child-centered", with an emphasis on individualization of instruction and affective growth, along with a program of traditional cognitive skills. Conceptualizing education in this

---

*Levels of implementation varied throughout the school, with at least one teaching "team" never actually using the team teaching technique, which was probably the central innovation among the "bundle" of innovations that constituted the school.

way -- as a non-uniform technology -- resulted in the intentional creation of a collegial organization, a type of organization congruent both with the value orientations of the faculty and with team teaching. The chief mechanism for guiding instructional tasks was the faculty's internalization of the values and norms of the school. The majority of teachers ignored the external environment; the main device for maintaining organizational boundaries was the delegation of authority to the principal to buffer, negotiate with, and possibly co-opt community groups.

Force and force threat. From the time of teacher selection until early implementation of the innovations, community criticism of the educational program intensified. Shortly after implementation, the result of persistent community pressure was a transitional period in the social relations of the school; there was at first disorganization, followed by a coercive compliance structure. During this period, the failure to maintain normal functioning of the organization was largely due to the lack of a clear boundary between the organization and its environment; there was no single power center or organizing principle. Community complaints and close scrutiny of school activities by many parents eventually resulted in a forced reorganization of two teaching teams.

Conflict bureaucracy. In reaction to the firing of a teacher, administrative ineptness and frequent intervention in school activities by community members, the faculty instituted rules within the school, and between the school and community, in an attempt to end what the majority of teachers considered the arbitrary use of force. In the process, the original goal of child-centered education was abandoned, and replaced with a modified "back-to-basics" educational philosophy. The evolved organizational structure -- bureaucracy --was no longer suitable for highly individualized, creative education (to which several teachers were still committed). Nevertheless, the objective of stabilizing the organization was achieved.

Stabilized quasi-collegial organization. In the second year, following succession to a new leader, the operating model shifted back toward the original collegial model. Hopes for re-implementation appeared, and several teachers actually used aspects of the first year's innovations, including team teaching. But bureaucratic procedures were still clearly in evidence, along with a cautious approach toward innovation.

B. ORGANIZATIONAL CHANGE AND THE ENVIRONMENT

Organizational change primarily stemmed from the educators' inability to maintain or create positive relations with the community throughout planning, and especially during implementation. We have identified this as the task of political stabilization, and noted that the dilemma associated with it is whether to confront outside groups or withdraw from contact with them. For the faculty of Lincoln Acres school, the political stabilization task became the central one; the accomplishment of all the other primary tasks eventually depended on it. The dilemmas associated with it were pervasive and never satisfactorily resolved. For example, during planning there was a distinct pattern of environmental avoidance. In the implementation stage, the teachers responded more actively by opening the organizational boundaries and attempting to resocialize the parents; eventually they engaged in pressure tactics similar to those used by the parents. Finally, the teachers withdrew from external contacts and created clear, less-permeable organizational boundaries. The patterns of interaction of the organization with its environment determined the configurations of and movement through the successive organizational types outlined above.

There are five factors associated with these organizational transformations that deserve some detailed discussion: the rate of change; organizational rigidity; the exercise of power; leadership; and organizational fragility.

1. The Rate of Change

Initially, the faculty and principal intended to implement the innovations slowly, and deliberately. By the time school opened, however, except for tactical assurances the principal gave the parents that the change would be "incremental", the original strategy was completely abandoned. The pattern was that as community complaints intensified, the faculty experienced an increasing need to defend their competence to their critics. Eventually, to establish their legitimacy as competent educators, they felt that rapid, tangible results were required; a demonstration that open education as it was envisioned would actually work. This determination increased the attempted rate of implementation substantially. It also altered the faculty's passive stance toward the community to one of confrontation.

Another consequence of the shift in change rate was that the time to accomplish the planning decreased, while internal organizational stresses accumulated. The pressure also increased the psychological and institutional costs to the faculty if the innovations were to fail. The hastily-revised planning strategy affected the accomplishment, not only of later planning, but all aspects of implementation.

Smith and Keith (1971), in their study of a new, innovative elementary school which attempted, unsuccessfully, to utilize educational techniques similar to those in Lincoln Acres, concluded that an incremental change strategy -- slow, deliberate installation of innovation -- is preferable to what they term "the alternative of grandeur," the implementation of a complex innovation more or less at a single time.

In their analysis, Smith and Keith in effect used a closed-system model of organizations; they did not examine the influence of the organizational environment on the degree of implementation of the innovation.* From this perspective, then, determining (and presumably

---

*Though they mention community dissatisfaction with the innovations in the school, and with the superintendent's performance, these are treated essentially as background factors, with no causal force.

controlling) the rate of change is a relatively straightforward matter; the planners choose a strategy and then manipulate the relevant organizational variables. The external environment, it is assumed, remains constant or is in substantial agreement with the planners' vision. We have suggested, however, that because of features in the context of American education it is extremely likely that new educational techniques will face resistance from various external forces -- resistance which must be dealt with.

The Lincoln Acres experience illustrates the fact that environmental pressure can under certain circumstances shift internal P/I groups toward the "alternative of grandeur" strategy. As in Smith and Keith's study, that strategy did not succeed. But it is <u>not</u> clear that a substantially slower rate of change would have increased the degree of implementation. The value differences between the school and community would still have existed; "personality" problems would probably still have developed to affect teaching teams adversely; and teacher understanding of the innovation and acquisition of the necessary skills would probably still have been deficient. Perhaps with increased time available, various mechanisms to gather feedback could have been established, creating opportunities for adaptation of the plans. That scenario assumes, however, that the organization would be responsive to signals from the environment. We can see from this analysis that rate of change, in and of itself, was not nearly as important as the problem of organizational boundary maintenance, and the flow of information across the boundary.

An implication for planning is that decisions about the rate of change -- a key variable and one that is directly related to implementation success -- should be contingent on several factors. Three are suggested by the Lincoln Acres experience. First, the complexity of the innovation (that is, whether it involves the learning of new roles and behaviors or only the use of new instructional materials) is important; more complex innovations should be implemented on a slower timetable. A second contingency factor is the skill level of teachers (including their previous teaching experience, familiarity with the proposed innovation, and willingness to innovate); low loadings on experience, familiarity and motivation suggest that a slower tempo is desirable.

Third, the political climate in which the school is embedded must be considered; the local community may be active or passive toward the schools -- and pro or con the particular innovation being attempted. Passivity leaves the field to the initiatives of professionals, but an active stance leaves the way open for community opposition or support. (As we have seen, there may be a sort of Gresham's Law in operation, where opposition drives out support, or at least pushes it into the background). So an active political climate suggests the desirability of a slower change rate.

We shall return to the question of leadership: here we should only note that managing the rate of change, using data about these three factors, is probably an important function.

In sum, we conclude that neither an incremental nor total approach is automatically appropriate as a strategy for school innovation. Instead a systematic, careful evaluation of the innovation's demand characteristics, the educators' skills and the context should be performed, and decisions made about rate of change.

Note that rate of change is closely connected with two other variables identified as important in Chapter 2: the evoking of commitment, and the nature of overarching goals. In Lincoln Acres, the dilemma of environmental contact vs. avoidance was poorly and unevenly resolved. This dilemma was intimately linked to another basic one: goal adherence vs. revision. Keeping out the community was at first seen as a way to avoid goal revision; once the shift was made to close contact with the environment, the pressures for goal revision became intense, and commitment had to be reluctantly shifted.

2. Organizational Rigidity

Faculty internalization of the norms, values and goals of the school was intended to provide the motivation to innovate and sustain the innovative effort and to support coordination of the teachers' actions. The social organization of the school also flowed from the values of a particular educational philosophy. Contingencies that arose in the performance of the non-uniform type of education that was planned were assumed to be within the range of abilities of the individual teacher and the teaching teams. There were no a priori rules governing all situations; initially, explicit school-wide rules were minimal. This approach provided a fairly sharp departure from the traditional school practice of bureaucratic administration; collegiality, which is what the under-emphasis on rules promoted, is not a common feature of most American elementary schools. Collegiality is also the essential feature in team teaching, the central innovation in Lincoln Acres school.

Two mechanisms were used to achieve internalization of the norms, values and goals of the school. First, only teachers with a propensity to work in an open space, team teaching school were recruited (cf. Kritek, 1976); teachers reluctant to participate in the planned changes would present serious obstacles to any attitude-change effort. Second, through the planning meetings, informal gatherings, the shared decision-making style, the communications workshop and the summer training program, there was a concerted effort to resocialize the teachers. This included socialization into the normative climate of the emerging organization, and an effort at training for the skills necessary for implementing the innovations. To a large extent the teachers absorbed the educational values more completely than the teaching techniques that would help to actualize them. This situation, we suggest, had multiple consequences for the school.

In bureaucratic structures, the phenomenon of the displacement of goals through ritualistic adherence to a priori rules has long been recognized as a source of dysfunctional behavior (Merton, 1968, pp. 249-260). Sources of dysfunctions in other types of organizations, particularly collegial structures, have been relatively unnnoticed. Indeed, the collegial type of organization is usually considered to be the opposite of legal-rational bureaucracy; it is viewed as being more flexible, primarily because power is decentralized and there are a limited number of a priori rules, facilitating problem-solving. This study suggests, however, that under conditions of rapid and large-scale change, there are some sources of dysfunctional behavior in emergent (and possibly mature) collegial organizations.

In this case, selective recruitment and resocialization into organizational values and goals were intended to help the organization innovate and manage internal contingencies. However, these features created inappropriate responses to environmental demands. Specifically, as a result of their high degree of commitment to the educational philosophy of the school -- an objective of the administration -- the faculty were reluctant to negotiate with the community or alter their plans voluntarily. The very rate of implementation effort was increased because of the strength of the teachers' values, and their fear of diluting the idealized vision of the school. In other words, rigid insistence on the accomplishment of abstract educational goals by particular means occurred largely because of over-resocialization. That in turn led to the heightening of conflict, and to the abandonment of the original vision -- including the collegial organization itself.

If the school had been initially organized as a bureaucratic structure, adjustment to parent demands could theoretically have occurred without major difficulties, since a change in policy at the top leadership level could have been communicated downward to the faculty and implemented.

But the members of a collegial organization by definition will not accept such "orders", and will tend to treat community demands in the same way. Thus, as we saw in the case, a painful second process of resocialization had to occur: the teachers had to give up many of their hopes and learn to live with a new internal organization.

The implication for complex innovative efforts is that it may be initially necessary to have a minimal number of rules, or a clear understanding that the administration can make unilateral policy decisions in specified areas or under certain circumstances.*

It also seems likely that different types of organization may be appropriate at various phases in the innovative process (cf. Duncan, 1976; Thompson, 1965). For example, a collegial form might be appropriate during the early stages when a plan is being formulated and a bureaucratic structure required at implementation. Or, as Kimberly (1980) has noted, the structure appropriate for launching an organization may be quite different from that required for institutionalization.# The structural shifts seen in Lincoln Acres were "forced" on the school; it seems likely that such a

---

*The reader may recall that Ellis and the teachers attempted just such a list. But many parts of it were left rather vague, and commitment to them was not strong.

#Some literature and much folklore connects this to the phenomenon of leader succession. New organizations often begin with charismatic, entrepreneurial figures, then shift to managers who are good at stabilizing things, and then to managers who are efficient operators. In Lincoln Acres, Ellis Brown was perhaps a quasi-charismatic leader, and Alberta Bard was clearly a stabilizer.

process could be managed to some degree. The lesson from our case, however, is that managed shifts in organizational form will require (a) a good means of collecting data from the environment; (b) buffering mechanisms to protect the organization while it deliberates; and (c) mechanisms that will support organizational responsiveness to the environmental data rather than denial or avoidance.

These remarks about dysfunctions of collegial organizations should be tempered by the observation that Lincoln Acres school was not a "pure" or fully-realized collegial organization; even from the beginning the faculty's participation in decision-making was less than full.* It could be argued that a "real" collegial organization would have engaged in better environmental sensing and problem-solving. But even so, a central risk that a cohesive, mutually supportive group of innovators faces is that of environmental avoidance, and rigid adherence to plans and abstract goals. The problem is how to maintain an innovative vision without becoming captive to it.

3. The Exercise of Power

The question of power permeated the events of Lincoln Acres through and through. The conflict between school and community occurred on two levels: the substantive level, where the issue was disagreement over the proper delivery system for education (open education and team teaching vs. self-contained classrooms), and the meta-level, where the disagreement was over the exercise of power itself. The question of whose influence should properly prevail was at many points more critical than the substantive issues.

The primary source of authority claimed by the teachers was expertise in education. However, as we have seen throughout the narrative, this claim was repeatedly challenged by the parents; there was a pervasive lack of trust in the teachers' abilities, and their legitimacy as professionals was never fully established.# When the conflict over the educational program intensified, and the parents convincingly displayed their own familiarity with educational matters, the teachers' reaction was to continue to claim -- in effect, demand -- recognition as professionals. But under the constant surveillance of the community, it became clear not only to the parents but eventually to several teachers as well that there were in fact serious pedagogical shortcomings in the school.

---

*Creating collegial organizations is a difficult process for many reasons (Rothschild-Whitt, 1976), not least of which is that members and leaders have much more experience with bureaucratic structures (and reluctance to leave them: see Argyris, 1974).

#To some degree, the parents may have been fighting back to recapture the legitimacy they felt they had lost when the voice of the people in the bond issue was ignored ("we have been lied to...shafted.")

As part of their effort to gain legitimacy, the teachers tried to demonstrate to the parents that the innovations were being carefully implemented and were working. In effect, they tried to re-socialize their critics. The intention was to convince skeptical community members, especially opinion leaders, that open education was a valid form of education from which all children would benefit. A variety of communication mechanisms were used in this effort: open houses, coffee-klatches, private conferences, visits to homes, and articles in the local newspaper. But the more exposure the parents had to the actualities of the activities in the classroom and to the teachers' explanations, the more dubious the parents became. The teachers' strategy to buttress their expert power -- claiming and demonstrating professionalism -- probably had the unanticipated consequence of heightening parents' expectations about teacher expertise. When evidence of expertise was lacking, the teachers' claims were seriously undermined.*

The educators in this case may have failed to persuade the community because the knowledge base of education is weak; there may not have been much supportive information to communicate. For example, if instead of avoiding expert knowledge, the Lincoln Acres teachers had made a systematic search of research literature concerning the two central innovations they attempted, they would not have found much to encourage

---

*The failed resocialization effort described above locates a significant problem for theories of organizational change. Some change theories assume that mechanisms exist to change not only the organization but also groups external to the organization (see Rothman, 1974). For example, the balance theory of school-community relations (Litwak and Meyer, 1974) assumes that through the appropriate use of "linkage mechanisms" between a formal organization and a primary group (family or neighborhood), the organization can reduce the social distance between itself and the external group, thereby increasing the possibility of changing the target population. When a primary group is characterized by high resistance to or open conflict with the goals of the organization, the theory suggests that the formal organization should use communication devices that increase trust and reduce the possibility of avoidance or distortion of complex information.

But the Lincoln Acres case suggests that when conflict between an organization and external primary groups is intense and the primary groups are well informed and powerful, the assumption of change through communication does not hold. There may be little the organization can do to influence the primary group, short of real "brainwashing" or inducing conversion experiences (Berger and Luckmann, 1966). On their side, the primary groups can act, as did the Lincoln Acres parents, to have personnel removed from the school; that is not easily done, but is possible under conditions of lay control of public education. A course of action open to the school is to restrict attendance to children from families in agreement with the school's educational philosophy, a strategy approximated in the "educational options" idea, where, within a district, school programs differ in explicit ways, and can be chosen by parents.

their efforts. In a thoughtful review of the research on team teaching Armstrong (1977:83) concluded that:

> ...one is struck by the very basic nature of the questions for which research has failed, after fifteen or more years of team teaching, to supply at least tentative answers. Team teaching, it is evident, represents one of those educational practices that have not been subjected to truly intensive and systematic investigation. Support for team teaching has been more of a validation through affirmation than a validation based on empirical evidence. At this juncture, little in the research literature provides solace either for team teaching's critics or its most ardent supporters.

Similarly, McPartland and Epstein (1977) report finding no relationship between open education and achievement, contrary to what the Lincoln Acres teachers assumed to be true.

Of course, there are other functions of knowledge utilization, among them establishing legitimacy by using knowledge symbolically. For example, experts with national reputations could have been used by the local educators to make presentations to community associations such as LAHA, thereby lending experience and prestige in support of the innovations. But the local educators' intuition reigned, and the rationale for the innovations seldom rose above the level of platitudes. Judging from the actions that the parents took against the school, the faculty presentations must have seemed like displays of ignorance.

The domination of Lincoln Acres school by the community suggests that under certain circumstances a community can exercise enough power over a formal organization to change it rapidly and fundamentally.* Several important features of the Lincoln Acres community permitted successful use of power against the school. First, there was a strong voluntary association, LAHA, whose members had previously experienced several conflict situations; techniques for organizing were well established, enabling the use of a wide array of strategies including petitions, the mass media, meetings, and personal influence. Second, a substantial portion of the community had detailed knowledge of education through experience as teachers. This gave them a claim to expertise and a foundation for their criticisms of the school. Third, the child-rearing stage in the life cycle and the relatively high economic status of most residents made the education of their children a central concern.

---

*The pattern of individual and collective action taken by the Lincoln Acres residents counters the view of industrial society as a "mass" society characterized by the reduction of intermediate levels of power, increased influence of the mass media, and a national network of bureaucracies that control major decisions (Nisbet, 1953; Marcuse, 1964; Mills, 1956). In particular, the power of the community in this case suggests that middle-class new suburban communities are not the disorganized product of industrialization, bureaucratization and urbanization that some observers (Stein, 1960) have decried.

4. Leadership

In new schools -- or, more generally, in new organizations -- is leadership central, one of several critical variables, or only a minor factor in implementation success?

Several studies of educational innovation view leadership -- the actions of a strong authority figure -- as the central factor in the achievement of the innovation (Smith and Keith, 1971; Gross, et al., 1971; Herriott and Gross, 1979). Indeed, the most recent of these studies places almost the entire responsibility for effective implementation of innovations on the leader, who must maneuver through an "Elaborated Leadership Obstacle Course" that includes features ranging from lack of motivation, skill and technical knowledge, to dysfunctional organizational arrangements, a wide range of conflict, resignations, role overload, and delays. We concur with Bailey (1975) in his critique of Gross, et al., which suggests that explaining innovative failure through presumably "omniscient" managers' failure to carry out their role obligations misses the fact that new roles for managers, teachers (and students) are being negotiated, resisted, and redefined. Similarly, Lighthall (1973) in his reanalysis of Smith & Keith (1971) suggests the importance of attention to the values and expectations of all parties to the change effort; "multiple realities" exist, and a shared reality must be negotiated.

Our view, as informed by the Lincoln Acres case, is that it would be a mistake to consider the behavior of educational managers as central to innovative success. Important, yes. But central, no. We can elaborate briefly.

First of all, there is an important caveat to keep in mind. An a posteriori analysis of "failed" leader behavior and its consequences does not tell us necessarily that "better" leader behavior would have made the difference. We can speculate that if the Lincoln Acres principal's leadership during the first year had been more sensitive to the community and faculty, or more politically astute at certain crucial points, the possibilities for success would have increased substantially. But as the old saying goes, "If your aunt had wheels, she'd be a trolley car." We cannot know with confidence what would have happened, only what did.

The leaders as persons. Ellis Brown's personal style is best described as aloof, intellectual and calculating. Like many successful entrepreneurs, he also exuded a feeling of self-confidence that at times bordered on arrogance. He was clearly familiar with educational issues and able to express his views coherently and cogently. Despite his espousal of a participative mode of decision-making, he tended to be manipulative -- and became more so as the conflict increased. His aloofness was not only interpersonal: it seems to have led him to withdraw from the scene for Boston or New Hampshire at several critical points.

Alberta Bard's personal style was quite different in many respects. She was candid, calm, warm and supportive (though certainly not "mushy"); there was little hint of the "charismatic", and she was clear about seeking teacher advice and collaboration in decisions. She was also quite active, staying with and solving problems.

It is tempting to conclude hastily that Brown's personal style was somehow a "bad fit" to the demands of the new situation, and that if only Bard had been selected as the first principal, all would have gone well. Against that speculation, we should note that the school under Bard, though it became quite stable, and was a "good" school, was still far from achieving its planners' hopes. More generally, we would like to note that the level of implementation in Lincoln Acres school seemed to depend on many factors in addition to leader style. For example, we have shown that the effects of teacher resocialization and commitment, the gaps between the ideology of open education and the skills it requires, and the likelihood of conservative critique as a function of general features of the American educational system were all important factors -- and they are all largely independent of what a principal does -- or at least, of the principal's personal style. One could say that a "good" principal "should" have dealt with such problems -- but that prejudges the issue in a tautological fashion, assuming from the start that the leader's behavior is the critical piece of the action.

Needed capabilities. We think it more useful to consider what the Lincoln Acres leader -- and the faculty group -- were and were not supplying in the way of capabilities for planning and implementation. Table 12.1 supplies a summary.

TABLE 12.1

P/I CAPABILITIES IN LEADER AND GROUP

	Year 1		Year 2	
	Leader	Group	Leader	Group
Legitimacy development	Strong early Weak later	Weak	Strong	Unknown
Investment development	Strong	Strong	Strong	Strong
Meta-planning	Moderate	Weak	Moderate	Weak
Political skill	Moderate	Weak	Moderate/ strong	Moderate
Reflexiveness	Weak	Weak	Moderate	Unknown
Decision-making skill	Moderate	Weak	Strong	Increasing

The table suggests some clear differences between the two years: before examining them we should remember that the contexts of the P/I effort were radically different. In the first year, the leader and group were struggling against parent opposition, beginning with damaged legitimacy, and trying to put together a new social system. In the second year, leader and group were attempting little that would invite opposition, had been given a license to proceed, and were fine-tuning an already partially-routinized system.

Keeping these differences in mind, we can see that the critical differences seem to have lain in three areas: legitimacy development, political skill, and decision-making skill.*

(1) Legitimacy development: Starting with strikes against him because of the "violation" of the bond issue mandate, Brown supplied strong legitimacy development skills early on. But as the conflict heightened, he (and, it might be noted, Biddle) faltered: they underestimated the depth of the community's value differences from the school's ideology. The teachers' efforts to build legitimacy were weak, and backfired frequently. In a sense, Brown was caught between two systems (which we have alluded to as democracy vs. expertise). He was not able to support legitimacy development efforts by the teachers, and when the community was invited to participate they often felt manipulated. Parent criticisms were often denied, treated by both Brown and the faculty as irrelevant quibbling; there was little effort to negotiate a legitimized, shared reality. Only force, ultimately -- the superintendent's intervention -- required that the parents' claims be seen as legitimate.

In the second year, Bard was careful to touch all bases -- even though she began the year with a stronger license than Brown had had. Since the teachers were not trying to claim expertise as a basis for pushing the innovation any longer, their weak legitimacy development skills were not crucial; we have no second-year data on this capability, in any case.

(2) Political skill: Though Brown sometimes proved politically astute, as in his negotiations with the Board and its chairman, he seemed to lack the patience for navigating among the shoals of the conflict. The faculty group was by turns bewildered and inappropriately militant. The tendency of both principal and faculty to withdraw from working contact with the environment at critical points -- and to drop the organization's boundaries at others -- exacerbated the problems.

The case suggests that boundary maintenance -- adequate buffering -- is an extremely important political capability. In a conflict of the sort that was present during the first year, the principal's role is perhaps unalterably "no-win", since parents and teachers want such different things. Brown's analysis was that he became a "target" -- a role he did not

---

*Investment development capabilities were strong both years, though as we have noted, _excessive_ investment in the first year made for rigidity and heightened conflict. Bard's approach the second year was to support existing investment rather than heighten it across the board. The two years' approach to meta-planning varied little. And reflexiveness, though its weakness in the first year intensified problems, was less of an issue in the stabilizing second year.

intend or wish to play. However, the role did have some buffering effects. The fatal problem, as we have noted, was the teachers' (and Brown's) belief, fueled by their own over-resocialization, that "involving" the parents in the school -- discarding the need to protect the school from hostile scrutiny during its early development -- would successfully coopt them.

In the second year, Bard was careful to protect the school from incursion, and equally careful to interpret it in politically-acceptable terms; the teachers for their part had learned some lessons about avoiding escalation and retaining parent endorsement. Buffering was aided by the physical walls as well -- which were simultaneously a symbol of the community's victory and a way to reduce visibility of role performance.

(3) Decision-making skill: Though Brown was reasonably clear and expeditious in his own decision-making style, his espoused hopes for collegial decision-making waned as the crisis rose. For their part, the teachers had little experience or skill in collaborating in joint decisions: even when Brown cleanly left decisions to them, they wandered, and avoided working things through. Only when Brown lost the teachers' respect and they determined to take power through formalistic means (the grievance, exclusion of him) did they manage to cope more productively. (This example illustrates well that the issue is only partly one of technical "skill" in decision-making as such: clarity surrounding decision-making powers is at least as crucial.)

We might note also that during the height of the conflict, both Brown and the faculty experienced the organization, in its environment, as alien to them, out of control -- and to some degree controlling them. Both Brown and the teachers lost the sense that they could collectively control their fate, and retreated more often than not to self-absorption and individual survival. That sense of powerlessness was especially frustrating to a group who had hoped to create a responsive organization that would realize their personal and professional vision.

In the second year, Bard made a point of being clear about when she was inviting shared decisions, and when she was inviting advice; the teachers' decision-making capabilities improved under these circumstances.

One final note: in the first year, on these three critical areas of capability, we note that the faculty was weak in all three, while the leader was strong/weak, moderate, and moderate respectively. During the second year, there was evidence of faculty improvement in two of the three areas, while the leader was strong, moderate/strong, and strong. Did Bard "build" the faculty's capabilities? Perhaps yes, in the case of decision-making -- but the faculty had learned a lot, shaken down as they traveled through the first year together. We continue to be dubious about the Great Woman theory of leadership in this case. In short, we conclude that leadership behavior in new systems is important, but probably not central; the degree to which participants deliver on needed capabilities -- both inside the system and in relation to the environment -- is also important.

5. Organizational Fragility

Finally, the "liability of newness" (Stinchcombe, 1965), a

characteristic of all emerging organizations, influenced the Lincoln Acres school and may have helped the community to prevail. Because of their newness, most elements of the organization were fragile. Roles were not well defined, communication patterns were irregular, and leadership uncertain. There was also considerable strain within the organization, because the interpersonal relationships and skills necessary for team teaching were untried and demanding. This fragility and strain was aggravated by the conflicting perspectives on education that were held by various segments of the community. The fact of newness made the school more vulnerable to its environment; the community battered down the figurative walls of an already weak organizational structure, only to put them -- and the literal ones -- back up. Paradoxically, newness -- one of the cherished assets of the innovators -- proved to be one of their chief liabilities.

APPENDIX A:
Methods Used in the Study

The first portion of this appendix describes our selection of and entry to the research setting. Then we review the methods we used to collect data, and discuss their limitations, problems and advantages. Finally, we discuss our data analysis techniques, especially the problems involved with making sense of large amounts of qualitative data.

A. SELECTION OF THE RESEARCH SITE

Based on the rationale that more could be learned from a positive example than a negative one, our primary objective in selecting research sites was to find new schools that were not only innovative but appeared to have a good chance of having the planned innovations successfully implemented. Crude indicators of probable "success" were: (1) the presence of resources, (for example, a building and qualified, interested personnel), (2) an innovative intent or vision, and (3) adequate planning time before implementation.

Potential sites were located through telephone calls to consultants, county superintendents, personnel at other innovative schools, local school people and others who might be aware of a new school's opening. The person who nominated Lincoln Acres school was a state department of education administrator of Title II federal funds. In her opinion, the Washingtonville school district had a reputation of being innovative and cooperative with researchers.

After interviews with the superintendent of schools and other central office personnel, it appeared that, compared with other available sites,* Lincoln Acres school ranked high on the selection criteria.

---

*For example, one site visited by the researchers was a new five-million-dollar regional high school that featured open space architecture. To estimate the probably degree of "success", we observed a meeting of the

It should be evident to the reader, however, that the selection criteria proved to be less than accurate predictors.*

B. ENTERING THE RESEARCH SITE

Gaining access to the relevant social groups in the school and community was accomplished in four stages. Entry began with the superintendent of schools, then turned to the principal, the community, and finally, the teachers. Each of these entry processes is briefly described below.

1. Entry I: The Superintendent

Initial contact with the school district was made through the superintendent. Robert Biddle had worked with Miles 20 years earlier in an action-research project; he was interested in learning about the current research project and trusted Miles.

In a preliminary meeting with Biddle, Little, and Smith, at which time the potential success of the school was assessed, it was mutually determined that both parties were interested in collaboration. It was agreed, however, that for the research to begin, the principal, who was to arrive in Washingtonville a month later, should be fully informed of the nature of the study and have the right to agree or decline to participate in the research.

The terms of a proposed contract between the project and the school were reviewed, but its completion was left for after the meeting with the principal.

2. Entry II: The Principal

Three days after Ellis Brown reported for work in Washingtonville, he met with members of the research staff to discuss the project and the possibility of participating in it. Brown's major concern was that the study

---

(footnote continued) planning committee, which was composed of department chairmen. Their primary concern was finding ways to partition the school and move the existing program intact into the new building. After further interviews with the people involved, including the superintendent of schools, it seemed clear to us that innovation of any type was unlikely. In other sites, planning had progressed beyond the stage when it could be meaningfully studied. In still another school, the school's principal was uncomfortable with being the object of research, and refused to participate in the study after several preliminary discussions.

*Apparently, predicting the success of an innovation is not an easy matter; of the six sites that were eventually selected by the Social Architecture project, only one realized intended plans during the first year of operation.

might interfere with the functioning of the school, especially the way in which teachers would behave under observation. After assurances that every effort would be made not to interfere with or intervene in school activities, Brown appeared satisfied. To protect both parties, a provision in the contract stated that the research could be terminated by either side, if discussion did not resolve problems that developed. Another provision was that teachers (as soon as they were selected) would have the opportunity to vote on whether or not to participate in the study. The contract also included statements on confidentiality and anonymity of data, and a clause offering periodic summary reports at mutually-agreed-upon times.

In this meeting the use of a consultant on a matching-grant basis -- $800 to be provided by the Center for Policy Research -- was also discussed. Brown did not view consulting help as either desirable or necessary; instead of being a tool for increasing the likelihood of collaboration and establishing positive relationships, as the researchers had expected, the offer of consultant help created some tension. As it developed, however, Brown, Biddle and the researchers did sign the contract,* including the consulting provision, and four days later research began, with Brown's being interviewed about his past educational experiences and the programs he envisioned for Lincoln Acres school. Soon after, retrospective interviews focusing on the history of the planning were held with the superintendent and assistant superintendents.

3. Entry III: The Community

Since the faculty was not yet selected, but Brown had been asked to present his plans for the new school to various community groups, the parents of children scheduled to attend LincolnAcres school became the next group that I# encountered. Initial contact was through observation of LAHA and other community groups. I was a silent observer in these meetings and did not actively interview anyone. Informal interviews did develop, however, when residents asked me if I were new in the community. I used these occasions both to gather information and to explain my objectives. In most cases there appeared to be understanding of what I was doing, and no fear of my presence.

During this initial period of attendance at community meetings, I tried to find out, through interviews with Biddle and his associates, which community members had been central in the early planning for the school. Most of these residents were then contacted and interviewed about the history of the planning, the history of the community (for example, the formation of LAHA), and the current state of the community. In these interviews names of other active community members surfaced.

---

*When Alberta Bard became principal, the original contract was renegotiated with few changes and signed by both parties.

#"I" refers to Gold, who carried out almost all of the field work. Miles conducted interviews at several points with Biddle, Holmes and Bard, and visited the school in operation a few times.

In general, entry into the community was extremely smooth. After several months I found myself able to sit in the living rooms of Washingtonville residents to observe meetings, or simply to ask them questions about recent events connected with the school. My impression was that in all but a few instances there was full cooperation and candor in the information supplied.

4. Entry IV: The Faculty

Sam Pennington was interviewed shortly after he had been appointed resource teacher. Pennington had participated on the building design and principal selection committees and was therefore viewed as an important informant. He also wanted to be assured that the proposed research would not interfere with the formation of a cohesive faculty, and that "the teachers won't think you're looking over their shoulders all the time." After discussion of our methods, he was convinced that the research would not be too harmful and agreed to participate.

At the first faculty meeting, without my presence, the research was informally approved by the teachers. At the second faculty meeting, Brown introduced me and I explained the research objectives and conditions. In particular, I stressed that all information would be confidential and anonymous, and that I would not intentionally intervene in school matters, nor perform an evaluative function. There were no questions.

In the next few faculty meetings, I made a strong, self-conscious effort to behave in accordance with the role I had described.* As a result my early interactions with the faculty were limited to greetings and note-taking. After several faculty meetings, once the teachers began to know each other and felt more at ease, my interaction with them also increased.

One important characteristic that may have increased initial contact with the faculty is that I was approximately the same age as most of them.# This reduced status inequalities and expectations of potentially threatening behavior, since I was probably not perceived as more highly educated or experienced than they were.

Another factor easing entry was that the faculty members were mostly new to each other. While this produced some tension and awkwardness in the first months of the group formation process for both the teachers and myself, it also meant that I didn't have to penetrate well-established friendship groups, or to learn and then manipulate strategically important facts about existing social relationships. Of course, the advantage of newness presented the problem of trying to avoid influencing

---

*My self-consciousness, in the sense of self-awareness, often with concomitant tension, remained high throughout the study.

#As research progressed, age assumed less importance; Regina, Sarah, and Priscilla, all middle-aged teachers, were as easy to talk with as the younger teachers.

the group formation process, while at the same time studying it and necessarily becoming a group member. This problem was managed -- successfully, I believe -- by maintaining a consciously marginal position in the organization. Marginality was usually not a difficult element of my role, since the teachers were usually too occupied with work to pay much attention to what I was doing. In general, a clear description of my role, followed by congruent behavior and a good deal of patience, proved to be the important ingredients of the entry process.

Entering the social systems of the community and the school with the endorsements of the superintendent and principal was beneficial; it helped establish the research as a serious and legitimate activity. One potential problem was the possible perception that the researcher was a representative of the school administration, who might be serving as a secret evaluator. Thus the behavior of, and information supplied by respondents -- particularly teachers -- could have been self-conscious, evasive or in some other way altered. In the early stages of research there were no indications that this was the case; maintaining an independent research role was not difficult. As the research progressed, however, problems with maintaining a credible research role did develop; they are discussed below. Before that, however, we turn to a general description of the qualitative data collection techniques.

C. NON-PARTICIPANT OBSERVATION TECHNIQUES

1. In the School

To gain a complete understanding of the school and avoid "elite bias", collecting information predominantly from organizational leaders, I made an attempt to sample the faculty members in each visit to the school. Sampling was necessarily imperfect because of the nature of school activities. For example, I did not interrupt teachers while they were teaching (on occasion, they would stop teaching to talk with me voluntarily), and teachers often left school immediately after meetings. Nevertheless, in almost all contacts with the school, at least five teachers, or approximately one third of the faculty, were used as informants.

My rapport with individual teachers varied; this also affected sampling, and data collection in general. In several cases, after initial greetings, a teacher would proceed to give a full running account of activities since he or she had last seen me. With other teachers, the information flow was less; they were either not well informed of school-wide activities (several consciously isolated themselves during the conflicts) or had difficulty expressing their attitudes. In only one case did I have a persistent feeling that the teacher seemed cautious in making critical or evaluative comments about others; this may have been a result of suspicions held concerning my possible use of the information. The important point is that there was variability -- as might be expected -- in the types of relationships formed between me and the various faculty members. These relationships were also internally variable, so that a usually articulate person would on occasion remain quiet and an ordinarily reticent teacher would bubble over with important information.

In addition to sampling the faculty, I tried to obtain as much volunteered information as possible (see Becker, 1958). Observation of meetings -- faculty, Board of Education, WEA, and PTA -- presented no problems; my role in them was as a complete observer. Informal interviewing during school hours, after meetings and, on occasion, at prearranged times, presented more of a problem, since my role shifted toward a more participatory stance. In these situations I made a conscious attempt to ask as few questions, as neutrally as possible. Fortunately, at informal gatherings teachers often asked each other questions relevant to the research, and listening was the only task I had to perform. These occasions also increased my feeling that the data I was collecting were valid; they indicated that my focus was similar to that of the teachers, and that the research was attempting to answer "significant" questions, at least from the participants' point of view. Beyond these comments, however, there is no easy way to demonstrate the proportion of volunteered information, other than presenting portions of the field notes throughout the text, and letting the reader make a judgment.

Careful sampling and reliance on volunteered information are both anti-bias procedures. Another protection against bias involves avoiding injection of the researcher's opinions into the social system under study. From the beginning of the research I was careful not to express my personal opinions on any educational matter -- or, for that matter, on most topics. Since the organization was still being planned and there were numerous unknowns, I reasoned that suggestions, or approval or disapproval could have significantly more influence on the actions taken by faculty members than they might have had in a chronologically mature, stable organization. If expressed, my opinions could also have been viewed as implicit evaluations of actions taken, resulting in inhibited responses. Even as the conflict with the community intensified, I did not give my impressions of the conflict to any faculty member, or indicate that I supported any group. When asked my opinion -- which was surprisingly infrequently -- I would either make a non-committal comment, or, more usually, simply reiterate that my role did not include making judgments. I assume, however, that because of my clear interest in them, the bulk of the teachers viewed me as somehow sympathetic to their efforts, not those of the parents.

To some extent, this non-interventive stance intensified a psychological sense of marginality from the teachers and parents (which I also experienced because I was an outsider). Although this sense of marginality was uncomfortable, it enabled a more detached, "objective", rapport with all groups during the two-and-one-half years of field work, especially during the height of the school-community conflict.

2. In the Community

Field work in the community was not as extensive as it was in the school, primarily because of time limitations. In the role of silent observer, I attended all LAHA, Board of Education and PTA meetings that had relevance in any way for understanding the school. In the initial stages of research, I conducted retrospective interviews with community members who had been active in the early school planning stages. These interviews were also useful for gathering information about the formation of the Lincoln Acres community, and about current community events. Throughout the year, I interviewed selected community members informally about a variety of specific issues. For example, Charles Frisch and his wife were interviewed shortly after they transferred their child from the Lincoln Acres school.

Because of the limited time available for field work in the community, the small number of regular informants tended to be community leaders. This was efficient, because they usually had a substantial amount of first-hand knowledge on a wide variety of issues. However, they were not representative of the community because of their elite positions, and because in many cases, they developed first into critics and then into opponents of the school. To correct for these biases, I conducted several in-depth interviews with less-visible community members who were relatively satisfied with the educational program of the school. The project's use of questionnaires also provided a correction of possible bias toward the attitudes and reactions of community members who were more involved and vocal at meetings, since a broad spectrum of opinion was tapped. Issues related to the questionnaires are discussed below.

The role I established with parents was the same as that used with teachers: a non-participant, non-intervening, interested observer. The only potentially serious break in this role performance concerned the faculty communications workshop. The Social Architecture Project made matching funds available to the school for support of the workshop, since there was no intention of using the money for a consultant. Selection of the Playboy Club was entirely a school decision; the project staff was considerably surprised by the choice of location, but raised no question about it. When the editor of the Washingtonville Courier discovered the source of partial funding, she telephoned the project director for more information. In a front page article headlined: "Lincoln Acres School Staff Meets at Playboy Club," the Board of Education reaction and Biddle's defense appear, followed by this account of the reseach project.

> Studying the Lincoln Acres School staff organization and documenting the planning process are Barry Gold and Dr. Matthew B. Miles, senior research associate, of the Center for Policy Research, Inc., New York City. With a National Institute of Education federal grant, the center is studying five new schools to document but not influence new school organization.
>
> The center is using Federal money to pay for half the Lincoln Acres communication workshop at the Playboy Club while the school board pays the rest of the cost.
>
> Dr. Matthew Miles says center researchers, who theorize failure of new schools in the sixties was due to poor planning,

hope to develop a strategy to avoid failure in the future. He says the center chose Washingtonville and the Lincoln Acres Elementary School because they wanted to study a success story.

"We are impressed with the planning we've seen so far. But we are not influencing planning but trying to be a fly on the wall," he adds, saying all Center studies are confidential and strive for objectivity.

At the next Board of Education meeting, one parent, in a far-ranging condemnation of the proposed school, accused the Center for Policy Research of promoting irresponsibility in the district's educators by both providing the money for and suggesting the Playboy Club as a meeting place. The following week a letter to the editor (quoted on page 137) also complained about the use of Federal funds for supporting the workshop. Fortunately, there was no further public discussion of the matter.

An unintended community intervention with some lasting effects developed as a result of the parent mail questionnaires. The first questionnaire was mailed just as a Board of Education election was beginning. The questionnaire had been cleared with Biddle and Brown* before it was mailed to parents. Shortly afterward, Tom Hassfelt, a first-time candidate for the Board, spoke to several Board members, raising the issue of the use of demographic data on the survey. (The reader may recall that this issue was also raised when the faculty conducted its survey at the beginning of the summer workshop, with the result that the demographic information was removed.) After consultation with the researchers, Biddle reported to the Board of Education that the demographic section was marked "optional", and that the questionnaires could not be altered since they had already been mailed to all families. The lasting result was that the two succeeding questionnaires had to be approved by the Board of Education. Each time objections were raised about the use of demographic data, but with the required indication that they were optional, both questionnaires were mailed as we had designed them. To a large extent the Board members used the questionnaires -- as they often did -- to harass Biddle, making him obtain their consent on otherwise routine matters.

An intentional but minor intervention was that selected results of the first parent questionnaire were fed back to the community, consistent with the terms of our agreement. At the suggestion of the superintendent, the method of providing feedback was to have a single report located in the Board of Education office. This enabled Biddle to explain the results to interested parents. To my knowledge, few parents actually consulted the survey results.

---

*Biddle found no questions objectionable, but Brown requested the removal of a set of questions designed to measure community satisfaction with the job performance of the principal, the superintendent of schools and the resource teacher, among other key positions in the school and community, such as the chief of police. These questions were removed.

In general, then, the research was not highly visible to most members of the community. For most parents, the only contacts with the research were a brief explanation by Brown at an early PTA meeting, the newspaper article, and the mail questionnaires they received. Relatively few Lincoln Acres residents were used continuously as active informants, though many were observed regularly at meetings. But during meetings, and after them in the form of interviews and eavesdropping, the amount of information I gained was substantial, especially since the problems with the school were the dominant topic in the community for many months. As with the teachers, the parents I interviewed cooperated fully, and appear to have provided honest, complete responses.

3. Field Work in a Conflict Situation

The first school-community conflict presented few difficulties for conducting field work; the school was not opened yet, and the parents and teachers met face-to-face infrequently. However, the second conflict -- once the school was in operation -- produced two major problems. First, there was tension over whether to abandon the non-participatory, non-interventive research role, and actively intervene in the school by providing information and support. Second, maintaining a "neutral" role performance -- once that appeared non-aligned with a specific group -- became problematic during the internal school conflict.

My impulse to participate actively in the affairs of the school and community was a result of prolonged observation of the conflict between them. By the middle of the second conflict, it appeared impossible for either side to gain an accurate, balanced view of the other which might lead to a quick, constructive resolution. Although it may have been self-serving, at the time I felt -- and still do -- that because of my special position I knew more about events in the school and community than most others involved. For example, I often attended LAHA or Board of Education meetings at which there were no faculty members. A day or two later at a faculty meeting, inaccurate rumors generated by events at community meetings would circulate; these were sometimes the basis for faculty actions and usually provided reasons for increased anger with parents, Biddle or the Board of Education. Similarly, Ellis informed me that he was actively looking for another job several months before he announced his decision to leave Lincoln Acres school to the faculty. Shortly after Brown told me of his intentions, I attended teacher meetings at which plans were formulated for punishing him to persuade him to seek other employment. My feeling at the time of these incidents was that I could possibly have played the role of conciliator between the community and school, and later between the teachers and Brown. This feeling persisted for some time and became especially intense when Katie was fired and the NBC and BJW teams were reorganized. Throughout this period I had a nagging feeling that I was in some way not acting in a responsible way by remaining silent. But after several conversations with the project director and others, I was assured, and eventually convinced, that my behavior was not unethical. In the end, I retained the original role, and did not offer either advice or other feedback to either members of the school or community.

In keeping with our non-interventive stance, several research design decisions were made at this time to decrease the possibility of having an effect on the school. For example, although it was not our original intention, we came to consider administering a questionnaire to students. As it developed, however, our intended date for administration coincided with parent demands for an outside evaluation of the school. To avoid the possibility of being viewed as evaluators, the student questionnaire was cancelled (we also were not certain that detailed-enough questions could be asked of elementary students to make data collection worth the effort). Similarly, the first questionnaire designed for parents was delayed for two months, at which time the conflict seemed to be well on its way to a resolution.

Despite these efforts, one unintended intervention did occur throughout the conflict. My presence as a person willing to listen to problems or complaints was taken advantage of by most teachers, Brown, Biddle and several parents. In some instances, this role operated as a "safety valve", that is, as an outlet for frustrations, grievances and disappointments. The unintended consequence was that the outlet was non-constructive; the information did not get channeled back into the organization for possible corrective action, even though on several occasions people seemed to feel relief or perceive a solution to a problem. In some instances issues aired with me were discussed at a faculty meeting, but not until several weeks after I was told about it. Throughout the research, I never discussed the content of my conversation with one informant with any other.

When the conflict changed from one between the school and community to one within the school, many members of the faculty became suspicious of each other. For instance, one charge made several times was that Sam and Lee Whitmore were giving Ellis information that the teachers wanted kept secret (for example, next steps with the grievance, or discussions of other plans for punishing Brown). The major effect of the distrustful atmosphere on the research was that for periods of time -- usually a week or two -- some teachers offered considerably less information than they had previously. My reaction to this was to rely on other sources of information, and patiently wait for suspicions to subside. It should be noted that there was never any direct indication that teachers were reluctant to talk with me because they thought that I had acted as an informant for the administration or community. Communication throughout the organization became guarded after the initiation of the punishment procedures against Brown.

At the same time, because he was ostracized by the faculty, Brown began paying more attention to me. For example, in the minutes before a faculty meeting he would joke with me, and often sit beside me instead of with the teachers as before. To avoid the impression of being aligned with Brown (or for that matter, with Pennington, Little and Biddle) I often had to use strategies for physically re-positioning myself in meetings. One successful ploy was the well-timed use of the bathroom or soda machine in the teachers' lounge. This ended the conversation without being excessively abrupt, and permitted me to re-join the meeting in another, presumably non-partisan, location. The basic objective of such maneuvers was to retain a role that presented me as interested in all groups within the school but as favoring and in the service of none, so that information could be collected from all participants.

As in the other phases of field work, I strictly maintained the confidence of informants. It is my overall impression that with the exception of a few weeks of reduced communication with several teachers, information came to me in an uninhibited, minimally distorted, fashion. For example, I was permitted to attend all secret faculty meetings, and information was often volunteered that could have been damaging to both sides in the conflict if divulged to the other side.

This examination of the field work procedures used in this study is at best partial; undoubtedly, certain tactics I used were beyond my ability to note and analyze as I became immersed in the recording of the events reported in the text. Similarly, it is probable that I influenced the social systems I studied in ways that I cannot imagine. Nevertheless, I believe that my attempt to interfere with the school and community as little as possible was reasonably successful and has resulted in an accurate, minimally distorted reconstruction of the events involved.

D. QUESTIONNAIRES

Three questionnaires each were administered to the faculty, and to the parents of all children attending the school. The faculty questionnaires were administered on December 8, 1975; June 14, 1976; and June 20, 1977. Time for answering the questionnaires was provided during regularly scheduled faculty meetings; several teachers took as long as two hours to answer the 40-page questionnaire. Considering that the faculty was not paid, and the questions lengthy, response rates were very high: 86% answered the first questionnaire, 71% the second and 83% the third.

Parent questionnaires were mailed at the same time that the faculty questionnaires were administered, except for the first questionnaire, which was delayed until February 20, 1976 because of the conflict.* After two reminder letters for each administration, the response rate for parents was: 52% for the first questionnaire, 35% for the second and, 44% for the third. Considering that the first questionnaire was 27 pages, the second 15 and the third 8 pages, the response rates are high. Code numbers (which could have reduced responses) appeared on both the parent and teacher questionnaires so the successive waves of data could be meaningfully analyzed, and in the case of parents, so that reminder letters could be sent to those who hadn't returned the questionnaire. The code numbers were not used for identification of individuals during analysis; as promised in the letter that accompanied each questionnaire, respondent anonymity was carefully maintained.

---

*Both Biddle and Brown suggested that the questionnaire be delayed until relations between the school and community showed signs of stabilizing. In view of our desire not to intervene, and the possibility that the questionnaire could have been viewed as an evaluation device, we agreed to delay the administration.

It should be noted that the community survey was not a random sample of all citizens, but was sent to the entire population of 226 families with students in the school. The survey results, then, are illustrative and not representative of the opinions of the entire community. It is also likely that the returned questionnaires overrepresent parents who were dissatisfied with the school.

The major objective in the construction of the teacher questionnaires was to measure variables that would document and explain the degree of implementation of the innovation (see Chapter 2 for the criteria of implementation success). The questionnaire was also intended to provide an in-depth view of the way the school was functioning at a particular point in time, to supplement field work.

In the construction of both questionnaires, field work findings influenced the questions asked (Sieber, 1973). For example, it occurred to a parent during an interview that many of his neighbors had been or currently were teachers; he speculated that this influenced their actions toward the school. As a result, a question asking if either or both parents had been or currently were teachers was included in the questionnaire. The finding was that 29% answered affirmatively, which suggested that expertise, or at least first-hand familiarity with education was high in the community.

There were two problems with the administration of questionnaires. First, the administration of the first teacher questionnaire coincided with the faculty meeting on December 8, 1975, when the firing of Katie Neustadt was discussed (see p. 251). This, the most intense internal crisis of the school year, undoubtedly influenced the teachers' answers. Of course, while the situation may have biased the answers (especially ratings of Brown's performance) negatively, the questionnaire did measure what it was intended to, the functioning of the school. Surprisingly, however, the answers were more positive than might have been expected. Several teachers even refused to answer some questions, feeling that they couldn't give "objective" responses under the strain of the removal of one of their fellow teachers. This suggests that they tried to be as honest as they could be without being swept away in the emotions of the moment.

The other complication occurred with the administration of the second teacher questionnaire on June 14, 1976. The date for administration was set a month in advance with Ellis. As it turned out, he was replaced as principal of the school a week before the scheduled administration date. This meant that a contract to continue research had to be negotiated with Alberta, and her permission granted to proceed with the questionnaire. After brief discussions, everything was agreed to and research continued. But when the teachers sat down to answer the questionnaires, Ellis had already not been the principal of the school for a week. This caused confusion among the teachers over whether to answer as though Ellis were still the principal, or under the actual conditions of Alberta's principalship. I made the decision that the questionnaires should be answered as if it were a week earlier and Ellis were still the principal. The reasoning behind this judgment was that the memory of Ellis was still fresh. Our objective was to measure the performance of the school for the previous six months, and Alberta had not been principal long enough for the teachers to answer meaningfully. As in the case of the questionnaire administered at the time of Katie's firing, the teachers' answers seem to reflect the conditions of the school accurately as they appeared in the course of field work. Nevertheless, the reader should be aware of the circumstances under which the first two teacher questionnaires were answered.

One advantage of combining field work with surveys is that the researcher can place the survey data in a meaningful context to evaluate the quality of the data. If, as is often the case, the researcher had not been present in the weeks before the questionnaire administration to observe respondent behavior, and/or the questionnaires had been mailed, the data would almost certainly be taken entirely at face value.

E. DOCUMENTS

A third source of data was documents that pertained to the planning and operation of the school. These were collected as the research progressed and proved to be invaluable aids for understanding events as they unfolded; they were also useful during data analysis, as discussed in the next section.

Documents were of several types: (1) internal organizational communication (memos, agendas); (2) organizational communication with external groups, for instance, parents, the Board of Education, the local newspaper; (3) communications from parents and parent organizations to the school or related organizations; (4) articles in local and state newspapers; and (5) miscellaneous (for example, a former mayor's autobiography, articles by residents appearing in professional journals and articles in national mass media).

F. DATA ANALYSIS PROCEDURES

We believe researchers using qualitative data owe their readers a careful accounting of the analysis procedures followed. We will not reconstruct every step exhaustively; only the major procedures and the logic supporting them will be described.*

1. Bureaucratic Beginnings

Since this study was part of a larger project, Social Architecture in Education, which aimed at comparing six new innovative schools, the original analysis schemes developed were standardized, and to an extent, bureaucratized the research process. Through rough standardization, it was reasoned, data collection could be controlled, then data could be categorized in similar ways and analyzed across all of the sites.

---

*For a critical review of our procedures and discussion of issues in qualitative data analysis, see Miles (1980).

To begin this process a coding scheme -- a set of labels to be applied to field work notes -- was constructed. This was essentially an a priori listing of factors that appeared to have influence on the planning of a new, innovative school. Most of these were of a social-psychological, small-group nature. As the field work progressed new labels were added and those on the original list that no longer made sense were eliminated.

For the actual coding procedure -- the attachment of labels to the field notes -- we developed the following system. After the field notes were typed, the field worker coded the notes and filled in several forms with questions such as: Who were the central actors in this contact? What decisions, if any, were made? and others. Then the field worker discussed each choice of category and the information on the forms with another project member, preferably one who was somewhat "distant" from the particular site but not totally unfamiliar with it. This procedure was designed to serve as a means for avoiding a biased view of the site; alternative explanations were always being sought in these meetings. In most instances, this method resulted in dozens of concepts being applied to a single field contact.*

Once the coding was completed, each fragment of field notes that had been assigned a concept was cut and pasted onto an index card, and filed with the other field work excerpts that had the same label. Despite lags between the coding, the discussion of the coding with another project member and the final cataloging system, this method continued for nearly six months, undergoing several revisions in both the substance of the concepts and the procedure.

As field work progressed, it became evident that more than a social-psychological small-group orientation would be needed to accurately and fruitfully code the field notes; increasingly we were discovering that planning was a political activity, and that planners and schools existed in outside environments that neither we nor they could ignore. Thus, the list of concepts expanded as it became grounded in field work data to include a variety of political terms and concepts for thinking about activities across the boundaries of the school, such as "resource acquisition" and "constraint management".

Eventually, after various shifts in emphasis, the list of concepts had expanded enormously; it lacked parsimony. In addition, the coding process itself became cumbersome, given the ongoing demands of field work, questionnaire construction, and project meetings. The result was that coding backlogs increased, and considerable energy was spent in meetings puzzling over ways to reduce them. Most importantly, it was also becoming considerably less clear what the purpose of this data analysis procedure was: it did not seem to be aiding in the generation of higher-level concepts that would lead to explanations: the categories were useful, but they did not lead to connections between variables.

---

*The length of field notes for a visit to Lincoln Acres varied, with the average being approximately 10 single-spaced pages.

After considerable effort, the lists of concepts were collapsed into 36 key themes which were dimensionalized (for example, Knowledge-seeking: Active . . . . . . Not Active). Instead of coding each segment of the field notes, we coded an entire field, contact using as few of these central themes as seemed to be meaningful. As with the original scheme, these were then put on index cards and filed.

The basic function of these procedures was that a common language and thus a more or less unified way of thinking about new schools developed among the project staff. Beyond this, however, it is fair to say that the coding schemes, despite the systematic approach they provided, did not closely influence the analysis presented in this study.

2. Later Analysis Methods

A project-wide analysis procedure that proved indispensable was staff "site analysis" meetings held approximately every two weeks to discuss recent events at a site. The focus of these meetings was on attempting to construct explanations for the activities, and to make predictions. Whenever it was possible, alternative hypotheses and explanations were proposed. The predictions were seldom correct, and we were continually being surprised. For example, I (Gold) was astonished that the teachers returned from the first year's Christmas vacation and took such a militant stance against Brown and the parents. I had predicted that their passions would be tempered by the distractions offered in the holiday season, and that they would adapt to the situation through passive non-compliance or resignation, but not engage in aggressive reprisal.

The products of these site analysis meetings -- including our learnings from failed predictions -- were memoranda, used to guide further data collection and the ongoing analysis.

Another regular analysis device was that in field notes (which were typed by the field worker immediately after a contact), a separate section was devoted to hunches, impressions or sometimes detailed analysis. These sections contributed to the more formalized analysis meetings, to memos, and to a comprehensive summary of the school made after the first six months of research. This summary provided an opportunity for a "trial run" at producing a case study.

Finally, shortly before writing of the final case study was to begin, a comprehensive site analysis memo was prepared. This paper integrated the previous analysis memos without substantially changing the interpretations that had preceded it. Included in it were: a chapter outline, the contextual features of the Lincoln Acres school, a brief chronology of salient events, a section on "planning and implementation as now viewed," and the key themes that had emerged in the site, with explanations in the form of propositions. This memo was critiqued by other staff members.

The next central task was the accurate reconstruction of the events of planning and implementation. Without this, our confidence in previous and future analysis would have been reduced, since, at minimum, the correct time sequence of events must be clear before one can make statements about causal relationships among variables. Because of the longitudinal nature of the study and the frequency of observations, reconstructing the flow of events was not overly difficult. It was done by creating a time-line of the major events, drawn from a careful reading of field notes, newspaper accounts and other documents. The time-line led to a detailed outline for use in writing the final report.

Once the chronology was established, Gold began writing the basic draft. The field notes were read carefully again, along with the documents, and at each stage the outline served as a guide. Most importantly, the site analysis memos that had been produced for project staff meetings guided the selection of materials -- including negative instances -- appropriate for presentation and analysis.

An example. We can usefully illustrate the general data analysis procedure followed. One central conclusion reached was that the school-community conflict was primarily between professional and democratic norms. This finding is more of a post factum interpretation than most; oddly enough, it was not until late in the analysis -- after writing had begun -- that this way of viewing the conflict emerged. Before this, it was of course clear that there was an intense, prolonged conflict -- but there were several alternative imterpretations for it, none of which seemed entirely convincing.

One interpretation was that the conflict was simply a matter of the community's opposing the innovations: the community members were locals and the faculty cosmopolitans; they had different reference groups. Another interpretation was that the parents were older, upwardly mobile first-time homeowners, and thus had a more conservative value system -- especially concerning education -- than the younger, less financially well-off faculty.

But there were few data to support either of these conclusions, and some countering information. For example, in terms of both educational and general societal values, the results of the questionnaires indicated that the parents and teachers had similar orientations. In the course of field work, only a few parents commented negatively on the teachers' value system -- they incorrectly wanted to be "friends" to the students or dressed too casually -- and the majority of parents, including the community leaders, were willing to give the innovation a try. In fact, several of the parents who had been anti-innovative before were completely satisfied immediately after the school opened.

These considerations led us to examine more closely the complaints that focused (in the first conflict) on the violation of democratic norms, and (in the second conflict) on the teachers' inability to perform their roles and present convincing arguments for the continuance of the innovation to parents whose expertise in educational matters was substantial. Although the educational orientation arguments were not entirely dismissed, the ovearching explanation appeared to be found in the tension between democratic and professional norms.

This example also illustrates one of the ways in which the quantitative data aided the analysis: here it permitted the examination of alternative hypotheses. The questionnaire data also permitted us to place more confidence in an interpretation based on a field work finding. In the illustration above, the possibility that the parents had considerable expertise in education was present from field work observation (for example, it was clear that Frisch was an expert, and a few other active parents mentioned past experience as educators), but the questionnaire results indicating that 29% of parents had first-hand familiarity with education as teachers or former teachers substantially strengthened our confidence in this as a possible explanation of the conflict, and provided further reason to explore its implications.

Overall, an attempt was made to base or "ground" the analysis in the data, while achieving a high enough level of abstraction to produce hypotheses fruitful for further investigation. It was not always easy to avoid the Scylla of mechanically applying a priori concepts to the body of data, and the Charybdis of producing sweeping generalizations unconnected to and far outrunning it.

Although in several instances interpretations were changed as "distance" or "perspective" from the flow of events increased (as in the example above), many of the original interpretations in the field notes and analysis memos remained unchanged.

The first draft of the case was read and critiqued by other staff members; Gold and Miles then added analysis and commentary sections tying the preliminary interpretations back to the study's general conceptual scheme (Chapter 2). The version of the case reported to the National Institute of Education was final-edited by Miles.

The present version of the case has been carefully reviewed and edited by both Gold and Miles. A few minor and peripheral details were excluded, and our general conclusions in Chapter 12 somewhat recast in the light of later reflection.

APPENDIX B:
Reactions to Feedback of the Case

We decided to feed back a draft copy of the case study to selected participants from the school and community. Participants would have an opportunity to correct factual errors, point out possibly-identifying or damaging material, and comment on the general thrust of the study and its conclusions. From the research perspective, participants' commentary offered an opportunity to evaluate the accuracy of the observations and the soundness of the interpretations; it also offered the possibility of producing more data to aid understanding of the complex flow of events.

The following key people were selected as possible commentators: Ellis Brown, Alberta Bard, Katie Neustadt, Regina Hanley, Charles Frisch, Sy Golden and Bob Biddle. In a letter at the end of December, 1977, we asked about their interest in providing factual corrections, and a two-page memo supplying alternative interpretations. All but Brown expressed interest, and copies of the case were sent to the next four people on the list in early January (Bard was asked to share her copy with Biddle, and Frisch his with Golden: this was done to save duplicating costs, but was in retrospect very desirable, since the teachers and Alberta could see the case before Biddle did).

Although the feedback of the report was an intervention, our stance did not vary significantly from that taken in the course of the project (that is, attempting to minimize influencing the social systems of the school and community). Thus, we avoided choosing highly interactive feedback procedures (e.g., using the case study as a basis for structured discussions or training sessions with the faculty and parents). However, the presentation of the case study to the faculty did develop into a fairly active intervention.

Participants' Reactions

On January 26, Alberta Bard called Miles saying that they had had three days off because of snow, and that "nearly everyone in the school" had read the case. She also said that several teachers were "uptight" about the case, wanting to know what they could do about material they considered damaging; some wanted all direct quotes stricken from the text, and one

376

was considering taking the case to the state teachers' association. A few were worried because the study was also accessible as a dissertation [Gold's] and could be examined by anyone interested.

Miles said that stiking out all direct quotes was not possible, but that those jeopardizing an individual would be de-attributed. He also stressed that changes would not be made if the case study had only "hurt someone's feelings." He suggested that she contact Gold for further discussion; that she and others send in corrections and proposed elisions by February 10, so a revised copy could go to Biddle; and reviewed with her who else had received copies. Alberta said she would call Frisch and Golden asking them not to share their copies with others. Miles' notes said:

> In general, she seemed to be very reasonable, and working well
> as a mediator between us and the teachers. I did not get the
> feeling she was upset about anything in the case.

A few days later, Gold went to Lincoln Acres, meeting individually with seven people. He wrote afterward:

> For the most part the people I met with were cordial and
> extremely understanding; only one person was hostile and
> resistant to my suggestions to reconsider the situation.

Some faculty members were personally offended: they thought they had been portrayed in an unfavorable light. For example, Bert White thought that some of the quotes attributed to him were "dumb", and that he couldn't have uttered them. Several teachers also thought that Katie's firing had not received extensive-enough treatment; they felt that the seriousness of the matter was slighted.

Generally speaking, the teachers tended to be preoccupied with what the case study said about individuals, and did not seem to be focusing on the school as an organization. The individual focus was not limited to self-protective reactions: for example, Rebecca thought Bert was "cast as a villain," and both Regina and Dori commented on the way Priscilla's actions had been depicted.

Alberta, on the other hand, did see more general implications in the report for the future of the school. Gold's notes read:

> The one implication she had drawn from the study was that she
> hadn't realized how committed the people were who tried the
> original innovations and how far she had retreated from them
> (that is, the original vision of the school) and become
> complacent. She said that she would try to increase the
> amount of creative teaching, and thanked me for having
> pointed out how comfortable the school had become with the
> old ways.

For the most part, passages to be omitted, corrections of factual information and differences of interpretation were minor; most problems were resolved in the face-to-face encounter between Gold and the teachers.

This outcome was in large part due to the fact that the most-concerned teachers had succeeded in defining the situation as one in which they could exert editorial control over the case.

Two instances, however, presented larger problems. The report contained references made by several participants to "emotional" problems on the part of a particular teacher. And another teacher insisted that all self-involving references be deleted from the text.

Gold came to feel after talking (cordially) with the first teacher and others that his inclusion of the "emotional" references had been a serious error of judgment. For one thing, some of the quotes, though reported accurately, were based on misunderstandings. The teacher had been under a good deal of stress, but allusion to the problems as "emotional" unsettled the teacher's status in the school at the time of the feedback, caused distress to the person and friends, and could conceivably affect future employment prospects adversely.

The other teacher's reactions were a surprise. Basically, there seemed to be no reason to suspect that s/he would have been offended by the (in the opinion of the researcher, positive) role outlined in the text.

But the teacher insisted that all named references be removed from the text. Interestingly, s/he did not find fault with the general role that s/he and other team members played in the school, but with many of the particulars, which were often seen as being, if not totally wrong, at least not the full story. S/he felt that the report "reflected badly on my teaching ability," attributing problems in the team's functioning to "me", rather than to other team members.

When Gold asked if s/he had read the entire report, s/he said s/he hadn't -- "only the parts about me." It was a "soap opera," s/he said; the only chapter of any worth was the last one, because it discussed the school as an organization (without, that is, reference to individuals). The teacher continued to be upset during the discussion with Gold, who left promising the option of specifying places in the case where allusions to the teacher should be deleted.*

On February 15, Alberta sent along photocopies of 57 marked-up pages of the report, with the changes and omissions requested by teachers. Since by this time Gold had taken another job, and Miles was out of the country from February through July, the revision process went very slowly.

No teachers, nor Alberta, ever sent interpretive memos supplying their alternative explanations of the events of the case. We infer that the meetings with Gold, plus the opportunity to provide corrections, enabled people to "set the record straight"; the conversations had also provided an opportunity for direct interaction and clarification that was reassuring. In any case, given the personalistic bias we have noted, there seemed to be little motivation to engage in general analysis.

We could not, of course, make this teacher into a "non-person," as if s/he had never existed: s/he was part of the social system of the school. But revisions in the case were made to be as fully responsive as we could to the concern.

Neither Frisch nor Golden supplied corrections or commentary. Considering the emotion-laden conflict between the school and community, and the ability of the community to use the newspapers, petitions, letters and other feedback mechanisms, this lack of reaction was somewhat of a surprise. Perhaps, because the community was victorious, there was nothing to complain about by the time the report was released. It may also be that Frisch and Golden were being responsive to the request from Alberta -- whom they seemed to respect -- that the case study not be shared with others.

Ellis Brown did not answer our letter asking if he would like to see and comment on the case. In one sense, this was congruent with earlier behavior: the reader may recall that Brown sometimes chose to ignore or selectively interpret messages from the school's constituents and the faculty. But in another sense, his non-reply was understandable. He had alluded indirectly at a number of points to the stress he had been under ("I'm 27 going on 81."), and it's likely that the Lincoln Acres experience was an extremely uncomfortable period in his career. So he might well be reluctant to rummage around in the recent past, even though a detached observer might have virtuously pointed out that mistakes and painful experiences can be instructive.

In mid-July, 1978, after final revisions were made in the case to include teachers' suggestions, it was sent to Robert Biddle for his corrections and commentary. He wrote back with a number of corrections, and commented:

> I have had difficulty responding to the study. My first reaction was anger; my second /that/ by and large, Barry did a good job....The study should make a real contribution.

As we have seen from earlier footnotes, Biddle was most angered by the "value judgments" that he had acted in a laissez faire manner, or tried to co-opt anyone, as well as by the implication that he was not interested in cognitive aspects of learning, and statements that he had not acted to support Ellis. He also stressed that his contact with the researcher had been minimal.

During a telephone interview, he said that insufficient attention had been given to certain constraining aspects of the early context, including: (1) increased construction costs after the first plans, resulting in rebidding and considerable construction and equipment delivery delay, which reduced Ellis' planning time; (2) the Board's refusal to hire the principal a year to 18 months ahead, which cut planning and community relationship-building time to an "impossible" six-month period; (3) the statewide budget crisis, which required much energy during the summer and fall of 1975; (4) the resignation of the central office personnel director who had served as a troubleshooter, followed by the Board's hiring an external negotiator, who "caused" the subsequent strike.

Biddle also re-acknowledged his misreading of the community as being mostly committed to open education, and his mistaken belief that he could "sit out" the "moaners and groaners." And he mused in his notes on the study:

A school is what the principal is. Ellis was, and is becoming /a good principal/and I have no doubts that when he internalizes the experience he will be or should be a very fine administrator.

/He/ is a bright guy. I hope he makes out well on Cape Cod and goes on to great things. He has the potential if he is able to conquer his feelings of superiority and arrogance. He wasn't the person for Lincoln Acres -- he might now be -- and had he known how to listen, he might have made it. We need people as bright as he. Alberta is still doing a great job.

Comments from the Authors

Biddle's comments, though they are occasionally and naturally self-protective, do add useful contextual information to the study. However, neither his comments, nor the specific changes and corrections made by the teachers, suggest that the general lines of analysis followed in the case are incorrect, or need expansion in any significant way. This adds to our confidence that we understood, essentially, the meaning of the events we were studying.

We do have further reflections in two areas: the role of students, and our feelings about the Lincoln Acres faculty.

Scattered throughout the study, there are references to the children who attended Lincoln Acres school, but their reactions to the events, their behavior, and the innovations' impact on them are not reported systematically. The omission of detailed information on students was intentional; we were interested in the planning and implementation of the school, and only peripherally in the impact of the innovations on students. A complete study should document and analyze the participation of all of the members of the organization.* We should note that Lincoln Acres students were lively, extremely well behaved, and intellectually curious. Though they were affected by the tumult around them, they appeared to weather the eruptions of their elders rather well.

The Lincoln Acres study raises several questions about the role of students in new educational settings. How do student characteristics and behavior influence planning and implementation processes? Do rapid change and conflict have substantial effects -- desirable or not -- on students?

---

*Studies of schools tend to focus primarily on one subpopulation, neglecting others. For example, Coleman's Adolescent Society (1961) hardly mentions teachers. Gross et al. (1971), and Smith and Keith (1971) largely ignore students, who did not seem to be considered as possible sources of influence. One of the few studies on new-school planning and implementation that tries to include both adult and student data carefully is Center for New Schools (1975).

What planning and implementation roles   might students play?   More generally, how can young students participate in school governance?*

We were sometimes asked by Lincoln Acres faculty what we thought of them. We naturally declined -- often with great difficulty -- to evaluate or advise, but some general comments may be appropriate.

It is clear there were many areas where the central administration, the school administration, <u>and</u> the teachers could have performed more thoughtfully, more professionally, or with more humane impulses. Despite these shortcomings, however, our view is that the majority of the faculty were sincere in their efforts, and attempted to provide the best possible education for their students. If nothing else, the depth of their disappointment and frustration at not having succeeded, which was evident during the first year and surfaced again in the response to the case study, attests to the sincerity and authenticity of their efforts.

Aside from their professional dedication to children, they were warm, friendly, and generous toward us as researchers. We gratefully acknowledge that without their trust, patience and introspection, the study could not have been written.

We had originally been looking for a setting where planning and implementation would be successful, so that useful lessons could be drawn for others creating new school programs. Even though the Lincoln Acres story was one of mixed success and some decisive failure, we think its lessons are instructive. And we hope the Lincoln Acres teachers -- and other educational innovators who read this account of their experience -- will have learned things that will stand them in good stead as they go about the task of improving the part of American education they can do something about.

---

*We should note that educational innovators, unlike researchers, do not have to obtain "informed consent" from students -- or even parents -- about the risks and benefits of a proposed innovation. In a sense, the Lincoln Acres story is in part one of parents' moving much closer to the arena of decisions about educational innovation than is classically the case. But even here, students were not involved in any systematic way.

APPENDIX C:
Suggestions for Using the Book
as a Teaching Case

What are alternative ways of proceeding when using a case of this sort for teaching purposes? Here we offer some procedures that have proved fruitful with this case and others like it.

Settings

The case can work well either in an intensive workshop setting, or in a course meeting periodically. Typical workshop or course foci might be planned change, innovation processes, educational administration and supervision, consulting skills, qualitative research methods, organization behavior.

Purposes and Procedures

Use of the case naturally depends on teaching objectives. Here we suggest several, and outline procedures that have proved useful for each.

Diagnostic ability. If the aim is to enhance the learner's ability to analyze a complex situation thoughtfully and accurately, one can proceed by "segmenting" the case. Ask participants to read a portion of the case (preferably beginning with Chapter 3); the segment read should conclude either at some critical point (a key meeting, an important event), or just before an analysis section in the case. Analysis sections are marked off by ( ) in the Detailed Table of Contents.

After reading, individuals write their analysis or diagnosis of the situation. Some typical formats:

Strengths and weaknesses in the situation.
Factors aiding or blocking movement toward some desired goal.
The main themes or patterns in the situation.
Explanations or causes for what happened.
What needs most to be changed or improved in the situation.

Groups may also be asked to prepare analyses: they too should be on paper. Newsprint provides an easy way to do this.

The analyses are reported to the entire group (photocopies of analyses, or newsprint), and discussed. Since all participants had the same basic data, differences in the diagnoses/analyses are usually very illuminating: they help to surface the differing assumptions held.

The question naturally arises of what a "good" or "correct" diagnosis is. Though there is no firm answer, one way to approach one is to assign an additional task: make predictions as to what will happen next in the case. A good diagnosis should lead to reasonably accurate predictions. The predictions can be compared (1) with each other, as above; (2) with the actual events in the next section of the case.

It may also be useful for learners to compare their analyses with those we have offered in the ( ) sections. The Index is concept-based, and provides a useful mode of retrieving analyses on particular issues.

Planning intervention strategies. The case can also be used to extend the learner's repertoire of things to do: how to intervene productively in a change process.

To do this, take a case segment as described above. Ask learners to think themselves into a particular role: principal, superintendent, resource teacher or external consultant. After reading the case segment, individuals or groups plan what they would do next in the setting (not what Ellis Brown, Sam Pennington, Bob Biddle would do).

When proceeding this way, the case segment should usually stop just before an opportunity for critical intervention is present. For example, learners might be asked to design the "communications workshop" after reading the material up through Chapter 5. Or, make a plan for the first faculty meetings (pp. 90-100), or a parent open house (p. 219).

Naturally, the interventions planned will require participants to develop a working diagnosis, set goals for their intervention, etc.

Intervention. If the aim is to consider what actual interventions might look like, it's possible to select out particular critical situations from the case for role playing. One example is the series of situations that occurred around the initial compromise plan (pp. 145-161). Others are Brown's first community meeting (pp. 81-85), and the tense faculty meeting with Brown (pp. 296-98). A simple way to proceed is to ask people to take the roles of the people depicted, start by reading out loud the text of the interaction, then continue the interaction spontaneously. Many different scenarios can be played out, and different people may wish to try their hands at "another way of handling it."

It may help to develop simple role briefings, outlining the interests and characteristics of various key actors.

Role playing scenes can be used in many different ways*: a few possibilities in addition to the "continuation" model above include: (1) recording a scene on audio- or videotape, then playing it back for analysis, critique, and development of alternative approaches; (2) role reversal (Katie steps into Ellis Brown's shoes, and vice versa); (3) coaching, in which role

---

*For additional suggestions on role playing, case analysis, and audio/videotape use, see Miles (1981a).

players turn to individual helpers during a break in the action and ask for suggestions on how they might operate more effectively.

Data analysis. The case can be rather helpful in aiding learners new to qualitative research methods. The approach is similar to that suggested under "diagnostic ability", but with more emphasis on conceptual and methodological issues.

For example, learners can be asked to read one or more chapters (excluding the ( ) sections), and develop a coding scheme to classify segments of the narrative. Alternative coding schemes can be compared. Or, a single coding scheme can be developed, and practice in achieving coder reliability carried out.

Learners can also be asked to develop an analysis of (a) the events in a particular chapter; (b) the flow of organizational change over time (ex: all events prior to Chapter 9, or to Chapter 12). Such analyses can be carried out without any recourse to the conceptual framework of Chapter 2 or the ideas in Chapter 12, in which case the learnings center on the process of developing and applying one's own conceptual framework. An alternative is to use the Chapter 2 framework, and to (1) log carefully the data analysis methods used to draw final conclusions; (2) compare the analyses reached; (3) assess how analysis methods followed led to the divergent conclusions.

General Working Principles

There seem to be some keys to success in using the case in the ways suggested above.

Segmentation. Deal with portions of the case, not the entire account.

Cumulation. Work chronologically from the start of the case onward. Allow time for the gradual development of understanding of the case events and characters. (The usual finding is that actors become more and more vivid and real in the minds of learners.)

Product orientation. Rambling discussion, as in the archetypal "case method" of Harvard Business School fame, is usually less fruitful than tasks which require the delivery of particular products (designs, analyses, interventions, etc.), on paper, audio- or videotape, etc.

Comparison. Looking at similarities and differences across products is usually extremely illuminating.

Adequate time. A productive session using the case material, even on a focused, segmented basis, requires at least 1½-2 hours. Time should be protected for individual and group work, for sharing/comparison, and for conclusion-drawing. Given the bulk of the data base, substantial time also needs to be available for reading itself.

If the choice is made to build an entire workshop around the case (which can easily be done), at least 2½ days should be available.

Leader familiarity. Those using the case for teaching should know the case well, to form an idea of which segments are most fruitful for the particular purposes at hand. There is no practical substitute for having read through it, preferably making marginal notes and analyses during the process. Notations in the detailed Table of Contents are also helpful, as is use of the conceptually-based Index.

BIBLIOGRAPHY

Argyris, C. 1974. Behind the Front Page. San Francisco: Jossey-Bass.

Armstrong, D.G. 1977. "Team Teaching and Academic Achievement." Review of Educational Research 47: 65-86.

Bailey, A. 1975. A Re-examination of the Events at Cambire School, 1965-67. University of Sussex. Unpublished manuscript.

Bass, G.V. 1978. A Study of Alternatives in American Education, Vol. I. District Policies and the Implementation of Change. Santa Monica, CA: Rand Corporation. R-2170-1-NIE.

Becker, H. 1958. "Problems of Inference and Proof in Participant Observation." American Sociological Review 23: 652-660 (No. 6 December).

Berger, B. 1960. Working Class Suburb. Berkeley: CA: University of California Press.

Berger, P., and T. Luckmann. 1966. The Social Construction of Reality. New York: Anchor.

Berman, P., and M.W. McLaughlin. 1974. Federal Programs Supporting Educational Change, Vol. I: A Model of Educational Change. Santa Monica, CA: Rand Corporation. R-1589/1-HEW.

_____. 1976. Federal Programs Supporting Educational Change, Vol. IV: The Findings in Review. Santa Monica, CA: Rand Corporation. R-1589/4-HEW.

Berman, P. 1981. "Toward an Implementation Paradigm of Educational Change." In Improving Schools: Using What We Know, edited by R. Lehming. Santa Monica: CA: Sage.

Biagioli, A. 1977. A Field Study of an Educational Setting: A Record and Analysis of the Creation, Planning and Beginning of an Innovative School, Ed.D. dissertation, Teachers College, Columbia University.

Bidwell, C.E. 1965. "The School as a Formal Organization." In Handbook of Organizations, edited by J.G. March, pp. 972-1022. Chicago: Rand McNally.

Blau, P.M. 1964. Exchange and Power in Social Life. New York: Wiley.

Bredo, A.F., and E. Bredo. 1975. A Case Study of Educational Innovation in a Junior High School: Interaction of Environment and Structure. Palo Alto: Stanford Center for Research and Development in Teaching.

Broad, L. 1977. Alternative Schools: Why, What, Where and How Much. Education U.S.A. Special Report. Arlington, VA: National School Boards Public Relations Association.

Buckley, W. 1967. Sociology and Modern Systems Theory. Englewood Cliffs: Prentice-Hall.

Burack, E.H., and A.R. Negandhi. 1977. Organizational Design: Theoretical Perspectives and Empirical Findings. Kent, OH: Kent State University Press.

Carr, J.C., J.D. Grambs, and E.G. Campbell. 1977. Pygmalion or Frankenstein? Alternative Schooling in American Education. Reading, MA: Addison-Wesley.

Center for New Schools. 1975. A Multi-Method Study of the Development and Effects of an Alternative School Learning Environment. Vols. I-IV. Final Report, NIE Project No. 3-2664, NIMH Grant 1-RO1 MH22248-01. Chicago: Center for New Schools.

Charters, W.W., Jr., et al. 1973. The Process of Planned Change in the School's Instructional Organization. Eugene, OR: Center for Educational Policy and Management, University of Oregon. CASEA Monograph No. 25.

Cherns, A. 1976. "The Principles of Sociotechnical Design." Human Relations 29 (8): 783-792.

Clark, P.A. 1972. Organizational Design: Theory and Practice. London: Tavistock Publications.

Cohen, D.K., and E. Farrar. 1978. "Power to the Parents? The Story of Education Vouchers." The Public Interest 48: 72-97.

Coleman, J.S. 1957. Community Conflict. Glencoe, IL: Free Press.

_____. 1961. The Adolescent Society. New York: Free Press.

Coleman, J.S., et al. 1966. Equality of Educational Opportunity. Washington, D.C.: U.S. Government Printing Office.

Collins, B.E., and H. Guetzkow. 1964. Social Psychology of Group Processes for Decision-Making. New York: Wiley.

Collins, R. 1975. Conflict Sociology. New York: Academic Press.

Cooper, B.S. 1973. "Organizational Survival: A Comparative Case of Seven American 'Free Schools'." Education and Urban Society 5 (4): 487-508.

Crozier, M. 1963. The Bureaucratic Phenomenon. Chicago: University of Chicago Press.

Czajkowski, T., and M. King. 1974. "The Hidden Curriculum and Open Education." The Elementary School Journal 75: 279-85.

Deal, T.E. 1975. "Alternative Schools: An Alternative Postmortem." In Managing Change in Educational Organizations, edited by T.E. Deal and J.V. Baldridge, pp. 482-499. Berkeley: McCutchan.

_____. 1978. "Muddling Through: A School Above a Bakery." In Alternative Schools: Ideologies, Realities and Guidelines, edited by T.E. Deal and R.R. Nolan, Chapter 9. Chicago: Nelson-Hall.

DeTurk, P.H. n.d. P.S. 2001: The Story of the Pasadena Alternative School. Bloomington, IN: Phi Delta Kappa and National Alternative Schools Project.

Duncan, R. 1976. "The Ambidextrous Organization: Designing Dual Structures for Innovation." In The Management of Organization Design, edited by R. Kilmann, L. Pondy and D. Slevin. New York: Elsevier.

Eastabrook, G., M. Fullan, J. Clifford, and N. Hood. 1974. Bayridge Secondary School: A Case Study of the Planning and Implementation of Educational Change. Vol. I. Planning. Toronto: Ontario Institute for Studies in Education.

Eastabrook, G., and M. Fullan. 1977. The Planning and Implementation of a New Secondary School: Bayridge. Paper presented at the American Educational Research Association meetings.

Edelfelt, R., and M. Johnson. 1975. Rethinking In-Service Education. Washington, D.C.: National Education Association.

Emrick, J.A., with S.M. Peterson and P. Agarwala-Rogers. 1977. Evaluation of the National Diffusion Network (2 vols.). Menlo Park, CA: Stanford Research Institute.

Flaxman, A., and K.C. Homstead. 1978. 1977-78 National Directory of Public Alternative Schools. Amherst, MA: University of Massachusetts, National Alternative Schools Program.

Friedmann, J. 1969. "Notes on Societal Action." Journal of the American Institute of Planners 35: 311-318.

Fullan, M., M.B. Miles, and G. Taylor. 1980. "Organization Development in Schools: The State of the Art." Review of Educational Research 50 (1): 121-183.

Fullan, M., and A. Pomfret. 1977. "Research on Curriculum and Instruction Implementation." Review of Educational Research 47 (1): 335-397.

Gans, H.J. 1962. "Urbanism and Suburbanism as a Way of Life: A Re-evaluation of Definitions." In Human Behavior and Social Processes, edited by A.M. Rose. Boston: Houghton Mifflin.

_____. 1967. The Levittowners. New York: Pantheon.

Gold, R. 1958. "Roles in Sociological Field Observations." Social Forces 36: 217-223.

Goode, W.J. 1967. "The Protection of the Inept." American Sociological Review 32: 5-19.

Graubard, A. 1972. "The Free School Movement." Harvard Educational Review 42 (3).

Green, A.C. 1975. "The Schoolhouse Revisited: Problems, and Missed Opportunities." Phi Delta Kappa 61 (5): 360-62.

Gross, N., J. Giacquinta, and M. Bernstein. 1971. Implementing Organizational Innovations. New York: Basic Books.

Gulick, L., and L. Urwick (Eds.). 1934. Papers on the Science of Administration. New York: Harper.

Herriott, R.E., and N. Gross. 1979. The Dynamics of Planned Educational Change: Case Studies and Analyses. Berkeley: McCutchan.

Katz, D., and R.L. Kahn. 1966. The Social Psychology of Organizations. New York: Wiley.

Kilmann, R.H. 1977. Social Systems Design. Amsterdam: Elsevier North-Holland.

Kilmann, R.H., L.R. Pondy, and D.P. Slevin. 1976. The Management of Organization Design. Amsterdam: Elsevier North-Holland.

Kimberly, J.R. 1980. "Initiation, Innovation and Institutionalization in the Creation Process." In The Organizational Life Cycle, by J.R. Kimberly and R.H. Miles, pp. 18-43. San Francisco: Jossey-Bass.

Kimberly, J.R., R.H. Miles, and associates. 1980. The Organizational Life Cycle. San Francisco: Jossey-Bass.

Kritek, W.J. 1976. The Design and Implementation of an Alternative High School. Paper read to American Educational Research Association meetings.

Lawrence, P.R., and J.W. Lorsch. 1967. Organization and Environment. Homewood, IL: Irwin.

Levin, M.A., and R. Simon. 1973. "The Creation of Educational Settings: A Developmental Perspective." Alternative Learning Environments Paper No. 2. Toronto: Ontario Institute for Studies in Education.

_____. 1974. "From Ideal to Real: Understanding the Development of New Educational Settings." Interchange 5 (3): 45-54.

Lighthall, F.F. 1973. "Multiple Realities and Organizational Nonsolutions: An Essay on 'Anatomy of Educational Innovation'." School Review February: 255-287.

Litwak, E., and H.J. Meyer. 1974. School, Family and Neighborhood. New York: Columbia University Press.

Maier, N.R.F. 1952. Principles of Human Relations. New York: Wiley.

Marcuse, H. 1964. One-Dimensional Man. Boston: Beacon Press.

McPartland, J., and J. Epstein. 1977. "Open Schools and Achievement: Extended Tests of a Finding of No Relationship." Sociology of Education 50: 133-143.

Merton, R.K. 1968. Social Theory and Social Structure. New York: Free Press.

Merton, R.K., and E. Barber. 1963. "Sociological Ambivalence." In Sociological Theory, Values, and Sociocultural Change, edited by E.A. Tiryakian. New York: Free Press.

Miles, M.B. (Ed.). 1964. Innovation in Education. New York: Teachers College Press.

_____. 1965. "Planned Change and Organizational Health: Figure and Ground." In Change Processes in the Public Schools, R.O. Carlson, et al., pp. 11-36. Eugene, OR: Center for Educational Policy and Management, University of Oregon.

_____. 1967. "Some Properties of Schools as Social Systems." In Change in School Systems, edited by G. Watson, pp. 1-29. Washington: National Training Laboratories.

_____. 1976. Thinking about How to Do It: Alternative Models of Planning and Implementation of New Schools. Paper read to American Educational Research Association meetings.

_____. 1977. On Networking. Washington: Group on School Capacity for Problem-Solving, National Institute of Education.

_____. 1978a. "New Schools as a Strategy for Educational Improvement." Chapter 2 in Final Report, NIE Grant NIE-G-74-0051, Designing and Starting Innovative Schools: A Field Study of Social Architecture of Education. New York: Center for Policy Research.

_____. 1978b. "Planning and Implementing New Schools: A General Framework." Chapter 3 in Final Report, NIE Grant NIE-G-74-0051, Designing and Starting Innovative Schools: A Field Study of Social Architecture in Education. New York: Center for Policy Research.

_____. 1979. "Qualitative Data as an Attractive Nuisance: The Problem of Analysis." Administrative Science Quarterly 24: 590-601.

_____. 1981a. Learning to Work in Groups: A Practical Guide for Members and Trainers. New York: Teachers College Press.

_____. 1981b. "Mapping the Common Properties of Schools." In Improving Schools: Using What We Know, edited by R. Lehming. Santa Monica, CA: Sage.

Miles, M.B., M. Fullan, and G. Taylor. 1978. OD in Schools: The State of the Art. Final Report, NIE Contract #400-77-0051, 0052, 1978. New York and Toronto: Center for Policy Research and Ontario Institute for Studies in Education.

Miles, M.B., and R.A. Schmuck. 1971. "Improving Schools through Organization Development: An Overview." In Organization Development in Schools, edited by R.A. Schmuck and M.B. Miles. La Jolla, CA: University Associates.

Mills, C.W. 1956. The Power Elite. New York: Oxford University Press.

Myers, L.A. 1973. "The Opening of an Open School." In Open Education Re-examined, edited by D.A. and L.A. Myers. Lexington, MA: D.C. Heath.

Nisbet, R. 1953. Community and Power. New York: Oxford University Press.

Nystrom, P.C., and W.H. Starbuck (Eds.). 1981. Handbook of Organizational Design. Vols. 1 and 2. New York: Oxford University Press.

Parker, L.A. 1977. The Individually-Guided Education Movement and Its Network. Cambridge, MA: Center on Technology and Society.

Perlmutter, H.A. 1965. Toward a Theory and Practice of Social Architecture. London: Tavistock Publications.

Pfeffer, J. 1978. Organizational Design. Arlington Heights, IL: AHM Publishing Corporation.

Rothman, J. 1974. Planning and Organizing for Social Change New York: Columbia University Press.

Rothschild-Whitt, J. 1976. "Conditions Facilitating Participatory-Democratic Organizations." Sociological Inquiry 46: 75-86.

Rubin, L. 1971. The In-Service Education of Teachers. Boston: Allyn and Bacon.

Sarason, S.G. 1972. The Creation of Settings. San Francisco: Jossey-Bass.

Schmuck, R.A., and M.B. Miles (Eds.). 1971. Organization Development in Schools. La Jolla, CA: University Associates.

Scott, W.R. 1965. "Field Methods in the Study of Organizations." In Handbook of Organizations, edited by J.G. March. Chicago: Rand McNally.

Sieber, S.D. 1968. "Organizational Influences on Innovative Roles." In Knowledge Production and Utilization in Educational Administration, edited by T.L. Eidell and J.M. Kitchel, pp. 120-142. Eugene, OR: CASEA.

_____. 1973. "The Integration of Fieldwork and Survey Methods." American Journal of Sociology 78: 335-359.

Simon, R.I., M.A. Levin, M. Fieldstone, and A. Johnston. 1973. The Development and Evaluation of an Alternative High School: A Report on S.E.E. (School of Experiential Education) Phase II. Alternative Learning Environments Project, Ontario Institute for Studies in Education.

Smith, L.M., and P.M. Keith. 1971. The Anatomy of Educational Innovation. New York: Wiley.

Stein, M. 1960. The Eclipse of Community. Princeton: Princeton University Press.

Stinchcombe, A.L. 1965. "Social Structure and Organizations." In Handbook on Organizations, edited by J.G. March, pp. 142-193. Chicago: Rand McNally.

Sullivan, E.W., and E.W. Kironde. 1976. Circumvention and Cooptation in the Planning of New Schools. Paper read at American Educational Research Association meetings.

Taylor, B.L. 1978. Mapping New Schools: A Series of New School Planning Guides. (Part 1: Setting the Stage for Planning. Part 2: Designing Your School. Part 3: Mapping Your School's Environment. Part 4: Making Your School Work.) New York: Center for Policy Research.

Taylor, F. 1922. Scientific Management. New York: Harper and Row.

Thompson, V. 1965. "Bureaucracy and Innovation." Administrative Science Quarterly 10: 1-20.

Walton, R.E. 1975. "The Diffusion of New Work Structures: Explaining Why Success Didn't Take." Organizational Dynamics Winter: 3-22.

Weber, M. 1947. The Theory of Social and Economic Organization. (Trans.) A.M. Henderson and T. Parsons. New York: Oxford University Press.

Weick, K. 1976. "Educational Organizations as 'Loosely-coupled' Systems." Administrative Science Quarterly 21 (1): 1-13.

INDEX

This index is essentially conceptual: it references the concepts used during analysis and commentary sections of the book. It can be used to locate themes, issues, key variables, and their importance at various points during the case.

To locate particular events or situations, use the Detailed Table of Contents, supplemented by Chart 9.1 (pp. 278-79), which lists the events of the first four months of school.

393

ABOUT THE AUTHORS

BARRY A. GOLD, a sociologist, is Assistant Professor of Management at Pace University, New York. He has also taught at Rutgers University, and was Research Associate at the Center for Policy Research, New York, and The Network, Andover, Mass. He taught elementary school for several years in Newark, New Jersey.

Dr. Gold holds a B.A. from Temple University, an M.A. from the New School for Social Research, and a M.Phil. and Ph.D. from Columbia University.

MATTHEW B. MILES, a social psychologist, is Senior Research Associate at the Center for Policy Research, New York. Until 1971 he was Professor of Psychology and Education at Teachers College, Columbia University.

He has published widely in areas including group training, educational innovation, and planned organizational change: his other books include Innovation in Education, Learning in Social Settings, Encounter Groups: First Facts, Measuring Human Behavior, Organization Development in Schools, and Learning to Work in Groups.

Dr. Miles has a B.A. from Antioch College, and an M.A. and Ed.D. from Teachers College, Columbia University.